Laughing Till It Hurts

Laughing Till It Hurts

The Complete Life and Career of
Carol Burnett

J. Randy Taraborrelli

William Morrow and Company, Inc.
New York

Library of Congress Cataloging-in-Publication Data

Taraborrelli, J. Randy.
  Laughing till it hurts.

  Includes index.
  1. Burnett, Carol.   2. Comedians—United States—
Biography.   3. Actors—United States—Biography.
I. Title.
PN2287.B85T37   1988   792.7'028'0924 [B]   88-8985
ISBN 0-688-08103-7

Printed in the United States of America

First Edition

1 2 3 4 5 6 7 8 9 10

BOOK DESIGN BY KAREN SAVARY

For Concetta Magistro—"Nona"

Foreword

IN A SELFISH, CYNICAL AGE SUCH AS OURS, IT'S DIFFICULT NOT TO be suspicious of Carol Burnett. So many of the people interviewed for this book, including those who cooperated without Carol's knowledge, agreed that she is one of the nicest, most unspoiled women in show business. Harvey Korman probably best capsulized the way people who know her feel about Carol when he said, "With her, you can be an ass and Carol Burnett still accepts you. She knows no other way." Then he added, only half joking, "I used to be an ass, so I know what I'm talking about."

But just as much as she's known for her affable personality, Carol is known for her cautious, guarded nature. "Oh, she's friendly, articulate, yet there's something oddly distant about her," someone once said of Carol. "There's something interior and removed, a wariness, a warning in her expression that reminds you of Dorothy Parker's gravestone epitaph: 'If you can read this, you've come too close.'"

During a Questions and Answers session on Carol's show, an amateur astrologist once predicted a rosy future for her, and then blurted out, "What blows my mind is that you're not a very open person."

Carol nodded solemnly. "Actually, you're right," she replied softly, without further explanation.

The friends of Carol's interviewed for this book were, above all, fiercely loyal to her and, at first, cautious about commenting on the hidden sides of her personality. But in time, as barriers to communication were broken, it became clear that her friends and coworkers understand, and even accept, the part of Carol that seems impenetrable.

"As far as what Carol presented as frontal personality, she was always enthusiastic, generous, and giving," Tim Conway ob-

7

serves. But then he hastens to add, "She is also a very difficult person to know. I never really attempted to know her because I felt she was well guarded by people, and by herself. She didn't want to get into anybody's personal life, nor did she want to welcome anyone into hers."

Harvey Korman comments, "If I let you into my life, I really let you in, pouring out all of my problems and fears to you. But if I'm going to be that way with you, I want you to reciprocate. Carol never did. She was always there when I needed her, when I needed someone to unload on. But she never let me, or anyone I know, in...."

Julie Andrews observes, "Carol has a wall behind which she retreats, and I think there is one part of her always behind it. I like to feel that, because of our friendship, she sometimes takes me back there, but it hasn't happened very often. Our relationship isn't the soul-baring kind...."

"She's open, but then again, she's not," Bob Mackie, her costume-designer, says. "She's very simple, yet very complex. For years, I didn't feel like I really knew her. There were things about her that fascinated me. Why should she be so open? She's not obligated to let everyone into her life, just because she happens to be nice."

From her technical crew to her costars, all agree that Carol Burnett rarely exposes any unappealing facets of her personality.

Jack Van Stralen, head of special effects at CBS-TV, recalls: "In eleven years of working on her show, I never once saw her lose her temper, and to me that's not normal. I would've respected her a lot more if Carol Burnett would have just shot off her mouth once in a while like Cher. There was always that effort to be 'nice Carol,' and it spooked me."

"Carol really isn't that unusual," Tim Conway insists. "You don't know a great deal about the comedy stars of years gone by, because as well as wearing a stage mask, they masked their personal lives. Carol has revealed a lot more about herself through the years than most of us have. But with Carol, you get it all or nothing."

Conway has a point. Carol Burnett has learned when, as a public person, she has to make a statement. She is invariably reticent until some aspect of her personal life begins to be a subject of rumor or gossip, and then she will purge herself of it and set the record straight by "coming clean."

In 1962, when she and Joe Hamilton fell in love and curious tongues wagged because he was married with eight children, Carol was silent and discreet. But when a desperate gossip columnist threatened to exploit the affair in an unflattering profile, Carol gave her an exclusive interview to squelch the unkind story. The resultant feature sounded like a love letter to Carol.

Two years later, when Carol became indisposed during the run of *Fade Out-Fade In,* her second Broadway play, the New York media speculated that she was faking her injury in order to extricate herself from the show. At first, Carol tried not to respond to the speculation. But, eventually, she became upset enough to hold a well-publicized, vitriolic press conference; she actually tried to have respected producer Jule Styne thrown out of the theatrical union. It was then that people began to learn that Carol Burnett can only be pushed so far.

(*The National Enquirer* can certainly attest to Carol's determination. When she sued that publication over an item that she felt implied she was publicly drunk, her law suit became the first against that tabloid to go to court...and Carol won. It's also interesting that Carol won't think twice about shooting off a note to the letters' page of newspapers whose reporters write nasty articles about other celebrities, particularly her friends.)

When her thirteen-year-old daughter Carrie was addicted to drugs and her Hollywood acquaintances gossiped about the "scandal," Carol shouldered the gossip without comment and waited until Carrie was in treatment. And then, rather than have the wrong story come out, she went public with the facts, and was one of the first entertainers to address the problem of drug abuse among America's youth.

There are many other instances, all discussed in this book, that portray Carol as a woman who knows how to be tough as well as honest, and also understands how to use a media known for using, chewing up, and then spitting out celebrities.

Still, Carol has probably whet as much as satisfied any curiosity about her private life. For instance, despite all the public brouhaha, we are still left wondering whether Carol's injury was her main reason for wanting to bow out of that Broadway play. And besides the immediate Hamilton family, who really knows why Carrie turned to addictive drugs? Carol lets her public into her home, but, as is her right, keeps some rooms decidedly off limits.

Carol apparently does recognize this duality, the irony of Hollywood-image making. In 1987, she said in an interview, "I talk a good game. Most performers do. There's a difference between what's in my head and what's in my heart."

Carol Burnett started her career in the theater, but the transition to television was a relatively easy one for her. In the early days, she expended a lot of energy leaning on the always-reliable gimmick of putting herself down. She used her looks as a whipping boy, probably because she knew that women who make fun of themselves have always been more readily accepted in the male-dominated field of comedy. If she can convince her audiences that she's an ugly misfit, the comedienne can be reasonably certain that they will side with her, not feel threatened by her. The act gives her vulnerability; audiences love vulnerability.

Still, sometimes humor reveals us—even betrays us. Carol's constant mugging and attempts to make herself look ugly in the early days were as much part of her need to entertain as they were a way of reinforcing in herself a nagging inferiority complex. When self-deprecation worked for her, gave her value and approval by validating her in her audience's eyes, she hung on to the gimmick with a vengeance. "The first time I ever forgot I was homely," she said in 1963, "was the first time I heard an audience laugh."

Carol certainly had the features for convincing self-deprecation. Someone once said that her rubbery, elongated face—with the sloping nose, those enormous teeth, the jutting lower lip, weak chin, and all of that improbably red (dyed) hair—was composed of equal parts silly putty and wizard's wax. She's said over and over that she always wanted to be prettier, but thank goodness she was never that fantasy image of herself—a more perfect face might have diminished her, made her seem less intriguing, less funny.

Yet, ironically, Carol was—is—oddly beautiful. A writer once said she had the "most eloquent, expressive eyes seen anywhere outside the silent movies." With those eyes, she conveys a gamut of emotions. Also, Carol is blessed with a sparkling peaches-and-cream complexion. In person, she has always been a very refined woman.

In interviews for this book, Don Saroyan, Carol's first husband, recalled trying to convince her that she didn't have to contort her features and make herself appear ugly in order to be successful. He said he was concerned about the impact this constant self-deprecation was having on her psyche. "But I have to do this, Don," he remembers her saying. "The people, they *love* me when I'm like this."

Carol's determined lack of self-confidence—in her looks, her music, her comedy—is maddening. But this pervasive inferiority complex has been integral to Carol Burnett's mass appeal. She's universally perceived as a guileless "Everywoman," mostly because that's how she sees herself. Carol has always made it appear that anyone can do what she does. She's the awkward girl next door, your kooky Aunt Grindl, your accident-prone cousin Clara.

David Greene, who directed Carol in the television movie *Friendly Fire*, recalls working with her on the streets of Stockton, California, where the film was made: "I was amazed at the proprietarial feeling the public has for her," he says. "People really feel that she's a personal friend, that they are entitled to stop her work, have a conversation with her, ask for her autograph.

"I would say, 'She's working! Can't you see that!' and the people would turn nasty toward me. I was robbing them of their Carol."

During the shooting of *Friendly Fire*, the cast stayed at a local Stockton motel. At breakfast in the coffee shop one morning, a woman came over to Carol's table. "I just can't believe it," she gushed. "It's you! Carol Burnett! *You're here and I'm talking to you!* And you know what's so *wonderful* about you?" she asked.

"Why, no, what's that?" Carol said with a smile. After all these years, she knew what was coming.

"You are just so...so...well," the woman concluded, at a loss for words, "You are just so *common!*"

"She has *time* for people," says Julie Andrews of Carol, "no matter how trivial or irritating their wants may be. I've never seen a chink in that attitude. It definitely isn't a gimmick. I guess I admire her all the more for it because I'm not capable of it myself. When she walks on a set, everyone calls her by her first name...."

"An entertainer can make an attempt at being nice, but if she really isn't, the public will know it," observes Tim Conway. "Closeups on TV are very revealing. TV picks out realism, and you better damn well be who you claim to be, or it just ain't gonna work. It's important that we *like* the people we laugh at."

Still, the life of a star is a privileged one. It's ludicrous to pretend that Carol Burnett is "just plain folks." Plain folks do not have access to limousines, expensive jewelry, opulent homes—all the accoutrements of stardom. Ordinary women don't socialize with Elizabeth Taylor, Julie Andrews, and Beverly Sills. They don't live in mansions. They don't have "help."

But you have to wonder how affected a woman can be who has to carry with her the memory of getting her foot stuck in a bucket of white paint the first time she met Jimmy Stewart. This same lady was so nervous about meeting Richard Nixon, she couldn't think of a thing to say to him when they were alone together in the Oval Office. After he pointed out the scars on the wooden floors made by Ike's golf shoes, the two of them stared at each other for an endless minute before Carol came up with this unusual icebreaker. "Gee," she said, "I guess *you've* been pretty busy, huh?"

And what can you make of a woman who writes to *Cosmopolitan* magazine (July 1980) to thank them for "a lovely story," and then notes, "I am not the age you printed. I'm three years older."

There aren't too many ladies in American history who have been accepted as comic icons. Lucille Ball comes to mind immediately. So do Ethel Merman, Nancy Walker, and Carol Channing in theater; Judy Holliday and Bette Midler in films; Imogene Coca and Mary Tyler Moore in television. In stand-up comedy—definitely not a woman's field—Joan Rivers, Phyllis Diller, and the late Totie Fields made an impact, all three queens of self-deprecation. And, of course, Lily Tomlin and Whoopi Goldberg have demonstrated rich comedic sensibilities as purveyors of analytical, "serious" comedy.

Social convention has had it that outrageous women like Carol Burnett—those who can do a pratfall or fall out of a window—somehow didn't fit into women's role in society.

"Women are trained from little girlhood not to grab the center of attention," Carol has observed. "A little boy is encouraged and called 'a caution' when he acts funny. Little girls are expected to be ladylike, not funny."

Certainly a double standard still exists in the world of comedy, long after the popularity of the pratfall has faded. The fact that Don Rickles is seldom criticized for being loud and abrasive while Joan Rivers is always chastised by her critics for doing the same kind of act speaks volumes for the kinds of roles women in comedy are expected to fill.

But Carol has always been unique. She's not a stand-up comic (she says she's always envied the kind of expressive, incisive comedic mind, like Lily Tomlin's, that can make social and political commentary). She's more versatile than most slapstick queens (whereas Lucille Ball must have a script to be funny, humor comes to Carol instinctively, as demonstrated by years of sharp repartee with her television-studio audiences).

Lucy played brilliantly, in many incarnations, a comical exaggeration of the everyday housewife, but Carol has essayed a wide range of characters in a plethora of situations. "She's the one performer I am jealous of," says Lucy, "because she can do it all."

Carol's comic genius is in finding and focusing on the camp absurdities and everyday inanities of life, and then reenacting them all in larger-than-life style by exaggerating their foibles. An important reason for her success as a wide range of characters is that she has always had a strong sense of the pulse and virtues of Middle America.

Carol managed to transform characters her writers created into living, breathing, people to whom we could relate; the devious girl scout Alice Portnoy, whose innocence belies her sense of blackmailing enterprise; the nagging harpy Zelda, who makes her husband's life a living hell; the doddering and victimized old woman Stella Toddler, who's "been hurt too much." And who can forget Carol's portrayal of the harebrained secretary Mrs. Wiggins, a woman who comes to work wearing an improbable hairstyle and tight black cocktail dress, and then spends the day waiting for quitting time in preoccupied, dizzy wonder.

In these characters, and in so many of Carol's other sketches, we see mirrored our relatives, friends, acquaintances, and sometimes even ourselves. The Burnett imagination has always been broad enough to appeal to everyone from big-city dwellers to country folk. It's never been difficult to relate to or laugh at Carol Burnett, because she has always been a clown, a totally original clown with a heart.

Carol's talent was nurtured in the late fifties period of slapstick humor, between the nonsensical brilliance of Lucille Ball and the cerebral satire of Elaine May. She was a part of the gradual evolution from light comedy to dark humor; between a time when a woman had to make herself look grotesque in order to get a laugh and a more enlightened time, when she would begin generating laughter by inventing compelling tragicomic characters. Carol has done both—slapstick and cerebral comedy.

This dissection of her work would no doubt annoy, maybe even puzzle, Carol herself. Not once has she convincingly attempted to examine her art for her public. She has said that she was influenced by Judy Holliday and Ethel Merman, but she has never really explained how. She has said that she's seen every Kay Kendall movie three times, that she even cried when the woman died, but she has never said how Kendall might have helped to shape her comic sensibility.

Instead, she has said, "I hate it when somebody tries to find some deep meaning behind why somebody crosses her eyes. It's so ridiculous."

In an *Esquire* magazine article in 1972, writer Harold Brodkey attempted to pore over every detail of Carol's mannerisms and characters. When the reporter encouraged similar examination from Carol, the results were less than enlightening, and she appeared superficial and uninformed.

At one point in the interview, Carol told him, "You know, Harold, I've been thinking, and, what it is, I think you overrate me. My comedy—you go into it too deeply. I wish all that was there but I don't think it is. There's no soap box to my humor...."

Carol Burnett seems oblivious to the deep inner workings of the comedic mind, but she certainly isn't alone. Johnny Carson has said that he knows virtually nothing about comedy, that he prefers *being* funny to *talking about* being funny. "If you try to analyze comedy, and dissect it, take it apart, it's no longer funny," he has said.

Or, as George Burns put it with such pithy eloquence, "If you laugh, it's funny."

Carol doesn't really know why people laugh at her work; she's just glad that they do. And her public, by the same measure, has never expected great depth from Carol Burnett. It just expects her to be funny, and Carol has had a gold mine of real-life material from which to draw upon for years of rich comedy.

She recalled some of her experiences in her recent memoir of her childhood, *One More Time*. Born on April 26, 1933, Carol Creighton Burnett was raised by a neurotic hypochondriac of a grandmother named Mabel Eudora (Mae) White. "Nanny" was, by most people's measure, a rather unlikable woman, what with her evil streak and selfish, stubborn nature, not to mention that nauseating Ben-Gay aroma of hers mixed with the smells of her farting and belching.

But for the little-girl Carol, Mae White was anything but cruel and repulsive. In Nanny's warm and secure embrace, Carol found refuge from the grim world outside . . . and the one inside, apartment 102, the one room in which she was raised. Nanny's love, though not unconditional, was certainly genuine, and Carol became Nanny's "little shadow."

While Carol's parents were usually lost in alcohol, Nanny was there to raise her to become a decent and, say her friends, loving and generous person. The adult Carol Burnett would instinctively infuse bits of Nanny into many of her characterizations. Whether comic or dramatic, she'd bring to her role those characteristics of Nanny she adored, the survival instinct and rich humor, as well as the grossness and vulgarity.

Carol's mother, Ina Louise Creighton Burnett, was a troubled woman and alcoholic who languished across the hall in an apartment even drearier and more pitiable than Nanny's. Over the years, she played out her life as the star of a depressing soap opera of indecision and insecurity.

As an adult, Carol could certainly poke fun at the regal side of womanhood; she hadn't seen all of those Irene Dunne movies when she was a youngster for nothing. But after observing her own mother, Carol would also have an innate ability to relate to women who might have been more than misfits "if only" this and "if only" that. Or who were always drunk and would fall all over themselves trying to cover up their hopelessness. (Carol always played drunks as losers in her sketches.)

When Carol was the melancholy Charwoman sitting on a bucket—the heartbroken cleaning lady to whom life had dealt a bad hand—there was Louise. When she was the headstrong, screeching, self-defeating Eunice shooting barbs at her mother, there, too, was Louise, sparring with Nanny. Both characters, the Charwoman and Eunice, have earned a real place in our hearts and memories, because both are—so honest, so real. Because of her life in apartment 102, Carol has that rare waiflike quality of Charlie Chaplin's little tramp—when her heart breaks, her audience's goes out to her.

One reason for Carol's success in television has to be because her second husband's career as a television producer paralleled hers as a TV comedienne.

Carol was married to Joe Hamilton for twenty years. Hamilton's overwhelming influence and expertise helped a talented comedic actress whose sights were set on the theater to change her direction and concentration to television. Her husband created an easy atmosphere in which she worked; he ran interference for her against the outside world. Everyone involved agrees that *The Carol Burnett Show* was really Joe's show, and that Carol was the star. He called all the shots, made all of the business decisions.

The Hamiltons' marriage and home life were played out strictly at home, never at work. There was a determined effort to avoid bringing any domestic squabbles to the studio. "The only time you knew something was ever wrong was when you read it in the papers," says Jack Van Stralen.

"None of us got an inkling about Carrie's drug problem until Carol and Joe went public with it," Ed Simmons, producer and head writer of the show, remembers. "As nice as she and Joe were to us, that's how removed they were."

We were all witness to the results of Carol and Joe's merger during the successful eleven-year run of *The Carol Burnett Show,* which he produced. The show was the longest-running comedy-variety show in television history; the series is still syndicated across the country as *Carol Burnett and Friends.*

Carol has usually tried not to downplay Hamilton's influence on her life and career. Still, today she does seem a bit embarrassed that she spent most of their marriage believing and professing to the media that he was the brilliant one and that she was just his talented shadow. Today, after years of consciousness-raising through the women's movement, she bristles when Joe makes statements that imply she has intelligence but doesn't always act intelligently, such as a remark he made for this book. "This is hard to understand unless you've worked with her," Joe said carefully. "She always knows what's wrong for her, but she's almost a hundred percent wrong when she thinks something is right for her."

Now, her friends say, Carol seems determined to chart her own course and put her ex-husband's influence in a new perspective. In 1985, when she was inducted into the Television Academy Hall of Fame, she thanked, in her speech, the two men who she said were the most influential in her life, her original agent, Arthur Willi, and Garry Moore. Most of her friends, and Joe's, were surprised and puzzled.

Joe Hamilton is reluctant to take credit for any of his ex-wife's success. "I don't think anybody 'makes' a star. The star makes himself," he says. "Either he has it or he doesn't. I saw right from the beginning that Carol had a lot of talent that hadn't been tapped yet, as an actress, a comic, a singer, but I give her the credit for developing it. Anyone who credits me or anyone else is wrong."

Most people are aware of the fact that Carol Burnett has won many awards—five Emmys, in fact, since the beginning of her career. There have been *TV Guide* Awards, *Photoplay* Gold Medals, People's Choice Awards, and practically every other award possible for an entertainer of her magnitude. This is mentioned here because there is no emphasis in these pages on that facet of Carol's career; not to diminish the importance of these honors, there's probably nothing more boring than a long recitation of such awards.

When Carol first became popular, her mentor, Garry Moore, predicted, "A talent her size is a terribly mixed blessing. She has a difficult life ahead...."

Carol would probably assert that though there have been some difficult moments, all in all it's been a rather entertaining life. Her secret? She knows how to play cards.

"I've come to believe that we're all dealt a hand in life," she has said. "God has given each of us a free will, choices to make. How we play our hand is up to each of us. You can be given a royal flush and still blow it," she concludes. "But if you're pretty good at the game, you'll play it right and maybe life won't be so tough.

"But then again," she hastens to add, "what do I know?"

Acknowledgments

CAROL BURNETT SAID THAT SHE FELT UNCOMFORTABLE ABOUT being interviewed for this biography; she was reluctant to talk about herself and her career because, I believe, to her it seemed self-indulgent. I think this is probably why Carol has chosen not to follow her childhood memoirs, *One More Time,* with a book about her adult life. As she's put it, "It would only be a Hollywood story about 'then I met this one and then I met that one.'"

This book might be a so-called "unauthorized biography," but these pages are certainly not uninformed—a tribute to Miss Burnett's unusually sensible attitude about her life and career and the way they relate to her public.

Carol, who's championed the cause of fair and factual reporting for years, and who's supported university journalism programs by her encouragement and personal donations, did not discourage her friends and business associates from cooperating with me on this book. As a result, I had free access to everyone I chose to interview. So, hopefully, the picture painted here is much more interesting and accurate than it would have been had I been forced to "go around" Carol and only interview people who wouldn't be concerned about her reaction to their involvement.

For that, I thank you, Carol Burnett.

And my sincere gratitude to the people I did interview:

Joe Hamilton, Carol's husband of twenty years, executive producer of *The Carol Burnett Show* and of most of Carol's television specials. His contribution to this book was, obviously, invaluable. He provided great insight into Carol, the comedienne and the woman.

Harvey Korman, Carol's TV costar for many years. Harvey is as articulate and honest as he is funny. What a gentleman!

Tim Conway, crazy man extraordinaire. Tim's work on Carol's series speaks for itself; he's just as offbeat offstage as you'd expect. Thanks, Tim, for a nutty afternoon.

Lyle Waggoner, who proved that old adage "you can't judge a book by its cover" to be true. He's more than a pinup boy, he's smart, too. Today, Lyle owns his own business, Star Wagons, the largest and most successful Winnebago-rental concern in Los Angeles. Continued success, Lyle.

George Abbott, esteemed Broadway producer and director, who directed Carol's Broadway shows. He celebrated his hundred and first birthday in June 1988. Congratulations, Mr. Abbott, and thanks. Your observations were invaluable.

Don Saroyan, Carol's first husband, mentor, and good friend. Thanks for sharing such a private time.

Robert Altman, who produced and directed Carol in *A Wedding, H.E.A.L.T.H.* and *The Laundromat*.

Robert Wright, associate producer of the Burnett series, most of Carol's television specials, and even *The Garry Moore Show.* Two in-depth interviews and phone-call follow-ups added a lot to this manuscript.

Bob Banner, producer of *The Garry Moore Show,* Carol's first five television specials, and the first five years of her series. And what a memory!

Ed Simmons, producer and head writer of Carol's show for five years. His time and energy made all the difference to the show, and to this book.

Dave Powers, director of Carol's series for ten years, a very busy man who gave of his time unselfishly.

Clark Jones, director of the series during its premiere year.

Ken Welch, who has written special material for Carol since 1956, and he's still at it today.

Mitzie Welch, who has also been writing for Carol for thirty years. Additionally, she understudied Miss Burnett in *Fade Out-Fade In*, and helped put that chapter of this book into perspective.

Artie Malvin, whose musical contributions to Carol's show for eleven years are still memorable (who can forget those great show-tune medleys!).

Harry Zimmerman, musical director for *The Garry Moore Show* and for Carol's early concert tours.

Irwin Kostal, another of Moore's musical directors and the arranger for Carol's first album for Decca and for *Julie [Andrews] and Carol at Carnegie Hall*.

Peter Matz, musical director for Carol's series and specials, who was one of the first people interviewed for this book. Thanks, Pete.

Bob Mackie, the wonderful costume designer who helped Carol develop many of her funniest characters. Carol calls him "the miracle worker." Diana Ross, Cher, and many others agree.

Roger Beatty, writer and assistant director on Carol's series for its entire run.

Gene Perret, another of the show's writers, whose amazing memory for sketches was invaluable.

Margaret Scott, script girl for Joe Hamilton for nearly twenty years. She gave me the opportunity to see some very helpful video material, and shared more than a few funny memories.

Pat Lillie Whelan, script girl for *The Garry Moore Show*, Carol's early TV specials, and the first year of her series. Pat provided archival photographs and allowed me to rummage through stacks of personal scrapbooks.

David Greene, who directed Carol in *Friendly Fire*.

Fay Kanin, who wrote the screenplay for *Friendly Fire*.

Paul Winchell, who gave Carol her first television job on his *Winchell-Mahoney Show*.

Marshall Barer, who wrote Carol's first Broadway show, *Once Upon a Mattress*. Marshall really inspired me to continue with this work; he was the first person I interviewed (for over three hours!).

Bruce Campbell, one of Carol's UCLA chums and a friend of thirty years. Bruce is the biographer's best friend. He provided many of the photographs used in this book, as well as an invaluable list of contacts and many memories.

Perry Gray, who maintained a close correspondence with Carol for many years. Perry and I spent many hours going over details of Carol's early Gotham years.

Joe Layton, who staged Carol's off-Broadway and Broadway debuts, and whose work with "divas" will always be remembered.

Don Crichton, Carol's lead dancer and close friend for many years.

Lester Osterman, who produced Carol's Jule Styne vehicle for Broadway, *Fade Out-Fade In*.

Pat McCormick, who played Carol's comic love interest in *A Wedding*.

Estelle Harmon, Carol's first dramatic coach at UCLA (who gave her a D + !).

Jack Van Stralen, head of the special-effects division at CBS-TV.

Ed Garcia, also an employee at CBS-TV, who helped me "get my feet wet" at the studio.

Lenny Weinrib, another of Carol's UCLA buddies. (Carol saved this comic from a life in dentistry.)

Roy Silver, the man who discovered Joan Rivers and Bill Cosby. He helped me understand the comic mind.

Elle Puritz, associate producer of Carol's TV film *Life of the Party—The Story of Beatrice*.

Bill Hargate, fashion designer for much of Carol's stage work.

Martha Raye, who gave Carol her first break on *The Garry Moore Show* by coming down with the flu.

Jeff Bleckner, director of Carol's miniseries, *Fresno*.

Dave Ketchum, Bob Emenegger, and Monty Hellman, who helped fill in the gaps for some of Carol's early years.

Steven Sullivan, Bill Bravard, Marsha Holland, and Basey Stewart, who provided invaluable insight into the CBS-TV machinery. And thanks to Michael Maron, John Redmann, and André Pittmon.

And, also, my thanks to the following people who shared so much with me: Susan Jenkins, Neal Peters, Timothy Van Buren, Stephen Spencer, Barbara Stephens, Peter Remmington, Brad Stewart, Peter Ivory, Frederick G. Gaines, Michael White. Thanks, also, Daniel F. Romo, Miss Velma, Scherrie Payne, Edward Jimenez, David Doolittle, Val Johns, John Passantino, Linda DiStefano, Robin Alexander, Mr. and Mrs. Joe Tumolo, Daniel Tumolo, Len and Lena Roth, Allan Roth, and Michelle and Nicholas Ragni. And a special nod to Reggie Wilson.

For additional comments about Carol, thanks to Julie Andrews, Lucille Ball, Beverly Sills, and Mary Rodgers.

Special thanks to Carol's publicist of more than twenty years,

Rick Ingersoll, for being such a thorough professional. The way Rick and I cooperated together could be a useful model for other biographers and their subjects' publicists. Thanks, Rick, for introducing me to so many other kind, generous, and helpful people.

Thanks also to Becky Mann, Joe Hamilton's secretary, for being so cooperative, and to all of the other employees at Joe Hamilton Productions, for their time and consideration.

Thanks to Carol's biggest fan, Steven Brinberg, for his assistance. And also to Jim Henkel, for all of the invaluable statistics, and to David Duarte, for the helpful research material.

My appreciation to the entire staff of the Margaret Herrick Library of the Academy of Motion Picture Arts and Sciences in Beverly Hills, for their cooperation on so many different levels.

Thanks to the staffs of the Library of the Performing Arts at Lincoln Center in New York City and of the American Film Institute.

Thank you, Ron Simon, and the rest of the staff of the Museum of Broadcasting, also in Manhattan, for allowing me access to Carol's earliest television appearances.

Carol Burnett and Joe Hamilton have donated much of their professional memorabilia to the University of California at Los Angeles. My sincere thanks to Sharon Farb, public services assistant at the UCLA Theatre Arts Library, for allowing me access to scripts, documents, and notes. Thanks also to Eleanor Tanin, director of UCLA's Television Archives, for allowing me so much valuable viewing time to catch up on thirty years of Burnett appearances.

Mrs. Freda Rosen, wife of the late Arnie Rosen who was a head writer and producer for *The Carol Burnett Show*, donated much of her husband's preliminary draftwork to UCLA, as well as hundreds of completed sketches and scripts. This material was vital to my research. Thank you, Mr. and Mrs. Rosen. To follow their example, the original manuscript of this book, as well as all of my notes, transcriptions, and supplementary material are being donated to UCLA's Department of Theatre Arts.

My appreciation to my agent, good-luck charm, and close friend, Bart Andrews. His trust means so much; thanks for such a good job, and for the title of this book. And thanks also to Robert Drake, and to the rest of Bart's staff.

To my esteemed editor, Lisa Drew, her assistant, David Means, my copy editor, Joan Marlow, and to their guiding force at William Morrow, Sherry Arden...thanks for sharing my enthusiasm.

Thanks to my business manager, James Perry, for taking care of all the headaches. You are the best...

Special thanks to Al Kramer, a good friend who read this book in its many incarnations and helped keep me, hopefully, on the right path. Thanks also to George Solomon and to Richard Tyler Jordan, for their invaluable input.

And, finally, thanks to my family—Rocco, Rose, Roslyn, Rocky, Rose Marie, and Nettie—for love, patience, and understanding.

J. Randy Taraborrelli
Hollywood, California
August 1988

Laughing
Till It Hurts

Prologue

Dear Dick,

    ... Then he had his accountant write us up *two $1000 checks*. Have you ever heard of anything so fantastic? He said we could pay him back when we were successful in New York. So I'm leaving in August ... determined to make a go of it. Other than this, nothing else is happening.

                         Love,
                         Carol ($)

P.S. The check is good—just purchased a toothbrush and watchband.

(a letter from Carol Burnett to UCLA classmate Dick DeNeut, July 1954)

A BALMY SATURDAY EVENING, JUNE 19, 1954. Twenty-one-year-old Carol Burnett, her twenty-five-year-old boyfriend, Don Saroyan, and eight fellow students were slated to perform for guests at a private cocktail party in La Jolla, an oceanfront community outside of San Diego, about a hundred miles south of Los Angeles. The entertainers were all enrolled in a musical-comedy workshop class at UCLA. Ordinarily, their final exam would have been conducted on a campus stage. Because of a scheduling mix-up, however, the stage was booked until the day after the class's professor, Dr. Jan Popper, was to leave on a European vacation with his wife. It was decided that the students would perform at this bon-voyage party for Popper given by some of his more affluent friends. In doing so, the students would fulfill the university requirement that they appear before an audience.

The opulent surroundings of the black-tie affair surprised

the students; they hadn't expected all the accoutrements of formality. The party area was romantically dark; people danced and exchanged pleasantries as they sipped drinks served by waiters bearing silver trays.

All of the students had their own material planned. Carol and Don, along with Allan Light, a friend who played piano, had worked up an act around "You Can Always Catch Our Act at the Met" from *Two on the Aisle*. Though they felt out of place at this gala, they were determined somehow to calm themselves enough to perform that routine. Then Carol would sing a number from *Annie Get Your Gun*.

When the Czechoslovakia-born Dr. Popper rose to introduce the talent, a significant hush fell over the crowd. "All of these youngsters are my students," he began explaining. "If you are entertained by them, they'll get A's. Their futures are in your hands," he chuckled. "So be gentle."

The show went well. The audience was impressed that Popper's students seemed to have such technical command of musical comedy despite their professional inexperience. These kids were no bashful tenderfoots, that was obvious.

Don Saroyan, a good-looking man with wavy dark hair and a very engaging smile, had a strong personality and a voice to match. Still, whenever gawky and clumsy-looking Carol Burnett was featured, she was the one who held the complete attention of everyone in the room. The partygoers laughed and commented to one another in hushed tones about Carol's wacky sense of humor as she performed "You Can't Get a Man with a Gun." The way her voice projected, it cut like a knife through an atmosphere that had, just a few moments earlier, been utterly subdued. She was really quite good; though she was nervous, she managed not to show it. The audience's approval was unanimous, and Carol basked in their enthusiasm and applause; it was a moment she would always remember with absolute clarity.

After their performance, Carol and Don, concentrating on looking casual, tried to mingle among the crowd and act as if they "belonged." As they sampled hot and cold hors d'oeuvres of every variety from the buffet table, a middle-aged man and his wife approached them. The gentleman, about fifty years old, was well dressed and impeccably groomed, though it seemed that he'd had too much to drink. His wife was attractive and sweet, rather timid.

"So, what is it you want to do with your lives?" the man asked Carol and Don, trying to make small talk.

They told him about their love for show business: It was everything to them, and energized their lives. They had such luminous personalities, both of them seemed warm and honest and enthusiastic. Their smiles were pure gold. When they spoke about musical comedy, their eyes sparkled.

"What we'd really like to do is go to New York," Don said.

"Why New York?"

Carol piped in, "Because unless you look like Marilyn Monroe or Tony Curtis, you have to get away from Los Angeles to be discovered." (She could hardly resist a crack about how much more she looked like Curtis than Monroe, but she bit her lip.) "And besides, the New York stage is where we belong...."

The furrows on his brow deepened as the man considered all of this. Then he asked very bluntly, "So, why not just go to New York?"

Carol and Don looked at each other incredulously and responded in unison, "Money!"

"What's money?" the man shot back. His speech was just a bit slurred. "When I started out, I was broke, a day laborer. I didn't have a cent. Today, I'm worth millions," he boasted. "You want New York, I'll send you to New York. The trip will be on me. How much will it cost? What'll it take?"

"Oh, I don't know," Carol said flippantly. "Maybe a thousand dollars. What do you think, Don?"

Don nodded his head and chuckled. "Sounds right to me."

The man handed Carol his business card. "Call me and we'll set it up," he assured her. His wife smiled and nodded her head in agreement. They shook hands and said good-bye.

It hardly seemed like a legitimate offer of help.

The following Monday at school, Don and Carol talked about what had happened in La Jolla. They confessed to each other that they hadn't been able to sleep the night before for wondering about the strange man at that party and whether or not his intentions were sincere. Was he drunk, or just eccentric? Either way, they had to find out. So they decided to telephone him at his office, using a pay phone on campus. (They could barely scrape together the change for the long-distance call.) First, they spoke to his secretary, and then he came on the line. He remembered them, and told them to stop by whenever they liked.

Don borrowed an old Buick that they would use for the trip, but they had no money for gas. A friend who lived in Westwood always seemed to have a couple of dollars to spare. They knocked on Bruce Campbell's door. "Either we'll come back owing you some money," Don promised with a broad smile, "or we'll come back with the money and a bottle of champagne."

Tuesday morning, June 22. Carol and Don left Hollywood at 6:00 A.M. for the drive to La Jolla. Three hours later, they were escorted into the mystery man's posh office; as it turned out, he owned a construction company. His personality was quite different than it had been at the party. Now, he had an aristocratic polish and seemed dignified. Apparently, they would later learn, he was a rare individual who had not been well educated but still managed to make a sizable fortune for himself by being a shrewd and tenacious businessman. He wasn't born in the United States, but he'd found opportunity here and had made it work for him. He was one of those "American Dream" stories.

Carol and Don awkwardly took their seats before his huge desk. For a few moments, no one said anything. Carol tried to mask her nervousness with good cheer. "Well, we made it!" she offered brightly. He stared at her from the other side of the desk; the fact that they'd managed to find their way to La Jolla from Los Angeles did not impress him.

Finally, he spoke. Again, he asked them what they wanted to do with their lives. Again, they talked about their dreams, their goals. "I know that I will never be happy doing anything else," Carol said simply. Don nodded his head.

"I believe you kids can make it," their would-be benefactor declared. "So here's the money for New York." He handed them two checks for one thousand dollars each.

Carol and Don were astonished. They listened to the stipulations but they were spellbound by now, and the rest of what the man had to say went right over their heads. "The money is a loan," he told them. "You have to pay me back in five years from show-business money, if you make it. And, also, you must never reveal my name. I don't want to be swamped with kids like yourself. And if you make it, maybe you two will help someone else. I hope so. It's a tough game," he concluded, getting up out of his chair, "so do what you can, and lots of luck."

He shook their hands. Carol and Don stuffed the checks in their pockets quickly, as if afraid he might change his mind. With as much dignity and as graciously as possible, they calmly walked out of his office, into the elevator, and then outside. They tried not to look at one another. Once out of the building, they threw themselves into each other's arms, squealing, hugging, and marveling at their amazing luck. Then they ran to the bank and cashed one of the checks. They had no choice; they'd forgotten to borrow gas money for the drive home.

That night, Carol and Don showed up at Bruce Campbell's door with his money and a bottle of the cheapest champagne money could buy.

After final exams a few weeks later, their friends gave Carol and Don a going-away party. It was a fun gathering, but also a little sad. Carol and Don had made a lot of friends at UCLA, and it wouldn't be easy saying good-bye. There were teary-eyed farewell embraces and kisses. Carol gave a sentimental speech, Don did the same. And then someone shouted out, "Hey, Carol, what'll be your first big Broadway play?"

She didn't even have to think about it. "It'll be a musical," she said decisively. "And you know what? George Abbott will direct it."

There was laughter. But she wasn't kidding.

1

High tides flooded Manhattan streets, LaGuardia airport
was shut down, traffic was hampered by uprooted trees and
rain floods. The storm called Hurricane Carol has hit New
York City...

—*The New York Times*
August 31, 1954

S HE WAS COMPLETELY ABSORBED IN THE WONDER OF IT ALL;
even her imagination couldn't compare to all of this neon.
She walked down Broadway in a daze, craning her neck to marvel at the illuminated theater marquees. Somehow, she had made
it to New York. Finally, it was Carol Burnett's turn to take a bite
out of the Big Apple.

Janis Paige, John Raitt, and Carol Haney were starring in
The Pajama Game at the St. James Theatre on West Forty-fourth
Street. George Abbott was directing them in this musical, and
Carol was determined that one day he'd do the same for her. As
soon as she had some extra money, she decided, she would purchase a ticket to see the show. Matinees on Wednesdays and Saturdays were cheapest.

Notices of Coming Attractions were everywhere. She saw
that next month something called *The Boyfriend*, starring someone named Julie Andrews in her Broadway debut, would be
opening at the Royale Theatre on West Forty-fifth Street across
the street from the Imperial.

Carol wasn't like a lot of other young people in 1954. Rock
music was about to revolutionize the entire record industry; most
of the under-thirty crowd was eagerly anticipating the onslaught.
Disc jockey Alan Freed had popularized the phrase "rock and
roll" that year as the theme of his show *The Big Beat,* which was

broadcast daily over WINS-Radio in New York. Carol couldn't have cared less about this music, or about people with names like Hank Ballard, Fats Domino, and Bill Haley. That year, when Haley encouraged the masses to "Shake, Rattle and Roll" and then to "Rock Around the Clock," Carol did neither. She much preferred Doris Day and Judy Garland any day of the week, thank you.

The seven-year-old medium of television was conquering the United States with a vengeance by 1954. There were 517 stations nationally, with an audience estimated at 32 million. But Carol was not among them. To her, TV was still an oddity. It had only been a few years since appliance shops used to display televisions in their windows, and crowds of people would gather on the sidewalks to gawk at the poorly defined images. Or, as Steve Allen once noted, "It was as if somebody put a Martian in the window. Everybody would stare, point, and say, 'Hey, get a load of that.'"

Carol's big romance was with the theater and its stars. To her, being a performer meant strutting the boards of a Broadway stage. She wanted to lose herself in the world of musical comedy. She longed to be Ethel Merman, and she certainly had the voice for it. Someone once said that "the Merm" could hold a note longer than the Chase Manhattan Bank. Carol wanted them to say the same about her one day. Hers was a big, loud clarion call that seemed perfect, at least the way she heard it, for the American theater.

She also wanted to be Martha Raye, and she did have budding ability as a comedic actress. Her talent was unrefined. Sometimes it got the best of her, and she didn't quite know what to do with it. But inside, she knew she was a clown. She had classic clown skills, gestures, and expressions, which she did not steal from Raye or from any of her other idols. They were hers, and with them she had an unquestionable ability to make people laugh. She hadn't won that UCLA Most Promising Newcomer award for nothing.

"I'm not afraid to make myself unattractive," she would say. "Most women are [afraid]. There's all that training you've had since you were three. 'Be a lady! Don't yell or try to be funny! Keep your knees close together.' When I was a kid, sometimes my mother would whack me when I crossed my eyes or screwed up my face. Now, the sloppier I am, the more comfortable I am, and the better I feel in a comedy sketch."

Though she wouldn't admit to it, deep down Carol was really convinced that she was one of the most unattractive women God had ever put on this planet. Rather than risk having anyone believe that she thought of herself as pretty, she'd contort her face and cross her eyes to underscore the "fact" that she really wasn't. This way, she decided, when people laughed at her for having the gall to get up on a stage, it wouldn't matter, because she was laughing at herself, too.

Perhaps she didn't know it at the time, but Carol Burnett had an abundance of what mattered most: sheer chutzpah and luck. She also had an optimistic heart that wouldn't quit. Quite simply, she was always certain that all circumstances in her life would magically arrange themselves in her best interest.

There were a lot of young, aspiring performers in Manhattan, but only a precious few would ever realize their goals in the theater. The unfortunate majority would go back to wherever they came from with a scrapbook full of wonderful memories and a litany of stories about how they probably would have made it big "if only..."

But not this girl. She had blinders on, and thank goodness she did; that the odds were stacked against her never really occurred to her. "I just *believed*," Carol has said. "My success was almost a given where I was concerned."

Carol's unflinching optimism wasn't particularly unusual. Who really goes to New York dreaming of Broadway stardom while thinking that it might *not* happen? But in the end, Carol's success would be proof of the power not only of positive thinking, but of *positive action* as well.

These were the Eisenhower years, a decade of enthusiasm for self-improvement and optimism, of competition and greatness—all values that were stressed at Carol's alma mater, UCLA, but certainly not in the apartment in which she was raised. Fortunately, she was always able to find a light side to any dark situation, because her childhood had been anything but carefree. The essential qualities of humor and humanity that would make Carol Burnett such a skillful comedic actress can be traced back to her days in apartment 102, the one-room dwelling—in a lower-income section of Hollywood—on Wilcox Avenue and Yucca Street, one block north of Hollywood Boulevard—where she was raised.

To the little-girl Carol, only the immediate family was privy to the "secrets" of 102. None of her childhood friends was ever allowed to venture into that room where newspapers, rags, jars, and all kinds of junk were stacked everywhere, laden with dust. The few pieces of cheap furniture in apartment 102 were scarred and dented. The air was thick and musty.

Carol's maternal grandmother and mother spent a lot of time fencing with one another. "Nanny had a way of just getting in under Mama's skin," Carol once recalled. "She had a way of pushing Mama's buttons and then...Mama would explode." When they argued, their fighting shook Carol to her toes. Did they really hate each other that much? she wondered.

They were on welfare; they had no money, but worse yet, by the time Carol left, they had no hope in their lives.

Carol's father, Jody, was an alcoholic who lived with his mother in Santa Monica until she died. After that, no one really knew where he lived. He was just around, here and there. He had no home; and even sadder, he had no dignity.

Carol's half-sister, Christine, a pretty, loving, and precocious child, was a source of inspiration for Carol; her laughter somehow made the darkest days a bit brighter. All was right with the world as far as little Chrissy was concerned, just as it should have been.

Carol was loved by all, despite the atmosphere of desperation. Still, she was glad to get out when the thousand-dollar check gave her the chance to escape to New York. Occasional pangs of guilt intruded on her relief, however, and sometimes flooded her conscience. She had been rescued, and now she was three thousand miles away from those bleak yesterdays, but who was to rescue Nanny, Louise, Jody, and Chrissy?

Agreeing to meet Don Saroyan in Manhattan later, Carol went to New York with a friend she had dated, Dave Ketchum, and his family. They attended a Ketchum family wedding in Milwaukee, and then, when they got to New York, they parted company. Ketchum stayed in Manhattan for two days and returned to Los Angeles, where he continued work as master of ceremonies for USO shows.

Carol checked into the Algonquin Hotel, which was lovely and quaint and steeped in theatrical tradition, but at nine dollars a night, much too expensive. She had already spent a portion of her thousand-dollar loan on dental work and a winter coat. If ever there was a time to economize, this was it. Boyfriend Don Saroyan was in Las Vegas, and it might be two months before he would be joining her as planned. For now, she was on her own.

A friend was staying at a four-story residence for actresses called the Rehearsal Club, located at 47 West Fifty-third Street. For eighteen dollars a week, which included the cost of two dietician-supervised meals a day (breakfast and either lunch or dinner), Carol was told she'd be able to share a single unit with four roommates. The fee also included use of the laundry room and the library, which had a television and a radio. One of the requirements for eligibility to live at the club was that she had to be in active pursuit of a career in the theater. She was allowed to work a part-time job to help pay her rent, but she and the other girls were discouraged from taking on any full-time employment that would distract them from their show-business goals. The only other restriction was that gentlemen callers were permitted to visit only in the lobby.

The Rehearsal Club was a well-known residence for young women who had show-business aspirations. The Edna Ferber-George S. Kaufman play, and subsequent film classic, *Stage Door* was based on the hotel and its charged atmosphere. It was founded in 1913 by Jane Harris Hall, an Episcopal deaconess, and Mrs. Franklin W. Robinson, daughter of an Episcopal bishop. The brownstone building that housed the Rehearsal Club had once belonged to the Rockefeller family. Former residents included Jo Van Fleet, Martha Scott, Shirley Booth, and Jayne and Audrey Meadows.

The fifty or so girls living there when Carol moved in were a lively bunch; all seemed to be in a perpetual state of frenzy, preparing for "the big audition" and poring over trade publications daily in search of "the big break." Carol was totally and happily absorbed in this new environment in no time; these people had dreams, they had goals. Now, if they only had jobs...

Carol had managed to find part-time employment as a hat-check girl at Susan Palmer's, a tearoom and restaurant on Forty-ninth Street at Rockefeller Center. She made thirty dollars a week for three days' work, which helped pay her room and board. The job left her plenty of free time to make the rounds in search of that elusive personage, an agent.

Susan Palmer's main dining room was on the first floor, with an oyster bar downstairs. It's curious that in an article published about Carol years later (in *Life* magazine, February 22, 1963), some former customers actually remembered her from her days at the tearoom. One of them was quoted as having said, "Suddenly this girl with the teeth showed up at the checkroom upstairs. She struck like a rattlesnake. One minute I was dashing down those stairs in the clear, and the next moment she'd be beside me grabbing my coat. I had no intention of ever checking my coat, but half the time she'd outwrestle me for it."

"You know those little cloth dingies you hang your coat up by?" Carol once asked a reporter. "If the thread was coming out even a little bit, I'd sort of help it along. Then I'd re-sew it with a different color thread. I'd tell the man what happened and what I'd done about it. 'I fixed your coat, sir,' I'd say innocently with this hang-dog face. Then I'd get an extra dime."

Probably the day Carol best remembers from her Susan Palmer's experience was the one when singer John Raitt walked into the restaurant. At the same time, he was appearing with Eddie Foy, Jr., in *The Pajama Game* on Broadway. On his way out, he tipped Carol a quarter. Two years later, she worked with him on Dinah Shore's *Chevy Show* and confided that she still had that quarter.

A friend back in Hollywood had once mentioned to Carol that he knew Eddie Foy from having had a small part in one of the actor's films. He suggested that if Carol ever got to Manhattan, she might consider asking Foy for advice, using her friend's name to get a foot in the door. So, one evening, Carol mustered her courage and ran down to the St. James Theatre, about ten blocks from the Rehearsal Club, to meet the actor. It was a miserable evening: Thunder boomed in the sky and rain pummeled the pavement. A good omen, thought Carol: She seemed to be luckiest when it rained. After working her way backstage by simply dissolving into the busy atmosphere, Carol was soon face to face with Eddie Foy, Jr.

"Please, Mr. Foy, help me," she began. "I want to, I *need* to be in show business. I'm new to New York and I have a friend who knows you and he said that you...and I thought that *maybe*... and then *possibly*..." She babbled on and on, telling the poor man every detail of her current life, where she was from, how she got to Manhattan, and how hopeless it all seemed.

Foy must have thought this person wearing two coats—a

cheap tweed covered by a plastic raincoat—was a certifiable madwoman. "What is it you want to do?" he broke in a little impatiently. Having just finished a performance, he was exhausted and eager to go home. "Do you want to be in the chorus, or what?"

She didn't think she'd be very good at that. She couldn't read music, a prerequisite to any chorus job. And she couldn't dance very well.

"To be honest," she said naively, "I think I would have to have a *featured* role."

Foy may have wondered at her brass, but he was nice enough to take Carol's phone number and say he'd be in touch. She thanked him profusely, and then ran off into the Broadway lights.

The following Monday, the Rehearsal Club's "community phone" rang in the hallway. The sound of that telephone's shrill ring was, as always, very quickly followed by a chorus of "I'll get it" before one of the aspiring performers picked up the receiver. "Carol, it's for you."

"For me? Is it long distance? Is it Don?"

Much to her amazement, it was Eddie Foy, Jr., calling to say that he had made an appointment for her to see his agent. It was a generous, not to mention surprising, gesture on Foy's part, for which Carol said she'd be "eternally grateful."

That week, she went to see the theatrical agent, her prized UCLA theater reviews and clippings in hand. While taking her seat before the fat, balding man, she couldn't help but notice that he seemed much more interested in his stinking cigar than in his visitor. She carefully spread her notices on his desk. "Now, this is the Homecoming Show," she explained breathlessly. "And here, well *here's* one of my *better* pictures."

"Yeah...right," the agent said, unimpressed. He blew a thick puff of smoke at the 8 × 10 glossy.

It wasn't going well.

"I can sing," she offered. "And I can dance, and I *think* I can act, and I *know* I can be funny, and I'll *bet* I could—"

He interrupted her suddenly. "If we need you for anything, we'll call," he said, making no attempt to mask his impatience. "Have a nice day, and close the door on your way out." She was dismissed.

Three months had passed. The irritating ringing sound of "that damn phone" cut into the early-morning quiet. There was no chorus of "I'll get it"—everyone was still sleeping. Carol crawled out of bed and dragged herself into the cold hallway. The call was for her. It was Mama.

Jody Burnett had died.

Carol adored her father, but he had nevertheless been a major disappointment to her. He was a tall, thin, gentle, good-looking man, with a full smile and a great capacity for love and understanding. He was probably one of the most sincere people she'd ever known; he was sensitive to the core. But for as long as Carol could remember, Jody had had a drinking problem. He wasn't a mean alcoholic, like her mother would become. He was just very, very sad.

Joseph Thomas Burnett, or Jody, as he was nicknamed, was born in Texas in 1907, the third and youngest son of Nora and John Burnett. Jody and Carol's mother, née Louise Creighton, met at Breckenridge High School in San Antonio and fell in love. Soon they were married, much to the chagrin of Louise's mother.

Mae never cared for Jody. Because he had no money, Nanny blamed any misfortune the couple had on the fact that her daughter had married this "worthless good-for-nothing bum."

Jody, Louise, and their only child, Carol Creighton Burnett, never really lived together as a family. Jody and Louise moved to California, leaving Carol in Texas with Mae. Jody became a door-to-door coupon salesman for a photographic business. Carol visited her parents once at their home on Montana Avenue in Santa Monica when she was about four, although she barely remembers it. When the marriage began to disintegrate, Louise sent the youngster back to Texas to live with Nanny again. There Carol attended the Crockett Grammer School.

At one point, before he ever left Texas, Jody Burnett was the manager of a movie theater in San Antonio. Little Carol would sit in the dark theater for hours, watching one film after another. (Louise liked to say that Carol was almost born in a movie house during a showing of *Rasputin and the Empress;* Louise barely made it to the hospital in time.)

Jody and Louise regularly wrote letters to Carol and Nanny, always sounding variations on a familiar theme: "As soon as things work out, we'll all be together." Louise would boast about the Hollywood magazines for which she was writing occasional features, the celebrities she was going to meet, and how in-demand she was becoming as a journalist. Though Nanny never believed a word of any of this, Louise really did get interviews with Bob Hope, George Montgomery, and Rita Hayworth.

Louise would usually have to cut her letters short because she was either too dizzy to hold her head up or too sick to carry on.

Louise thought it was entertaining when Jody drank. However, when he became an alcoholic, she was frightened and angry. She would break liquor bottles into the sink as he stood by helplessly, humiliated because she called him weak and hopeless. But by the time Carol was about nine and Louise was in her early thirties, she had become an alcoholic as well.

Carol grew up always hearing from Nanny—and after her parents' divorce, from Louise—about what a "miserable lump" Jody was. But how could a father who would carefully fold a scribbled "Dearest Punkin" letter around two one-dollar bills be a "miserable lump"? He would mail the letter to her from California, and it would arrive in Texas three days later. With genuine indifference, Nanny would snort and hand the envelope to Carol. When the child unfolded the letter, the two bills would fall out and she would squeal with delight. Her daddy loved her.

Once, in a letter to Carol, who was about five years old at the time, he wrote that he had finally stopped drinking. He wouldn't take another drink, he promised, as long as she prayed for him. For years, Carol would feel guilty because Jody would fall off the wagon and she knew that it must be her fault...she hadn't prayed long and hard enough. Her father surely never intended to give his daughter a guilt complex about his drinking, but that's exactly what he did.

Little Carol would come down with a cold, and Nanny would write to Jody and Louise to complain about the cross she had to bear, what with this sick kid and all. That was Nanny's way—she loved Carol and would do anything for her, but if she couldn't complain about it, somehow it just wasn't as rewarding. Jody would send a "Dearest Punkin" letter to Carol telling her to get well because her Mommy and Daddy loved her. Then he would enclose a couple of bucks for Nanny to buy medicine. The coupon business was slow, he would apologize. "Coupons!" Nanny would say, exasperated. "*Coupons!*"

When seven-year-old Carol and Nanny moved to Holly-wood, Carol was able to spend time with her father every now and then. Sometimes he was sober, and then he seemed to her the most wonderful man in the world. They would go to the movies, talk, and laugh for hours. He was Jimmy Stewart. But when he was drunk, he was such a letdown. After a couple of belts, he didn't care about anything: He didn't even seem to care about her. She wondered how he could hurt her like that...how he could drink.

The years passed. "I took her to see her father once," Don Saroyan recalls. "It was the last time she ever saw Jody. He was sort of out of it. I felt great sympathy for him. When they were together, it was like no one else in the world existed."

That was in August 1954, just before she moved to New York. Jody was forty-six years old. He was sick and in the tuber-culosis ward at Olive View Sanitarium in California; it was sur-prising to Carol that he'd become so whippet-thin and frail-looking. His once-smooth face was etched with lines that be-spoke years of frustration and underdog humiliations. When he spoke, he seemed infinitely tired and sounded pained. His eyes looked permanently glazed. Joseph Thomas Burnett had made such a mess of his life, and who knew why? Who even remem-bered how?

It wasn't a somber meeting. Carol told her father about the man in La Jolla who had lent money to her and Don so they could go to New York. Jody listened intently; he was a bit sad, guilt-ridden. "I wish I could have given you the money, Carol," he said, tears in his eyes. She believed him.

He had never seen her on the stage. Proudly, she showed him some of the reviews and clippings of her UCLA perform-ances. Carol had selected each article carefully, and when Jody slowly read every word, it made her smile. She explained that what she wanted most was to become a famous theater-actress like the great Ethel Merman. He wasn't surprised. To his kid, the whole world had always been a stage.

Father and daughter made a pact. At the time of her Broad-way debut, she would send him the money so he could come to Manhattan. There would be a center seat for him in the first row. It would be their night. She would be a success, and they would be proud together.

Now, three months later, he was dead. She felt cold and lonely.

Carol didn't go to her father's funeral because she had no money for the train fare back to Los Angeles. Memories of Jody haunted her. She could not get him out of her mind. The days turned into weeks and, suddenly, it was October.

Nanny had said that if Carol didn't become famous by Christmas, she should just come home and forget about this pipe dream. "Either they like you, or they don't," she sniffed.

Carol hadn't told Nanny—it would probably have floored the old woman if she knew—but she had very generously given herself five years to make it...not to become a star, but just to get some kind of paying job doing *anything* in front of an audience. She was learning the ground rules quickly: No agent was interested in an aspiring performer unless that performer was already working on the stage, and no one could work on the stage unless he or she had an agent. It was a theatrical catch-22.

Even life in New York was not what she had anticipated. Everyone she met had his or her own life and problems; no one was really concerned about hers. And even though her friends at the Rehearsal Club all had the same aspirations and faced the same obstacles, there was still something oddly impersonal about her relationships with them. Though cordial, they all seemed self-involved and remote. There was really no one to encourage Carol on the days she felt most rejected, days that were becoming more and more frequent.

Previously when she was depressed, a stroll down Broadway could lift her spirits. But not these days. If anything, that seemed to make matters worse. *Those* people had jobs in the theater; *she* was a hatcheck girl in a tearoom. And at this point she couldn't fathom a more thankless job. Self-pity was rapidly setting in— she was sure that everything and everybody were working against her.

So when Don Saroyan finally completed his work in Las Vegas and arrived in Manhattan, Carol had never been so happy to see anyone in her life. She loved Don, and having him here with her was a much-needed comfort. The reunion was a tearfully happy one.

Carol hadn't had many boyfriends, and was absolutely determined to "remain pure" for her eventual husband because that's what all "good girls" did. Still, she was curious. But sexuality was not an open subject in 1955, so she and Don rarely discussed it. That could wait. The important thing was that they were together again. She wasn't going to pressure Don into marriage.

One reason Don had been in Las Vegas was in order to establish the six-week residency that Nevada state law required before a divorce could be obtained there. Now he was a free man again (Don and his former wife had long been separated). He intended to marry Carol as soon as possible—as soon as they could afford such a commitment. "Apparently, Carol has indicated that I was not eager for marriage. I don't remember it that way at all," he says, "and maybe she'd be surprised to know that. I just assumed that we'd be married, and that's why I went to Vegas to get the divorce."

Don was enthusiastic about his and Carol's future in New York, and was also riding a crest of optimism thanks to a successful Las Vegas production of *The Happy Time,* which he produced for the parks department. In order to be near Carol, he moved into a one-room apartment in a three-story brownstone at 44 West Fifty-fourth Street, near the Rehearsal Club.

The unit was hardly large enough to accommodate one person, so there was barely room to breathe when two friends from Los Angeles who had relocated to Manhattan moved in with Don. Bruce Campbell, just discharged from the army, and Frank Wolff, an aspiring actor, were new to the East Coast and in search of their own show-business destinies.

No one in this optimistic triumvirate was making any money yet. Perhaps, they mused, when they started working they could move into an apartment in which the sink worked. Meanwhile, they rigged up a dish-washing system in the bathtub—plates and glasses piled on a tray, all of which were rinsed off by shower water. Carol would smuggle food in from Susan Palmer's for her hungry friends.

"We were also eating a lot of potato sandwiches back then," Campbell remembers. "I was going to be a writer, producer, and director. Don was going to be the great musical-comedy star. Frank, who was to be a brilliant actor, was the first to get some work, off-Broadway."

Of the three, Frank Wolff was considered the most likely to become famous. He had played the lead in *Macbeth* at UCLA, and was said to have been a great influence on fellow-student James Dean's acting style. Yet Frank never made it. Years later, he committed suicide in Rome.

Bruce Campbell remembers the evenings he, Carol, and Don would walk down Broadway, the three of them gawking at the neon-lit marquees. Carol would always find the brightest, most mesmerizing one and announce decisively, "One day *my* name will be up there in lights. Just wait and see."

"Sure, Carol," her friends would respond, teasing her. "That'll be the day."

This isn't to say, though, that Carol's optimism was unwavering. "I can't tell you how many nights we sat on the steps of St. Thomas's Church on the corner of Fifty-third and Fifth, with me telling her she was wonderful, she was sensational, she had to stick it out and persevere because she owed it to herself," Don remembers. "I think that during those talks I believed it more than she probably did."

Anecdotes of Carol's struggling days in New York abound from the people who knew her best. One of her former vocal coaches, Edna Wood, remembers: "She was Gracie Allen when it came to handling money. She would pay me from her Susan Palmer tips. She'd clank when she walked, from all the change in her pockets. And as she handed me nickels, dimes, and pennies, she once said, 'You will live to see the day when somebody else handles my money.'"

No matter how hopeless their situations in New York were, the UCLA contingent seemed to find the proverbial silver lining to every cloud. Even if there was an occasional lapse of determination.

One February evening in 1955, Carol and a group of her friends, including Don and Bruce, went to see a revival of William Saroyan's *The Time of Your Life,* starring Gloria Vanderbilt, at the City Center Theatre. The temperature was a frigid twenty degrees. Hungry and freezing, the group stopped off at the Stage Delicatessen, where Broadway's elite congregated; just being in this atmosphere was usually a morale booster, but not this evening.

"We'll never make it in this damn town," Campbell announced, ordering yet another beer.

"Brucie, you shouldn't drink so much," Carol warned. (Because of her background, she was always very cautious about alcohol and never overdid it. To this day, if she has one drop too much, she will get ill. Don was just as sensitive about alcohol and says that he never drank when Carol was around.)

"I've had it with New York," Bruce announced, by now feeling the effects of his beers. "Carol and Don, you guys suffer and starve, if that's what you want. I've had it. I'm finished. I'm leaving town...."

"You'll be back," Carol said solemnly.

Bruce left town, hitch-hiking to Florida with twenty dollars in his pocket. That evening, his roommates divided up his belongings. In a couple of days, Bruce was back.

"That's how we were back then," Don recalls with a grin. "The pull of Broadway, the magic of believing. It was so damn irresistible."

The search for work continued. Don was now employed by the R-K-O Roxy Theatre on Sixth Avenue at Forty-ninth Street. His G.I. Bill brought in about twenty dollars a week, so his small Roxy salary came in handy. Work as an usher was boring and monotonous; he saw Van Heflin perform in *The Black Widow* dozens of times.

Also, he recalls, the job was humiliating. He had come to Manhattan to set the Broadway stage ablaze, and instead he was cooling his heels and showing movie patrons to their seats. "So close, yet so far," he lamented. Later, he took a job as a waiter at a bar on Forty-sixth Street. He was fired on the third day, when his boss realized that he didn't even know how to arrange a proper table setting.

It seemed that Carol and her circle of friends needed a shot in the arm, and one day she came up with the perfect motivator. She remembered a passing comment Eddie Foy's agent had made when she complained about not being able to get a job without an agent, or an agent without a job. "Hey, kid, why don't you just put on your own show?" he said absentmindedly, while he puffed away on that fat, disgusting cigar.

"Why don't I put on my own show!"

Finally, an idea that made sense.

Carol was now president of the Rehearsal Club, duly elected

because none of the other girls wanted the distinction. Most were too busy to be bothered. Some were now actually working; there were a couple of Rockettes here and there in the hallways. Most of the others were still always on the run, chasing after agents and job leads. The rest were hatcheck girls.

One evening after dinner, Carol called an official meeting. She told the girls that she had some information to pass along that would make a difference in all of their careers, "...our very *lives* even," she said dramatically. Usually, the only time anyone ever called a meeting of residents was when she wanted to file a complaint about the food. So the girls were less than enthused.

They filed into the parlor slowly.

"Listen, girls, I think we ought to put on our own show," Carol began nervously. Blank faces stared at her.

"What for?" someone asked.

"Who has time to play make-believe when we're trying to find real jobs?" another skeptic added.

Carol went on to explain that they had all seen practically every agent in Manhattan, but to no avail. It was time for them to take matters into their own hands, to create their own showcase for their talents. "If we put on a show, maybe some agents will come to see us and they'll realize how good we are and they'll put us to work and...and...and all our problems will be over," she stammered away.

There was silence. Then a smattering of applause.

Twenty of the girls decided to put on a revue that would be about a bunch of girls putting on a revue. There would be solo numbers as well as group numbers: The showcase would be called *The First Annual Rehearsal Club Revue*.

Carol recruited Don as producer/director. "If you could actually say it was produced and directed," he jokes. "It really was one of those 'Hey-kids-let's-put-on-a-show' kind of stories, like *Babes in Arms*. We rehearsed at the Showcase Rehearsal Studios on Seventh Avenue. At the end of each practice session, we would take up a collection from everyone involved in order to pay for the studio."

For one hundred dollars an evening, the residents could rent the Carl Fischer Hall on West Fifty-seventh Street for two nights. The girls came up with half the money, and the women who financed the Rehearsal Club donated the balance. One of the club's board members, popular Broadway actress Katharine Cornell, was persuaded to endorse the show and sign the invitations, hastily printed penny postcards that could be used for admittance.

March 3, 1955, 8:00 P.M. Carl Fischer Hall was packed with invited agents, directors, producers, and friends. The air was charged with electricity as the girls noisily ran about backstage fixing seams, practicing harmonies, and chattering about how nervous they were.

"Is it too late to back out?" someone asked. "I'm so scared, I think I might throw up."

"What rotten luck!" another girl complained. "*Bus Stop* opens tonight on Broadway, of all nights!"

"But did you see those people out there?" someone else asked. "The place is *packed.*"

"You're *kidding!*" Carol said as she made a beeline to the curtain. She pulled it back just a crack, enough to sneak a quick look out into the audience. Not a good idea. "Oh, no! Oh, no!" she screamed. "Oh, no! Oh, no!"

She had spotted Marlene Dietrich and Celeste Holm in the busy crowd. Now, she was dazed, almost unable to register.

"Please, God, let me be good. Let me remember my music," Carol prayed, her knees shaking. Already she was perspiring, and she hadn't even gone on yet. "Let them like me."

In less than two hours, the verdict was in. The show was a success; the audience approved of the girls' creation. But more to the point, Carol Burnett was a revelation to more than a few ticket holders. In the first act, she sang a straight, mournful number called "I Love New York, but I'm Scared." It hit close to home, and Carol's delivery was strong and convincing. In the second act, she performed an ingenious rendition of "Monotonous," Eartha Kitt's number from *New Faces of 1952.* This was the evening's showstopper.

Kitt's version was memorable: She oozed sex appeal and lounged on six elegant chaises as she sang about the monotony of fast life and high-rolling, and how dull it was to be lusted after by fascinating men. But Carol's concept was to perform the number in a dowdy housedress, an old pair of "sensible shoes," curlers in her hair . . . and with three beat-up wooden kitchen chairs. She was the bedraggled frump who suffered from the same problems Eartha sang about.

There was obviously more than a bit of self-revelation in her sense of irony. "I knew I wasn't going to win any glamour prizes," she said later. "I was going to have to establish myself as a slob." In many ways, Carol's performance of "Monotonous" was the precursor to her Charwoman character, which would be developed years later.

Somehow, Carol's performance gave the entire revue an aura of excitement. The other girls were just average, but Carol was special, like the smart kid in class who drags the whole grade-curve up.

"Easily, the winner in the parlay was Carol Burnett," wrote Leo Shull in *Show Business,* the actors' trade publication. "She's a character-actress comedienne who stole the honors. She can sing and pantomime with the best of them, her timing is top notch."

Theatre Arts published two photographs taken during the first performance, including one of Carol alone in her big number. This magazine was considered the show-business "bible" to girls registered at the club, so recognition of their efforts here was quite a morale booster.

In the weeks to come, many of the young performers who'd been in the show were contacted by agents for possible representation. Twenty called on Carol. Her head was spinning; everyone around her was making suggestions as to whom she should ultimately choose to represent her. She remembered that after the show Celeste Holm had come backstage and offered to counsel her if she had any problems or questions. Holm was very gracious; as it happened, she would spend an entire Saturday afternoon with the novice Burnett. Eventually, they agreed that Carol should sign with the prestigious William Morris Agency and start at the top.

The agency sent Carol out on a job on April 18, but it wasn't the most rewarding work. She was one of the "stars" of what was called an industrial show for the Aluminum Corporation of America at the Eighth Street Theatre in Chicago. The cast came out in skirts made of aluminum foil, and they sang and performed in sketches about how great the foil was as a wrap. Carol delighted in the work, and the money wasn't bad; it afforded her the opportunity to go home to Los Angeles for a ten-day visit.

Don Saroyan remembers: "The big number was something about 'I have the best-wrapped garbage in town. Why? Because I wrap in aluminum foil.'"

Carol Burnett was finally on a stage, and there was some satisfaction in that despite the odd surroundings. Indeed, she was on her way . . . sort of.

2

S HE READ ABOUT THE AUDITION IN *SHOW BUSINESS* MAGAZINE. "Old hands, new hands, the great and the small," the ad read. Producer/director Gus Schirmer was holding auditions for summer stock. Schirmer had a lock on casting for summer musicals and theater in New York at that time. To please him was to be guaranteed a whole season's work in some show somewhere. Carol knew that everyone even remotely involved in New York theater would want to audition for Schirmer, but she made the call anyway and set up an appointment.

Hopefully, she would soon go on from industrial shows to something closer to her dreams, but in the meantime, Carol at least had some steady work. Don had also managed to find a bit of security directing some of these productions. On one, they took the lyrics to "Whatever Lola Wants" from *Damn Yankees* and changed them to "Whatever Hotpoint Wants." That worked, so then they tried "Whatever Motorola Wants."

Gus Schirmer could deliver Carol from all of these household appliances; he could be a godsend. Carol recruited an accompanist, Peter Daniels, to play piano for her audition. Daniels had played for the Rehearsal Club revue, so she trusted him and decided to use his arrangement of "How About You?" When she arrived, she discovered that Schirmer's studio was filled with confused and nervous young actors, actresses, and singers. It was the so-called "cattle-call" situation where, despite prearranged appointments, everyone seems to arrive at exactly the same time. Still, it was hard not to be awed by all of this show-business energy and activity. Carol stood in a corner for a few minutes just to savor and enjoy the moment. More people with dreams and goals; it was all so intoxicating.

Schirmer had hired a young pianist/vocal coach by the name

of Ken Welch to play at the audition for anyone who didn't have an accompanist. Welch had been the musical director of the Pittsburgh Playhouse, and among his protégés there was the young Shirley Jones. He persuaded Jones's family to allow him to take her to New York to audition for a few theatrical producers and agents. First, she auditioned for Schirmer, but that didn't work out. That very same day, she sang for Richard Rodgers, who eventually cast her in the film version of *Oklahoma!* The rest is Shirley Jones legend.

Of Carol's tryout for Schirmer, Welch remembers: "A girl walked into the audition, just radiant and healthy, with a California complexion. She was wearing a simple skirt and blouse, and even before she performed, I liked her. But once she started, I was hooked."

Carol performed the song from *Babes on Broadway* in a straight, very upbeat manner, with few comical affectations. Basically, she was auditioning as a vocalist. Ken Welch thought she was marvelous, but Gus Schirmer didn't agree.

"Thank you, miss. Next."

Carol meticulously gathered up her sheets of music. "Better luck next time," she said to Peter Daniels as she walked away, disappointed. It was obvious that she wouldn't be working for Gus Schirmer. As Carol exited and the next girl came through the door, Ken Welch asked to be excused. He followed Carol down the hall.

Trying to catch up to her, he began, "Excuse me, I just have to tell you this...."

"Yes, what is it?"

She stopped abruptly and looked at the stranger. He was out of breath.

"I think you are absolutely brilliant."

Carol was astonished. "You do? You *really* do? But he didn't like me, did he? Maybe I should've chosen another number. I shoulda done...and I *coulda* done..." Again, she was babbling.

"It doesn't matter what Gus thinks," Ken broke in. "You were wonderful." He introduced himself and then scribbled his name and phone number on a piece of paper and handed it to her. "Call me anytime. Maybe I can help you."

"Thanks. Thanks a lot, Mr. Welch."

Ken recalls: "What I felt from the audition was that she had the ability to communicate gut to gut. There was no pretense about her. She was straightforward and honest. Plus, she had this voice that projected so well. And also, she was extremely attractive. I thought maybe Gus had made a mistake in not accepting her."

Ken trotted back into the audition studio. "Gus, that girl, that Burnett girl! She's terrific. Don't you think?"

"She's okay," Schirmer said halfheartedly. "But she needs work. She needs *a lot* of work."

One of the best places to get "a lot of work" at that time was at an adult summer camp in Warrensburg, New York, called Green Mansions. It was one of a dying breed of summer-stock workshops where actors, actresses, writers, directors, and other show-business people benefited from the experience of working in a different Broadway-style show every week. The audiences consisted mostly of young people and their parents on summer vacations.

In *The Borsht Belt,* their excellent book about resort hotels and camps in the East Coast area, entertainer Joey Adams and lyricist Henry Tobias wrote of places like Green Mansions: "The entertainment had to be good, for the youngsters were far more discriminating than their entertainment-hungry parents. Neither rain, nor storm, nor sun, nor shows would stop them from trying to score (sex), so the show had to be not just original but even, if possible, better than sex to keep them diverted...."

Carol left for Green Mansions on June 18, 1955, but not before getting a job as an extra on a segment of *The Colgate Comedy Hour,* starring Martha Raye. This was Carol's first time in front of a TV camera, and what an auspicious debut it was: She spent the entire sequence kissing a male extra she didn't even know in a "tunnel of love" sketch. When it aired, Nanny sat glued to her television set. Not bad, she probably thought. Maybe next time she'll get to talk.

Ironically, the sketch was written by Ed Simmons, who would, in twenty years, go on to become the head writer and producer of *The Carol Burnett Show.*

At Green Mansions, Carol had the opportunity to play a number of different characters in productions of *Three Penny Opera, I Am a Camera,* and Dorothy Parker's one-act *Here We Are.* The training Carol received here, in terms of discipline, imagination, and skill, would prove invaluable. Plus, she was paid five hundred dollars for the whole season, which included room and board.

Don had a job at MCA with the industrial-show circuit; he was now assistant to the director, so he wasn't able to join Carol at Green Mansions. It was difficult, though, for him not to be jealous of her situation there; it was the perfect environment for anyone interested in theater.

At around this time, the William Morris Agency sent Carol out on an audition for Rodgers and Hammerstein's *Pipe Dream* production, set to open in the fall. She took a bus down from Warrensburg for the audition. In what was probably one of the most exciting, if not terrifying, moments of her life, Carol found herself onstage at the Cort Theatre on the morning of July 28, in front of both Richard Rodgers and Oscar Hammerstein. As she sang "Monotonous," her voice seemed to bounce off the walls of the near-empty theater, and even she was surprised at how big it sounded. Carol was so bewitched by this experience, the day would be stamped on her brain forever.

"That was quite marvelous, Miss Burnett," Mr. Rodgers said to her from his seat in the audience. "Do you think you could come back in two weeks and do that again for our director, Harold Clurman?"

Did he need to ask? Harold Clurman had directed *Bus Stop*. Rodgers and Hammerstein were, well, *Rodgers and Hammerstein*.

"Yes, oh, yes, sir!" Carol said excitedly as she looked down at him from the empty stage. She probably had to pinch herself to make sure she wasn't dreaming—was she really standing on a *Broadway* stage, talking to *the* Richard Rodgers? If only Nanny could see her now.

"Yes, sir. I'll be back," Carol said confidently. "Thanks. Thanks a lot..."

As far as Carol was concerned, these were to be the slowest-passing two weeks in show-business history. When she finally returned, she sang again, and then was told that they'd like to see her for a third call-back. She gazed at them in utter disbelief.

Now this was almost too much to bear. All she could think of every day at Green Mansions was *Pipe Dream*, and how thrilling it would be if she got this job. Her problems would be over. Good-bye, Susan Palmer's! Hello, Broadway! But when it was time for her third audition, she caught an ill-timed flu. "What am I going to do? Oh, no, not now! *Not today!*" she sobbed.

She auditioned anyway. What else could she do?

"Uh, thank you, Miss Burnett. We'll, uh, be in touch."

It took a moment for that to sink in, but she knew what it meant. She didn't get the job.

It was fall 1955. All of that summer excitement, and to what end? Carol was back to work as a hatcheck girl.

While at Green Mansions, she mentioned to a choreographer friend on staff that she thought she might like to work with a vocal coach. "The best coach in town is Ken Welch," he told her. ("He had choreographed a couple of revues for me, so he was a bit biased," Welch laughs.) The name clicked in Carol's head, and she promised herself that when she returned to Manhattan she'd give Welch a call.

"Hello. You won't remember me..." she began.

How could he forget? They arranged a meeting.

When they got together, Ken encouraged Carol to sing every song in her growing repertoire. She had a wide range of material by now, everything from zany comedy to straight ballads. Ken immediately noticed that she sang her serious material with a pained resolve, as if she were tremendously uncomfortable with it. When she wasn't being funny, she lacked character and personality, or, as Ken put it, "down would come a mental block."

Despite that, he recognized an earnest, if rather vaguely focused, desire to be a star. She made it clear that she'd never shy away from hard work.

"I offered her a couple of choices," he remembers. "I told her that I could probably come up with some outrageous stuff, because she was good at mugging and making faces. She could do this material and become the rage of Greenwich Village. But that would be it. She'd never be taken more seriously than that.

"Or, we could work on some long-range plans, material that would be well thought out and would give her career some direction. Which would it be? A quick buck or a long career?"

The decision was obvious. Carol hadn't come all the way to New York just to make "a quick buck."

After the first session together, Carol and Ken agreed that they'd work up a rendition of the raucous "Everybody Loves to

Take a Bow" from the Broadway show *Hazel Flagg*. Afterward, it was time to talk business.

Carol looked at him levelly. "Look," she began, "I don't have much money. I can't come here every week. How about every other week?"

"No! No! *No!*" Welch insisted. "If we're to make this work, you have to come twice a week."

"I gotta tell you," she said firmly, "I'd be lucky to be able to afford to come here twice a *year*. I really want to do this, but I think we'll just have to forget it for now...."

Welch remembers: "I told her she could owe me the money. It was so little, I don't even remember the amount. But she said, 'No way!' I was really fond of her, and knew that she'd never get any work if someone didn't start coaching her. If not me, someone else. And I wanted it to be me. So I went to a drugstore and got a tablet of promissory notes. And we agreed that every time she came she would sign a note. Then, if she ever made any money, she would pay me what she owed me."

It's fortunate for all concerned that Ken trusted Carol. Today, thirty-two years later, he and his wife, Mitzie Cottle Welch, are still writing Carol's special material. "Eventually," he smiles, "she did pay me what she owed me."

Welch picks up the story: "We started going on a lot of auditions all over Manhattan. None of them resulted in any work. We found that the musical-comedy roles that existed for Carol's type were almost all for older women, so that was a roadblock. To me, she was a leading-lady comedienne, even back then. So we decided we needed some special comedic material for her to audition with rather than songs identified with other singers. She'd be the only newcomer with her own standards..."

Carol had met agent Arthur Willi as a result of the Rehearsal Club show. Even though she signed with another agency, she and Willi maintained a friendship. When he heard that ventriloquist/entertainer Paul Winchell was auditioning girl singers for a regular role on his then-popular *Winchell-Mahoney Show,* he suggested that Carol set up an audition. The job would pay only $115 a week, but it would offer her national television exposure.

Paul Winchell recalls of the audition: "She was extremely nervous. I remember her telling me that if she didn't get this job, she might consider going back to Los Angeles. She was having no success in New York, and I felt that she was at the end of her rope. I told her not to get hysterical, just go up on that stage and do whatever she thinks she can do best. She auditioned some song ["Somewhere Over the Rainbow"], in a very big voice and I hired her personally."

Winchell was reticent about discussing Carol's thirteen weeks on his program, out of modesty, it appeared. "Don't say that I gave her her first television break," he cautioned, "because compared to the marvelous things she did after that, it seems presumptuous."

The Winchell-Mahoney Show had been one of the most popular children's programs since 1947. Winchell was named television's most versatile performer in 1952 and in 1953. (Incidentally, years later he would be credited, along with Dr. William J. Kolff, with the invention of the earliest artificial heart.) So appearing as a regular on his show was a real coup for Carol. She was excited about it, but there was still an empty feeling in her gut. It wasn't the theater; and Winchell wasn't George Abbott.

Carol was amazed that Winchell had actually hired her; she and Don celebrated over dinner, and then she called Nanny collect to tell her the news. Immediately, her grandmother wanted to know how much Carol would be paid. Considering that Mae was paying $34 a month rent, Carol's making $115 for 30 minutes of work must have seemed rather outrageous. "Say hello to me on the air, will you?" Nanny suggested. "That would be real nice."

Carol tried to explain that NBC wouldn't appreciate it if she broke into their scripted program to say hello to her grandmother on the West Coast. "NBC can't be hurt by one little hello to your grandmother," Nanny argued.

That's when they came up with the signal: Carol would tug on her left ear at the end of each program. This would be an acknowledgment that Nanny's girl was thinking about her. It was a signal a couple of Carol's friends who were dancers had invented to tell their little boy that they loved him when they knew he was watching them perform. Of course, this went on to become one of Carol's trademarks. (Once, it was reported that a newspaperman measured her earlobes after years of tugging and discovered that one was now longer than the other.)

December 17, 1955. Carol made her television debut on *The Winchell-Mahoney Show* singing "Somewhere Over the Rainbow" to dummy Jerry Mahoney.

Over the next couple of months, Carol would become a favorite personality on the series. Usually, her spot was a quick song arranged by Milton DeLugg and somehow relating to the show's premise that week. For instance, Jerry vanished on one episode, and so Carol wailed "Where Oh Where Can Jerry Be?" (He was eating breakfast with Paul Winchell.) On another show, Mahoney and Winchell were troubled by a pesky draft in their clubhouse, so Carol bellowed out "Little Sir Echo." Another week, NBC sent out a hastily prepared press release that urged, "Don't miss young Carol Burnett's wonderful rendition of 'Here Comes Peter Cotton Tail.'"

For Carol, this job gave new meaning to the cliché "everybody has to start somewhere."

"It was exciting for her," Don Saroyan remembers. "But, let's face it, not much of a showcase. As I remember it, she sang but did no comedy. But it gave her hope. It gave us *both* hope that this kind of thing really was possible."

Don certainly needed the reinforcement, because he was now driving a cab part time to help make ends meet. Despite the disparity in their careers at this point, Don and Carol were committed to their relationship.

This news would not make Nanny's day. Her goals for Carol were simple and nearly engraved in stone: She should marry someone who had a steady job and a decent bank account. "Get the ring," she would preach. "Go to Woodbury secretarial school, become a secretary, and marry the boss. *Get that ring!*" To Nanny, there was no one more hopeless than an old maid.

But despite what Carol saw in him, Don Saroyan was still an unemployed actor with no money. As far as Nanny was concerned, he certainly wasn't good enough for her granddaughter. "She was born in 1885, when the men had all the power," Carol has observed. "If there was any money, the men had it. Her thinking was, 'Get somebody and get him for all he's worth.'" Nanny didn't think Don was worth very much.

To most of their friends, Carol and Don seemed like the perfect couple, and in many ways they probably were. They were compatible in the sense that they shared common goals and ambitions related to the theater. Their struggle against what sometimes seemed like insurmountable odds since they had moved to New York City had drawn them closer together. Each of them had a wonderful sense of humor and was able to make light of their mutual dilemma; they spent a lot of time laughing.

Carol's vibrancy was a tonic for Don. He loved the way she couldn't wait to roar into the new day. It inspired him to do the same. Her naiveté was refreshing; she was such an innocent, and her vulnerability aroused his deepest interest.

Don was quite a catch for someone like Carol, a girl who'd look in the mirror only to agonize over the reflection. He was a warm, gentle man, "tall, dark, and handsome." She noticed that on campus his presence seemed to electrify everyone within range. Before Carol came into Don's life, he had a reputation for being quite the ladies' man. But after he met Carol, there was no other girl for him. She knew this, and it gave her a sense of security and fulfillment. Also, she valued the way he bolstered her self-confidence with pep talks and encouragement.

Don was five years older than Carol, much more mature than she, and seemed able to handle any situation. She could rely on him where others had failed her. To her, it seemed as if he'd already lived a full lifetime of experiences.

An only child, Don is from Omaha, Nebraska. A brother died when Don was a few months old; his mother, Anna, also passed away when Don was a child. His father, Harvey Saroyan, owned a dry-cleaning plant in Omaha, and later a successful drive-in restaurant. He died when Don was in his late twenties. It's often been written that Don was a relative of author William Saroyan. In truth, the two were not related. Don had, however, met the playwright and fiction writer on several occasions.

Don acted in college at the University of Omaha, but unlike Carol (who remembers that despite their financial plight, she and Nanny always managed to figure out a way to see eight movies a week), he was not a film buff. He starred in several shows in the Omaha Community Playhouse, and at one point he and his singing instructor formed a vocal duo and hosted a thirty-minute television series in Omaha called *The RCA Master Show Room*. It was a local success, airing opposite a community show with a similar format, hosted by local boy Johnny Carson. When Omaha was given access to network television, both shows were canceled. Johnny Carson went on to do a few other things with his career. Saroyan joined the navy.

He married at the age of eighteen, relocated to his wife's hometown of Philadelphia, and had one child, a daughter he adored. After the couple moved back to Omaha, the marriage broke up, and his wife returned to Pennsylvania with the child. Eventually, Saroyan moved to Los Angeles, where he hoped to be "discovered" as a singer and actor. He enrolled in a UCLA graduate-studies program.

"We all looked up to Don Saroyan," Lenny Weinrib, Don's fellow UCLA student recalls. "We thought of him as being a real theater-experienced fellow because of his theatrical background in Omaha. He was a real showman, the veteran of show business, in our eyes, with this young, funny, up-and-coming comedienne at his side. Also, he was a good four years older than everyone else, and that made all the difference."

Don and Carol met on the UCLA campus in 1952, at the beginning of the fall semester, through a mutual friend, Peggy McKenna. "Peggy told me that there was a wonderful girl on campus who would be great for me," he recalls. "'You'll *love* her, you'll *adore* her,' she said. One afternoon, the two of us were eating lunch near Royce Hall when this gangly creature came bounding across the yard. My immediate reaction was, 'My God, Peggy! You've got to be kidding...' But then I met her, and I was hers. Instantly hers." Soon, they were dating.

"Carol never tried to hide anything from me about her background," he remembers. "I never had the feeling that she thought her life was so bad, that she was some kind of 'brave soul' going through a struggle. She was a great overcomer, coping with her difficult home situation, living with it."

Don and a roommate settled into a $130-a-month apartment in Westwood, a bustling neighborhood just outside of the UCLA campus where many students lived in fraternity and sorority houses. It was about five miles from the one-room disaster area that Carol, Chrissy, and Nanny shared. Sometimes Corey Allen, a friend who would go on to become a successful movie producer, would lend Don his automobile for the weekend. Don would drive to Hollywood to pick up Carol for dates. They would spend hours at the Village Delicatessen in Westwood ("We called it the V.D."), talking about show business, the theater, and what the "good life" would be like when they became Broadway stars.

Carol always seemed to have a confident sense of herself as a performer in UCLA productions, and Don, like a lot of other people, was awed by her onstage savvy. As insecure as she may have been before going on, this girl could stand up in front of an audience and suddenly be totally in control. Carol knew that she was different from those students out there in the audience. She was onstage and they weren't. There was something powerful about that. And it felt damn good to her.

"She was everything I enjoyed in a performer, even back then," Don remarks. "She had vitality, showmanship, a broadness about her characterizations, and also generosity. She was eager for that give-and-take between a performer and her audience. I think she really *cared* about her audiences...."

It wasn't long before Carol and Don started working together, sometimes with a fellow student named Alan Light. They complemented each other beautifully, and had a good time singing together.

When the wealthy La Jolla benefactor gave Carol and Don the money to move to Manhattan, they knew that it was the beginning of a wonderful dream come true. Together, the two of them hoped to realize all of their Broadway fantasies.

Carol knew that being in New York with Don would be fun. But it's difficult to believe that she really understood what she was getting into when she decided to marry him. Young and terribly naive, she had never really seen anything more than cold, passionless communication between her parents. Carol had idealized marriage from what she'd seen in the movies, and from what Nanny had told her to expect if she played her cards right with the perfect—as in rich—mate.

Carol grew up in a subculture where women were supposed to marry in their mid-twenties, if not earlier. So that's what she did. Her relationship with Don may have been "the right thing to do," but it doesn't suggest the romantic involvement of a young girl desperately in love.

As one of Carol's friends from Los Angeles says, "She always wanted to do the right thing, that's how she was raised, really. I'm sure Carol probably thought that she and Don would have a family and live happily ever after. She'd cater to everyone's needs, and somehow squeeze her career into the cracks. The fact that she wanted a career at all was the progressive side of Carol. Where Nanny was concerned, women didn't have careers, they had husbands."

The afternoon of the Paul Winchell show, Don borrowed an

automobile from his boss at MCA so that he and Carol could drive to Yonkers—"where true love conquers"—to be married by a justice of the peace in a small ceremony. Peggy McKenna, the woman who introduced them at UCLA, was a witness to the ceremony. Saroyan is hazy about the brief honeymoon, saying that he has only a vague memory of going "somewhere in the mountains" to be alone together.

Nanny and Louise were very unhappy about Carol's news when she called to tell them that she was now a married woman. Ordinarily, Louise was a complete romantic, in love with the idea of love, but Nanny's negativity had rubbed off on her. Nanny kept harping on Carol's "misfortune," and soon Louise was just as upset.

Perhaps Mae and Louise's reaction would have been understandable if they had been concerned about Carol being trapped in a marriage for which she was unprepared. But that wasn't it at all. They simply believed that she was a fool for marrying someone who was, in their view, as badly off as she was. He had no money, no real job, and, worse yet, he was Armenian, "and you know how they are . . . you'll end up with a house full of kids."

Moreover, they probably felt that they'd really "lost" Carol to this interloper. So the two women harassed her with letters that condemned the marriage. Carol craved their approval, and so their bitter criticism hurt her more than they probably even realized; though in time the wounds would heal, there would always be scars. Their opinion of her marriage didn't do much for Carol's self-image, and only served to intensify her deep-rooted feelings of self-doubt. *Had* she made the right choice in marrying Don?

Yes, she decided, she had. Maybe. "Why don't they just leave me alone?" she wondered angrily. And then Carol desperately tried to keep Nanny and Louise's opinion of him from her new husband. Apparently, she did a good job. Don never really knew how Nanny and Louise felt.

He remembers: "They never said anything at all to me about the marriage. I heard that they warned Carol against marrying me because I was Armenian. Today, I don't have any pertinent feelings about Nanny or Louise," he concludes. "There was never any unpleasantness between us, and never any great feeling of warmth, either."

Obviously, the time had come for Carol to move out of the

Rehearsal Club. The Saroyans settled into a simple one-room apartment on West Fifty-fourth Street between Sixth and Seventh Avenues. "It was humble," Don remembers, "but what did we care? We were newlyweds and very happy. We had a lot of friends, and New York was still exciting to us. It was a good life."

(Carol wouldn't forget her Rehearsal Club beginnings. In 1963, she began sponsoring an annual production by girls at the club. The winner was awarded the Carol Burnett Fund, money applied against room and board at the Rehearsal Club, which allowed her to use her own money for drama lessons or other expenses for a period of a year. By the time the Rehearsal Club closed its doors in 1980 after more than fifty years in operation, it was said that over ten thousand girls had lived there.)

The Saroyans' efficiency apartment was above the La Scala Italian restaurant, and when they had guests over for an Italian dinner, Carol would use canned sauces and leave the windows open so that the aroma of what was simmering downstairs would waft into the small apartment. "In that apartment, it always smelled like Carol was the greatest cook in the world," says a friend, "but then when you ate her food, the jig was up."

For just a couple of months, Carol and Don had nothing on their minds but the concerns of being newlyweds and trying to find work. It was a happy, frivolous existence. But in March, they were faced with tragedy. Don's young daughter was hit by an automobile in Philadelphia. She was in critical condition; Don and Carol immediately went to the hospital to be by her side. The girl died a couple of days later.

Suddenly, everything had changed.

"In all fairness to Carol," Saroyan says thoughtfully, "what happened didn't make me very easy to live with."

Don was devastated by his daughter's senseless death. A proud man who refused to reach out in "weakness," he withdrew into a dark world that Carol couldn't seem to penetrate. Rather than cling to her in this time of deep grief and bereavement, he pushed her away. He wouldn't confide in her, or share his emotions. Instead, he kept all of his misery to himself and became sullen and despondent, impersonal and distant. He was turning himself inside out, and there was nothing she could do about it.

"Carol has always been a very passive person," says a friend of Carol and Don's. "She shied away from confrontation. And she simply didn't have the experience to force Don to deal with feelings of anger and pain. Plus, I think that she was very much afraid of those emotions."

Don began to reconsider his goals. Becoming a show-business success no longer mattered to him; musical comedy wasn't as much fun as it used to be. It was as if all of the humor in his life was swamped by the pain—a human reaction to a devastating personal loss.

Carol really didn't know how to handle this immense sorrow. The dynamics of their relationship were such that Don and Carol rarely dealt with the serious, dark sides of life. They could usually punctuate the saddest stories with a joke that drew gales of laughter. Their romance up until this point had been one long, funny, happy improv.

Carol would try to counter her husband's grief with humor and cheerfulness, but that rarely worked. She sympathized with Don, but mostly she felt helpless. She knew that this wasn't the ideal way to start off a marriage.

"And also," Don adds, "it's Carol's basic personality that she's always on such a high. The wind had been knocked out of my sails. I was a drag to be around, I'm sure. I was changed, but she was still the same."

Carol has never publicly discussed Don's tragedy, and apparently, she purposely omitted it from her autobiography, "out of respect for my privacy, I'm sure," Saroyan acknowledges.

They threw themselves into their work: Don at odd jobs and on industrial shows, Carol on the *Winchell-Mahoney* program. But then Paul Winchell's ratings dropped. NBC moved his show from its popular Saturday-morning spot to an obscure Sunday air time, and then canceled it altogether. Later, ABC would pick it up, but without a girl singer. Carol was disappointed but not devastated. She still thought of herself as a stage actress who dabbled in television. "I was not hooked on it," she has said of TV. "I always felt that the stage was for me. If someone offered me an opportunity on television, I wouldn't turn it down. But, still, I wanted to be Ethel [Merman]."

Months passed, and on the outside it seemed that Don was coping fairly well. So, in the summer of 1956, when Carol was asked to join another theater workshop as she had done the previous year at Green Mansions, she and Don decided that she should go.

The resort, called Tamiment, was in the Pocono Mountains

of Pennsylvania and was also the last of the popular resort hotels of its kind. Just as at Green Mansions, every week three sketch writers and four songwriters would put together a different Broadway-style major production. Expedience was the name of the game. Says Mary Rodgers, one of the writers at Tamiment (and daughter of composer Richard Rodgers): "An hour and fifteen minutes was the staying power of a Tamiment audience. They were revered and renowned for a lack of staying power."

"I was one of the last who had a chance to learn and make mistakes in summer stock," Carol would say years after the fact. "I did summer stock where nobody was a star. Everybody was a beginner hoping for the best. I don't know where young people can practice and learn their crafts in front of live audiences anymore. There are comedy clubs for stand-up comics, places where people can hone that skill. But where do people go to learn to play sketches today?"

Back when Carol made her first big impression in Manhattan with *The Rehearsal Club Revue*, there were quite a few people in the audience who would cross paths with her later on. One was then-thirty-two-year-old lyricist-composer Marshall Barer, who made his own New York debut in January 1955 with the musical *Once Over Lightly*. A writer for Tallulah Bankhead and Beatrice Lillie, he was also part of the Tamiment writing staff. He and Mo Hack, Tamiment producer, were scouting for talent in 1955 and attended the Rehearsal Club show hoping to make a major discovery.

"I flipped out over this young girl Burnett," Marshall Barer remembers. "'Hire her! She's sensational. She has that *Je-ne-sais-quoi* quality. She's top-banana material,' I told Mo Hack."

"Hell no!" Hack shot back. "She's too inexperienced. She's good, but not top-banana material. Second banana, maybe."

That was the summer Carol ended up at Green Mansions. The next year, in the summer of 1956, she *was* chosen as top female banana at Tamiment, where she would work with up-and-coming top male banana Arte Johnson. Barer was senior writer, and Kenny Welch was special-material junior writer. Don, who was working at MCA, would visit the troupe on weekends, just as he did when Carol was at Green Mansions.

One Thursday evening a couple of weeks into the summer season, Carol called her husband with some good news.

"They've fired the stage manager here," she said brightly. "I told them about you, Don. Why don't you come up here?"

"How can I?" Don asked. "What about my job?"

"You need to be here," Carol said. "I think it'll do you a lot of good."

Don remembers: "It was a good idea. First of all, it would get me into an entertainment-related situation with new, interesting people. And also, we could be together, Carol and I. At this point, I was terribly unhappy at MCA because I didn't feel I was getting what I should have been getting. So I went into my boss's office the next day and told him I wanted a huge raise. He said, 'No way,' so I quit."

Don drove straight to the Poconos, where at Tamiment he made, according to his recollection, forty dollars a week, plus free room and board.

"We had a helluva good time at Tamiment," recalls Ken Welch. "Everyone loved Carol and Don, they were like the perfect couple. I remember Carol in Sol Berkowitz's opera *Fat Tuesday*, where she played a chorus girl who, by the way, looked terrific in her little chorine outfit. (Mitzie Cottle, whom Ken later married, played the lead.) We did a lot of revues; in one, Carol sang a knockout number I wrote called 'Destroy Me.' Day in and day out, all we thought about was theater."

"It was such an exciting atmosphere," Don adds. "Some of the things we did there I still recall well today and hum the melodies to. We worked very hard, but it was the kind of work we craved."

3

ON SUNDAY, OCTOBER 7, 1956, CAROL MADE AN IMPORTANT AP-
pearance on the outstanding ninety-minute weekly cul-
tural program *Omnibus*. This segment, the first of the series' fifth
season and written and narrated by Leonard Bernstein, paid
tribute to musical comedy with scenes and music from shows
such as *South Pacific* and the operetta *The Mikado*.Wearing a
flouncy eighteenth-century costume and an elaborate white-pow-
dered wig, Carol performed "(Give Him the) Ooh-La-La" from
Cole Porter's 1939 hit *DuBarry Was a Lady* (which had originally
starred Ethel Merman on Broadway).

Perry Gray, one of Carol's UCLA friends who maintained a
regular correspondence with her at this time, organized a small
party of West Coast friends to cheer on her appearance. Carol
had no introduction (none of the singers did), but her enthusiastic three-minute performance was memorable to her school
chums just the same. Says Gray, laughing, "It was sensational to
us, even though we might have gone down the street and asked
someone else about it only to hear, 'Oh, yeah, you mean that
noisy lady on TV?'

"As we were watching, Bruce Campbell [who loaned Carol
and Don the money to visit their benefactor in San Diego in
1954] stood up in the room and announced, 'There she is, the
star of tomorrow!'" At the end of the program, her friends
cheered as Carol was quickly acknowledged on the credits as
being one of fourteen vocalists.

On October 12, Carol wrote Gray a note to thank him for a
complimentary letter he'd sent to her about the appearance. She
always responded to his letters immediately in clear, graceful
handwriting. In a few instances, she typed impeccably. "I've
made some great contacts through the *Omnibus* show," she

wrote. "So keep your fingers crossed." She was talking about the fact that she was getting ready to audition for *The Garry Moore Show.*

By October 1956, Garry Moore had become an enormously popular staple of daytime television. Moore was a kindly-looking man who always wore a crew cut, a bow tie and a friendly, down-home grin. He looked like the neighborhood barber, but actually he'd been a media personality for years. He started out in radio as a writer and first became popular on the air as a result of a five-year performing partnership with Jimmy Durante. Moore became master of ceremonies on *Take It or Leave It,* the quiz show that popularized the phrase "the sixty-four dollar question."

In the fall of 1949, he began his own daily variety show for CBS-Radio. Later, he began hosting a daily talk-variety show for CBS-TV, thirty minutes Monday through Thursday, ninety minutes on Friday. The show was live. "That's what makes television so exciting," he said at the time. "It's the unexpected, the feeling that what is happening in front of you has not been planned."

In that great tradition of television talk-show hosts, Garry Moore could not sing, dance, or act. Like Johnny Carson today, Moore was capable in comedy sketches and an adept monologist. He was well liked by his crew, and often called writers' conferences on weekends aboard his yacht, *Red Wing.* But even more important, he was a congenial, warm, and charismatic personality who made viewers feel comfortable and anxious to tune back in.

Garry was constantly thinking up gimmicks to involve his public in the program. For instance, in the spring of 1954, he "gave away" his announcer, Durward Kirby, in a "Why I Would Like to Have Durward Kirby for My Very Own" contest. The viewer who wrote the best letter got Kirby for a weekend. The winner was a woman who lived in a small town just outside of Cleveland, Ohio. On a Friday show, the six-foot-four Kirby, a good sport if ever there was one, stepped into a crate that was sealed and sent on to Cleveland. He was delivered to the winner's front door by special messenger, and spent the entire weekend with these people. (He remained friends with them afterward.)

Even Garry's stage name is a product of public conception. His real name is Thomas Garrison Morfit, and back in his early radio days he offered fifty dollars to anyone who could come up with a new name. A woman in Pittsburgh suggested Garry Moore.

Garry also developed some interesting, quirky habits. "At one point, on every show Garry would say something that only related to John F. Kennedy and Jackie," says musical director Irwin Kostal. "They watched the show regularly. Often no one else would understand the joke except for the Kennedys."

Moore's daytime show was one of the few network programs that actually held auditions for new talent. In his book *Ladies and Gentlemen—The Garry Moore Show*, the show's producer, Herb Sanford, explained why. "We needed more than built-in format changes," he wrote of the series. "We needed new faces, not as in a variety or talk show where guests are essential, just an occasional different face that would give viewers a change from the regulars. The fact that we did not have a budget for big names gave us an additional reason for doing what we wanted to do anyway—look for new faces."

Helen Keane organized general talent auditions for CBS Casting, and she selected people for the Moore show to see. Some of the entertainers first discovered at auditions for Garry Moore include George Gobel, Don Adams, Kaye Ballard, Don Knotts, Jonathan Winters, and Dick Van Dyke. (Van Dyke was at the end of his rope in New York, struggling to become a comic actor, when Garry Moore gave him a shot on his show and changed the course of his life.) But this isn't to say that *The Garry Moore Show* contingent was infallible. Some of the entertainers who were turned away after their auditions include Tony Bennett, Carol Lawrence, Rosemary Clooney, Louis Nye, Nipsey Russell, and a seventeen-year-old Steve Lawrence.

Carol was only vaguely familiar with Garry's history. In a 1962 article she penned for *TV Radio Mirror* titled "That Marvelous Man Moore," she said, "I suppose if I wanted to make points, I should go on record here as saying that he was my idol at an early age. But that would be nonsense. I suppose that I should say that his [daytime] program thrilled me. It didn't. I never saw it".

When the William Morris Agency no longer seemed interested in her, Carol chose Martin Goodman Productions, where Arthur Willi worked, to replace them. The Goodman agency firmed up the *Garry Moore Show* audition for the afternoon of November 9, the first Tuesday of the month, in a CBS-Radio studio on East Fifty-second Street where Arthur Godfrey did his radio show. This was a large, very empty-looking room when all of the folding chairs were removed; there was no audience for laughs. When Carol arrived, she immediately noticed how lonely the place seemed. In a sound booth, a few stray chairs were set up around a piano. A solitary microphone faced a long glass window. Garry and his staff watched the auditioners from the other side of that window, where the central control room was.

"It was an unnerving situation," Ken Welch recalls of the audition, "because anyone auditioning couldn't help but feel so alone at that mike."

Prior to Tamiment, Ken Welch had prepared a seven-minute audition piece for Carol entitled "The Singers," in which she caricatured different types of girl singers and the way they auditioned for jobs in New York. It was a very clever piece of material, and they decided to use it for their audition.

Carol and Ken were ushered into the sound booth. Moore watched on the other side of the glass. She began with "the nose singer" (all off-key, nasal vocals), "the jaw singer" (exaggerating every movement of her mouth), and then "the hand singer" (with every word a choreographed hand movement).

Next up was her "Miss Big Deal" character, the self-possessed type who thinks of herself as the greatest talent to walk down the pike. "Please wait to discuss the signing of my contract," she said, dripping phony sweetness, "until after I complete my first number." And then she sang a horribly off-key chorus of "The Lady Is a Tramp." Stopping the song, she turned to Ken in mock frustration and snapped, "Excuse me, but must you play *so much melody? I'm* auditioning, *not you!*"

"And then," Carol announced, "there is always some refugee from the local high school who managed to slip through," the golly-gee, gosh-almighty star-struck novice dummy. "A ballad?" she sweetly asked the unseen audition director, "Gee, I don't know . . . I only brought this one song and, heavens, I don't *know* if it's a *ballad* or not!"

Welch began playing a song introduction and then suddenly a series of arpeggios; on and on he played melodramatically, until finishing with a final flourish up and down the keyboard. Carol stood transfixed, staring at Ken with her mouth agape and her eyes like saucers. She walked over to him and, acting as if she'd forgotten that she was in the middle of an audition, she said in her shriekest, loudest bellow, "O-o-o-oh, that was wo-o-on-der-ful! Oh, do it *again!*"

Garry Moore said later that he didn't pay attention to the rest of the audition. Carol had won him over with that one line. "No one else could have said it quite that way...or quite that loud," he recalled.

Carol once remembered, "As I went through the audition, I couldn't hear Garry's reactions but I could see him laughing. I just didn't know if he was laughing at me or with me."

When Carol finished her routine, Garry motioned for her to come out of the studio and meet him in his office. When they finally met face to face, she was surprised at how young he looked. Considering all of the years he'd spent on radio and television, she'd expected someone much older. He had a kind, pleasant face. "Do you have anything else?" he asked.

Oh, God! she thought. He didn't like what I did and now wants to know if I have more material. And I don't!

She swallowed hard. "No. No, sir, that's it."

"You're on this Friday," Moore announced flatly. Then he shook her hand and walked away, leaving her suspended somewhere in the clouds.

"She had the air of a college kid," Garry would say years later. "Only one out of maybe fifty candidates would ever be of any interest at those auditions. But with Carol, I'd never seen anyone so young with such finish. It was as if she'd had years and years of experience."

On Fridays, Garry featured new talent on the ninety-minute version of his morning show. If an artist made it through the audition, it was ordinarily two weeks before he or she would be booked on the program. But Moore didn't want someone else to feature Carol first, so he juggled around the scheduling. Carol got her shot on November 9, 1956.

Garry's show was broadcast live at 10:00 A.M.—in black and white, of course—from the former Maxine Elliot Theatre on West Thirty-ninth Street where Ed Sullivan's *Toast of the Town* also originated on Sunday evenings. Two cameras were stationed at the back of the theater next to the control room, and a third, movable camera was positioned on a ramp at one side. It was an ideal situation because the audience had an unobstructed view of the stage, and Carol had a clear view of her audience. This would be the basic floor plan for Carol's own shows years later. To her, there's nothing worse than having huge cameras block the energy from her audience.

"So here is a young lady to whom big things have already started to happen," Garry began in his introduction. "We feel confident it is only the beginning. Let's give a large welcome to Carol Burnett."

Carol walked onto the stage in a simple skirt and blouse. As soon as she reached the mike, she froze for seven seconds. "Well ...uh, you know, uh..." she began nervously, "when I first came here from California a couple of years ago, to try my luck in show business, I was amazed at all the mobs of enthusiastic people whose lives are completely normal, except for one thing. They sing. And another thing is that they use practically every part of their body to sing."

Then she launched into her routine. She gave exaggerated comical examples of "the nose singer," with nasal coyness; "the jaw singer," with dramatic Anthony Newley-isms; and finally "the eye singer," with pop-eyed Lena Horne-style gusto. "Even then," she would joke years later, "my extensive training as a method actress was apparent in the subtlety of every word and gesture...."

Amazed at Carol's versatility and range, Moore invited her back for another appearance. For her second shot, Carol and Ken Welch decided to do a variation on "The Singers" by including a couple more types. Much more at ease in her second spot than she was on her first, Carol added "the gear shift singer, the musical comedy girl," she explained, "with three completely different voices—high, low and over-drive!"

The act continued: "And we have the best paid singer of them all...the non-singing singer. This is the Hollywood movie starlet whose price per motion picture is not quite as high as her mother would like it to be. So our Hollywood movie starlet has been booked into a top Las Vegas nightclub, backed by four of the hardest working chorus boys you ever saw..."

Then Carol introduced her "all female" character, Miss Pepper Grinder, a flamboyant, clumsy Las Vegas showgirllike personality—with a bit of Dinah Shore thrown in for good measure. While singing her number "I'm Lovely to Look At," she opened her coat with a flourish. "How do you like it?" she gushed. "I made it myself with a Jiffy pattern."

The sketch closed with a speech: "I would like to thank all you wonderful devoted people who have made my spectacular career in show business the phenomenon that it is....Without your support I would never have been able to expose myself here tonight."

From this point on, Carol had carte blanche with *The Garry Moore Show.* "Come back any time you have new material," Garry encouraged. "Just call, and you'll be booked."

Now Don and Carol were able to move into a larger one-bedroom apartment on Eighth Avenue. Don was happy about Carol's success, but he was still having no luck at all where his own career was concerned.

"I was never the right type," he remembers. "In fact, I don't think I ever really got to sing for an audition. I'd get up there with fifty other guys onstage, and I would always be too tall, too ethnic-looking, or some other thing." For Saroyan, what was happening now for Carol was bittersweet victory. He wanted her to be successful, but he wanted that for himself as well. But their goal was still the Broadway stage, and neither had yet made it into any theater. So he and Carol continued to have common ground. They shared a distant common goal.

Arthur Willi, a brilliant career strategist who is now deceased, always managed to keep his finger on the pulse of what was happening in the burgeoning New York television industry. Most interesting to him at the time was the news that Max Liebman (best known as producer of the Imogene Coca and Sid Caesar weekly, *Your Show of Shows*) was producing a television vehicle to star Buddy Hackett. The rotund comic was a hot property as a result of his Broadway success with *Lunatics and Lovers.*

Despite the NBC network's pressure to feature Hackett in a variety format, Liebman was determined to produce a situation comedy that would be broadcast live. The show evolved into *Stanley,* a thirty-minute farce about "a well-meaning nincompoop" (to use NBC's press-release language), who managed a hotel-lobby newsstand in the fictional Sussex-Fenton Hotel in New York City. Paul Lynde was cast as Horace Fenton, the owner of the hotel, who was never seen, only heard dispatching orders.

The series debuted on Monday, September 24, 1956. Competition from the other networks was strong (*Arthur Godfrey's Talent Scouts* on CBS and the *Firestone Variety Show* on ABC), and so after *Stanley's* premiere, penned by Neil Simon, the ratings dipped. It was decided to bolster interest in the program by introducing a girl friend for Hackett as a comic foil.

Arthur Willi heard of the open call, and along with Mickey Ross (who had directed Carol in Green Mansions), arranged an audition for Carol. She read with Hackett and was hired immediately for the role of Celia, described by Liebman as "Stanley's wacky, daffy, nutsy girlfriend."

Naturally, Carol was ecstatic. She and Don celebrated her good fortune over dinner. It wasn't theater work, but it was steady employment and terrific national exposure.

Monday, November 19, 1956. Carol made her prime-time network television debut on *Stanley*. The plot synopsis of that episode, as described by the network's press release that week, read: "Stanley has a date with a new girlfriend, Celia (played by young comic Carol Burnett). But she is irate because he has trouble keeping the date due to a series of unusual events."

The best way to describe Carol's first appearance on *Stanley* would be with one word: frantic. She played everything very broadly, and she was probably the loudest comedienne on the air at that time. But after her appearance, the ratings did improve. It's hard to say, though, if that was because of the addition of Carol to the cast, or because NBC managed to secure a cover story in that week's *TV Guide* for Hackett.

Working with Buddy Hackett was not easy for Carol. Hackett was never considerate of his costars; he ad-libbed a lot, and no one ever knew what to expect or how to react. Irwin Kostal, the musical director on *Your Show of Shows*, who also worked in that capacity on *Stanley*, laughingly recalls: "Buddy didn't rehearse much. He was a great ad-libber. On the very first episode, he skipped about twenty pages of script. The show was live, so you can imagine what kind of scene that was. We spent the next sixteen weeks having one hell of a time trying to keep up with him.

"Hackett was very funny at what he did, and we had to agree that most of the time his changes saved the show. However, when he began ad-libbing and skipping about, Carol had to react accordingly. After the show, she'd come up to me and be just exasperated. 'Did you see what he did to me?' she'd say. 'My God! I didn't know whether I was coming or going for half the show.'"

What was uncanny about Hackett's comedic timing on *Stanley* was that he adhered to the one cardinal rule of television: Make room for the commercials. Commercials would often be plugged into a live broadcast automatically, whether a plot break allowed for one or not. Somehow or other, even though he wasn't following a script, Hackett always managed to come up with a brilliant punch line at the exact moment it was time to go to a commercial. "And," says Kostal, "the band would have just enough time to play 'ta-da!' before the commercial happened."

Carol's job on *Stanley* was to hold everything together as Hackett skipped about the script. Often, her next line would either make or break a whole scene. There were no retakes. Millions witnessed whatever happened as it happened.

One evening after a show, Hackett snapped at Carol, "Hey, look, stop stepping on my lines out there, will you? You're supposed to support the show, not try to steal it." But Carol certainly wasn't trying to "steal" the show, and if she'd stepped on his lines she didn't even realize her blunder. She was simply trying to make a plot bridge when Buddy jumped from page 2 to page 19 of the script. But she wasn't the star of the show, so she apologized and never made any waves. "She quietly kept the peace," Kostal remembers.

Any improvement in *Stanley*'s rating didn't last long. For the next few months, the show limped along: In one episode, Celia nagged Stanley about his lack of aggressiveness; in another, Carol had the chance to sing with Hackett in a Christmas fantasy sequence.

That holiday season, the Saroyans had a small Christmas gathering of what a friend refers to as "a raggle-gaggle of loners." It had been a difficult, very emotional year, but Carol and Don always enjoyed their holidays together. One season, a group of Saroyan friends went out into the streets to sing Christmas carols. They dared to sing "Jingle Bells" in the lobby of the plush Plaza Hotel, and then they spread their vocal cheer outside of the swanky new Playboy Club. The doorman there, a regular "Scrooge," shooed them away and threatened to call the police and have them all hauled off to jail. Afterward, the chilled carolers ended up at their old stomping ground, the Stage Delicatessen on Seventh Avenue, where they took refuge from the ten-below temperature. They ate pastrami sandwiches and cheese blintzes and drank sweet hot chocolate until sunrise.

No matter how bittersweet the year, there was nothing like Christmas in Manhattan.

4

T ODAY, MOST PEOPLE AREN'T EVEN AWARE THAT SUCH A SHOW
existed, but the *Stanley* series was a major breakthrough
for Carol Burnett in terms of national exposure and recognition.
Though she was far from being considered a brilliant comedy
figure, it wasn't difficult for Arthur Willi to arrange a booking
for her on Ed Sullivan's popular Sunday-night program on January 6, 1957. Elvis Presley was also making an appearance on the
show, his final Sullivan guest shot, so the ratings were very
strong, and it was a wonderful way to start the year.

Besides Presley, who was allotted most of the sixty minutes
of air time, other guests included a Brazilian singer, a rhythm-
and-blues singer, and a ballerina, none of whom anyone had ever
heard of before, or has heard from since. And also, Carol Burnett.

Fresh-faced and wearing a flowing knee-length dress, Carol
walked out onto the stage to moderate applause. She surrepti-
tiously pulled on her earlobe, signaling to Nanny. Not the exaggerated tug Carol would become known for, this was more like
an incidental scratch. She seemed quite nervous as she spoke for
a moment about Presley and how his success "gives all of us
young singers and people like that new hope and new courage to
make all the countless rounds of auditions." Then she performed
her "Singers" routine.

She and Ken had added a new character, "Miss Old Timer,"
a wonderful takeoff on Judy Garland. Brimming with cocky self-
confidence, Carol sang Garland's trademark "I Feel a Song Coming On," using all of the stereotypical Garland mannerisms and
gusto. "Hit it, baldy!" she said to the pianist as he wrapped up
the finale and she kicked off her shoes.

Nanny, Louise, and Chrissy watched Carol's performance in

Hollywood and were proud. It was a good show. "I love that Elvis Presley," Louise said later. "Sure would like to meet him. He's my kind of man. . . ."

In March, *Stanley* was taken off the air. "I remember that we were all heartbroken when our little show was canceled," Irwin Kostal says. "Carol was very disappointed. Most of us, with the exception of Carol, were already committed to doing other work. I told her at the time, 'Don't cry, kid. This is just a little show, and you're going to become a big star.'

"Now I'm not bragging about that," he hastens to add, "because I might have been saying that to everybody on the set. She did make an impression with the Celia character, though. Five years later, in 1962, I introduced her to my mother. Mother shook Carol's hand and greeted her by saying, 'Well, hello there, Celia.'"

For the next few months, Carol was back on unemployment; Don returned to his job at MCA. Nothing much was happening for either of the Saroyans at this point; they made plans to go to California in the spring, and then to spend another summer in stock theater. But when March came around, Don couldn't take time away from his job, so Carol went on to California alone to visit Nanny and Christine. While she was there, she had a chance to rekindle warm relationships with many good friends from UCLA. She'd never lost track of any of them. They were a link to her roots, and she somehow managed to maintain communication with constant letters and phone calls. They cheered her on and encouraged her; Carol always valued their support.

On March 22, 1957, old friend Perry Gray threw a surprise party for Carol at his parents' home in Los Angeles. The gathering was lovingly planned by a group of Carol's friends, all of whom had been watching as she became a budding known show-business personality. Gray fashioned a handmade mobile and positioned it above the front door that Carol would walk through when she arrived. On the cards were his attempts to copy the logos of *Omnibus, Stanley,* and *The Ed Sullivan Show.*

Around the doorframe, Perry carefully taped taut tracing paper. Then, when Carol showed up, someone behind her gently pushed her through the paper so that she could make a grand entrance. Her friends yelled out, "Surprise!" In the background,

Eartha Kitt's "Monotonous" played in tribute to the success of *The Rehearsal Club Revue.*

"Oh, no!" Carol squealed. "You didn't!"

"She was truly stunned," Gray recalls. "There were probably two dozen people there. It was all a very good-natured tribute to the fact that she had made it and the rest of us were still hoping to...."

Her friends led Carol to a back room where there was a cake. On the frosting was an astronomical number in the millions—the number of people estimated to have watched Carol's performance on *The Ed Sullivan Show.* "Some of those millions probably tuned in to see Elvis Presley, too," Gray joked.

The partygoers made a tape recording of the entire celebration so that Don could listen and enjoy. It was a wonderful, generous outpouring of affection from some very proud friends. For Carol, it was a memorable evening. Two weeks later, the Gray family received a letter from her, written on Sunday, April 7, 1957, from the Saroyans' apartment at 142 West Fifty-fourth Street in New York:

> Dear Mr. and Mrs. Gray and Perry,
>
> Well, what can I say? I just finished playing the tape from the party for the umpteenth time, but I'm still overcome. Such a wonderful memory to be able to capture over and over again. I arrived home Wednesday evening after a lovely flight only to be greeted by a white welcome mat—it was snowing, and in April! It sort of rounded out the whole trip. And to think, only a few days before I had played baseball on the most beautiful campus (UCLA) in the world, with a group of the most beautiful people in the world.
>
> As always, after such a long trip, it's wonderful to be home. Doubly so because I can think back over some very wonderful experiences this trip afforded. Topping it all off with that superb blast, a wonderful evening at your home on that beautiful Friday evening.
>
> Love Always,
> Carol

Carol's next television appearance was on Jonathan Winters's program on April 24, 1957. Then, on May 8, she auditioned some more material for the Garry Moore program, which promptly booked her for another appearance. While all of this was going on, someone from the Martin Goodman Agency—either Arthur Willi or another ambitious agent, George Spota—showed some kinescope tapes of a few of Carol's television spots to the owners of the popular Blue Angel nightclub on the East Side. Carol was then booked there for a three-week engagement that would commence June 5.

The Blue Angel, one of the trendiest and best-known nightclubs in the city, was a breeding ground for new talent. Its policy allowed show-business novices the opportunity to hone their skills and work out new material before a paying, mostly very supportive upper-crust audience. Harry Belafonte, Orson Bean, Mike Nichols and Elaine May, and many others were first seen by New Yorkers at the Blue Angel. It was a small, simple place, with tables the size of dimes. About two hundred people could be squeezed into the showcase room.

Carol and Ken Welch spent every spare moment working up new material for the engagement. "I'm scared silly about this," Carol said to friends. "It's just the thought of club work that frightens me."

Carol had never done anything like this before, but she understood that her performance had to be unique and interesting enough to distract two hundred people from conversation and liquor. Standing alone onstage as herself, "working in one," as show people call it, was a discomforting thought. She would not be playing a character as much as she would be playing herself, exposing Carol Burnett.

"Working in one is the loneliest thing in the world to do," comic friends had warned her. But Don encouraged her; he knew she could handle it.

On opening night, she was a wreck. "When I entered the club and saw those people sitting there, I felt every single one of them was an ogre, waiting to devour me," she once remembered.

Perry Gray flew from Los Angeles to New York in order to attend opening night. He recalls: "There were three acts before Carol's: One was a lovely Latin singer who I remember broke Carol up with her broken English and strange translations of blue expressions; there was a guitarist and singer of folk songs; and I think there was an elderly woman who played piano. Then the lighting changed, and Carol walked out. She stared at the audience, reared her head over the piano, and then suddenly hesitated. I thought, My God! I hope she didn't forget her lines. It was all part of the act. She composed herself and then started singing her opening number, 'I'm Getting the Feel of the Room' She was saying, 'Don't worry about me, I'm just pulling myself together, and here I am!'"

Carol received a good notice in *Variety*, and New York critic Martin Burden also reviewed Carol's act in his popular "Going Out Tonight" column. "We will guess fearlessly that Carol is due for big things in the cafes and she is bound to be a best bet for TV," wrote Burden. "In a word, the girl is good."

When the booking was over, the club closed for a month, as it had traditionally done every year. The owners were impressed with Carol's fourteen-minute act, and they told her that if she was able to come up with twenty minutes of new material, they would renew her contract. She was working two shows a night, every night, and making only two hundred dollars a week, but at least it was steady.

Carol and Ken had decided that it would be a good idea to use "Destroy Me," one of the Tamiment numbers, as a song in her Blue Angel act. The concept had her playing the part of a dowdy housewife madly in love with an unnamed show-business idol. It was always a crowd-pleaser.

For the second engagement at the Angel, Ken Welch thought that the "Destroy Me" routine would be an even bigger hit if he reworked it a bit and personalized the song. "I was always intrigued by the spectacle of people who feel themselves to be nothing," Welch explains, "who live their lives vicariously through celebrities. The whole business of irrational passion and obsession from fans, that's where 'Destroy Me' came from.

"It occurred to me that the idea could be taken a bit farther by actually naming a celebrity that the girl, Carol in this case, was infatuated with. Not Elvis, or someone obvious like that. Instead, someone very unlikely would be the target for her obsession. One day I asked myself, 'Who would it be absolutely nuts for anyone to be infatuated with?'"

Carol thought the idea was a good one. "What about Khrushchev?" she asked. The Russian leader had recently visited New York, and Ken began to work on the song. "But then I was afraid that it was going to be misread as some kind of political statement," he remembers. "So I scrapped that concept and started over again."

One morning, it hit him. John Foster Dulles. Who better? Dulles was secretary of state under Eisenhower, and was known for his austere, dignified, and somewhat stuffy image. The idea of a whacked-out fan having a crush on this conservative states-man was absurd enough to be funny. Not only that, but if the concept was misread as a political statement, at least the subject of the farce was American. Welch wrote the song in one day and called it "I Made a Fool of Myself Over John Foster Dulles."

When they debuted "Dulles" at the Blue Angel, it was an instant crowd-pleaser. Welch's idea: A nervous, frantic young girl is explaining why she has been sentenced to a seven-year prison term after having been classified a threat to national security. Apparently, the first time she laid eyes on John Foster Dulles at the United Nations, she swooned and made a complete fool of herself. She became obsessed with Dulles. Eventually, she ac-costed him in an airport and, unable to control her overwhelm-ing passion, she tried to grab onto his sleeve but accidentally got hold of his briefcase. Now despite her protestations, the govern-ment is sure she's a spy.

The number worked well because Carol really delivered, in a brassy yet naive characterization. The first time she sang it, she got a standing ovation. Word spread quickly all over the East Side: "Have you heard about this nutsy girl who sings about Dulles? Is she for real?" Soon, the Blue Angel was packed every night.

When the talent coordinators for *The Tonight Show,* starring Jack Paar, heard about the number, they called to ask if Carol would perform it on the show. They felt that it would be an interesting novelty, and Paar's late-night audiences would proba-bly enjoy its outrageousness. Paar's show was one of the most popular of the era, and went on to become renowned for its unusual controversies. In his five years as host of *The Tonight Show,* Paar would pick fights with NBC censors, Ed Sullivan, the United States Senate, Walter Winchell, Jimmy Hoffa, and anyone else he decided to harpoon with his caustic wit.

"Hey! That's great!" Don said to Carol when she told him the news. "Everyone watches *The Tonight Show!*"

"Yeah, I know," Carol said nervously. "That's what I'm afraid of."

"There was a big conflict in her mind as to whether or not

she should do that song on television," Saroyan explains. "She couldn't decide how it would be perceived, whether it was too political or not. We talked about it, and the only thing we were sure of was that the song was a definite attention-getter."

Tuesday night, August 6, 1957. After her first show at the Blue Angel, Carol and Ken hopped into a cab headed for the Hudson Theatre on Forty-fourth Street to do the Paar show. "You know, Don and I were talking," Carol began, "and I'm not sure about this. The show is live, and what if someone gets angry over this song? Maybe we should do 'Puppy Love' instead." ("Puppy Love" was another of Welch's special-material numbers written during this time.)

"Look, Carol, what have you got to lose?" Ken reassured her. "Take a chance. See what happens."

Paar introduced her, and Carol walked out onto the stark stage. She was wearing a plain dress, buttoned all the way to the neck. Her hair was curly and brown. Her face was scrubbed clean, with hardly any makeup. This was a simple, down-home girl if there ever was one. She was tremendously nervous and it showed, but it didn't matter, because it all seemed part of the act.

The camera came in for an introductory closeup. As part of her routine, Carol shuddered and hid her face behind her hand. Then she turned away from the audience for a moment, as if what she was about to disclose were the most humiliating piece of self-revelation ever to air on network television.

Finally, "I made a fool of myself," she began tentatively, "over John Fo-o-o-oster Dulles." When she sang the word *Foster* and held the note, her mouth opened so wide you could almost see straight down her throat. Her face moved as if it were made of Silly Putty; she mugged, crossed her eyes, and held her ears when "the drums started pounding." It was the performance of an eager neophyte, and caused quite a little uproar.

When Carol got back to the Blue Angel for her second show, she has recalled, "the phones were ringing off the hook. AP, UPI, *Life, Time,* and even Washington. The Washington call scared me. I thought maybe they were going to deport me to Texas."

The caller was John Waters, Dulles's television advisor. He told Carol how much he had enjoyed the performance and mentioned that he planned to request that Paar have her back on so that Dulles, who had just returned from a NATO conference, could see the routine himself. So that Thursday evening, Carol went back on the Paar show and sang the song again.

Hundreds of viewers wrote to and called the network applauding the performance, and 152 people called to register protests charging that the young comic actress had overstepped the bounds of good American taste. The *New York Post* ran a photograph of Carol with the headline PROTESTS, and a brief story explaining what the furor was about. The newspaper called the song, "an original ditty, 'I'm In Love With John Foster Dulles.'"

When Dulles appeared on the *Meet the Press* news program that Sunday, he was asked to comment on the news that this bright young comic had a crush on him. "I make it a policy," the ordinarily pompous diplomat quipped, "never to discuss matters of the heart in public."

It's interesting that, historically, it is Jack Paar, and not Carol, who is credited for the uproar that took place those evenings onstage at the Hudson. A *TV Guide* reporter once analyzed:

> [On *The Tonight Show*] the first real moment of Paar-like tension was when Carol Burnett sang a parody entitled "John Foster Dulles." This kind of irreverence over a stately government figure was new; the nation gasped. [Paar] had created a moment, and it is as a merchant of moments, a retailer of the unexpected, that he has thrived ever since.

Ed Sullivan, never one to be outdone by Jack Paar (they feuded for years) brought Carol back on his weekly CBS program to perform the routine. "Here is the girl who's become the TV sensation of the year," Sullivan said in his introduction. "Here is young Carol Burnett." It was her second appearance on Sullivan's show, and her third national media exposure in one week.

On the morning of Wednesday, August 28, 1957, Carol was astonished to find an article about the brouhaha in *The New York Times*. "The song is being sung on radio and on television and in a nightclub in New York," the story explained vaguely. She must have been disappointed. There wasn't a single mention of her name, nor of the name of the club in which she worked.

Better publicity came in the form of a *Life* magazine two-column article that same month. Entitled "A Love Song to Mr. Dulles," the very brief feature was accompanied by a picture of Dulles walking at the White House, briefcase in hand. Next to that photograph was a shot of Carol, described as "a newcomer to nightclubs," onstage, "with briefcase," the caption read, "she claims to have swiped from him."

Incidentally, Carol never met Dulles before he died in June 1959. ("I feel as though I've lost a friend," Carol would say. She stopped using the number in her act when it became known that Dulles was suffering from cancer.)

Suddenly, the Blue Angel nightclub was more popular than ever, crowded with people eager to see the young sensation Burnett. It was difficult for her to imagine that she had amassed such a legion of local admirers in such a short time. The sudden fame went straight to her head.

"Yes, I had changed a bit," she admitted. "It didn't take me long to feel just a little self-important. I thought that I'd finally made it. No longer would I ever have to feel nervous. This was such a snap, so very easy. Who knows why I ever worried about it all in the first place, I wondered."

After about two weeks of steady ego buffing from her new fans, Carol discovered why the expression "fleeting fame" came into being. She walked out onto the stage at the Blue Angel on a Monday night, opened with the "Dulles" number, as she always had, and received the most lackadaisical reaction she'd ever encountered. There were a few chuckles here and there, and she noticed one or two grins, but no genuine enthusiasm. Undaunted, she performed the lampoon on young romance "Puppy Love," and now the reaction was even worse. No one was laughing.

It wasn't that the audience was preoccupied by conversation. They were listening and paying attention to her. But what they heard was an abrasive woman they did not find at all humorous.

Besides being a very funny performer, Carol was so appealing in part because she was vulnerable, innocent, and unpretentious. Her audience enjoyed those qualities about her. She was one of them.

But when the "Dulles" number became a national sensation, she no longer felt a part of the commonality. Because she is such an honest performer, that loss of humility immediately registered in her act. She discovered very quickly that "cocky" does not work for most entertainers, certainly not for Carol Burnett. Or as Jimmy Cagney used to say, "As soon as you're sure, you're through. Always doubt."

Defeated, Carol cut the act short and hurried off the stage, hoping against hope that there would be enough applause to warrant a curtain call. There wasn't.

Once backstage, she began to cry. "What happened?" she wondered aloud. "I've lost it! Whatever I had, it's gone. I don't even know what it was, but now it's gone! And I still have another show to do tonight!"

Out of the corner of her eye, she noticed a man who had obviously had one drink for the road too many. He lurched his way around a corner and headed in her direction. Bouncing from one wall to the other, he muttered something about trying to find the bathroom. When he saw Carol standing there sobbing, he stopped short.

"Say? Aren't you the little lady that was just onstage?" he asked. His speech was slurred, and he squinted as if his vision was blurry.

"Why, yes...yes, sir. That was me," she responded. She wished that she hadn't been recognized, but this man seemed to have sympathetic eyes. Anything he could say, even in his drunken state, might make all the difference in the world.

"You know what?" the man asked, sizing her up.

"No, what?" she said.

"You really stink."

The rest of 1957 was exciting. Carol had never been so busy. In July, she and Don were able to move into a nicer and more spacious apartment, number 3-C at 901 Eighth Avenue. "It's only three blocks from where we lived before," she told friends, "but —golly!—you can roller-skate in it, it's so big!" She reopened at the Blue Angel on July 8, and then made another Garry Moore television appearance on July 19, singing "Puppy Love."

In August, Carol and Ken Welch went into the studio to record a single of "I Made a Fool of Myself Over John Foster Dulles" backed with "Puppy Love" for ABC Records. Most people felt that Carol's comedic interpretation of the material was so largely physical that the songs didn't translate well onto vinyl. The record wasn't a hit; the "Dulles" phenomenon was over.

After the recording session, Carol and Don planned a brief

vacation on Long Island before she reopened at the Blue Angel on September 5. Her third four week-stint at the Angel was pleasant, but nothing like the engagement a month before that had crowds lined up in the streets to see Dulles's kooky admirer.

In October, she spent a week in bed with a flu. A full-page article in the New York *News* Sunday magazine on October 13 did wonders for her spirits, though. "Carol Burnett is a young comedienne who loves her husband," the article began. Two photos accompanied it, one of Carol in a simple green lace dress, another of her and Don in their apartment. They talked about how thrilled they were to be able to buy an eighty-five-dollar lamp with Carol's salary from the Blue Angel. They posed with a sofa that Don had made himself.

Carol continued her Blue Angel commitment, closing there on Wednesday, October 30. Next up were rehearsals for *The General Motors NBC 50th Anniversary Show,* which aired on November 17. It was an exciting appearance; the show was hosted by Kirk Douglas, and the other guests included Helen Hayes, June Allyson, and Claudette Colbert. Carol could hardly believe that she was in such august company. In some respects, she felt as if she was really beginning to make some headway with her career. After the taping, she went to Dallas for two weeks to perform her Blue Angel act at a small nightclub called the Tree Club.

It had been a busy time, and by the end of the year she was exhausted and anxious to go home to Hollywood. She would visit just before Christmas, she decided, because Don wouldn't be able to take any time off from his job, and she wanted to be with him for their first wedding anniversary on December 17. Maybe, she mused, she'd bring Christine back with her for a visit. Her sister had never seen New York, and the experience could be a lot of fun.

Chrissy had been on Carol's mind a lot lately. When she went back for visits, she could never really gauge how well her sister was faring. She seemed all right, but how could Carol be sure?

One morning, Carol asked Don how he would feel if Chrissy came to live with them. "I think that would be great!" he encouraged, "as long as we're ready to take full responsibility for her. It's a big decision."

That it was. But Carol would not postpone it; she knew from her own experience that 102 was hardly an ideal environment for a girl Chrissy's age.

5

"There comes a time when you realize they did the best they could with who they were, and considering what they were going through at the time..."
—Carol Burnett, 1986

IN CAROL BURNETT'S WONDERFUL CHILDHOOD MEMOIR, *ONE MORE TIME*, she discussed and examined her background with considerable depth and perception. *One More Time* started out as a letter to her three daughters, and ended up a fascinating book written as much for Carol's own peace of mind as for her offspring. The book got its name, Carol explained, because in writing it she relived her childhood "one more time." The major portion of Carol's memoir deals with her upbringing in the one-room apartment in the center of Hollywood from which, in December 1957, she contemplated rescuing Chrissy.

Unlike many other celebrities, who paint varying pictures of their backgrounds from time to time as they see fit, Carol has been amazingly consistent about her memories, from her earliest interviews with the press all the way through her promotional book tour in 1986. She has always loathed the image of a "Pitiful Pearl," and despite a lot of evidence to the contrary, she insists that what she had was a rough childhood but certainly not an unhappy one, because she was loved.

Her family was poor and on welfare, but that was not unusual, she maintains, because most of the people in the lower-class Hollywood environment in which she was reared didn't have much money. She was likable and had a lot of friends, and a lot of fun, too. She remembers the nights she, Mama, and Nanny would laugh and sing "I'll Get By (As Long As I Have You)" in the kitchen area as Louise strummed her ukulele.

There have been cynics who have taken a dim view of Carol's candor. "Mae White made a lifework out of raising Carol," one reporter sneered, "and in return Carol made a saint out of Mae."

Mae White was born in 1885 in Belleville, Arkansas. She was known as the Belle of Belleville, and her father, F. C. Jones, had been a very prestigious and wealthy man in Arkansas until he lost all of his money (and to this day, no one seems to remember how that happened). He died penniless and humiliated. She married a railroad employee, Bill Creighton, and had two daughters, Eudora in 1907 and Ina Louise, Carol's mother, in 1911.

In all, Mae went on to have so many husbands and affairs that even her close family lost track after Mae died in 1968. "I think she married them for what she could get out of them," Carol once said. "And then she discarded them. It was survival of the fittest, because in her heart she was a loving woman." But the fact that Mae had had so many men in her life never stopped her from condemning Louise, her daughter, who had rotten luck with the other sex.

Carol loved, respected, and feared this lady she called Nanny, a confused and confusing woman. She was a strong-willed, feisty survivor, with a big heart and a secure hug, someone sober (most of the time, anyway, though she did like her sherry) to watch over Carol and, later, Carol's sister, Chrissy. She pulled the girls through the tough times.

But Nanny was a study in contrasts. She was as weak as she was strong, as mean as she was kind. Her love was not unconditional; she expected loyalty and undivided attention, always.

Out of insecurity, she could be manipulative and unbelievably cruel. She would feign being deathly ill and stuff newspapers inside her belt "to keep my insides in," as Carol watched, horror-stricken. Carol was terrified to leave her grandmother's side even long enough to attend Selma Avenue Grade School and LeConte Junior High.

"I'm having a hissy fit," Nanny would suddenly declare. Then she would take deep, gasping gulps of air and frantically feel for her pulse and heartbeat. "God help me now!"

Turning to the wide-eyed youngster, she'd warn, "Watch me, Carol, I'm dying. Just watch..."

The frightened little girl would scream to the Lord, "No! No! Take me first! Take me first!"

Nanny may have been a selfish hypochondriac, but she loved

her granddaughter, and never for a moment did Carol feel neglected as a child. "Nanny was interested only in Carol," Don Saroyan says. "Her every thought, every word, was about Carol."

"Grandmother was the main vein," Carol's sister, Chrissy, has said. "I mean, powerful, like an empress. Carol was the real love of her life."

Mae White was Carol's rock, her foundation, and also one of the funniest people Carol had ever known. She would take out her dentures and then put her chin clean up over her nose to make Carol hysterical."

Much of what Carol has lovingly said and written about Nanny has taken on a mythical charm. She and Carol would get on a bus, and Nanny would look down the aisle and find that there were no empty seats. "I'm an old lady and I'm having a heart attack!" she would scream. "Get up, somebody!" A horrified rider would jump up and offer her a seat. As Carol stood by her side, the contented old woman would pass gas. It must have been humiliating, even if now it seems funny. "And also, she could belch louder than any woman I've ever known," Carol remembered proudly. "'Well, there's more room out than in,' Nanny would say."

"I was raised by a grandmother who was a Christian Scientist but who covered her tracks with phenobarbital," she told an audience of publishing executives at an American Bookseller Association press conference in May 1986.

"Before going to the movies," Carol told the audience, "she would take me to the Thrifty Drug Store for lunch." Nanny had what Carol calls "a big Mary Poppins-like bag" which she would open on her lap at the counter. When no one was looking, she'd dump in all of the knives, forks, napkins, and salt and pepper shakers. "Then, after the movie, we would go into the theater bathroom and dump all the toilet paper into Grandma's purse. Now we were set for a month."

When Carol was about thirteen, she and Nanny moonlighted as cleaning ladies in an office building owned by Warner Brothers on the corner of Hollywood Boulevard and Wilcox. But she says that this experience wasn't the basis for her popular Charwoman character years later. "We didn't dress that way," she recalled, "and I didn't even have a mop. . . ."

"She was an incurable pack rat," Carol continued about

Nanny in another interview. "She would save everything, always saying 'you never know when you're going to need this.' So we had 150 peanut butter jars. She'd stuff everything she had in the little closet behind the Murphy bed that pulled out from the wall, including all the junk she brought from Texas, trunks and all."

In all of the fourteen years Carol lived there, they never could get that bed back into the wall. There were magazines, newspapers, clothes, rags, and all sorts of junk in the space where the bed was supposed to go. Carol had no place to hang her clothes, so she carefully arranged them on the shower rack above the bathtub. Her wardrobe was always rather nicely steamed, but sometimes smelled a bit moldy. Nanny would never let her open the air shaft in the bathroom because she was certain she'd die of pneumonia from the cool, fresh air.

When she wanted to take a bath, Carol would push her clothes aside and get into the tub. There she would fantasize about being the most beautiful of all the mermaids in her secret undersea world where she, and only she, could visit.

Carol has described her mother as "petite with beautiful legs, slightly plump in a sexy way. She had a great figure. Beautiful eyes. Joan Crawford eyes. She would spend hours looking at herself in the mirror, putting on make up, posing. She kidded all the time— really effervescent but a fiery woman with lots of temperament."

As time went on, Louise became a rather tragic person. She came to believe that life had thrown her just too many bad-luck curves; she'd run out of ways to cope. She'd had a wonderful singing voice, and probably could have had a career if she'd had some direction or ambition. But after following her husband's lead into alcoholism, she became blind to her strengths and spent all of her time concentrating on her weaknesses and mistakes. Often, she wasn't very coherent. There were times when Carol felt anger and hurt and even hatred toward Louise. "I felt obviously that Mama didn't love me," she explained, "or she wouldn't be drinking."

By the time Carol was approaching her teens, her mother was barely a shell of the vivacious woman she once was. She was miserable about the way her life was evolving. She was lonely, unhappy, and could be mean-minded and vicious. Her constant criticism of Carol slowly eroded most of the girl's self-confidence.

An affair with an Italian actor in Hollywood got Louise pregnant. She was determined to have the child and keep it. It was a courageous act at that time and spoke volumes for Louise's inner strength; while in labor, she got on a streetcar in the middle of the night, and went to the hospital to have the child. Nanny, of course, taunted and berated her mercilessly. Little did Louise know that Nanny had become pregnant with *her* as a result of an affair she had while she was married to another man. She then lied to Louise about the identity of her father. Carol's mother went to her grave never knowing the truth about her paternity.

Louise felt as if she'd lost her Carol to Nanny, and so now the new baby would be hers. Antonia Christine was born in December 1944. After Chrissy arrived, Louise was fine for a while. But then she fell back into a rut, and the drinking got worse. There were many days she wouldn't even get out of bed; she kept the drapes closed and lay in the dark all day.

Years later, Chrissy said of her mother, "On one hand she could be just delightful and witty and wonderful. On the other hand, with the drinking problem, she could be very sad, morose, and just tired."

To escape from it all, Carol would sing and dance when she was alone in 102. She was too embarrassed to let anyone see her pretend to be a star. "I used to be a closet radio performer," she once remembered. "When I was alone, I would open the window and pretend I was a radio show. I would shout out 'Welcome to our show this evening. Our guest today is . . .' and I would make up a name. 'Would you like to sing a song for us?'

"'I certainly would,' I'd say, changing my voice.

"'Do you need any music?'

"'No, I sure don't.'

"And then I would sing a song at the top of my lungs."

One afternoon, somebody in another apartment yelled, *"Turn that damn radio off!"* Carol was stunned, and also rather thrilled. She'd fooled her neighbor; he'd heard her sing and thought she was good enough to be on the radio. Yet she was also invisible. She had the best of both worlds that afternoon.

When Carol enrolled in Hollywood High School, she was a gawky, lanky, and terribly insecure teenager. "Unless you're a baby Lana Turner or Marilyn Monroe, adolescence is just one big walking pimple. There's nothing worse," she once observed.

She was five feet, six inches tall, had long, stringy brown hair, an overbite with slightly bucked teeth, a weak chin, and she weighed about ninety pounds. Louise's streak of self-pity would come out now and then in her daughter's thinking: "Why do I have to be the ugly girl in class? *Why me?*"

She remembers these years as being her most difficult. "High school remains a muddle because I blocked a few things out," she told *USA Today*. "I certainly was not what one would call a beautiful girl. And I always wanted to be beautiful. My sister was beautiful, my mother was beautiful. For a while, I thought I was adopted."

Carol once remarked of her mother, "She always wanted me to have as many dates as she'd had, and of course I never did. I think it came as quite a shock to her that she didn't give birth to a beauty."

She was a good girl in high school; being "good" was what she excelled in. She explained to Phil Donahue, "It was the best thing I could be. I wasn't rich, I wasn't that smart, I didn't know what I was going to do or be. So the way to survive was to have all of the teachers and kids say, 'What a good kid.' I was everybody's friend who could blend into the paint in the wall. I got by that way. . . ."

She got her first acting role in a ninth-grade play, but the experience was uneventful and didn't make much of an impression. However, something in her made her wonder what it would be like to be an actress; it was a wonderful, secret fantasy she would keep to herself.

She loved going to the movies with Nanny. To her, the cinema represented a way out. Becoming an actress seemed like an exciting, if distant, bit of hope. There wasn't much she could do to work toward her goal now; unbelievably, Hollywood High didn't have a drama department.

A personal highlight for Carol was when she began writing a column, anonymously, for the school newspaper. At one point, she even interviewed actor Joel McCrea for a feature story. Her mother approved; Louise remembered better days, back in the forties, when she herself wrote celebrity profiles for *Pic* and *Collier* magazines. She would have been a great writer . . . "if only" this, and "if only" that.

"Write, kid," she advised her daughter. "Because no matter what you look like, you can always write."

Carol didn't dare reveal her secret, that she really wanted to be an actress, because she knew that Louise and Nanny would demolish her dream. "What, are you crazy?" she knew they would say. "You're not pretty enough to be an actress. And you certainly have no talent."

Carol didn't have many boyfriends, and she did her best to keep the few she did have out of apartment 102. "The place was a shambles," she has said. "I could never let a boy into the apartment. I was too embarrassed." When she was a child, she wouldn't even let her girl friends into the room. "Use the bathroom across the street at the gas station," she would suggest.

Chrissy, who always called Carol "Sissy," has concurred: "Her home life was a terrific embarrassment to Sissy. She was trying to date fellows and at the same time trying to keep them away."

Another problem was the way Carol's mother would sometimes react jealously to her daughter's beaux. Carol has recalled incidents when boys would come to call only to be intercepted in the hallway by Louise, in a drunken bad mood. There would be an inevitable confrontation, and Carol would always end up humiliated and in tears.

When Carol graduated from high school in the winter of 1951, Nanny encouraged her to go to secretarial school. But she envisioned herself on the Westwood, California, campus of UCLA. It seemed impossible, though, because tuition at that time was forty-two dollars, which, of course, they did not have. (Rent for the whole month was thirty-five dollars!) "It wasn't that I wished I could go, that I had faith I could go," Carol has said. "I *saw* myself on that campus."

Carol recalled for *McCall's* magazine: "Every morning, I used to open the apartment door and look across the lobby to the front desk, and I could see our mail slot, the second one from the left. One morning I saw we had an envelope and I ran across the lobby in my blue chenille robe. It was a plain envelope with just my name typed on it in capital letters. It was stamped but it hadn't been mailed. There was a $50 bill in it."

To this day, Carol doesn't know where the money came from. She didn't know anybody with a typewriter, let alone that kind of money. She used it to enroll in UCLA, much to Nanny's chagrin.

Carol originally planned to major in journalism, but UCLA

had no undergraduate journalism department. She registered as an English major, and in short order began to gravitate toward theater-arts English so that she could take a course in playwriting, to appease Louise. While enrolled, she knew that she would be able to investigate the world of theater arts a little more closely. Deep down, she knew she wanted to be an actress, not a playwright. But she wouldn't admit this to herself. Being an actress meant performing in front of an audience; the mere thought was numbing.

As a part of her curriculum as a theater-arts major, she had to take a basic acting course, Acting 2. It took her about two weeks to sort out her roster of classes, so she was late signing up for the class. The professor who taught that course, Estelle Harmon, is today a gregarious and beloved acting coach in Hollywood. She recalls: "It was a pretty big class, and scene study was an important part of our work. One day, this frail-looking girl came in looking very scared, very pulled back. I remember asking her why she was late, and she could barely give me an answer. She mumbled something, and then, self-consciously, she quickly scrambled to the back of the room.

"Everyone had already been paired with someone else for the first scenes we were doing. So Carol came in as the oddball ...in many ways. I looked at her sitting back there and thought, Oh, Lord, what have you sent to my class?..."

Carol had a choice for her first assignment, either a scene from *The Madwoman of Chaillot* by Jean Giraudoux, or a monologue from *The Country Girl* by Clifford Odets. The monologue was shorter, so she chose that. It never occurred to her to read the play to see what she was getting herself into. She just memorized the small scene on the 5 X 7 card.

"I gave her a D minus, and I was being quite generous," Estelle Harmon laughs. "But, even though I don't think I ever told Carol, I thought her reading was very funny. It was accidental comedy and certainly not what the play required, but I had to hold back a chuckle."

Two weeks later, Harmon gave Carol another scene, partnering her with a student for a dialogue from Noel Coward's *Red Peppers*. Carol was catching on; Harmon gave her a A. "I didn't get the impression that she knew what she was doing, exactly, but she made the kids laugh," Harmon remembers. "And I think she enjoyed the sound of their laughter. But, still, she would not admit to wanting to be an actress. She always insisted that she was going to be a writer."

Later in the term, Carol tried William Saroyan's *Hello Out There* and was given a grade of C for that performance. Says Harmon: "The play was about a girl who feels like a reject and works as a clean-up woman in a little jail in a small Southern town. One prisoner there, in order to get her to help him escape, begins to treat her like a real person. It's his 'hello out there,' but it's also hers, the inner call of a misfit. Her portrayal needed work, but she did seem to identify with the role. I had the impression that she was afraid to reveal herself totally.

"Carol was an extremely private girl," Harmon concludes. "Most of her fellow students and the faculty weren't remotely aware of any of the details about her home life, about her family."

Lenny Weinrib, a college friend Carol would go out with now and then, recalls: "When we'd make plans to go to a movie, Carol would always say, 'I'll meet you over there. Don't worry, it's not very far from where I live. Don't you worry 'bout me."

One day, Lenny suggested on the phone, "Look, Carol, I'll come over and pick you up. See you at six."

There was silence on her end.

"Well, uh, gee, uh..." she stammered.

"C'mon, Carol," he pushed. "We'll go to the movie together. It's on my way." He became exasperated. *"What's the matter with you?"*

"It's just that the place is a little...messy."

Lenny showed up at the apartment building, and Carol was waiting for him in the lobby. "I thought to myself, What the hell is going on here?" he remembers. "But I made no comment."

After the fourth time this happened, Lenny confronted Carol outside of the building.

"Carol, why do I always have to wait in the lobby? Why can't I come in and say hello to Chris and Nanny? What is it? Are you ashamed of me, or what?"

She felt trapped. A couple of excuses quickly rolled off her lips: "Well, the place is an awful mess and nobody's dressed... and...and—"

"Big deal!" Weinrib cut her off. "So your grandma puts on a robe, I come in and say hello, and then I leave." He was insistent, and now his feelings were hurt. Carol had no choice but to let him into 102.

"I went in, and then I realized why she didn't want me in there," he remembers with an understanding smile. "The first thing I noticed was the Murphy bed. Then this little stove in the corner. I looked around quickly as Carol shuffled from one foot to the other. The place looked as if a cyclone had been through it. Nanny was as pleasant as could be, a lovely midwestern-looking woman, like something out of a Norman Rockwell painting. She was apple-pie American. That was also the first time I met Chrissy, a sweet, precocious kid. Then we left."

Afterward, Lenny asked Carol, "Why wouldn't you let me into your apartment before?"

"Well, it's not much to look at, is it?" Carol said, just a bit defensively.

"So what?" Lenny shot back. "What do I care? Carol, *your friends don't care.*"

She knew he was right, but still it was hard not to be embarrassed. The friends that she met at college knew nothing about her secret world in 102. With them, she could try to be whoever she thought they wanted her to be.

"It" happened one night during a performance of a twenty-five-minute student-written comedy called *Keep Me a Woman Grown.* In two scenes, Carol was to play the role of Effie, a hillbilly woman. The first act went well: The audience seemed to enjoy her Southern accent and exaggerated walk. When she came back for her next scene, her opening line was simply "I'm back." The audience erupted into screams and applause. Carol Burnett had suddenly arrived. It was as if she had been born again. After hearing the sound of that laughter, she knew she would never again be the same.

"It" was a moment that would become a lifetime.

The next semester, someone asked her if she could carry a tune for a student musical; she wasn't sure that she could, or would even dare try. But when she opened her mouth to sing, a voice came out and it was loud. "My mouth is so big, the sound must bounce around in there," she joked to classmates, somewhat self-consciously. She won a role in the chorus of *South Pacific* (she was so powerful they had to ask her to tone it down) and then a featured role singing "Adelaide's Lament" in *Guys and Dolls*. It was her first solo onstage, and she was a hit.

Then she began winning roles in most of the school's major musical comedies. In the summer of 1952, she joined the Stumptown Players, a prestigious student summer-stock group that worked in northern California. (She'd go back in 1953.)

The semester after she returned in 1952, she started working in campus sketches with Lenny Weinrib, who had become the school clown. They performed together in the Homecoming Show at Royce Hall in front of the largest audience she'd ever seen. The next day, everyone was talking about "this girl, Carol Burnett." And that was the day she met Don Saroyan, who would become her first husband. Along with other students recruited to play piano, Don and Carol began their act of singing popular show tunes. They began working together in school plays and starred in the three-act *Tobias and the Angel* in December 1953.

Finally, Carol felt a genuine camaraderie with her peers at school. She quickly became part of the inner group of students who lived and breathed theater arts. It was an exciting, happy life.

It usually seemed that the prettiest girl got all of the attention in the academic world. But Carol discovered that in a theater environment, the rules were very different. The other students seemed to flock to the most talented. And frequently the most talented was not at all the most attractive or most fashionably dressed. Suddenly, Carol had value as a performer; her new self-esteem was validated by the acceptance of her peers. It changed her perspective of life; all of a sudden, she had a goal: to be a musical-comedy actress.

She cherished her good reviews in the college paper, *The Bruin,* carefully cutting out each one and pasting it in a scrapbook she would one day take to New York with her. The February 9, 1954, issue said she was "the funniest gal since Martha Raye." That month she won the lead in the school play *Love Thy Coach,* which ran for two days in May; she had a showstopping number called "Give Me a Man's World." The musical's producer, Bruce Campbell, joked at the time, "This score will not soon be forgotten, and after we finish here we plan to move to the Imperial Theatre on Broadway in New York for a three-year run."

The Daily Bruin ran a picture of Carol on its front page on March 15, 1954, with this headline: VARSITY SHOW FEMININE

LEAD OLD HAND IN TA (theater arts) PRODUCTIONS. "Upon graduation," the article said, "she plans to enter the musical comedy field." One wonders how many times *The Bruin* said that of other students, and how many of them actually fulfilled that promise.

Probably Carol's most precious memory of her college years was the evening she invited Louise, Nanny, and Chrissy to a student revue in which she was to perform a scene from Irving Berlin's *Call Me Madam.* Her family had no idea that she had become so engrossed in musical comedy; she was afraid to tell them, to have Nanny or Louise burst her bubble. But this evening, she decided she wanted them to see her work. There was nothing they could say, she decided, that would disillusion her or make her change her ambition.

In an interview with Barbara Walters, she remembered, "I was a wreck, an absolute wreck. We were all backstage and they hadn't come yet. I thought, Oh God, maybe Mama's drunk. What if she shows up drunk? Then I was hoping they wouldn't come. Then the back door opened in the lecture hall and I saw this familiar figure."

Carol couldn't believe that Louise, along with Nanny and Chrissy, had actually showed up. Louise hadn't been out of bed in a very long time, but she was there, shaky but sober.

The *Call Me Madam* scene was a showstopper. Nanny and Louise looked around the room at the smiling faces, they saw for themselves the standing ovation, they heard the cheers echo in the theater. They must have been utterly dazed. Who ever would have dreamed that their Carol had it in her?

Afterward, there was pandemonium in the theater as everyone gathered around Carol congratulating her. Nanny made certain all the ticket holders within hearing distance knew that she was Carol's grandmother; suddenly, she didn't seem very feeble at all.

Carol felt a tap on her shoulder. She turned around. It was Louise. Her eyes were damp.

"You really *were* the best one," she said.

It was a moment Carol would never forget.

"You really were the best one."

"She devoted all of her energies into getting out of 102," Carol's sister has said. When Carol finally did make it to New York, she saw a whole new world of possibilities open to her.

Emotionally, she had a long road to travel before anyone would venture to call her self-confident, but she would not define herself by her limitations as Nanny and Louise would have expected of her. Much to her surprise, she could do a lot with her talent, maybe even with her life.

When she returned to 102 in December 1957, memories of all that had happened since she'd left two years earlier made her head spin. Paul Winchell, Garry Moore, Green Mansions and Tamiment, *Stanley,* the Blue Angel, and "John Foster Dulles." She would wake up in the morning on that couch in the one-room apartment and wonder which was her real life, and which was the one she dreamed.

Apartment 102 was no longer home, of that she was certain. But New York didn't seem real at all. Carol couldn't wait to get back to make sure it was.

Despite the uncertainty of her life in Manhattan, she sensed a bright future for herself. But what was in store for Chrissy? Nanny and Louise had chosen their lots in life, but did her kid sister even have a chance?

The area was more run-down now than ever; tough, streetwise boys terrorized the neighborhood—the same one in which the child Carol loved to come out of her shell and, with her friend Ilomay, scream down the bathroom shafts of her building or play at being spies. But in 1957, the scene was right out of *West Side Story.* Twelve-year-old Chrissy was playing with undisciplined hoodlums-in-waiting.

"Carol was very concerned about the way the girl was being raised," Don Saroyan remembers, "and about the people she was hanging out with. She and I talked about it long and hard, about whether it was the right and fair thing to do, taking Chrissy away from Nanny and Louise. Also, how we would be able to handle the girl both financially and emotionally. But we agreed that it just wasn't right to keep her in Hollywood. It was Carol's idea to bring her to New York."

Chrissy had shaved off her eyebrows and was wearing makeup and tight sweaters to accentuate her already-full figure. She wasn't even a teenager yet, and she was headed for certain trouble.

Christine remembered: "I was getting wild and rather streetwise. I think Carol saw the scene coming. I probably would have been an unwed mother at fourteen, and struggling. I think

Carol wanted to help me out of that. Mama just didn't have anything left...."

Carol has said that she somehow convinced Louise to allow
her to take her sister back with her, not just for the holidays but
permanently. Louise understood that this would not be a temporary stay for Chrissy, that the girl would not be back after New
Year's. It was a painful but necessary parting, and deep down
Louise knew that it was best.

But Nanny would never have been able to deal with it. She'd
already lost Carol to show business, and Chrissy was now the one
bright light of her dark, empty life. They would have to keep this
plan from Nanny. And from Chrissy, too, for if she knew she
wasn't coming back, she surely would never leave. She loved her
life on Wilcox, was happy in school, and could never imagine
being without her close-knit group of friends.

Louise kept their secret and, ironically, it seemed to bring
her and Carol closer together. Maybe one day they would actually get to know one another, Carol hoped. It was a comforting
thought.

After the sisters left, Louise told Nanny that Chrissy would
not be returning home to live. A week after Carol and Chrissy
left Union Station for the train ride to Manhattan, Perry Gray
received this note from Nanny, dated December 19, 1957, and
mailed from the apartment at 1760 North Wilcox:

Dear Perry,
  So sweet to remember me, dear. I'm lonely and ill.
Collapsed when got home from station. Bruce and Lenny
took us. Carol will return about February 1 to do the Dinah
Shore Show. I had to have a doctor after they left. Still having
daily treatments. Chris won't get to come back with Carol.
That makes me very unhappy. I miss her so. Thanks again
for your lovely Xmas card.
                                     Merry Xmas,
                                     Nanny

When she got to New York, Chrissy brought new, young
laughter and joy into the Saroyan household. "We were married
two years and had a thirteen-year-old daughter," Don laughs. "I
became sort of a stepfather to her. It was fun showing her
around New York, helping to raise her. She was never a problem

for me. Chrissy was a very pretty girl, growing up fast. She was more physically developed, probably, than most kids her age. Also, after having dealt with such peer pressure in Hollywood, she was a bit rebellious. Underneath that façade of rebellion was a very, very sweet girl.

"She had reached a point," he continues, "where she was becoming someone that she didn't really want to be in her heart. She wanted somebody to say, 'No, don't do that, don't *become that.*'

"I don't remember too many details," he adds apologetically. "But when I think of it, I get a warm feeling."

They had enjoyed a lovely Christmas together, and were now looking forward to a festive New Year's celebration. It was a day or two before the New Year's holiday, and Carol and Christine were carrying groceries home from the market. As they crossed the street, Chrissy turned to her older sister and said, "You know, I'd better be going home soon. I have to go back to school."

Carol decided that now was as good a time as any to break the news to her sister. "You're not going back home," she said cautiously, all the while trying to appear nonchalant. "You're going to stay here with me."

Chrissy's eyes became saucers. Shocked, she dropped a bag of food onto the sidewalk. Oranges, apples, and carrots tumbled out of the paper bag, over the curb, and out into the busy street; speeding automobiles and buses made instant fruit juice out of them.

"I won't stay! *I won't stay!*" she screamed at the top of her lungs. *"You can't make me stay, Sissy!"*

Chrissy threw a temper tantrum on Forty-eighth Street and Eighth Avenue that Carol has never forgotten. She said later that if her sister's performance could have been caught on film, Chrissy would have been hailed the new Anne Bancroft.

"Why are you doing this to me?" she whined and sobbed all the way back to the Saroyans' apartment. *"You've kidnapped me!"*

Carol tried to explain that Louise was ill and tired. Nanny was getting on in years, and could no longer be expected to raise a teenager. "I think I can take care of you," she tried to reason with the girl. "If things keep going well with me, we'll be real happy." Chrissy began to calm down when Carol promised her new braces and talked about the private school she would attend, the fun friends she would make, and how exciting her new life would be. Out of emotional desperation, Carol decided to place a long-distance phone call to Louise for reinforcement.

Bad idea.

As soon as she heard her mother's voice, Carol knew that Louise was drunk.

"You're kidnapping my little girl!" Louise screamed into the phone. "I want her back! Please don't take my baby from me," she started to weep. "Please, Carol..."

The expression on Carol's face immediately registered with Chrissy, and she began to scream at the top of her lungs in the background, "I wanna come home, Mama. Please don't make me stay here!"

Carol had never expected such an awful scene. Finally, she was able to control the situation and persuade Louise all over again that Chrissy really would be better off in Manhattan with her.

"Please give me a chance to make her happy, to show her a good life," Carol pleaded. By now, she was crying, too. "She'll come back to visit, Mama, I promise. We'll both be back, Mama..."

There was silence on the other end.

"Mama?"

"Take care of my baby, will you, kid?" Louise finally said.

"I will, Mama. I love you..."

"I love you, too. I love you, Carol."

"Good-bye, Mama..."

A week later, on January 10, Ina Louise Burnett died, at the age of forty-seven.

6

CAROL AND CHRISSY COULDN'T GO BACK TO LOS ANGELES WHEN their mother died in 1958. Again, there was no money for train fare. Louise was cremated.

Carol knew there was nothing inevitable about her mother's early death. Once, in an interview, she was asked, "If you could talk to your mother today, what would you say?" Her voice shaking, Carol responded quickly, "I would put my hand on her shoulder and I would say, 'Mama, you're gonna get through this.' I can't help but fantasize that if I had done well before she got so sick, maybe, just maybe, she might be alive."

Nanny was alone now. She told Carol that she couldn't bear to live among all of the memories in apartment 102. The place seemed so empty now, and it would obviously be best if she moved. Nanny had devoted her life to taking care of Carol; now it was Carol's turn to make sure Nanny was taken care of. But it wasn't going to be easy; with Nanny nothing ever was.

Carol was booked to appear on *The Chevy Show,* starring Dinah Shore in February, but that was postponed for a month. She would go back to Los Angeles then. "I am looking forward to seeing all of you again," she wrote to a West Coast friend. "But it will be a sad homecoming, I'm afraid. However, it *has* to be done, and I have Christine to work for and think of."

Carol was more determined now than ever to get Christine on the right track. As for the matter of education, she felt that enrolling her sister in a public school would be a mistake. "Putting her in a New York City public school would be like taking her out of the frying pan and throwing her into the fire," she told friends. She found a private school about an hour away from Manhattan, a rural New Jersey area. The school was run by Episcopalian nuns; Carol and Don decided that the strict discipline would be good for Chrissy. The girl agreed to attend only if Carol promised that they would be able to spend weekends together.

Tuition for this schooling would amount to fifteen hundred dollars, which, of course, Carol did not have. Arthur Willi, from the Martin Goodman Agency, agreed to cosign for a bank loan.

"Carol did everything in the world to protect her sister and make sure that Chrissy would have the best she could afford," Lenny Weinrib recalls. "I think she was proud of the fact that they figured out a way to put Chrissy in that private school. She was riding horses for recreation; going to school with girls who would be a good influence."

Chrissy would call every other day. "I'm homesick," she'd cry. "Sissy, can I come back?"

Carol would assure her that they would be together for the weekend. But she knew that Chrissy felt alone and isolated; the first few months of adjustment were difficult ones.

"Maybe you should reconsider a public school," Don suggested one day. "Her phone calls are tearing you up, Carol. Why feel so guilty?"

"No. I think I'm doing what's best," she said.

Don was proud of her. She was really taking charge.

Weekends with Chrissy were always fun, but even then there would be the problems inherent in a relationship where sister is suddenly guardian.

"You are *not* my mother!" Chrissy would yell at Carol when Carol tried to keep her in line. "*Don't tell me what to do, Sissy!*"

Carol once remembered: "When I was just Sissy, everything was fine. When I had to be Mother, we had a few fights. But I had to be both, just the same."

March arrived and Carol flew to Los Angeles for the *Chevy Show* taping. When she got to Hollywood, the first thing she had to do was move Nanny into a one-bedroom apartment not far from the former residence. Somehow, Nanny wasn't quite the same, Carol noticed. She seemed older and frailer. For the first time, she even seemed a little defeated.

The next few months were more of the same. A *Jack Paar Show* appearance, another Ed Sullivan. Then, in early April, Carol was booked as a semiregular on *Pantomime Quiz,* a charades program featuring a celebrity panel, hosted by Mike Stokey on ABC-TV. (The show was the precursor to the perennial favorite

Stump the Stars.) The appearances were worthwhile because Carol didn't really have to perform so much as just play the parlor game. It allowed her a chance to show her own natural, warm, and humorous personality to millions of viewers.

In July 1958, Carol was booked into the Desert Inn Hotel in Las Vegas as part of an Ed Sullivan revue. The four-week engagement was exciting in that she had the chance to see many of her UCLA classmates who flew in for the performances. They opened on Tuesday, July 1. Her act wasn't more than seven minutes long; for two shows an evening she sang the "Dulles" number, did a few routines, and was off. "God! It's like stealing!" she laughingly told her buddies. She reserved a table for them close to the stage and then had Sullivan introduce her former classmates from the audience.

"I remember that engagement well," Don says. "Being in Vegas with Ed and Sylvia [Sullivan]. We stayed at the Bali Hi Motel on Desert Inn Road. I think the Ames Brothers were there also." The Saroyans brought along their new female Yorkshire terrier, Bruce, named after their good friend Bruce Campbell.

"I didn't know whether or not to be honored," Campbell jokes.

"Actually, I remember that engagement as being a bit rocky," he continues. "Don was still taking odd jobs and doing industrial shows, and I remember thinking that this was really eating away at their marriage. They didn't seem to be real happy together. In Vegas was the first time I'd ever noticed."

He recalls a particularly disturbing incident. "Either we were checking in or checking out, and there was luggage all over the place. Somebody from the motel walked over to Don and said, 'Oh, Mr. Burnett, what would you like us to do with these bags?' Don was a gentleman about it, but he's a man with enormous pride; it had to affect him."

"There was resentment building on my end," Saroyan frankly confesses. "I began to feel shut out of Carol's life, which caused bad feelings. This is why so many show-business marriages fall apart. When one has a career that is so demanding, as Carol's was, almost all of your waking thoughts have to be centered on yourself. I began to see that this was becoming the case with Carol, and I didn't see any way around that. In fact, in the beginning I encouraged that thinking in her.

"I really got no support or encouragement from her as I had

given her," he continues. "I was getting none of that back at a point where I really needed it."

Another friend adds, "When Carol started becoming a national figure with the television appearances and concerts—something more than a New York personality—Don wasn't able to handle it. He had, after all, helped to nurture her every step of the way. And now she was surpassing him. But what could she do? Give up her career to spare Don's feelings? Plus, Don was never as concentrated on his career as Carol was. He was never as focused as you have to be to be successful in show business."

Carol and Don had always found it difficult to break through their reserves and discuss their deepest feelings. Most of the time, Don recalls, they repressed their emotions when they desperately needed to communicate them. Also, they hadn't been spending much time together lately. The marriage was not going well.

After the Vegas engagement, Don went back to work in New York. Carol and Chris went on to Los Angeles, where Carol was booked on a couple more Chevy shows at the NBC television studios in Burbank. Dinah Shore was on vacation and the program was being hosted by other stars, like Janet Blair and Edie Adams.

The *Chevy Show*'s producer and director, Bob Banner, best known today for his creation of the successful *Star Search* television program, recalls the way Carol was booked on the show: "George Spota from Marty Goodman's office had been calling me constantly about this new young comedienne. Well, I got a lot of calls like that. I did what I could to see them all, but I never did.

"Every year NBC sent us to New York to do a couple of *Chevy Show*'s from that location. When we were there, Spota called again about this Carol Burnett person. He tried to set up a time for an audition. 'I just don't have the time, George,' I told him. 'Send us a picture at the office and we'll consider her.' Whatever it took to get him off the line, that's what I said."

Banner was having a breakfast staff meeting in his hotel suite when there was a knock on the door. It was George Spota, with a film projector under his arm and a kinescope of one of Carol's "John Foster Dulles" television appearances. Banner was exasperated. "Can't you see we're in a meeting here?" he said impatiently. "Three minutes," he decided as Spota quickly plugged in his equipment. "That's all I'll give you for this. Three minutes."

The agent didn't have a screen with him (he probably knew he wouldn't have enough time even to set one up.) Carol's fuzzy, distorted image appeared on a yellow wall in the suite's living room. The recording of her voice sounded thin and tinny. Three minutes into her performance, Spota nervously turned off the projector.

"Hey! Turn that back on!" Banner demanded. "Let me see the rest of that."

The talent for the next three *Chevy Show*s had already been booked; Banner signed Carol for the fourth. "And then I thanked George Spota for being such an irritation," he said with a grin. "You might say that for me Carol's success was written on the wall."

Perry Gray recalls of one *Chevy Show* taping, "It was Sunday, September 7, 1958. I still have the ticket stub," he says, grinning. "John Raitt, Janet Blair, and Edie Adams were the performers, and Carol was the newcomer on the program. It was broadcast in color, so we were all very impressed with the picture when we looked at the television monitors. Up until this time, I don't recall seeing Carol on TV in color. During a break, she came over to me into the audience. She knelt by my side and whispered into my ear, 'I'm so nervous. Poor Edie Adams, her father died. She's very upset, and they want me to sing more in the medley to relieve her.' She didn't have to worry. She was more than fine."

Harry Zimmerman, musical director of the orchestra for *The Chevy Show*, remembers the first time he met Carol: "Those were fun shows because on them we showcased a lot of up-and-coming talent, like Streisand and Burnett. I recall Carol doing a parody of Cole Porter's 'Don't Fence Me In.' I had never heard of her before, so I didn't know what to expect.

"The orchestra started the number and Carol came in. But she was late and slightly off-key. I discreetly stopped the performance.

"We started again. And again she came in late, and this time very flat.

"Finally, I went over to her and said very quietly so as not to embarrass her, 'Miss Burnett, I think we should do this again. You're singing off-key, I'm afraid. And also, you don't seem to know your cue.'

"'Why, Mr. Zimmerman,' she said, all wide-eyed. *That's* the idea. I'm *supposed* to come in late. I'm *supposed* to sing flat. It's a joke. Don't you get it?"

"'Oh, sure,' I lied through my teeth. By now, I was very red-faced. 'I get it. Funny, too . . .'"

After the *Chevy Show*, it was back to Manhattan. Don was off working on the crew of a road-show production of *The Tender Trap*. When he returned, he would help assist in restaging singer Denise Darcel's act for an engagement at the Latin Quarter. ("She's replacing Anna Maria Spaghetti," Carol joked, referring to Anna Maria Alberghetti.)

Carol appeared on a *Garry Moore Show* on Tuesday, October 7, 1958. Another appearance was scheduled for his Christmas show on December 23. All of this television work had its good points, but also bad ones. Carol was at the mercy of the staff writers employed by the shows on which she appeared. She wasn't always able to use her own Ken Welch material. Often, the material she was given to perform was simply not funny or imaginative. Many times it was similar to what she'd already done on other shows, making it seem as if she had no comedic depth or stylistic range. This was particularly frustrating given the fact that she came to New York to be a theater personality, not a television comedienne-singer.

Perry Gray wrote to Carol after her October appearance on *The Garry Moore Show*: "It strikes me that the fewer people involved in creating your material, the better it will be. It seems strange and a great waste that a show with Hermione Gingold and Marion Lorne was not funny. I have a feeling that you *must* continue working on your own material with Kenny or you'll become a victim of [television] writers who are told to prepare something for you and their first query is, 'Oh, and what does *she* do?'"

Carol agreed that at this point she really wasn't able to challenge her potential. Her response to Gray's comments in a letter she wrote on October 11: "I couldn't agree more with your impressions of Garry's show. I wish for his sake that it improves as he deserves the very best. It's a shame that his writers don't agree. I'm working on new stuff with Kenny. Actually, nothing seems very 'new' to me anymore. God! For a legit show! But I just have to be patient."

On Tuesday, January 6, 1959, Carol auditioned for Richard

Rodgers, who was mounting a revival of the 1937 Broadway hit *Babes in Arms*. The show would go on the road in the spring and summer, beginning with an engagement in Florida. If successful, Rodgers planned to take it to Broadway. "Say a huge prayer for me," Carol told friends. "This could be it!"

Rodgers enjoyed Carol's audition, and she felt good about it herself. He told her they would be in touch, but she decided not to sit by the phone waiting. She auditioned for the lead in a summer-stock company of Jule Styne's *Bells Are Ringing,* and it looked as if she'd be playing the lead. That was an exciting prospect even if it wasn't New York theater. At least she'd be on the stage.

Sunday, February 15, 1959. The telephone rang at eleven o'clock in the morning in the Saroyan residence. Carol picked it up.

"Miss Burnett, are you available to fill in for Martha Raye on Garry Moore's new prime-time show?" the voice asked. "We've been rehearsing all week. You'll only have until Tuesday to learn the whole show. We go on Tuesday night. Live!

"Hello, Miss Burnett? Hello....are you there? Hello?"

Garry Moore had been such a success in daytime television, the CBS brass gave him a prime-time variety series to augment his daily chores for the network. The new show aired on Tuesday evenings at ten o'clock, immediately after Red Skelton's program. It wasn't his first prime-time exposure; Moore hosted an evening variety show five nights a week in 1950, and another series in 1951, but neither show was a success.

The new series was highly touted, and when it first aired on September 30, 1958, the ratings were quite good. The program pulled in an amazing 53 percent share of the television viewers. But Moore was utilizing much the same format he used in daytime; the writing wasn't strong, and the production seemed scattershot. After six shows, he was only pulling in 17 percent of the viewership, and his show was on the verge of being canceled unless a new producer could breathe some life into it.

Mike Dann, head of programming for CBS, contacted Bob Banner in Los Angeles to see if he would be interested in replacing producer Ralph Levy. Banner agreed to go to New York; he formed his own production company, Bob Banner and Associates, with Joe Hamilton as producer, Bob Wright as associate producer, and the late Julio deBenedeto as director. They were contracted to overhaul the program during its Thanksgiving hiatus, and then to produce six shows. They ended up staying six years.

Two or three Banner-produced episodes had aired by the time popular comedienne Martha Raye was booked for an appearance. Other guests on the show were Buddy Hackett, Jaye P. Morgan, and Johnny Desmond. Raye rehearsed on Thursday and Friday and then left the set complaining of a sore throat. She was scheduled to go back to work on Sunday, and the show would air live on Tuesday evening.

Associate producer Bob Wright picks up the story: "It was Sunday and one of those blustery, rainy winter days in New York. I remember that the phone was ringing as I was putting the key in the lock of our office in the old Sheffield Milk Building they called CBS Production Center. I ran in to get it. It was Martha's husband calling to tell me that she was deathly ill. She couldn't even move her head, he said, and there was no way she could do the show on Tuesday. And I said, "But...but...but...""

Raye would have to be replaced by someone who resided in the New York area since there was no time to fly anyone in from Los Angeles. She had to be a relatively familiar personality and versatile enough to step into Raye's three major sketches, but not so well established as to be able to demand any major rewrites. Above all, she had to be a quick study. Banner, deBenedeto, and Hamilton had all worked with Carol Burnett on *The Chevy Show* and thought she would be the perfect replacement. Garry Moore had always liked Carol's appearances on his daytime series, and so they called her.

"Hello, Miss Burnett? Are you still there?"

Carol pulled herself together. "Yes...I'll have two days? I'll be right down. I can do it," she said with appropriate resolve.

"My God! Carol, that's great!" Don enthused when she told him about the call.

"It's *nuts*!" Carol exclaimed. Suddenly, she wasn't quite sure about any of this. "How can I learn all of that material? What if I bomb? Then what?"

There was no time to think about that. It was raining out, at least, so that was a good omen as far as Carol was concerned.

One hour later, she was deep into rehearsal. "And you'd be surprised at how fast you can learn when you're hungry," Carol would later admit.

Carol came dashing into the studio soaking wet. She'd left so quickly she'd forgotten to bring an umbrella. She looked rather pitiful, but the moment was deceptive. She was ready to work.

"When we started rehearsing, you knew from those first moments that something wonderful was happening," Bob Wright recalls. "The writers started reworking sketches. Even though there was no time, Carol was so good they felt like they wanted to take the time. They started taking out Raye-isms and throwing in what would go on to become Burnett-isms."

Ernie Flatt, the show's choreographer, says, "Martha was supposed to do a sketch where she was the carved figurehead of a ship. With her, shall we say, *ample* figure, it promised to be very funny. But when Carol did it, she struggled to stick out her small figure, pushing out and pushing out to hopelessly fit the image of a sexy carving. She made the bit even funnier than the writers had intended it for Martha. Everyone knew at that moment that she was *in*...."

Garry Moore was absolutely enchanted by Carol, by how adept and professional she was. She seemed to be such a natural performer. For the next couple of days, he watched her flipping and flapping all over the studio, doing pratfalls, working her face at a mad pace, and being game enough to do anything for a laugh. Somehow, she seemed to make everybody else on the set play better. "This is unbelievable," he kept saying to the crew. "This is Cinderella. It's Cinderella time."

The broadcast on Tuesday evening, February 17, 1959, was a success. Carol was given a solo number: She sang a rip-roaring rendition of "Johnny One Note" from Rodgers and Hart's *Babes in Arms* (and she probably hoped Richard Rodgers, who hadn't yet made a decision about casting her in that revival, was watching the program). During the final commercial, Moore went into the control booth. "Give me about three minutes at the end of the show," he told the producers. "Cut whatever you have to cut. I gotta tell America what happened here tonight."

Says Bob Wright: "He told the story and brought Carol out for one more bow. The whole audience just rose en masse, screaming and yelling when she walked onto the stage. Carol just stood there crying. What a moment..."

When she got backstage, Carol found herself surrounded by crew and costars all congratulating her on her performance. She had been working on sheer nervous energy for two days, and now she just wanted to drop. Then someone told her that she had a phone call. It was Martha Raye calling to warn her that she would never become ill again and allow Carol to fill in for her. "You were too good," she scolded. After Carol hung up, a security guard gave her two dozen roses. They were from Martha. The crowning gesture to an amazing evening.

"Ain't show biz grand?" she remarked to Bob Wright on her way out of the studio. She already knew the answer.

7

CAROL HAD MADE SUCH AN IMPRESSION WITH HER APPEARANCE on Garry Moore's program that the next day the producers approached Moore with the idea of hiring her as a regular member of the cast. The writers said that they'd had a terrific time working with her. It seemed obvious that adding Carol Burnett to the weekly show could only enhance the series' continually sagging ratings. "Mike Dann, vice-president of CBS, had seen the show the night before," Bob Wright says, "and he absolutely agreed. Carol should be on every week."

But Garry wasn't ready for the likes of Carol . . . at least not at this point. "I approached him with the idea, and he didn't want her on as a regular," Joe Hamilton remembers. "'She's really kind of strong,' he told me. 'No. We'll book her occasionally. That will do fine.'

"'Well, Garry,' I told him, 'I really think you're passing up something kind of super.' But he had made up his mind, and it *was* his show. He was under a certain pressure, I think; we were still wondering if the ratings would pick up, if he could actually succeed in hosting his own prime-time series. He was obviously a bit insecure about adding someone as overpowering as Carol to the show."

Carol wasn't aware of what was happening behind closed doors in the Garry Moore offices, and that was probably for the best. That "big break" would come in 1959 anyway, but it wouldn't be before television cameras; rather, it would be where she had always intended it, in the theater.

The circumstances that led to Carol's first theatrical experience in Manhattan are a textbook example of the way lives and careers in the theater often intersect. They also demonstrate how a typical theatrical production is cast and mounted

By 1950, comedienne-actress Nancy Walker had become one of the brightest and most acclaimed new stars in New York. She had made her Broadway debut in October 1941 in the George Abbott opus *Best Foot Forward,* followed by three more Abbott vehicles, including the tremendous 1948 success *Look Ma, I'm Dancing* at Broadway's Adelphi Theatre. Walker, then twenty-nine years old, was touted as the logical successor to Martha Raye; she was so grateful to Abbott—and so valued his opinion—that she used to retrieve notes from his wastebaskets and paste them all over her dressing-room walls.

Walker went on to achieve her biggest fame on television some thirty years later as Valerie Harper's mother, Ida Morgenstern, on the popular *Rhoda* TV series. That abrasive persona was the kind of personality for which she had become typecast on the stage, a lady cab driver, a lady cop. In 1950, she was looking for something different.

A mutual friend suggested that she contact lyricist Marshall Barer for ideas. Barer says, "It's always better to go for the surprise in comedy, for opposites. Before our meeting, I remembered that the funniest Nancy had ever been was a moment in *Look Ma* when she wore a tutu and got up on her tippy toes for a delicate dance routine. Suddenly, I had this image of Hans Christian Anderson's *The Princess and the Pea,* with Nancy climbing up on top of the bed and trying to sleep despite the presence of a single pea under the mattress. It struck me as very funny."

He shared the idea with Walker. "Sounds like a cute bug," she decided, "if you don't step on it too hard."

She told Barer to work up a script, but he procrastinated, and before long Walker found another project to devote her time to. That was the end of *The Princess and the Pea*...until eight years later.

In August 1958, Marshall Barer collaborated with his then-fiancée Mary Rodgers (daughter of composer Richard Rodgers) and Jay Thompson on the *Princess* concept as a Tamiment production, directed by Jack Sydow and choreographed by Joe Layton. On closing night, the producers invited forty of New York's theatrical elite—producers, directors, agents, and actors—to the performance. Nancy Walker was in the audience. She enjoyed the play and agreed to allow Barer to use her name to secure a television deal for it. Unfortunately, Nancy Walker wasn't a television name at that time, and no one wanted to sponsor her in a network special.

Five months later—in January 1959—Mary Rodgers was dining with set designers William and Jean Eckart, who had also seen *The Princess and the Pea* at Tamiment. After Rodgers explained the problems in financing the show as a television special, the Eckarts suggested that perhaps the one-act play could be expanded to two acts for off-Broadway theater. The pair had assisted in the successful Marc Daniels production of *Phoenix 55* starring Nancy Walker at an off-Broadway house on Second Avenue in the East Village, the Phoenix Theatre. As it turned out, the Phoenix Theatre Production Company was scheduled for a summer hiatus and the theater would be empty for a few months. Perhaps, they mused, *The Princess and the Pea* could fill the down time.

Jean Eckart remembers that there were peas with the chicken that night—"a definite omen."

So on January 19, the Tamiment version of *Princess* was auditioned for T. Edward Hambleton and Norris Houghton, directors of the Phoenix Theatre. Their reaction was, "If you can get George Abbott to direct, the theater is yours for the summer."

George Abbott had just finished producing *Drink to Me Only* at the Fifty-fourth Street Theatre. He told the Eckarts that if they came across a strong property to produce, he would consider directing it for them.

The stage was quickly being set.

Ten days later, Barer, Thompson, and Rodgers auditioned the show for Abbott. They sang their hearts out and waited for his reaction.

The bald, blue-eyed, and very intimidating Abbott, then seventy-one years old, deliberated a moment over what he'd just heard and finally concluded, "You've got a lot of funny stuff there...but it's too precious. You know what I mean by precious, don't you?"

The three nodded fiercely even though they had no idea what the man was talking about. He was the great George Abbott, after all, and if the play was "too precious," then so be it. Abbott was off to Acapulco for three weeks, and as he walked out the door he said that if they could "get all of the preciousness out" of the book, he'd consider directing the show. "But, frankly," he concluded, "I'm afraid the preciousness is permanently built in." (Years later, in his autobiography, *Mr. Abbott,* he would write that he found the original book "too sweet and naive.")

They considered trying to find a new director. However, without Abbott they realized that there would be no show, at least not at the Phoenix. So another writer, Dean Fuller, was recruited by Barer to work on a complete book revision. His input was invaluable, and three weeks later, on a springlike February 9, another appointment was set with Mr. Abbott. The last page of the new play was hastily typed out on Thompson's portable Olivetti in a cab on the way to Abbott's office in Rockefeller Center.

Patient and newly tanned, Abbott listened again, and this time he liked what he heard. He was ready to go to work immediately. *Once Upon a Mattress* (as *Princess* was eventually retitled) would become the first, last, and only off-Broadway production ever directed by George Abbott.

He suggested a number of rewrites; sets and costumes were discussed. Eighty-thousand dollars was raised by Mary Rodgers without benefit of auditions for potential backers (there could be no auditions because the show hadn't even been cast).

When it came time to cast the play, Abbott decided that he didn't want to work with Nancy Walker again even though that's who the show had originally been written for. The two had had a disagreement over an unrelated matter. Somebody mentioned Carol Burnett's name, and he recalled years later, "I didn't think that would work either, at first.

"I had seen her sing the 'John Foster Dulles' number a year earlier when she performed by special invitation at a Dutch Treat Club show. It was a private club for show business people, and Carol was fine entertainment. But, still, I wasn't certain that she would work out as the princess. The part was brassy, tough, like Nancy Walker, not like Carol Burnett. I had my reservations...."

Of that Dutch Treat Club show, Carol has remembered that she wasn't at her best that evening. The audiences gave her a mediocre reception. When she heard that Abbott was sitting somewhere in the crowd, she thought to herself, Oh, no! That finishes me!

Abbott felt that comic actress Pat Carroll, who had been appearing in a revival of *On the Town,* would be ideal for the lead in *Princess.* Carroll was essaying the same role Nancy Walker played in the Broadway play, Hildy the cab driver. Mr. Abbott sent his daughter Julie to the show, and the next morning he asked for her appraisal of Pat Carroll's appearance.

"She was okay," his daughter began carefully. "But she's a bit ... old."

"Old?" the then-seventy-two-year-old Abbott shot back, his voice rising. "We don't want 'old.' Find somebody young ... somebody no one ever heard of."

Carol was on pins and needles about the Richard Rodgers revival of *Babes in Arms*. This seemed like the opportunity of a lifetime. "So what if it's not George Abbott," she decided. "At least I'll finally be working on a Broadway stage." There were many call-backs; the director thought she had potential, and he even came to the Saroyan home to coach her personally. But Carol had no name value, and Rodgers seemed interested in trying to find a major personality for the role.

In the end, Carol didn't get the job.

The afternoon of her final audition, she came home frustrated and defeated. Christine, home from school on a spring break, tried to console her, but it seemed hopeless. Carol couldn't stop sobbing.

"Cheer up, Sissy," Chrissy began optimistically. "You know what you always say: 'One door closes, another opens.'"

Carol had to laugh. That's what she'd said, all right.

Meanwhile, the same afternoon Carol was singing the blues in one part of Manhattan, Mary Rodgers was complaining to Marshall Barer in another. "We have tested every single young actress in this city," she groaned, "and we still haven't found anyone for this play. We'll *never* open at this rate. It's March, for chrissake!"

"Suddenly, I got this flash," Barer recalls dramatically. "With just a few small changes, I thought the part might be right for Carol, after all. I got out my pad and frantically started scribbling notes."

The way he had written it for Nancy Walker, the role was that of a very tough, urbane princess. It occurred to him that with some alterations, the lead could be an awkward, gangly, country-girl type: Carol Burnett. They found her home number.

Carol was in the kitchen fixing dinner when the phone rang. Chrissy picked it up.

"Sissy, it's for you. . . ."
One door closes. Another one opens.

The scene was Marshall Barer's apartment on Third Avenue. Ken Welch was playing piano as Carol sang "Everybody Loves to Take a Bow" from the show *Hazel Flagg* with everything she had in her. An audition for George Abbott was set for Friday, March 6, at 4:00 P.M. at the Phoenix Theatre. Rehearsals would begin in two weeks.

The thought of working with George Abbott had Carol in a daze. This was exactly what she had envisioned as her break when she left Los Angeles five years ago. Somehow, she would recall later, she now felt as if she were home free. "I knew I had the part before I even got on the subway," she's said. She knew the role of the princess was hers in the way she knew she'd find a way to go to UCLA . . . the way she knew she'd figure out a way to get to New York. Somehow, somehow.

As Carol sang the song, Marshall Barer was a rapt audience. By this time, Ken had stretched Carol's vocal range; her voice was fuller and more vibrant than Barer had remembered it being when they worked together at Tamiment. It was all the difference between the acceptable and the remarkable. Everybody agreed that this would be the number Carol would sing for George Abbott.

Marshall Barer says of Carol's audition for Mr. Abbott, "Here was this girl from nowhere auditioning for one of Broadway's leading masters. She was enchanting; that 'star quality' was there, and Mr. Abbott recognized it immediately. And those choppers! She had great teeth. Mr. Abbott always said that if you didn't have great teeth, your smile would never make it to the balconies."

"That's the smile that will light up the Phoenix," Abbott decided after he gave Carol the role.

George Abbott celebrated his one hundred and first birthday on June 25, 1988. He arrived in New York as an actor in 1913, and by the 1920's had become a successful writer, producer, and director. By the time *Mattress* came along, he had produced, directed, or otherwise been involved in ninety-five shows. They used to call him the "Show Doctor" because of his skill at resuscitating dying productions. His work on Broadway in the

1940's and 1950's is legendary, and includes big, brassy shows like *Call Me Madam, Wonderful Town, Pajama Game,* and *Damn Yankees.*

Abbott is a stern no-nonsense type, known to be sometimes blunt and dictatorial. Not a man given to idle chatter, he never uses two words when one will do. A perfectionist, he has no patience for mediocrity. And while he is known for his work with Broadway stalwarts like Helen Hayes and Mary Martin, he's always been a habitual booster of new talent. "Besides saving money," he said, "it saves wear and tear on the nervous system."

A favorite story in Broadway circles is that an actor once said to Abbott, "Sir, I don't understand this script. What's my motivation?" Abbott shot back, "Your job!"

All of those who've ever worked with him call him "Mr. Abbott." He never demanded it; it just somehow seemed natural.

To *Once Upon a Mattress* George Abbott brought an aura of unchallenged authority, a feeling of security. He was Papa at the head of the table. And though Carol may have been intimidated by him at first, that didn't last very long. She knew that she could discuss anything with him, as long as she kept it short and to the point. He wasn't an ogre.

Abbott's patience with Carol was unflagging. "He taught me so much without ever raising his voice or overworking me," she once recalled. "When he said, 'That's good,' it was like a bouquet of roses thrown at me."

Humorously enough, while so many people involved in Carol's career refuse to take credit for their contributions, Mr. Abbott won't hear of such humility. "Oh, yes, I *discovered* Carol," he says succinctly.

"I was enchanted by her, but, oh, I don't think I ever let her know that," he laughs. "One thing about Miss Burnett, I would not stand for any mugging from her. I demanded that she play the part of the princess seriously, even though it was farce. I told her that if she played it seriously it would be ten times funnier.

"What amazed me most about Carol is that she is as funny a personality as she is a good actress, which isn't always the case. Carol could also sing, so she was very much the consummate stage performer. I remember she was nervous about the opening. She would never for a moment express that to me, because she certainly wanted me to think she was confident. But I'd heard she was a bit frightened.

"One day I told the cast, and this statement was directed to

Carol: The whole point of theater isn't to have someone applaud your performance but rather the pleasure of doing the best work you can and the knowledge that you've done it well.

"And also," Abbott concludes with a laugh, "if you don't get too emotional when the audience gives you standing ovations, you'll be a lot less emotional when they don't."

His words must have touched Carol. It seems that she's never forgotten them.

March 7, 1959

Dear Perry,
 Well, at last I have some exciting news. The Phoenix Theatre is presenting a musical comedy spoof of the old fairytale, *The Princess and the Pea* to open on May 12. I auditioned yesterday and got the title role! (NOT THE PEA!) And the best part—it's to be directed by George Abbott!!
 I signed for a year and needless to say, I'm speechless. THIS IS WHAT I CAME TO NEW YORK FOR! And IT has finally happened. I wish you could be in the audience opening night, Perry. You bring good luck. Anyway, you will be, in spirit. I know that. I'll write again soon with details.
     Love,
     Carol

Eighty-five dollars a week. That's what Carol was told she'd be making in off-Broadway theater. The show was guaranteed a six-week run. "But even if it were to close after the first day," she said later, "I felt it would be worth it. I would have paid them to let me do it."

Don was happy for Carol; this is what they had been working toward. But it was a bittersweet victory in a way, because, for Don Saroyan, nothing at all was happening. "Certainly for Carol it seemed like things were coming together," he remembers. "George Abbott had been one of my idols, too. The show was perfect for her; she was perfect for the show. To be honest, I'd have to say that I was jealous," he concludes frankly. "I was jealous of her extreme good fortune and my extreme lack of it."

Carol couldn't help but feel guilty about her sudden coup in the face of Don's bad luck. So she tried to keep him as involved in what was going on by filling him in on every detail when she came home from rehearsal each evening. Somehow, though, that seemed to make matters worse. When the opportunity arose for Don to go to Cuba and work as a sound technician on a film about the Castro revolution, *Cuban Rebel Girls,* he decided to take the job. The movie starred Errol Flynn's girl friend, Beverly Aadland. Don promised that he would return in time for Carol's opening.

For the next few weeks, Carol walked around in perpetual astonishment, amazed that "all of this good stuff" was really happening to her. It never occurred to her that it could all come to a crashing halt in just a few weeks. There was no room for that kind of pessimism, not when there was so much work to do.

The cast was a strong one: Joe Bova, Jane White, Jack Gilford, and other familiar names in New York theater.

Somewhere along the way, the title of the musical had been changed from *The Princess and the Pea* to *Once Upon a Mattress.* Author Marshall Barer hated the new title ("I thought it was crude and salacious"), but Abbott didn't, and so it stayed.

Carol loved the script; she devoured it line by line. In Hans Christian Andersen's fairy tale, the princess of a royal kingdom was so sensitive that she could not sleep on a bed of twenty mattresses when a single pea was placed beneath the bottom one. In *Once Upon a Mattress,* a few twists were added to that theme.

Carol played Winnifred Woebegone, a hapless princess who is tricked by an evil queen into taking a "sensitivity test" to prove that she has royal blood. The queen will only be satisfied if Winnifred is kept awake by a pea she doesn't even know has been placed under the bottom of her bed of twenty mattresses. If she falls asleep, she flunks the test and can't marry the queen's son, Prince Dauntless.

In the end, the princess tosses and turns and passes the test —because, unbenown to her, a sympathetic minstrel has placed a lute, a helmet, a large spiked ball, and a couple of lobsters under the top mattress. Princess Winnifred gets her prince, and everyone in the kingdom lives happily ever after (except the evil queen, who is struck dumb by a royal curse).

One of the most interesting castings in *Mattress* was that of Jane White as Queen Aggravain. White is a respected black actress and daughter of Walter White, one of the founders of the

N.A.A.C.P. Her portrayal marked the first time a black woman had ever played a non-black character in a full-scale professional Broadway production (*Mattress* was destined for Broadway). Abbott was dead-set against casting White because, as he put it, "a Negro playing a Caucasian was unheard of." He was convinced but only with the stipulation that not one word of publicity would ever be written about the unique casting. He considered exploitation of White's role to be gimmicky casting, and he wouldn't hear of that.

Rehearsals went smoothly, and Carol loved the group spirit on this production. Marshall Barer recalls having a problem with one of Carol's big numbers in the show. "It was very difficult coming up with a song show people call 'the eleven-o'clock spot,'" he remembers. "That's the moment in the second act when the star, Carol, comes out and does her big star number. The one we'd written with Nancy Walker in mind was all wrong. Mr. Abbott rejected everything we'd written for Carol. We were getting close to opening night, and still no big number for the second act. I was frantic...."

In desperation, he called Carol at home one evening and suggested that perhaps there was a special-material number in her nightclub act that could be adapted to the play. Carol mentioned a novelty number Ken Welch had written about a girl giving her valedictory speech. Since the vacant spot in the play was at a point where Winnifred was "studying" for her "sensitivity test," the Welch song seemed like it could work. Carol, Ken, and Marshall spent the evening adapting the number.

The next morning, they auditioned the number for Mr. Abbott in the basement rehearsal hall of the Phoenix. Carol ran through the song breathlessly. Ken played frantically. They were *selling*. As Mr. Abbott watched, Marshall Barer studied him carefully, hoping for any sign of approval.

"Ta-da!" Ken proclaimed when the number was over. Carol took a triumphant bow.

Abbott looked at them blankly. He walked over to Carol. "This is going to break your heart, kid," he said, "because I can see you think you've got it. But you don't. It's no good."

As they left the rehearsal hall, Carol and Marshall agreed that even though the song wasn't as good as they had thought it was, "it's a helluva lot better than *he* thought it was."

It was raining as the two of them tried unsuccessfully to hail a cab in front of the Phoenix. "Look, Carol," Marshall began. "I am going to come up with a number for you. I want to know, I *need* to know, that you believe I can do it." He began to apologize, "I'm so sorry . . . I really am."

Carol's soaking-wet hair was plastered to her forehead, and standing there, drenched, she looked like something out of one of her comedy sketches. She considered Barer's apology and said, "Listen, if I had to pack up my gear and leave the theater after the first act, and never even come back for the second, I would still already feel that more than enough had been done for me."

"Whether or not she meant what she said that evening in the rain—and I must say that I believe she did—it was certainly the right thing to say," Marshall Barer recalls with a grin. "Carol's attitude could inspire any writer to bend over backwards to come up with the perfect vehicle. I finally did. It was called 'Happily Ever After,' and the critics loved it. Oh, and so did Mr. Abbott."

April 11, 1959

Dear Perry,

Goodness! I'm pooped! I haven't worked this hard since The Homecoming and Varsity shows at UCLA, nor have I had as much fun! It's almost too good to be true, Perry! If I had sat down and listed all of the things I'd want to do in my first show, this would have been it! It's all there. I just *have* to work like the devil to make sure everything comes out as it should. The book is hysterical, the music tuneful and the lyrics biting. And the people wonderful.

Mr. Abbott is all I ever imagined: wise, silent, at times funny, and very kind. I discovered muscles I never knew existed. This is the most physical part I've ever had. So we run all summer—I'll be in excellent shape come September.

Don's in Cuba and will be back in another two weeks. I really miss coming home and telling him everything about the show. Bruce and Fang [the dogs] seem interested enough, but I think they're just being polite.

I work all day, study my lines and then go to bed.

Dull but delicious.
Much, much love,
Carol

The month flew by. There were five preview shows at the Phoenix, which were, according to the frazzled writers, equivalent to five weeks of advance performances on the road, with book changes every night suggested by Mr. Abbott. And then, on Monday evening, May 11, 1959, *Once Upon a Mattress* finally made its wobbly way to the stage.

It was obvious from the reaction of the audience on opening night that the play was a hit. It was even more apparent that New York had discovered a new star. Carol proved herself to be one of the most engaging performers Manhattan had seen in years.

The song that introduced her to New York's theater audience was a big, boisterous Marshall Barer composition titled "Shy." Carol performed it as Winnifred's first number; she was supposed to be dripping wet from having swum the moat to get into the castle. In a clarion Ethel Merman roar, she sang of being "terribly timid and horribly shy." Judging from the animated way she performed, she seemed to be anything but...

Barer explains that "Shy" was originally written for comedienne Buzz Holiday at Tamiment in 1958. He refashioned it for Carol. "We wanted a number that would bring Carol into the world of theater in an unforgettable way," he says. "When she walked out onto that stage and sang that song, the faces of everyone watching registered the same thought: Oh, my God!"

Roy Silver, the former personal manager who discovered Bill Cosby and Joan Rivers, remembers: "It was *A Star Is Born* time for Carol. She walked out on that stage and blew everyone away. She was so self-assured, so vital. It was a strong, wonderfully healthy, and typically 'legit' musical-comedy performance.

"In those days, I don't believe they miked the stage. So a performer had to be a belting vocalist in order to really be heard in the far reaches of the theater. Carol could be heard not only in the balconies, but probably out on Second Avenue. She had that kind of force and sustaining power that made Ethel Merman a star. It was Carol's night, and no one would ever forget it."

Bill Hargate, a fashion designer who would go on to work with Carol in years to come, was also in the opening-night audience. "I can't even remember how many standing ovations Carol got that night," he says enthusiastically. "And ovations like that were a lot harder to get in those days. I've never been to a show since when it was so unanimous that the audience felt it had truly made a major discovery."

(As for Richard Rodgers's revival of *Babes in Arms,* the show never even made it to a New York stage; it closed in Florida.)

Don and Chrissy sat close to the stage and watched Carol's performance. Unfortunately, Nanny couldn't be there. She was too ill to make the trip. "And," laughs a West Coast friend, "you can bet that she was busting a gut at home about that."

"It was the most exciting night of my life," Carol has remembered of that evening. "I think it was probably everything I had dreamed it would be." Afterward, she was exhausted. She had completely forgotten to be nervous. She didn't dare acknowledge the degree of stress she was under until it was all over, and then the tears started to come. She was bone-tired, but it had been well worth it.

Carol Burnett had a dream and the guts to make it happen. It wasn't Broadway, but it was awfully close. The little girl from apartment 102 had finally turned herself into her own fantasy.

8

"YOU CAN NEVER BE TOO COCKY," GEORGE ABBOTT WARNED his charges backstage after opening night. "You never know what the critics are going to think."

"Who cares what the critics think?" someone said. "We're a hit!"

Abbott certainly knew better. One bad review from any of the New York press can kill a show that took months longer to mount than *Once Upon a Mattress*. The producers decided to hold the opening-night party at the Phoenix Theatre and have the cast wait there for the reviews. If the notices were favorable, then the whole group would catch cabs to Sardi's restaurant and celebrate their good fortune. William and Jean Eckart were smart enough to know that it's deadly to have the whole cast and crew gather in a classy restaurant only to learn that the show has been panned. "The paté just turns to crap when that happens," one writer notes.

As the cast members waited for the verdict, the Phoenix press agents were on the phone with their media contacts, hoping to get advance word of the reviews. The first one was from Brooks Atkinson of *The New York Times*. It wasn't a rave. But it wasn't bad either. Of Carol, he wrote: "[She] is a breezy comedienne who comes brawling into the story about half way through the first act and gives it a wonderful lift for the rest of the evening. Miss Burnett is a lean, earthy young lady with a metallic voice, an ironic gleam and an unfailing sense of the comic gesture."

The rest of New York's critical elite seemed to agree. "George Abbott enriched the ranks of comics last evening," Frank Ashton of the *New York Telegram* wrote. "His contribution is Carol Burnett. She is the funny find of the season."

Cast and crew headed to Sardi's, where they celebrated the arrival of, if not an unqualified theatrical success, certainly one of the most exciting newcomers in quite some time. And also, they presented George Abbott with a wastebasket lined with the sheet music to the many songs he threw out of the show during pre-production.

On May 28, Carol opened a four-week engagement at the Blue Angel. She would do her shows at the Phoenix, and then run down to the Angel and do her nightclub act. She was appearing on a bill with Ken and Mitzie Welch doing their singing and piano-playing act. "It'll be rough," she told a friend of the double-duty. "But I think it will help the show if I'm kept busy at two places at once." She was still making appearances on *Pantomime Quiz,* and on Tuesday, June 9, she had one of her best appearances on *The Garry Moore Show,* singing "Bill Bailey, Won't You Please Come Home?" on a program, that also featured Buddy Hackett. Garry devoted a portion of his show to a re-creation of one of the scenes from *Once Upon a Mattress,* and that promotion was invaluable. There was still some idle talk that Carol might be asked to join the cast as a regular, but at this point she was too busy to listen to the gossip.

On June 16, the original-cast album of *Mattress* was released, and it sold fairly well (it's still available today, in reissue). Perry Gray bought a copy of it the day it came out and rushed over to Nanny's apartment on Cherokee Avenue to play it for her before Carol had a chance to put one in the mail. At first, Nanny wasn't even sure how to use the record player, how to play the record without scratching the vinyl with the needle. "I decided that I'd better buy her two copies in case she ruined the first copy," Perry says. "She enjoyed the record as if she were actually seeing the show. At the first sound of Carol's voice, she smiled from Cherokee Avenue in Hollywood to the Phoenix Theatre. I still have the second copy. Sealed.

"Somehow, I felt that she was just so all alone," Perry recalls of Nanny. "Even though Carol was concerned and obviously in constant communication, this old lady was watching her grand-daughter's ascendancy and there was something oddly sad about it. Her existence seemed to be one of living out of jam jars and funny little glasses; you just had to wonder if she even ate enough. When I'd visit, she was always pleasant; she used to call me 'sweetie.'"

Nanny stayed in touch with Gray through letters. "They would always be of sentences alternating between what Carol was doing, to how sick she was, then back to Carol, and then back to how sick she was and why she had to go to the doctor that particular week. Nanny wasn't amazed by Carol's success. She rather expected it, I think. After one of Carol's big TV appearances, I remember her saying, 'Now that girl will never change...all those *faces!*'"

On Monday, June 22, 1959, Carol and Don paid back the loan to the La Jolla businessman who had staked them five years ago to the day. Each sent a check for one thousand dollars. "I don't remember if it was all Carol's money," Saroyan recalls frankly, "or our money. We were just grateful to be able to pay him back."

It's interesting, and probably says a lot about Carol's growing popularity, that all of the Manhattan newspapers carried stories about the repayment of this loan.

Carol had written to the gentleman she's called Mr. C. many times over the previous five years, but he never responded. In 1971, seventeen years from their first meeting, his wife called Carol at CBS-TV. Carol was stunned; after all these years, they'd finally gotten in touch. The three of them had a pleasant lunch; he was shy but obviously quite proud. Carol had the opportunity to thank him one more time for having confidence in her, for loaning her that money. He died shortly thereafter.

(Don never again laid eyes on their generous benefactor. Ironically, though, years later he worked in a summer-stock company in San Diego, and an apprentice there turned out to be the man's daughter.)

Once Upon a Mattress was a tremendous success at the Phoenix through the summer months. Carol started receiving scripts of other plays and began lining up ideas for what she'd do if and when the play ever closed. "It's very exciting, this business," she wrote to a friend. "However, I am in no hurry to leave *Mattress*. It's too much fun.

"Mary Martin came back to say hello last week," Carol enthused in her letter. "I nearly fainted. She was so lovely. This has been the most exciting experience I've had since I've been in New York."

Summer stock looked as if it would be a thing of the past for a while, so the Saroyans decided to move into a larger apartment so Chris could have her own room. They moved to an older building at 200 West Fifty-fourth Street, apartment 10-L, not far from where they had been living. Their tenth-floor apartment overlooked both Broadway and Seventh Avenue. Carol had to pinch herself every morning when she looked out at the view. Don wasn't around much; most of the summer he was out of town with the Motorola Industrial Show.

Though the success of *Once Upon a Mattress* was a triumph on many levels, the directors of the theater considered it a personal victory. One of the main reasons T. Edward Hambleton and his partner Norris Houghton established the Phoenix was to give young artists a chance in the theater. But just prior to *Mattress*'s opening, the theater had slid into its worst economic state since the directors took over the old Stuyvesant Theatre in 1953 and renamed it the Phoenix. Right before *Mattress*, Graham Greene's *The Power and the Glory* lost $148,000 after just three performances. The show was canceled; the theater was to close for the summer, and then the Eckarts brought in *Once Upon a Mattress*. The Phoenix rose from its figurative ashes.

But despite this success, the theater directors were determined to maintain their policy of regular subscription plays in the fall. They had no choice. A schedule of plays was announced and tickets had been sold. Rather than kick *Mattress* out of the theater, they leased the Coronet Theatre on Broadway and opened Eugene O'Neill's *The Great God Brown* there. But when the Coronet was unavailable for the future Phoenix subscription play *Lysistrata*, Houghton and Hambleton decided to end *Mattress*'s run.

"We were faced with an unexpected predicament," Mary Rodgers recalls. "No theater and no prospects for one, either."

The cast was understandably disappointed when told by the Eckarts and Abbott that the play would have to close. How could this happen? they wondered. They were a hit! "What am I going to do now?" Carol fretted to a friend. "I'm not going back on unemployment. Not after all of this . . . no way!"

Someone suggested that the cast take affirmative action. So they organized a mock "strike" to draw attention to their dilemma. At the close of the matinee performance on a freezing Sunday, November 1, 1959, Carol and cast went from backstage to the sidewalk at five o'clock with placards and hand-painted signs that said, "Why Close a Hit Show?" "Our House Is Not a Home," "Our Kingdom for a House," and "We Need a Theater." In full costume, they marched up and down Second Avenue. Carol called out to patrons as they left the Phoenix, "Write to your newspapers! Write letters to the editor!"

Carol had become fast friends with many of the neighborhood children she used to meet at a candy store near the Phoenix Theatre that was owned by a friendly couple known only as "Boris and Sylvia." The youngsters would wait at the store for Carol to walk by on her way to the Phoenix, and then they would follow her down the street as if she were some kind of pied piper. One newspaper reporter called her "the best loved girl on Second Avenue." Once, on a Saturday afternoon, they saved their money and bought garlands and crepe paper with which they decorated the store. Then they purchased a cake and threw Carol a party for no particular reason. These youngsters helped out in the picket line.

The next day, the strike was novel news on Manhattan's television-news broadcasts and in the newspapers. One writer suggested in his column that Carol's candy-store friends were paid fifty cents an hour to join the demonstration. She was quite angry about that and contacted his editor. A retraction and apology were printed shortly thereafter. As one witness puts it, "There wasn't much happening in New York that week, so this was big news."

One evening close to the final night, Carol even made an impassioned plea from the stage after the show. "There has to be another way..." she said.

Later, during the week, the show's publicist arranged an interview with New York *Daily News* writer Charles McHarry to publicize *Mattress*'s plight. Carol was picked up at her apartment by the publicist, and on his way to the interview he gave her a pep talk.

"Now look, kid," he warned, "ya gotta come on strong. Really lay it on thick. This could be a *major* piece, and it could very well make the difference between you working and you being on unemployment." Carol listened intently and nodded her head obediently as he wrapped up his little speech. "So, you go in there and knock 'em dead."

The next day, Wednesday, November 4, the *Daily News* ran an article headlined CAROL'S IRISH IS PLENTY UP.

"Carol is outspoken when riled," wrote McHarry, "and she is riled right now. She's saying, 'We pulled the Phoenix out of the red and now they're kicking us out. It's ridiculous. It's a crime that the Phoenix people didn't have foresight enough to get us another house. Why don't they take *Lysistrata* someplace else? It'll probably be a *bomb* anyway.'"

McHarry continued to quote Carol as having said, "Don't tell me about Phoenix policy. Let's face it! They sure do some *lousy* old plays. They shy away from anything that entertains people."

Though this might have been tantalizing copy, it was horrible representation for a young up-and-coming theater actress. "Suddenly, that week in New York Carol had a reputation as a hothead that was worse than Shirley Booth's," Marshall Barer remembers solemnly. "To say those things about her bosses and about a play her peers were struggling to get off the ground just looked terrible. It was a bad moment in career strategy, to be sure."

The day the story broke, Carol was in the publicist's office. Marshall Barer was present also. "She was in tears when she read that," he remembers. "Very emotional and upset. She had simply done what she was told, and look what happened as a result. The press agent didn't give a damn about her reputation, and when the article appeared it was without any evidence of her innocent naiveté."

"It's not exactly what I said," she told Barer. "I hedged. I said I thought *Lysistrata* would *probably* be lousy."

But Carol realized that that wasn't much better, and that she was backed into a corner. She slammed the newspaper down on the publicist's desk. She was angry at him for manipulating her, and also at the writer of the piece for exploiting her. She must also have been upset with herself for allowing such a thing to happen. "That's Carol," McHarry concluded in explanation of her tirade.

"I have tried so hard not to be like this," Barer recalls Carol as having said. "I am not like this woman in print. But, dammit, maybe I'll end up being that way if they're going to portray me as that."

"I think it was one of her first hurts where the media was concerned," Barer concludes. "I think that some of her innocence was chipped away that day...she was certainly a lot more guarded about what she said to the press. And also about what she was *told* to say to the press...."

It was probably a lesson well learned.

A felicitous piece of luck suddenly made the Alvin Theatre on West Fifty-second Street and Broadway available when *The Boys Against the Girls,* a musical revue starring Dick Van Dyke and Nancy Walker, closed on November 14, 1959, after sixteen performances. *Once Upon a Mattress* was booked into the theater as a two-month interim engagement before the next scheduled play.

George Abbott's *Fiorello!* was about to open (eventually he would win a Pulitzer Prize for directing this musical version of Fiorello LaGuardia's life), and the general feeling was that it would be a smash. Even though *Once Upon a Mattress* would now be the most inexpensive musical on the so-called "Great White Way," with Abbott's name connected to the publicity the show was sure to be a hit.

And the fact that *Lysistrata* crashed and burned on takeoff didn't hurt matters. It opened on November 24, the night before *Mattress*'s Broadway premiere, and the reviews for Dudley Fitt's version of the Aristophanes play were merciless.

"If the Phoenix people are thus endeavoring to regain their fortunes with this sordid exploitation of poor taste, they would have been better off hanging on to *Once Upon a Mattress,*" John McClain wrote for the *Journal American.* "That was a truly funny show chased away for this tasteless and revolting catastrophe."

The following Wednesday evening, *Once Upon a Mattress* opened at the Alvin. At last, Carol was the star of a *Broadway* play directed by George Abbott. And what made the night even more special was that Nanny was well enough to fly in to be there. She stayed with Carol and Chrissy for a four-week visit and had a terrific time in New York with her granddaughter the Broadway star.

By 1959, Nanny was more a character than ever before. She was healthy and fit, and feisty as usual. Carol described her appearance at around this time to Barbara Walters: "Nanny had great gams. She wore her skirts very short. She loved pastels or bright colors. She wore makeup and she was punked out ahead of anybody's time. She had lavender hair; she wasn't the blue-haired grandmother. The hat with the flowers. I mean, she did a number!

"I was numb," Carol has remembered of the opening night. It's all a blur to me, really. To be on Broadway after all of those years of wishing it, dreaming it, and knowing that it would happen. I was absolutely numb."

A friend of Carol's remembers opening night at the Alvin: "Carol tried to act like this was just another opening night, but we all knew better. First of all, the excitement was high energy because the play had found a home. And, Carol was a Broadway star, so that made the event all the more thrilling. After the show was over, she cried. She just stood backstage, and she cried away years of anticipation."

Despite the prevailing optimism and good word from the media, the show opened to less-than-enthusiastic ticket sales. Eventually, though, sales did pick up, and the show became a certified Broadway hit. It was the first show ever to make the move from off-Broadway to Broadway and make a profit in doing so. It was also the first full-scale American musical to have a score composed by a woman, Mary Rodgers.

But then, one evening just seven weeks after they opened, the cast arrived at the Alvin to be greeted by the news that Frank Loesser's *Greenwillow* would indeed open as originally scheduled. *Mattress* would have to find yet another home.

By now, television-writer Neil Simon had jokingly called *Once Upon a Mattress* "the most moving show on Broadway." The musical was relocated to the austere Winter Garden Theatre, another temporary booking. Carol has recalled this brief engagement as being a career highlight. She was given the same lavish dressing room that Rosalind Russell had when she appeared in *Wonderful Town*. The suite comprised three rooms, and a huge bathroom with an enormous pink bathtub. Nanny, who had returned to Hollywood by this time, would certainly have had a "hissy fit" if she'd been able to see this.

The room in which Carol changed clothes was bigger than a lot of apartments in Manhattan. "Let's just live here," she told Don, only half joking.

Carol had made quite a few appearances on *The Garry Moore Show,* and many of the program's writers were still eager to bring her into the fold as a regular.

"Garry, I still think you're passing on something kind of super and for the wrong reason," Joe told him.

Moore's reluctance was understandable. He was the star of the series and wasn't anxious to have a more compelling performer than he was in the regular cast. Up until this point, Garry's show had been anything but consistent in terms of quality comedy. The addition of Bob Banner and Associates as producers certainly helped, but the program still needed a boost.

Eventually, Garry was persuaded, and Carol joined the show permanently on November 19, 1959. Moore was to find that the addition of Carol Burnett to his cast wouldn't take anything at all away from him; rather, it would add to the entertainment value of his program. When Carol became a regular, the show's ratings picked up immediately.

Carol's addition to the cast also gave Durward Kirby an opportunity to stretch his talent. Basically, he was an announcer with a great sense of humor. He knew how to get a laugh, but he had always been Garry Moore's straight man. With Carol in tow, Kirby began to be utilized as the perfect foil for her antics. Soon, he was portraying a variety of characters, including the eccentric Mayor Quagmire, and a comical impression of poet Carl Sandburg called Carol Sandbag. Most popular of all was a recurring routine in which he and Moore in bustles and wigs played two crochety, high-spirited biddies, Martha and Jenny. Jenny (Kirby) always had a straight-end cane at the ready with a healthy supply of sherry in it. She'd unscrew the top, pour two shots, and propose the toast: "Tippecanoe and Tyler, too!" Martha (Moore) would always respond with, "Down with the Kaiser!" And then they'd drink up. (A couple of times, unbeknown to the stars, the crew substituted real sherry for whatever was usually in the cane, and to very funny effect.)

Carol considered before accepting Garry's offer, wondering if it was possible for her to appear nightly on Broadway and also do weekly television. "Twenty-four million people will see you every Tuesday night," he told her.

The value of that kind of exposure was obvious; Carol would become a genuine television star. But was that really what she wanted? She had come to New York to be on the Broadway stage. Now that she had achieved that goal, she decided that as long as she could continue performing on the stage she would do the TV show. Words like *pressure* and *overwork* never crossed her mind; she was just trying to forge her way.

By this time, Garry's show wasn't live; it was taped on Friday evenings from seven to eight for broadcast the following Tuesday evening. This permitted the use of theatrical performers as guest stars, as it allowed them to make their 8:30 P.M. curtain after the taping. Carol would rehearse for the Moore program every day for the Friday taping, do the Broadway show every night (except for Mondays, Broadway's traditionally dark night), and perform matinee performances on Wednesdays and Saturdays. Her days on the unemployment line certainly seemed to be over, but this kind of hectic schedule over the next couple of years would take its toll. Her weight would plummet to 106 pounds, and she'd complain to friends, "I look like John Carradine in a wig."

Carol would first see the script on Tuesday, and by Wednesday she usually had it memorized. Garry and his sidekick Durward Kirby, who used cue cards, weren't used to this. "But I can't look at an idiot board and concentrate," Carol said.

"That's the only thing I have against her," Garry would joke. "Then Durward Kirby got smart and started to learn his lines. So then I had to, too.

"She couldn't any more deny show business than Picasso could give up painting," he would later say of Carol. "It's compulsive, of course. There is not one ounce of contrivance to her makeup. She has *got* to be a star."

There was some discussion among her friends as to whether or not Carol had made the right decision by joining the ranks of weekly television, where the material was often mediocre.

"She has been burdened by some of the soggiest material that the producers and writers of weekly television ever foisted onto a star strong enough to bear it," one critic wrote of early Carol.

After her first couple of appearances on the show, Perry Gray sat down to write Carol a very long and emotional letter to express his dismay over her decision to join *The Garry Moore Show*. "I fear that from now on you will be taken for granted on the show," he wrote, "and shoved into such unfortunate skits as that hassle with the portable radio. It's brutal but true, it wasn't funny."

Gray wrote that he felt Carol had settled for something second rate, "and it's very hard to move up to class after that. You are a first-rate performer... And unless something happens soon, you'll look back one day and lump *Omnibus, The General*

Motors Spectacular, Sullivan and Shore in the group of pleasant appearances, and lump Garry Moore with *Stanley.* Carol, you're cheating yourself and wasting your time...."

Perry didn't mail the letter because, after he wrote it, he felt that it was too cruel. He explained, "I also felt that she was someone to nurture and take care of, and not be cruel with in any fashion."

His instincts about Carol were on target. Later, she would admit, "I was very thin-skinned. If anybody was to give me the Bronx cheer or a raspberry, I'd shrink to nothing. I'd die...."

On the Garry Moore shows, and even on the earliest episodes of her own series years later, Carol was known as one of comedy's chief muggers. She'd said that she didn't feel pretty inside, and the way she'd contort her face was, though often very funny, obviously an attempt to generate humor from self-deprecation. Sometimes, she was like a child testing the rules of good behavior: "How many faces can I get away with before I'll be sent to my room without supper?"

Ernest Haveman described Carol this way for an article in *Life* magazine: "Above an endlessly receding chin, her lower lip juts like a hitch-hiker's thumb. Her long, sensitive and disdainful nose swoops down to greet it. She is perhaps the only woman in the world who looks in profile like a monkey wrench." Not really a very pretty picture. And she did her best to exaggerate it.

"To be frank, it was a personality problem," Garry Moore once observed. "She could go barely two minutes without making herself look ugly. Even at the end of the show when we were taking bows she'd be crossing her eyes and making faces. I'd tell her that it wasn't necessary, that she should let the people see her out of character, as Carol the person rather than Carol the face maker. She had no security on any stage unless she was mugging or making fun of herself."

None of this was news to Carol. She openly admitted to all of it. "I have to be somebody else to do *anything* at all before a camera. Take photographs. If I'm doing character stuff, I horse around happily all afternoon. But if I have to be myself in a picture, I'm stiff as a popsicle. I'm never myself on a stage...I have to be introduced as 'And now, here's Carol Burnett, who's playing Lady Dither' or some such character. Then I'm fine...."

When she did an interview for *The Saturday Evening Post* in 1962, the reporter, who quipped that her face was "as mobile as the horsy countenance of the French comic Fernandel," felt that she was trying to camouflage her natural beauty during their meeting. "The Carol Burnett I was seeing was thoroughly feminine, but it was as if she were trying to conceal that fact under a bulky sweater, a pair of nondescript slacks, feet clad in soiled socks. No shoes," wrote Pete Martin. He also noted, "Off stage, she is free from the self-uglification which exposure to a TV camera seems to throw her into."

"What the TV camera never saw," Bob Wright, the show's associate producer, says, "and in black and white it was even more difficult to pick up, was her terrific luminous skin. Her complexion was all peaches and cream, her eyes were sparkling green. None of that came across on TV. For some reason, her features, particularly her mouth, were exaggerated by black and white television. She made it even worse with all of the faces.

"Her big mouth, like Martha Raye's, was always part of her cartoon persona. And then the receded chin, the big teeth, and sleepy eyes. She always hated all of that in herself, but she felt that exaggerating these features was what the public wanted in Carol Burnett . . . and it made her feel secure in front of the audience to say, 'Yeah, I know I'm not pretty. In fact, I can make myself even uglier. Watch this!'"

"Miss Burnett is resigned to the fact that the TV cameras do not flatter her," John P. Shanely wrote in a *New York Times* profile in March 1960. "She says, 'Friends who have seen me on the screen sometimes ask, "Why do you make yourself look so awful?" I can't tell them that I spend hours in the make up room *trying* to look beautiful. . . .'"

"Carol, you've got to stop all of that," Don Saroyan scolded her one night after a show. "You're better than that. You don't need all of those gimmicky expressions and faces."

Right away, he remembers, her feelings were hurt.

"How can you say that?" she asked, her puppy-dog eyes filling with tears. "I'm just trying to be *funny,* Don. The people, they like me when I do those things."

And then she said something her husband used to hate to hear: "And let's face it, Don. I'm no beauty."

Saroyan remembers: "Suddenly, I was this guy saying to her, 'Carol, you can be better than this. Be better.' I felt she was relying too much on mannerisms and mugging that were too predictable. There was room for growth, so, yes, I voiced that. But there were fifty highly successful people on the other side telling her that she was fantastic, that she knew exactly what she was doing by making herself look ugly. And the television viewers were saying, 'Yes, yes, *yes,* you *are* wonderful.' To pick that particular time to be critical was probably bad timing and strategy on my part."

A friend of Saroyan's adds, "Don thought that Carol's face making and the way she handled herself wasn't very ladylike, very feminine. I think he was more worried about her self-image than about her career."

Don's assessment of his wife's work probably did little to bring the two of them closer at a time when they already seemed to be drifting apart.

Carol must have been torn by Don's criticism. She certainly wasn't confident enough of herself as a comedic artist to completely disregard his comments. In fact, whenever anyone would compliment her work on the set of Garry's show, her response was usually to insist that she had messed up something else. Once Garry came over to her and said, "Carol, you don't have to be embarrassed when someone pays you a compliment. It's all right to accept praise. All you have to do is say 'Thank you.'" For Carol, that was easier said than done.

On the other hand, some of Carol's comments at this time suggest that she may have thought that Don was just being prudish. "Most women are obsessed with an outmoded sense of modesty," she said. "They labor under the necessity of being ladylike. They are afraid that being funny is unfeminine. Most men seem to have the same idea about comediennes. They laugh at us but they're wary of us as women. Men might date a comedienne, but marrying her is different.

"Women are afraid to make themselves unattractive," she added. "I'm not afraid of that, goodness knows! But all but one in a million women are afraid to mess up their hair, not wear lipstick, slouch, look flat-chested. Me? The sloppier I am, the more comfortable I am, the better I feel in a comedy sketch. I'm not terribly chic. I'm not *soignée.*"

A secure artist would likely have taken Don's comments in stride, analyzed them, and then gleaned from them whatever she chose to. But, despite some of her pronouncements to the press that seem to indicate otherwise, that wasn't Carol at this point. She'd always valued and respected Don's opinion, and perhaps he did have a point, maybe she was overdoing it. If so, what did that mean? Would she have to reevaluate her comedy just when she'd found an approach that had given her national acclaim?

Or was Don just jealous? After all, she had been a lot luckier than he'd been. Not only had she achieved her Broadway goals, she'd extended her ambitions to television. She was making it, while he was still looking for work. He hadn't gotten a single major break since arriving in Manhattan.

Certainly, with all of this angst in the air, when Don would ask "How was your day, honey?" she thought twice before answering. She told friends later, "I was so engrossed in everything. But then I'd come home from work and couldn't talk about it. I hated to, it depressed Don so."

Don certainly has no delusions of grandeur where his show-business career is concerned. "God knows I haven't made stardom," he says pragmatically. "So maybe I was completely wrong about my opinion of Carol's work. It is true that the faces, the postures, and all of those things that bothered me so much about her work did become her trademark."

Twenty years after all of this happened, Carol would look back and have to admit, "Making faces and being loud, that *was* my whole comedy. But at the time I started, that's what people accepted, it's what they liked. Now, I like to be more real. I've become much less grotesque."

The relationship between Carol and Don had been a lovely friendship but a complicated marriage, off to a tragic start when Don's daughter was killed in Philadelphia, and strained by the divergent paths he and his wife began to travel in their careers. Their lives were totally different now. They didn't have very much in common, and hardly saw each other anymore due to their conflicting schedules. They'd grown apart.

In March 1960, they went their separate ways.

9

CAROL NEVER EXPECTED THAT SHE WOULD HAVE A FAILED MAR-riage. But the problems at home had culminated in a logical conclusion. In retrospect, when she and Don separated, it seemed more an evolution than a tragedy.

"It was really Carol's idea," Don remembers. "For me, it was a very painful separation. Strangely enough, I can't even remember the details. I don't even remember which of us left the apartment...."

Pat Lillie, script girl for *The Garry Moore Show* and a close friend of Carol's, recalls: "We were in the middle of a complicated week, and I had to call and change rehearsal schedules for Carol about a dozen times one day. She was not there, and Don would always answer the phone because I think he wasn't working at the time. About the sixth time I called that day, I very stupidly said, 'Oh, Don, I am really sorry to be making you a messenger to Carol....' Right away, I felt so dumb. He said, 'That's all right. I'm used to taking messages for Carol.'

"The next day, Carol came into rehearsal, and I remember so vividly the moment she told me what was happening. We were on the third floor of the production center, and we had to go down to the second and into the rehearsal hall. We were in the crook of the stairwell, and she stopped me and said, 'I gotta tell you something. I don't want you to tell anybody else because I don't want anybody else to know. But Don and I are separating.'

"Well, I wanted to die," Pat remembers. "All I could think of was the day before, when I made that tacky crack about making him Carol's messenger. He was such a nice, genial guy."

"I never heard anyone say a negative word about Don Saroyan," UCLA chum Lenny Weinrib says. "Boy, he sure killed himself to help Carol, I'm tellin' you. And then to end up 'Mr.

Carol Burnett.' What could he do? What could she do? Not much."

At the time of the breakup, Don was driving a taxicab for a living. He had to do something, he said, to maintain his self-respect, and he didn't want to rely on Carol's income for support. He insisted on making his own way.

"He could have said, 'Okay, my wife's working, so I'll just sit on my duff,'" Carol said to friends in Don's defense. "He didn't do that. It bothered him that I was making more money than him, though. The situation was unnatural to him."

Publicly, Carol remained circumspect about the failure of her marriage. In press interviews, she gently evaded any overly personal question. "The fact that I've been successful far beyond anything I deserved did have something to do with it," she said graciously. "What made it particularly rough was that Don wanted to be an actor too. If he'd wanted to be a director, maybe it wouldn't have been so hard."

There were no attempts at a reconciliation, but it would be years before a divorce was final.

"I purposely stayed away," Don remembers. "Perhaps I saw her now and then, but I have a tendency to withdraw from things that are painful."

Today, Carol still wonders how Don really felt about their marriage, whether he was pressured into being supportive and cheerful, whether he resented her tremendous success. "I don't really think I was that supportive a lot of the time," Don says frankly. "And I probably did resent her career. She was very busy, had very little time, and I felt shut out."

"But," he hastens to add, "I'm not bitter about any of it. When it was happening, I had feelings that she'd gotten too big, that maybe I was no longer good enough for her. But now I realize it wasn't as simple as that: It was me, it was her, it was the time."

Carol has said that, in retrospect, perhaps Don was intimidated into marriage by Nanny's old "get the ring" philosophy. Don doesn't feel that this was the case. "Maybe that's the perception Carol has of the relationship, but it certainly isn't mine. I loved her and was eager to marry her. I think she really loved me as well. One thing is certain, we never yelled at each other. Never. There was no fighting."

After the separation, Carol only dated occasionally. There

was no time. Nineteen fifty-nine had been a milestone year for her, and she was juggling a full career load. She had the spirit, drive, and creativity to tackle anything where her career was concerned. To those on the outside, it all seemed so effortless (and the fact that Carol made it appear that way spoke volumes for her professionalism). To fill what little time she had, she volunteered for work in a handicapped-children's hospital.

Pat Lillie remembers the days when she and Carol were Manhattan bachelor girls: "We used to go out to dinner almost every night after rehearsal, because we were both girls on the loose with no social life. We paired up, and a wonderful friendship grew from our being lonely gals. We used to walk from the Production Center on West Fifty-seventh Street to a restaurant and, because the show was in black and white, Carol wasn't always recognizable by her flaming-red hair. But when she *was* recognized, it was always a hoot.

"We would go into restaurants and then into the ladies' room. I would be washing my hands, and Carol would be in one of the stalls," Pat recalls, laughing. "Someone would follow us in there, take a paper and pencil, and slide it right under the door of the stall. 'Miss Burnett,' the fan would say, 'can I have your autograph?'

"I remember her telling me that she was walking down Broadway one time on the way to the theater, and this touristy-looking couple came up to her—tourists were most likely to recognize her, since New Yorkers were often too blasé to notice—and the guy with a camera came up to her and started gawking. He grabbed his wife and said, 'Hey, Martha, look, it's that Carol Burnett girl.' Then he turned to Carol, sized her up, and said, 'You know, you ain't such a *dawg* after all.' She loved that."

There has always been a general perception that the Carol Burnett on the television screen is not unlike the one you might meet on the street, in a restaurant, or even in the bathroom. Happily, Carol has never held her public at arm's length. On the contrary, anybody can approach Carol...and say the most amazing things.

Once, in a dress shop, a saleswoman greeted her by taking both of her hands and gushing sincerely, 'Carol, Carol, *Carol!* I see you every single Tuesday night and never, *never* enjoy you. *Never!*"

Another day, a man came up to Carol in a restaurant and said, "You know, until you came along, my son's idol was Bela Lugosi. He just loves monsters."

And she once received this fan letter: "My daughter looks just like you, Carol. Would you please write back and tell her that there is hope? Thank you so much."

Those incidents, and many others, provided Carol with years of self-deprecating anecdotes for magazine and newspaper features. They really were funny, but Carol's friends insist that they may have done more harm than good. The psychological effect of being perceived as particularly unattractive was something she would deal with for years. She already had an inferiority complex, and now it was being engraved in stone. It's one thing to feel ugly inside but quite another to have a total stranger verify and validate those insecurities, however unintentionally.

One of Carol's most popular sketches on *The Garry Moore Show* was written by Neil Simon. In it, Durward Kirby played the president of the safety council and Carol his secretary. Pat Lillie, script supervisor, remembers the sketch: "Durward was dictating points about safety to Carol, and every one of the calamities he was talking about happened to her. He put cigarettes out on her hand, poured hot coffee in her lap. He turned to a blackboard with a pointer, and when he turned back, he whacked her with it on the neck. He picked up the telephone, and then, when he put it down, he clamped it on her hand. The point of a pencil went into her eye. By the end of the sketch, Carol was this gnarled person with her arms and legs bent in every direction and one eye closed. And then, at the end of the sketch, she gets knocked right out of the window, head first. It was one of her favorite sketches."

Irwin Kostal remembers another funny moment: "Carol was doing a sketch with Red Skelton, and at some point, she decided to trip him up and pull an ad-lib. Now Red wrote the book on ad-libbing, he's an expert. She did this one-liner on him, and he looked at her and said, 'Hey, that's not in the script!' and then he jokingly pushed her. There was a table behind her, and she made the most of the opportunity and fell over it and onto her back. As she was lying there on her back, Red looked down at her and said, 'So *that's* how you got your job!' Carol never laughed so hard in her life. It took thirty minutes for all of us to regain our composure and retape the sketch for the world to see."

Another popular bit was one Carol reputedly conceived herself. Elegantly dressed in a black gown with white pearls, she was seen singing a sultry rendition of "Come Rain or Come Shine" while sitting on a gazebo bench. During the second torchy chorus, a trickle of water hit her forehead. By the end of the last chorus, buckets of water were being dumped onto her head as she valiantly tried to finish the number.

Because of the myriad of technical problems, she had to be "rained" on four different times. Carol had to dry off and change after each take. That morning, she went to work with a headache and sniffles; by the time she finished for the day and returned home, she was quite sick.

Garry Moore recalled later that one audience member felt such empathy for the soaked Carol, he tried to pick a fight with the star of the show.

As Moore tells it: "This man started coming down from the audience shaking his fists at me, saying 'Look at her, just look at that poor girl! What the hell is wrong with you, you sadist!'

"As the gentleman made his way down to the stage, screaming and shouting all the way, I tried to explain that the whole thing was Carol's idea, not mine. 'She *wants* to do this,' I said rather nervously. She *likes* this stuff...."

Carol's injuries as a result of her madcap antics and pratfalls on Garry's show began to add up during the next few years. She used to describe herself as "a happen-to type," and certainly if self-visualization worked for Carol in other areas of her life, it worked here as well. Over the next couple of years, she would seriously sprain her back while somersaulting over a sofa; tear the cartilage in her foot while falling out of a prop window; permanently render her right hip black and blue while sliding down a department-store-counter set; and sustain a rather serious neck injury doing one of her famous falls. This last injury caused pressure on one of the nerves on her neck vertebrae and, combined with injuries she'd sustain in an automobile accident a few years later, would cause the cancellation of her second Broadway show.

"There must be something psychological about all of those injuries," notes one observer. "It was as if, self-consciously, she was injuring herself intentionally. As if she was saying, 'I'm ugly, so I punish myself.'"

Carol won't hear of any such analysis. "I just loved to throw myself around," she once said with a laugh. "I learned to take pratfalls the hard way, I never practiced them, I just did them because I wanted the job.

"I remember one time I was supposed to jump out of a window on 'The Garry Moore Show.' It was a Neil Simon sketch called 'Playhouse 90 Seconds.' I told them, 'Oh yeah, I can do stunts.' I just headed out, head first, and never even thought to check on whether or not there was a mattress out there. The crew had obligingly put one down for me. When I landed I said (dazed), 'Oh, hey, thanks for the mattress, everybody!' And they said (sarcastically), 'Yeah, we can tell *you* do a lot of stunts. Right.'"

On April 27, 1960, *West Side Story* was scheduled for a revival at the Winter Garden. *Once Upon a Mattress* would have to find yet another theater. This time, the tiny Cort Theatre was leased.

On the evening of Wednesday, April 27, the first and only annual presentation of "the Schumie Award" took place at the Cort. The award was given to "the most moving musical in town, *Once Upon a Mattress*." The show was now known as the only production ever to tour New York (and the pit stops weren't over yet, either). The Schumer Theatrical Transfer Company, paid to load and unload the production every time it was forced to move, sponsored the festivities as a practical joke. Most of the crew couldn't attend the party because, as Mary Rodgers put it, "They were unpacking. They were always either packing or unpacking. That's why we got the award."

Carol accepted the handsome, bronzed replica of a theatrical moving transfer van called a "Schumie." The Schumie is the only award *Once Upon a Mattress* ever won.

The play stayed at the Cort for all of two weeks. In early May, the Eckarts chose to move it to the St. James Theatre on Forty-fourth Street. The theater was bigger, it was available indefinitely, and would be home to *Once Upon a Mattress* for the duration of its run.

"Carol always wanted to play the New York stage, and she certainly got her wish, didn't she?" George Abbott muses. "She appeared on one off-Broadway stage and four Broadway houses in the course of one year."

That summer of 1960, Carol received Daniel Blum's *Theatre World* magazine's annual award for "Most Promising Personality" along with twelve other hopefuls, including Warren Beatty,

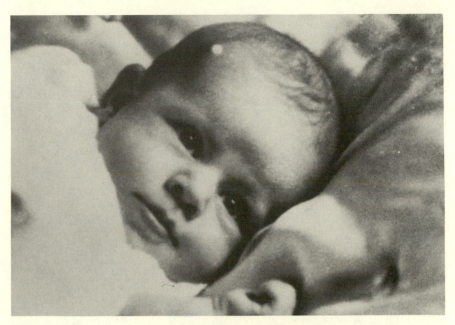

Carol at three months old in San Antonio, Texas

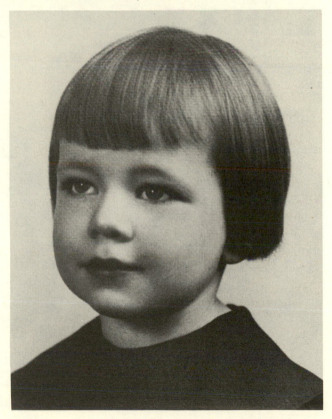

Carol at age three,
1936

Carol and her half sister, Christine, in the summer of 1949. Even though Carol was only sixteen, she practically looked like Chrissy's mother. Chrissy would turn six in a couple of months. *Neal Peters Collection*

Carol and Chrissy, 1949 *Neal Peters Collection*

Carol in high school, 1949. "I certainly was not what one would call a beautiful girl," Carol has said of this period. "My sister was beautiful, my mother was beautiful. I thought *I* was adopted." *Neal Peters Collection*

Carol (eighteen), Chrissy (seven), and Nanny (sixty-six) just after Carol's graduation from high school in the winter of 1951. Carol's mother, Louise, who was by now sick and an alcoholic, also attended the graduation ceremony. "She didn't look too hot," Carol had to admit, "but at least she was there." Carol's father, Jody, was in a charity hospital. *Neal Peters Collection*

The graduation girl
Neal Peters Collection

Carol, at twenty years of age, performing
"Laura de Maupassant" from *Hazel Flagg*
at the Homecoming Show in 1952 at
UCLA's Royce Hall *Bruce Campbell
Collection*

Here, Carol and classmate
Lenny Weinrib are in
costume to entertain at
UCLA's annual Mardi Gras
Benefit on April 9, 1954.
Weinrib also went on to
become a comic and comedy
writer. *Bruce Campbell
Collection*

Carol with a fellow student at UCLA, 1954. Carol had quickly become part of the inner group of students who lived and breathed theater arts. It was an exciting, happy life. *Bruce Campbell Collection*

On February 24, 1954, Theatre Arts junior Carol auditioned for and won the lead in UCLA's Fourth Annual Varsity Show, *Love Thy Coach*. Here she is in costume as Coach Christy Adams. The school newspaper called her "the funniest gal since Martha Raye," and noted that "upon graduation, she plans to enter the musical comedy field." *Bruce Campbell Collection*

Twenty-one-year-old Carol with her cast of football-playing misfits in *Love Thy Coach*, May 1954. Tickets for the show were $1.50 each. Carol would leave for New York shortly after this photo was taken. *Bruce Campbell Collection*

Carol and Don Saroyan were college sweethearts who went to New York together to become Broadway stars. Theirs was a lovely friendship and they married in December 1955. The fact that Carol became a star and Don never did caused problems; they divorced in September 1962. *Robert Emenegger Collection*

Starring in her first "big break," an off-Broadway production of *Once Upon a Mattress* at the Phoenix Theatre. Here, Carol, at twenty-six, is in costume as Princess Winnifred Woebegone, with Joe Bova as Prince Dauntless. The role won her the American Guild Variety Artists Award as Most Outstanding Comedienne. *Love Child Enterprises*

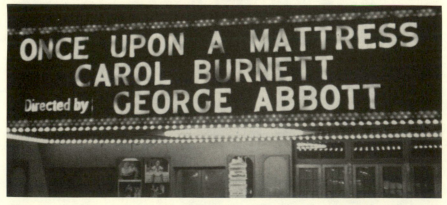

It wasn't long before *Mattress* made it to Broadway and Carol had her name up in lights, November 1959. *Daniel F. Romo Collection*

Circa 1960 *Love Child Enterprises*

"On the seventh day, God created Carol Burnett," says Garry Moore, "and then he rested—because he was all worn out." Carol and Garry Moore were quite a team by 1960. *Neal Peters Collection*

Nanny was at Carol's side when she won the *TV Guide* Award for Favorite Female Performer on June 13, 1961. Carol beat out Loretta Young, Dinah Shore, and Barbara Stanwyck for the honor. Nanny, at seventy-six years old, was still kicking. *Neal Peters Collection*

Carol's first album for Decca, released in August 1961. Carol wasn't eager to make the record because she never had confidence in herself as a vocalist. *Love Child Enterprises*

Taking bows at the end of a segment of *The Garry Moore Show* (left to right): Durward Kirby, Marion Lorne, Julie Andrews, Garry Moore, television actor Allen (*The Deputy*) Case, Carol, and Arthur Treacher. This was Julie's first appearance on the program, and the springboard for a television special in which she would star with Carol. *Pat Lillie Whelan Collection*

Carol with Julie Andrews, who had by this time made a name for herself on Broadway in *My Fair Lady* and *Camelot*. Carol was twenty-nine, Julie twenty-seven. *Pat Lillie Whelan Collection*

Here, Carol and Julie share a light moment behind the mike at Columbia Records' Thirtieth Street Studio in New York while recording the soundtrack to *Julie and Carol at Carnegie Hall. Neal Peters Collection*

Julie and Carol performing the "Big D" finale production number during taping of *Julie and Carol at Carnegie Hall* on March 5, 1962. Carol won an Emmy a year later for her work on this program—a real victory for her since CBS-TV had to be talked into buying the show. *Neal Peters Collection*

On May 22, 1962, Carol was awarded her first Emmy in the category of Outstanding Performance in a Variety or Musical Program or Series for her work as a regular on *The Garry Moore Show.* Her competition in the category included Perry Como and Judy Garland. To date, Carol has won five Emmys. *Neal Peters Collection*

Carol, as Jane, appearing on *The Jack Benny Show,* October 5, 1962. Benny is a beefed-up Tarzan. *Groove Tube Photos*

Carol made an art out of self-deprecation, much to the chagrin of Don Saroyan, her first husband. "You don't need all of those gimmicky expressions and faces," he'd tell Carol. Hurt, she would counter with, "Let's face it, Don. I'm no beauty." *Groove Tube Photos*

The advertising campaign for Carol's first film, *Who's Been Sleeping in My Bed?,* December 1963. Carol is still embarrassed by the movie. "I should have been given the award for Worst Performance Ever Given in Movies by an Actress," she has said, only half-jokingly. *Daniel F. Romo Collection*

As Carol and her new husband, Joe Hamilton, honeymooned in Hawaii in May 1963, controversy was brewing over the fact that Joe's family was loyal to his ex-wife and dead set against his new marriage. "But I am hardly the home-breaker type," Carol defended to a reporter on the telephone from Hawaii. *AP/Wide World*

Carol and Johnny Carson, circa 1963, chatting during a break in the taping of a television program *Pat Lillie Whelan Collection*

FADE OUT-FADE IN

Carol as Lila Tremaine on the *Playbill* for *Fade Out-Fade In*, May 1964.
Carol, displeased with the show, wanted the Broadway opening delayed.
Eventually she tried unsuccessfully to negotiate her way out of the play.
"It was the most miserable time of my life; I felt incompetent and un-
professional," she has recalled. *Steven Brinberg Collection*

Dick Van Dyke, Patty Duke, Eileen Brennan, and Jane Fonda, all of whom made Broadway debuts in the 1959 season.

As much as Carol enjoyed her work in the play, and the acclaim it garnered for her, she began to feel the strain of carrying such a heavy work load, juggling the Moore show with the play. She always seemed to be exhausted. "I remember one night after I'd done the show for a long while, I was in the middle of a song and thinking things like 'Well, I'm out of oranges. I need milk. I have to take the dog to the vet. I wonder how Chrissy is?' And all of this time, the words to the songs were just coming out like rote. That's when you know you've been at something for too long...."

One night Carol climbed on top of the mattresses to do her six-minute pantomine of not being able to fall off to sleep...and she almost fell asleep!

Her contract was up in the fall of 1960, and after 460 performances she decided to leave the show.

Was it possible that this production could continue without Carol Burnett? George Abbott didn't think so. "How could it?" he asked years later in retrospect. "But we had to try, because we owed that to the rest of the cast."

Ann B. Davis was hired to replace Carol as Princess Winnifred. Davis had won two Emmy awards for her role as Bob Cummings's secretary, Schultzy, in his TV series of the late fifties. Because she was such a strong television personality, at the time it was thought that she might be able to carry the show. (Davis went on to seventies TV fame as Alice, the maid on *The Brady Bunch.)*

Ann B. Davis was in her mid-thirties at the time, and somehow she seemed too old for the role. After a couple of weeks in rehearsal, she debuted in the role on June 27, 1960. "Broadway Hails a New Princess," the advertisement campaign proclaimed, but in two weeks, the show closed. The audiences came to see Carol Burnett, and when they realized that she was gone, they wanted their money back.

"It was not good," Davis recalls. "I spent the whole time doing a bad imitation of Carol. I never got into the part as myself."

"As it turned out, it really was Carol's show," Abbott affirms.

"Very often, it's been said to me that my show made Carol Burnett a success," Marshall Barer remarks. "My reflexive response to that is that Carol Burnett made my show a success. The minute she left, it was curtains for *Once Upon a Mattress* on Broadway."

The show continued to run a thirty-week national road tour with actresses like Dody Goodman and Imogene Coca essaying Carol's role, and Edward Everett Horton and Buster Keaton (in their last stage appearances) as King Sextimus. In October 1960, *Mattress* went abroad, without Carol. The cast was entirely British, with the exception of American actress Jane Connell, who played Princess Winnifred (Connell is best known for her portrayal of Agnes Gooch in the stage and movie productions of *Mame)*. It was said that the producers didn't think any British girl could ever muster up a voice big enough to handle any of Carol's numbers. The reception abroad was devastating; the audiences actually booed. After only thirty-nine performances, the show closed.

(Carol herself went to England for the first time in August 1960 for a tour. Curiously, the British press seemed most interested in the controversy Carol's comments about *Lysistrata* caused. "I don't think I said it would be a bomb," Carol said in London. "I hedged. I said I thought it would *probably* be lousy." While in Manchester, she and comic Milt Kamen taped a television special called, prophetically enough, *The Carol Burnett Show.)*

Today, *Once Upon a Mattress* continues to be a favorite in amateur community theater; over the last twenty-five years literally hundreds of versions have been staged in small towns across the country.

Carol also considered leaving *The Garry Moore Show* at the end of the 1960–61 season. The work was going well, and she enjoyed it, but wondered if the time had come for her to go on her own. She had made a number of close friends on the staff, one of whom was the program's producer, Joe Hamilton. Joe was quite an amazing person—at thirty-two years of age, he was the youngest producer in television. Usually, after a taping Carol and Joe and some of the others would socialize in an intimate bar next to the theater called the China Song. One day, she asked Joe if she could talk to him privately.

"She told me she was thinking of leaving Garry's show," Joe remembers. "Marty Goodman, I believe, wanted her to leave the program and go out on tour. It seemed like the logical progression. I said, 'Carol, I think you're making a mistake by about a year. If you wait a year, your stock-in-trade in the business will go up. You'll be happier making the transition, and you'll make a lot more money."

She listened intently as he concluded, "You're not ready. You have the name, almost. But not quite."

She would take Joe Hamilton's advice and it wouldn't be the last time.

Nineteen sixty-one was a whirlwind. Carol's appearances on *The Garry Moore Show* continued, and to much acclaim.

On Tuesday, June 13, 1961, she won *TV Guide's* award for Favorite Female Performer in a color telecast on NBC—Carol was nominated in that category along with Dinah Shore, Barbara Stanwyck, Donna Reed, and Loretta Young, who had won the award the year before. Carol never expected to win the poll (288,000 *TV Guide* readers filled out ballots); when her name was announced as the winner, she was dazed. Someone pushed her out onto the stage, and for a single, endless moment, as she stood at the podium with her gold cup, she couldn't remember Garry Moore's name, the name of his network, or the name of the network carrying this presentation.

"I did all of those things I hate people doing at those shows," she said, embarrassed. "All of that bumbling and fumbling...." (Carol went on to win this award in two consecutive years.)

This was also the year Carol's first solo album was issued on the Decca label. It wasn't difficult for the Martin Goodman Agency to secure a record deal for her, because of her tremendous exposure on prime-time television. "The Decca people obviously thought that Carol would sing some of the songs on the album on Garry's show," Joe Hamilton observes. "And back then, doing a song on TV was equivalent to a hundred-thousand-dollar plug in advertising for the album it came from."

Carol wasn't eager to make the record; she never enjoyed performing as Carol Burnett, only as a character. Perhaps she thought that it would be different in the recording studio, where there would be no audience. Without scrutiny, she may have considered she would be freer to be herself. But she was wrong.

The first day in the studio, she began singing Vivian Blaine's "Adelaide's Lament," and, somehow, it just wasn't working. Her performance was dull, lifeless. "Uh, Carol, do you think you could try that again?" Irwin Kostal, who was arranging the album, asked. She did. It was worse. Carol looked out through the window of the sound booth and noticed the puzzled expressions on the faces of the Decca executives who'd come down for the sessions. They huddled in a corner with Kostal. The arranger, nodding his head in agreement, got up out of his chair and came into the recording booth.

"Carol, we've got a problem here," he began carefully. "And I think I know what it is."

"Well, tell me and we'll both know," Carol said nervously.

Kostal, a tremendously patient arranger who was musical director of *The Garry Moore Show* and would go on to win Academy Awards for *West Side Story* and *The Sound of Music,* pulled Carol aside and calmed her down.

He remembers the moment vividly: "A recording studio is a terrible place for a performer; you sing with a mike in your face to no audience. Carol is a performer who grows with an audience. So I said, 'Carol, from now on I am your audience. And it's pretty hard to knock me out. Besides me,' I told her, 'you have to remember how many hundreds of thousands of people are going to be your audience listening when this record is released. You gotta sing it for them, kid.' Carol lit right up and she really put on a show that night...."

The album, entitled *Carol Burnett Remembers How They Stopped the Show,* was released in August. The record is a collection of show-business standards, including Ruth Etting's "Ten Cents a Dance," Ethel Waters's "Happiness Is Just a Thing Called Joe," Bert Williams's "Nobody," and Judy Garland's "The Trolley Song."

John Wilson of *The New York Times* gave the record a sparkling review (September 21, 1961) in which he favorably compared Carol's debut to the ever-popular *Judy [Garland] at Carnegie Hall.* Wilson admitted that he thought Judy was the last in the tradition of old-time belters, but added that Carol's album "reveals that this versatile comedienne has the vocal range, the show biz know-how, the vitality and the style to carry it on."

Irwin Kostal smiles at the memory of that review. "I never tried to elevate Carol to the status this gentleman suggested," he says. "But there are a lot of theories about talent: One is that when a person does the best she can, she's great.

"Imagine if we had had some *real* time," Kostal concludes with a chuckle. "I hate to say it, but I think I arranged the entire album in one weekend."

Carol must have been impressed with her work as a singer on that Decca album, for she did accept a steady job as a vocalist on CBS-Radio. She starred with Brooklyn-born singer Richard Hayes (who had made a name for himself on *The Arthur Godfrey Show*) in *The Carol Burnett-Richard Hayes Show*, a twenty-minute program Monday through Friday evenings at 7:10. The show debuted September 4. (Carol would continue with the program until January 1962.)

Considering her already full schedule, and the fact that the television medium had become such a strong vehicle for her, most people were mystified as to why Carol would want to have anything to do with a radio show. "I had never done a radio show before, and it's part of show business," she said at the time. "In TV, a puckish face can help build laughs, get you an audience reaction. Radio has no such built-in advantages. You reach your audience by voice alone; that's a challenge to me."

Toward the end of the year, Carol was signed to make an appearance on *The Twilight Zone*. She would star as misfit Agnes Grep in a thirty-minute dramatic-comedy episode called "Cavender Is Coming," and it would be filmed in Hollywood.

Carol treated "Cavender" as if she were making a Hollywood movie; she scared herself half to death thinking about it. She had done a couple of films in college, but how could they compare to this? In *The Fiend That Walked the Beach*, she and Don sat on the sand and watched as school friend Bob Emenegger, "the fiend," came out of the ocean in an overcoat; Carol reacted appropriately to the horror of it all. It was a fifteen-minute short produced by Bruce Campbell, who also produced another one with Carol and Lenny Weinrib called *Blue Moon in January*. "These movies still exist as blackmail footage," Campbell jokes. "I showed *Blue Moon in January* at a party for Carol about twelve years after we did it. She *screamed* at her appearance."

Rod Serling was a big admirer of Carol's, and he wrote a script that drew from some of her real-life experiences, and also from her image as a clumsy, but well-meaning good ol' girl.

As produced by Buck Houghton and directed by Chris Nyby, Serling's story was about Agnes Grep, an usherette at Plotsky's Bijou of Famous Hollywood Hits movie house. When she is fired from her job, an apprentice angel named Harmon Cavender (portrayed by Jesse White) is assigned to aid the forlorn and discontented Grep for a period of twenty-four hours. If he changes her life in some positive way, he will have earned his wings. Cavender gives her opulence and an exciting life-style, but Agnes decides she misses her old life and her friends. After much discussion, Cavender gives her back her former world, and she lives happily ever after, having learned an important lesson.

The episode served as a pilot for a TV program to star Jesse White. It eventually aired on May 26, 1962, but the spinoff series never materialized.

Perry Gray was with Carol during a couple of days of filming "Cavender" on the MGM lot: "She considered this her first film, and here she was at the great MGM Studio. But she was very surprised that the lot was so, as she put it, 'tacky.'

"One day, Carol said to me, 'I don't know *what* all of this is about,'" he laughs. "She was quite dismayed because they were filming out of sequence. She wanted to start at the top and run straight through, as she was used to doing in theater. She really had to depend on her director to tell her where they were in the story and what she was supposed to be doing. It wasn't an easy shoot."

"I really tip my hat to those film actors," Carol said during a break when she was interviewed by the *Hollywood Citizen News*. "This is the first film I've ever made. I knew all of my lines before I got here. But the problem is getting the momentum, building up to the scenes. They just won't do any of them in sequence. At first I just couldn't cope with it, but now I'm getting the hang of it."

The reporter asked Carol if she'd considered doing a major motion picture. She responded by saying she would appear in a film for free if Billy Wilder directed it and Jack Lemmon starred. "But you don't see them knocking down my doors," she joked. "A movie type is somebody who is absolutely glamorous and, as you can plainly see, I don't fit the bill."

"Carol was always rather star-struck," Perry Gray remembers. "One day, we were in the commissary talking, and suddenly her attention was distracted. Richard Chamberlain came into the room. 'Oh, my God, just a minute,' she said. 'I'll be right back.' She scooted over to Chamberlain and began complimenting him on *Dr. Kildare*. She was rather dazed...."

Serling based part of his script for "Cavender Is Coming" on Carol's actual experience as an usherette in a movie theater. The summer of her first year at UCLA, Carol worked at Warner Brothers Theatre on Hollywood Boulevard for sixty-five cents an hour. The Arabian-styled pants and gold-braid epauleted tops Carol wore as a uniform were similar to those designed by Serling for her early scenes in "Cavender." Just as on the show, Carol's maddening boss had used hand signals to give orders, and he appointed Carol as "spot girl." Her job was to give directions to the entering patrons, all the while standing in a spotlight.

Once, when Alfred Hitchcock's *Strangers on a Train* was playing at the theater, a couple arrived late for the screening. "You can't go in now, you'll ruin the end of the movie for yourselves," Carol warned.

"But we want to sit down now," they insisted.

"I'm tellin' you, it'll just *kill* the whole movie for you," Carol argued. She extended her arms and blocked the entrance to the theater.

They argued like this for a few minutes; Carol tried to explain the importance of suspense to an Alfred Hitchcock plot line as the disgruntled customers made faces at her. Her boss overheard the ensuing argument.

"Burnett, you are *fired!*" he fumed.

"But...but...but...," she stammered.

And then he ripped off her epaulets.

About twenty years later, in May 1975, the Hollywood Chamber of Commerce offered Carol a star on the Hollywood Walk of Fame. A true connoisseur of irony, Carol asked that the star be laid right in front of the movie house on Hollywood Boulevard from which she had been fired, now the Pacific Theatre. Sweet Hollywood revenge.

After the Walk of Fame ceremony, Carol and Chrissy took a walk one block up the street to Yucca and Wilcox Avenues, to the building in which they were raised. They walked into the rundown structure, down the hall, and to the door of the apartment where their mother died. They touched the wooden door gently, as if trying to feel Louise's presence, and wept.

Regaining their composure, they approached 102. A young Mexican woman cautiously answered their knock. Reluctantly, she let them in. The room, despite the twenty years that had passed, hadn't changed; Carol said it was like going on "a trip back into the twilight zone."

"This apartment is calling me back," she told Christine. "I

have dreams about one-oh-two. Maybe there's something I have to find out about." She promised herself that, one day, she would again go back to 102, and after apologizing to the new tenant for the intrusion and thanking her for admitting them, she asked, "May I come back someday?"

The woman nodded, closing the door behind them.

10

U P UNTIL THIS TIME, THOUGH POPULAR AND WITH A HIGH PRO-
file, Carol Burnett was still generally considered by the
public and entertainment world to be a second banana. First,
with a modicum of exposure she was a supporting player to Paul
Winchell, then in prime time to Buddy Hackett, and now, with
much acclaim, to Garry Moore. She was eager to make a broader
impression, and though she didn't know it at the time, she would
have to help create her own vehicle, which wouldn't be easy.

Fate always seemed to have a hand in Carol's destiny, and it
just so happened that another entertainer in New York faced a
similar problem. Julie Andrews, who had starred in the Broadway musicals *The Boyfriend, My Fair Lady,* and *Camelot* was her-
alded as the sensational new musical find of late-fifties and
early-sixties Broadway. Yet though *My Fair Lady,* in which she
costarred with Rex Harrison, is considered one of the greatest
musicals in theatrical history, it did little for Julie in terms of
national exposure. She wasn't really known west of New Jersey.

Carol Burnett had always been awed by the regality of Julie
Andrews. "The first time I saw Julie Andrews close up, she came
into Whelan's drugstore at 44th Street and Broadway, the Sardi's
of the unemployed actors, to buy a refill for her eyelash curler,"
she remembered in a 1962 article she wrote for *Good Housekeeping* titled "My Friend Julie Andrews."

"Having stood through *My Fair Lady* four times, I rose as she
entered out of force of habit, as though Queen Victoria had arrived. I watched her leave and then I bought the same refill for
my eyelash curler . . . only I could never get it in straight."

Two years later, Carol was appearing in *Mattress,* and Julie's
manager, Lou Wilson, came backstage after a performance. He
met Carol and was delighted by her personality.

"Why don't you, Bob Banner, and I have dinner with Julie Andrews?" he suggested.

"Me and *Julie Andrews*?" Carol asked incredulously.

"Why not? I think you'll like one another. You've both got the same personality. Kind of wacky..."

Carol looked at him suspiciously. "Julie Andrews, *wacky*?"

Carol was eager to meet Julie, having seen her on stage so many times. Julie, on the other hand, was a bit ambivalent. She and Carol Burnett were from different worlds, she thought. "I resisted it in the same way my daughter resists having me introduce her to a new friend I think is just right for her," she recalled later. "I met Carol with some trepidation."

The two women finally met at Ruby Foo's, a Chinese restaurant, accompanied by Lou Wilson and Bob Banner, who had worked with Julie a few years earlier in London. Carol and Julie hit it off immediately. "Lou and Bob are two very verbal types," Carol remembered. "But that night they never got in five words edgewise. Julie and I conducted a two-hour filibuster; it was like *Open End* without a moderator.

"When she wrote about me in *Good Housekeeping,* she described our first meeting, how she, the panic stricken ingenue, was ushered into the presence of the Big Broadway Star—me," Julie remembered years later. "That's nonsense. The only people who had heard of me were the relative handful who had seen *My Fair Lady.* Carol had built a huge following on *The Garry Moore Show; she* was the one who was recognized and fussed over, not me."

Despite appearances to the contrary, they had a lot in common. About the same age—Julie was twenty-six and Carol twenty-eight—they shared views about show business and its effects on their personal lives. Julie was married at the time to scenic designer Tony Walton. Over sweet-and-sour pork, Carol explained some of the problems she and Don faced, and then admired the way Julie and her husband seemed to manage similar situations. "The fact that at times Julie makes more money than Tony doesn't bother either of them," she observed later. "Julie earns more than President Kennedy, let alone her husband. She just counts her blessings, saves her pennies and is taking up cost accounting."

They also had their self-protective natures in common; neither one is easy to get to know. "Julie is encased in an iron sheath of charm that is impossible to penetrate," Sheila Graham once wrote. "I have never been able to cut through the metal and neither has anyone else, to my knowledge." Similar observations have certainly been made about Carol in the past.

Carol could understand Julie's reluctance to be totally open with strangers; she understood Julie's insecurities. Like Carol, Julie is not an ivory-tower person from a privileged world. Her parents were vaudevillians, and Julie Elizabeth née Wells was, as they say, born in a trunk. Her parents were divorced when she was young, and Julie lived in poor conditions in a low-income neighborhood outside of London. She had a difficult time proving herself in the American theater, and was by no means the most confident actress ever to walk onto a Broadway stage. But, like Carol, she's a survivor. "Julie has that English strength that makes you wonder why they lost India," her director Moss Hart once said.

Also, Julie is a brilliant practical joker, the author of hundreds of off-color limericks, and a very bawdy, fun person. "You must not be deceived by that grande-dame façade," Carol insisted to friends. "Underneath her Rule-Brittania face beats the spirit of a rampant lion cub. Julie is not Queen Victoria; she's an irrepressible British kook."

By the time they'd finished dinner, Julie had confessed that she could never get her eyeliner refill to work right, either; they decided that they simply had to work together. Carol called the decision "the idea of teaming Miss Raggedy Ann Burnett, Girl Kook, with the remote, ladylike silver-throated Miss Andrews, 'ere from England to grace our 'umble U.S. shores."

On May 2, 1961, Julie made a guest appearance on *The Garry Moore Show,* her first. Besides the fact that she wanted to work with Carol, she also agreed to appear for two reasons: "I needed the money. And, also, they promised I wouldn't have to sing anything from *My Fair Lady.*"

As far as Moore's creative staff was concerned, Julie's Broadway image *was* Julie, and without benefit of her show tunes they hardly knew what to do with her. So when she playfully started giving Carol Cockney lessons one day, that was worked into a hilarious sketch. When asked what she would like to do for a finale number with Carol, Andrews responded that she'd enjoy doing something totally out of character, or, as she put it, "absolutely inappropriate."

Julie always had a knack for choosing the most obscure material to perform on her TV appearances; often it worked to her detriment, but not this time. She and Ken Welch settled on a raucous song about Dallas, "Big D," from Frank Loesser's 1956 musical *The Most Happy Fella*. As arranged by Ernie Flatt and Ken Welch (who was working his first week as special-material writer for the show), the uproarious production was a success; Carol and Julie clowned it up in cowboy hats and oversize chaps.

On the first day of rehearsal, Carol and Julie arrived wearing almost the exact same outfit. It was as if they'd planned their wardrobe the night before on the telephone. Remembers Irwin Kostal: "Carol came over to Julie and said something very proper, like 'I've so looked forward to working with you,' as if she still thought that's what Julie expected. Julie responded in a Cockney, harsh, unladylike put-on comment, and the two of them fell out laughing. Julie always knew how to take the stars out of Carol's eyes where that relationship was concerned."

Joe Hamilton remembers: "I've been in television a long time, but I'll never forget what happened that night they did 'Big D.' The audience, a typical studio audience, mind you, got to its feet and gave them a standing ovation as if it were a Broadway opening."

"What Julie most had in common with Carol is that basic uncluttered honesty about her work," says Ken Welch. "No come-ons, put-ons, and pretentiousness. On this Garry Moore appearance, the camera magnified Julie's directness for the first time."

Garry Moore, Bob Banner, and Joe Hamilton were delighted with Julie's performance, and she was immediately booked for five additional visits. Meanwhile, Hamilton and Banner thought that the idea of teaming the two performers for a television special would be beneficial to both their careers. They knew that there weren't many women who worked well onstage with other women: Gwen Verdon, Lucille Ball, Eileen Farrell, and, of course, Mary Martin and Ethel Merman, but precious few others. Julie and Carol as a team would be unique and maybe even exciting.

"But specials at that time were very hard to sell," Bob Banner recalls. "So we still had to try to find a hook for it other than the fact that the girls would be performing together. At that time, I had been asked to work on a special to try and save Carnegie Hall because they were thinking of tearing it down. We'd gotten Jack Benny, Isaac Stern, Eugene Ormandy and the Philadelphia Orchestra, and other names to do the show. I went from that meeting directly to dinner with Julie and Carol, where I promised to have a premise for their special.

"I frankly didn't have any ideas at all. Grasping for straws at the last minute, I just blurted out off the top of my head, 'What about Julie and Carol at Carnegie Hall?' They immediately sparked to the idea, and everyone thought it was brilliant. No one ever knew it was just a passing thought. . . ."

"No network would buy it," Joe Hamilton says. "The excuse was that nobody knew Julie west of the Hudson River. And Carol was a second banana, a sidekick you saw every week on TV, why'd she need a special?"

Hamilton remembers that Carol was actually the catalyst for the realization of this show on network television. It was just before the Christmas holidays in 1961, and she was attending a CBS-TV luncheon at the Waldorf-Astoria in New York. She dined with Jim Aubrey, then president of CBS, Mike Dann, East Coast programming vice-president, and Oscar Katz, vice-president of network programming. When it came to socializing with network executives, Carol apparently was not the proverbial shrinking violet.

"It's a shame you boys passed up your chance at doing a show with Julie and me," she said matter-of-factly. "But then, now that I think of it, we do look *so* much better in color anyway. (At that time, NBC was the only network that had regular color telecasts.)

"What are you talking about?" Aubrey asked suspiciously.

"Oh, haven't you heard?" Carol responded ever-so nonchalantly. "Julie Andrews and I, we're doing a television spectacular. Probably over at NBC. Should be a big deal . . ."

There was silence. Then someone changed the subject.

"The fellows left the meeting about five minutes after Carol did, and they found her standing out on a curb on Fifth Avenue hopelessly trying to get a cab," Joe remembers. "She was headed back to her apartment on Central Park West. 'Don't worry,' she told the guys, 'I'll probably get a ride somehow. I always do in this town.'

"At that very moment, a beer truck appeared from out of nowhere. The burly trucker yelled out, 'Hey, Carol, want a lift, sweetheart?'

"'Central Park West, whaddaya say, bud?' Carol answered.

"'Hop in, honey. I'll take you anywhere you wanna go.'

"The three CBS guys helped her into the cab of the beer truck, and as she pulled off, she said something like 'See you fellas at Carnegie Hall!'" Joe Hamilton laughs. "Then off she went down Fifth Avenue in a beer truck!"

The driver stuck a tattooed arm out of the cab window and flashed the CBS executives a "thumbs-up" sign. The three of them stood riveted to the curb, astonished at what they'd just witnessed.

"Mike Dann called her late that afternoon and said, 'You just sold yourself a special at Carnegie Hall,'" Hamilton recalls. "'Anybody who is that well known by the truckers in Manhattan, who has the guts to do what you did, she should have her own show....'" And he clearly thought it shouldn't be on NBC.

It was a Wednesday afternoon, and Julie had just finished her matinee performance as Lady Guinevere in *Camelot*. Carol called her backstage at the theater and told her the news about what she called "the poor man's Ethel Merman-Mary Martin Show."

"It's in the bag!" Carol told her.

"Well, who's sponsoring the special?" Julie asked excitedly.

"Lipton Tea . . . I think," Carol answered.

"Well, Carol, if it has to be in a bag," Julie concluded properly, "it might as well be Lipton's."

Julie was heartbroken at around this time, though she would never admit to it, from having been rejected by movie mogul Jack Warner when he chose Audrey Hepburn to star in the film version of *My Fair Lady*. Julie knew that this big-budget Hollywood movie would have provided her with great national exposure and could change the course of her entire career. But Warner decided to go with the more bankable star. Ever gracious, never once did Julie publicly criticize his decision.

Meanwhile, Walt Disney, who had once attended a performance of *My Fair Lady,* was trying to lure Julie to Hollywood to star in *Mary Poppins,* a fantasy musical that was still in the storyboard stage. She was undecided as to whether or not to take the job; she needed time to think. Working with Carol was a pleasant respite from this period of professional indecision.

Since Julie and Carol had hectic work weeks, rehearsals for the show had to be conducted in twelve-hour-day sessions during weekends. Julie talked about Carol's insecurities to a writer who was visiting the set: "For some reason, Carol feels I can pick up dance steps more quickly than she. After dance rehearsals, she always tells me to go off somewhere and do something else while she keeps plugging away at the dancing." Later, as the writer watched in disbelief, Julie pulled up her satin gown and started belting out "Ol' Man River." While she did a soft-shoe clog, Carol crossed her eyes and contorted her face.

One segment of the program featured a takeoff on the Moiseyev Ballet (called "the Nausiev Ballet"), and the women were so overly ambitious about learning their dance routines as quickly as possible that Carol sprained an ankle ("the left one, the one I always sprain"), and Julie took a tumble and nearly blackened an eye. They lived on tea and pep pills and developed psychosomatic colds. "I got through this show with the help of Carol," Julie said. "Mostly Carol." As Julie lost weight, Carol said she gained it, "right in the bags under my eyes."

During the rehearsal period for this television special, script girl Pat Lillie recalls that Carol and Joe began to feel attracted to each other. "It's just an instinct I had," she remembers. "They would go off into the corner together and have deep conversations, and then they'd laugh a lot.

"They loved to laugh. One Sunday afternoon, we were all in the studio cramming as much rehearsal time in as possible. At six that night, we broke, and Joe said, 'Carol and Julie, you ladies have been so nice to give us your time on a Sunday afternoon, I'm going to take you both out to dinner.' They went up to the rehearsal hall to get their coats, and from the third floor you could look down on them and see them as they waited for their cab. I don't know why, but I went to the window and watched them walk out to the curb. Joe was in the middle, with one arm around Julie and one around Carol. But there was just something about the way he held Carol, a closeness. And a voice inside of me said, 'Something's about to happen here.' Then they started dating each other, very discreetly though, because Joe was still married even though he was separated...."

In the weeks to come, the relationship would begin to blos-

som and Carol would enter a new—and extremely controversial
—phase in her life and career.

Monday March 5, 1962. *Julie and Carol at Carnegie Hall* was
taped performance-style in front of a black-tie audience. Because
CBS had scheduled it to air as a summer special during a season
considered a poor ratings period, it was a low-budget production: $160,000. Today, a ten-minute show couldn't be produced
for that kind of money. For scenery, the cracks in the Carnegie
Hall stage were simply covered with a white backdrop. The hall
was rented for a twenty-four-hour period, from midnight to
midnight. In that time, the crew had to set up all of their equipment; the cast had to rehearse before the cameras for purposes
of staging; background vocals had to be prerecorded; and then
two shows had to be taped before a live audience. Afterward,
everything had to be moved out and it had to look as if nothing
had ever happened in Carnegie Hall that evening.

Joe Hamilton, who produced and directed the show, remembers a hitch they came across right before taping: "Carol
was scared to death to do her solo; she simply decided that she
couldn't do it. I told her, 'Carol, you can't go out and do a show
that's billed as Julie and Carol at Carnegie Hall and have Julie
sing a solo and not you. That doesn't make any sense.' 'Give Julie
another song, she's good at that. I won't do it,' she said.

"She didn't like anything Ken and Mitzie had written for
her, and we had gone through something like fifteen songwriters
before finding one song someone had written called 'Meantime,'
not specifically for Carol but good for her just the same. She was
scared more of doing that song than of doing anything else on
the show. I had to badger her into doing it. . . ."

Carol has never enjoyed singing alone on a stage. She never
did, and she still doesn't. If she can sing in comic character, as
someone ridiculous or outrageous, she's comfortable. Also, she's
usually at ease when onstage when with another singer. Oddly,
Carol has never been particularly intimidated by sharing the
stage with great vocal talent, which suggests that perhaps she's
not as insecure about her voice as she is about being Carol Burnett alone onstage *as* Carol Burnett. "It was a definite problem,
always," Ken Welch says. "It's just something we learned to accept. The amazing thing to me was that she would still do it, even
though she was frightened. She'd somehow conquer the fear for

that moment. But then, afterward, she was a wreck worrying about the next time."

(Originally, Carol and Julie were each to have two solos; Carol was going to perform "Meantime" along with "Johnny One Note," but the second solo for each performer was cut because of a time problem.)

Pat Lillie remembers of the taping: "The black-tie audience looked stunning, and we were all holding our breaths waiting for this magnificent moment we'd worked so hard for. Joe cued the music, and then the announcer. Julie and Carol walked onstage to a tremendous rush of applause...then, in a big, important voice the announcer said, 'And now ladies and gentlemen, we proudly present *Julie Andrews as Carol Burnett.*'"

Lillie cringes at the memory. "Nobody in the booth heard the mistake, because they were so involved with all of their technical work. But I was tuned in, because as script girl that was my job. I started screaming, *'Joe, Joe, you gotta stop, it's all wrong, all wrong!'* The moment was so sad, because it took all the juice out of that initial entrance. We laughed at the party afterward, but we were certainly not laughing when it happened."

Carol and Julie took to the stage in floor-length voluminous gowns with matching long gloves, holding feather fans by jeweled handles. Julie looked regal; Carol a bit awkward (she struggled to keep her shoulder straps from dropping through much of the opening song). With a full orchestra in the pit before them, the women sang live; there was no lip-synching as there always seems to be on today's telecasts.

The opening number was a piece of special material called "You're So London," written by Ken Welch and Mike Nichols. The song contrasted Carol's down-home American ways with Julie's "austere" British background, Carol's simple pleasures with Julie's supposed extravagance, each preferring the other's life-style. It was an ingenious spoof on the images the performers had presented to their audiences up until this point: Carol as a hopeless girl-next-door misfit and Julie an unapproachable Broadway starlet.

The Nausiev Ballet satire was an effective mockery of the onslaught of Russian dance troupes in the United States at that time. The two women also spoofed *The Sound of Music* in a sketch called "The Pratt Family" (the comedy here was prophetic; Julie would, of course, go on to star in the movie version of this hit

Broadway play). Andrews did a pristine solo of "Oh, Dear, What Can the Matter Be?"

Despite her apprehension, Carol performed "Meantime" alone on the cavernous stage in a simple black gown before a lone microphone. It was very impressive.

Together, they performed a strong nineteen-minute medley, "The History of the Musical Comedy." The show culminated in a reprisal of the "Big D" routine from *The Garry Moore Show.* As before, they sang and danced in oversize cowboy hats with furry chaps and gun holsters.

At the end of the concert, the company of male dancers brought out one floral arrangement after another and laid them at Carol and Julie's feet as the audience stood cheering. A fine moment of show-biz fantasy, until the announcer put the commercial aspect of this event back into perspective when he proudly proclaimed, "This fall look for *Calamity Jane* starring Carol Burnett, brought to you by icy Lipton Tea, the change-of-pace drink."

A soundtrack album was released shortly after the show aired on Monday evening, June 11, 1962. The "original soundtrack" was actually recorded in Columbia's Thirtieth Street studio in Manhattan rather than live at Carnegie Hall. Though Irwin Kostal went on to win a much-deserved Emmy award for his musical direction of the special, the album falls a bit flat. The appeal in combining Carol Burnett with Julie Andrews was as much visual as it was aural. Without the sight gags in the long sketches, and considering the fact that the two rarely achieve any kind of vocal blend in their duets, the album doesn't do the televised event justice.

Most of the press was unanimous in its approval of the show, particularly of Carol's performance. "Last week's special was Burnett at her manic best," wrote a reviewer for *Time* magazine.

Julie also benefited a great deal from the experience. In his biography of Julie Andrews, Robert Windeler credits the Carnegie Hall special as being "Julie's single most important television appearance," mostly because it showed her great versatility and exposed her to American audiences as an approachable, homespun girl, in contrast to her distant ice-princess image.

Julie and Carol at Carnegie Hall was rerun in the fall and, says producer Bob Banner: "That was good money, finally, because we lost a bundle on the first airing." Carol went on to win an

Emmy award for her work on the special; it completely validated her as a viable television property and was probably one of the most important stepping stones to her future as a television star. The show itself won the Rose D'Or Award from the Montreax Festival in 1963, the first American TV program to do so.

The following spring, Julie went on to film *Mary Poppins,* which became the biggest-grossing picture ($31 million) of 1965, and garnered a *Time* magazine cover for her, not to mention an Academy Award for "Best Actress." Ironically, if she had been signed to play Eliza Doolittle in the screen version of *My Fair Lady,* she wouldn't have been able to appear in *Mary Poppins,* because the production schedules would have conflicted. Audrey Hepburn wasn't nominated for an Oscar, but most observers had to agree in retrospect that if Julie had starred in *My Fair Lady,* she probably would have won for that role, too, that's how popular she had become. When Julie accepted her Academy Award for *Mary Poppins,* she coyly thanked Jack Warner, the man who rejected her in favor of Hepburn, "above all the rest for making this award possible."

Julie went on to star in *The Sound of Music,* which earned her another Academy Award nomination and is one of the highest-grossing movie musicals in history.

The friendship between Julie and Carol has remained strong through the years. "She was the first person I told when I suspected I was pregnant," Julie says. "I'd confided to her that I'd just sent off a specimen, and if the little mouse died, I'd know for sure. And she said, 'Send me a message no matter where I am when you find out.'"

When Julie discovered she was expecting, she phoned CBS to tell Carol the news. Carol, who was in the middle of a rehearsal, couldn't come to the phone. So Julie asked the operator to relay the message. Minutes later, all of the public-address speakers at CBS announced, "We have a message from Julie Andrews to Carol Burnett: 'The mouse is *dead.*'"

Julie's baby, Emma Kate Walton, was born in November 1962 in England. ("Julie felt that such an occasion called for British soil," Carol joked.) That night, Julie sent Carol a telegram: "She's here, known officially as Emma, Stop, Start leading a good clean life, Stop, you're her godmother." The message was signed "Mother Walton." The next day they talked on the phone continent to continent about Julie's success at breast feeding.

(Emma Walton would go on to follow in her mother's footsteps and become an actress. Nearly twenty-five years later, she was one of the stars of the Julie Andrews/Jack Lemmon 1986 vehicle *That's Life,* produced by Julie's second husband, Blake Edwards.)

Carol and Julie wouldn't appear together again until January of 1965, when they and Mike Nichols were asked to perform in Washington at President Johnson's inaugural ball. What stands out in Carol's mind from this experience is a practical joke she and Andrews tried to pull on Nichols.

While waiting for Mike to come out of an elevator in the posh hotel in which they were staying, they decided to do something outrageous to break him up. Sitting on a settee across from the elevator, Julie in old slacks, Carol in a worn bathrobe, they tried contorting themselves into various positions, hoping to come up with something that would shock Nichols when he exited the elevator.

"I know *wot,*" Julie said mischievously. "Let's be necking!"

"Gee, Julie," Carol responded. "I like you a whole lot, but I don't know about this. . . . Okay, let's do it. . . ."

The elevator door opened. Julie and Carol went into a mad embrace. An older, very prim woman got off of the elevator and, appalled at the scene on the settee, hurried away.

"Oh, I'm *so* embarrassed," Carol said.

"Yes, isn't it *marvelous,*" Julie concluded, giggling.

(Later, when Julie would tell this story at parties, she would say that the shocked woman was Lady Bird Johnson. It probably wasn't, but that does make for an even better story.)

The elevator doors opened again. Another mad embrace. This time, a dozen gentlemen exited, none of them Nichols, all of them stunned. Carol and Julie could barely contain their laughter as the gentlemen walked by them, all the while craning their necks for a closer look.

The woman, still watching the whole scene from down the hall, came back toward Julie and Carol. "Excuse me," she inquired. "You're Carol Burnett, aren't you?"

Carol wasn't about to be the only one recognized in this ridiculous situation. "Why, yes," she answered cheerily. "And this here is Miss Mary Poppins!"

The elevator doors slid open again. A mad embrace, this one more exaggerated than the others.

Mike Nichols walked out of the elevator and glanced at the two women making out on the settee.

"Hi, girls, how's it going?" he said, unimpressed. Then he casually sauntered right by them and walked into his room, closing the door behind him.

"Why the *nerve* of him," Julie said, nonplussed.

11

A TIME OF TRANSITION.

Julie and Carol at Carnegie Hall was such a success on network television that Bob Banner and Associates booked the two performers for a summer concert tour together. But when Julie became pregnant, the plans were canceled. However, Joe Hamilton thought that Carol could go on the tour by herself and be a success as a solo attraction. He never had any doubt that she would draw sellout audiences on the road and make a profit. The booking agencies agreed, and so dates were confirmed for Carol's first major tour.

At this time, she was faced with a difficult decision. The last few years had been grueling, and those close to Carol couldn't help but notice that she was overworked and looking haggard. Chrissy, now preparing to enroll as a student at Moravian College in Bethlehem, Pennsylvania, would usually write a three-line letter every week just to keep in touch or to ask for money. But one week in 1962 she sent this note:

> Dear Sissy,
>   I miss you very much. It just killed me to see you look so thin. I know that you are working very hard, but money can't buy good health. So, please take good care of yourself. You can't live on sweet rolls and coffee.
>   I love you,
>   Chris

It was obvious that the time had come for Carol to stop doing weekly television for a while. She said at the time that she was "desolate" about it, but that she would be leaving Garry's show after her June appearances and before the summer tour. It wouldn't be easy. She would be leaving behind three irreclaimable, amazing seasons.

"I feel I have done as much as I can on Garry's show," she said in an interview on June 9, 1962, to United Press International writer Jack Gaver. "I don't mean just for myself. I mean for the program, too. After all, that exposure every week—and I'm expected to be funny all the time, not just sing a couple of songs or dance—can reach a saturation point as far as the television viewers are concerned. It's best not to wear out your welcome."

"It was entirely her decision," Joe Hamilton recalls. "And not an easy one to make. She loved the Moore show, the camaraderie of everyone on the set, and she especially had strong feelings for Garry. It's ironic, because during the first year the relationship between Carol and Garry was a bit rocky since he didn't want to have her on as a regular. But then he really took her on as a protégée. They became great friends."

"If Garry has a funny line in a sketch and he thinks it would be even funnier if I said it, he gives it to me," she said at the time. "He doesn't want to be the whole hog. It's one of the secrets of his TV indestructibility." Moore was setting a good example for Carol, one that she wouldn't forget when she finally starred in her own series.

"Carol Burnett was born of Garry Moore," associate producer Bob Wright observes. "She was an open book when she joined the show, very naive and unknowing. Garry filled in the pages for her. He was probably one of the greatest things that ever happened to her. He taught Carol more about television than any one person, fostering her, coaxing her, and being her mentor in every way."

Though Moore was amazed at Carol's development as a television personality over the last couple of years, he still saw room for growth. "I've said to her that the only area she's not already expert in is developing a Carol Burnett character on the screen so that she can work alone," he observed at around this time. "But more and more, she's gaining confidence. She knows now that an audience is not some giant waiting to devour her.

"Our biggest problem is trying to persuade her of her feminine charm," he remarked. "She simply won't believe in that. She won't let the public see her as a gracious young lady. She still wants them to see her as a kook."

Moore also respected Joe Hamilton's business acumen, and had become quite fond of him, as well. At one point, he asked Hamilton to run his entire multimillion-dollar company. Joe turned him down because he didn't have the time to devote to Moore's affairs. "But he was one of the nicest men I've ever had the pleasure of working with," Hamilton says.

Even though Garry would often not listen to Joe's advice, he was struck by the fact that Joe always seemed to have his finger on the pulse of what was happening in the entertainment world. For instance, after seeing Barbra Streisand in her first major play, *I Can Get It for You Wholesale*, Hamilton booked her on Garry's program to do comedy, not to sing. It was on *The Garry Moore Show* that Barbra was given her theme song, "Happy Days Are Here Again," a treatment of that old standard written by Ken Welch.

"I could have gotten Barbra as a regular on the show for almost nothing," Joe said with a grin. "I could have owned her for two and a half years for seven hundred fifty dollars a week the first year and twelve hundred fifty a week for the second. After that she would get fifteen hundred. But Garry said, 'Absolutely not! She goes right through the set. She's too strong.'" (Note: What Barbra was to have made might not seem like much in retrospect, but considering the fact that in 1962 the starting salary for a secretary at CBS was eighty dollars a week, show business was being good to Streisand.)

Hamilton was not able to convince Garry otherwise, as he and Bob Banner had eventually done when Moore felt the same way about Carol Burnett. Streisand was never hired as a regular on the Moore show. All of this is interesting because had Garry hired Streisand, she might never have become a movie star but rather a television attraction in the Burnett tradition.

At first, Garry wasn't eager to let Carol go. "He was willing to literally give Carol half the show if she would stay. He wanted to make her the costar, give her half the money, the whole works. *The Garry Moore Show with Carol Burnett*, Joe Hamilton recalls. "She talked to me about that, and I told her not to do it. I said, 'If you do, you'll be married to him for life....'"

Garry eventually did reconcile himself to Carol's decision, and he was proud of the way she'd decided not to jump into another series but rather explore all of her options. "She would be foolish to continue with our show after the next season," he told *TV Guide* in an interview (September 20, 1961). "She's been offered series, situation comedies and that sort of thing. Nothing artistic in them, though. Oh, they're fine all right for old age—residuals and so on. But she can wait with the certain knowledge that when she's 40, she will have become so big she can then take on something with an annuity in it. It's *she* who doesn't want to go too fast. . . .

"She's got a glimmering, but no real idea how important she's become."

Carol made her final appearance on Moore's show in June 1962. She called it "the saddest last show in the world." Because it was such a sentimental episode for Carol, she wanted it to go as smoothly as possible. But the rest of the cast, Garry included, had other ideas.

They decided to play a practical joke on her. During the taping, while Carol was offstage changing costumes, Garry told the studio and home audience that the next sketch, titled "Found Money," would be played a bit differently from the one Carol had rehearsed all that week.

As written, the sketch is about a middle-class couple. The wife is out looking for work, and the husband, Durward Kirby, is home housecleaning and listening to the radio. He hears on the news that ten thousand dollars in a Pan Am travel bag was left in a taxicab. At just that moment, Carol as the wife walks in with a Pan Am bag under her arm.

"Guess what's in this bag?" she asks Kirby.

Instead of saying he didn't know, as per the script, Kirby blurted out, "Ten thousand dollars."

Carol was aghast. He had stepped on her line, she thought, and had blown the entire sketch. But she proceeded gallantly. She was to open the bag and pull out the money. When she tried to, she discovered that the bag had been wired shut. She'd always had a recurring nightmare in which every detail of a sketch goes awry. Now, it seemed to be coming true. What made it worse was that Garry had told the audience to laugh at all of Kirby's lines but none of Carol's.

The sketch continued. Carol was to make a phone call, and just as she was about to pick up the receiver, the telephone rang. She answered it, hung up, and it rang again. She picked it up and the cord fell out. The doorbell rang and, according to the script, Garry, dressed as a policeman, was supposed to be at the door. But when Carol opened the door, she found no one there. Over her shoulder, she noticed Garry slipping in through the window.

It was a hilariously funny prank, and not easy to pull off, because Carol was always very meticulous about her props; she tried to insist on seeing the bag before airing. "She was going nuts backstage saying, 'I gotta check the bag, I gotta check the bag!'" Pat Lillie remembers. "She still didn't have the pocketbook when the cameras started rolling, and then the stage manager just threw it at her. When she tried to open it and it was locked, the expression on her face was pure terror. Later, she said she thought everyone had gone out between the dress rehearsal and air show and gotten drunk."

"I had never been so scared in my life," Carol recalled. "I thought I was on *The Twilight Zone.* I was ready to burst into tears when Garry put his arm around me and told me it was all in fun."

After Carol left the program as a regular, the series never really recovered. By November, Carol had returned for four visits, but her spot had still not been filled. The producers used Nancy Walker five times, Judy Holliday four, Tammy Grimes twice. When Carol appeared, according to *The New York Times,* the ratings would be up 35 percent from the weeks she wasn't on. Dorothy Loudon eventually replaced Carol, and though she was capable, the show had run out of steam. Garry gave it up in June 1964. (*The Garry Moore Show* returned two years later with a new format but lasted only four months against formidable competition, *Bonanza.*)

Monday, July 2, 1962. Carol's first major concert tour kicked off in Pittsburgh; the one-week engagement would gross $116,748. In the next two months, she would perform for SRO audiences in Kansas City, Dallas, and Indianapolis. In Detroit, the second balcony of the Shubert Theatre was opened for the first time in years in order to accommodate the full houses. The tour would wind up in Las Vegas. Along with a full orchestra conducted by Irwin Kostal, the comedy team of Allen and Rossi, a troupe of sixteen male dancers, and the George Becker Singers from *The Garry Moore Show* (just the fellows, not the ladies), Carol reprised some of her most popular sketches of recent years, including "The Singers" and "The Princess of Monrovia." In the latter, she played an austere dignitary complete with jeweled gown and tiara, "Her Royal Highness Princess Marianne of Monrovia." The princess gets looped to the gills by drinking too many wine toasts while rehearsing the taping of a tribute to an American doctor.

Carol also sang a few songs, such as her opening number, "Oh How Lovely Is the Evening," and "Johnny One Note," from her debut album, "Meantime" from the Carnegie Hall soundtrack, and a melancholy rendition of Bert Williams's "Nobody." Her Charwoman stripper mime was always a crowd-pleaser, as was a Questions and Answers spot (which she borrowed from Garry Moore—he did it every week on his show, though as a warm-up spot it was never taped—and which would go on to become a regular opening segment on her own series). The concert always closed with the "Big D" routine; the dancers tossed Carol into the air so many times that she ended the tour with a fresh new set of black-and-blue bruises (at the end of the show, for her closing bows, they carried her onto and off of the stage in a Red-Cross-type stretcher).

Chrissy went along with Carol on the road. It was a strenuous tour, though, and sometimes the entire cast was onstage rehearsing from midnight to three in the morning preparing for the next evening's performance. All sorts of props had to be kept track of, including twenty flags (for the Nausiev Ballet routine), guns with blanks (for "Big D"), and also twenty pairs of black horn-rimmed glasses, wineglasses, coffee tables, end tables, lamps, two thick twin-size mattresses for pratfalls, and quite a few other bits and pieces (not to mention a scrub bucket, mop, and scrub brush for the Charwoman routine). The cost of the production wasn't that high, Joe Hamilton remembers with a smile, "because I managed to steal—or I should say *borrow*— all of the costumes for the singers and dancers from the wardrobe department of every television show in New York."

"She wondered if people would actually come and see her perform," Don Crichton, lead dancer in the show, remembers, "and as it turned out, we were all bowled over by the reception. In Pittsburgh, when she walked out onto the stage, the audience stood up and started to scream, 'We love you, Carol! We love you!' After the show, they stood cheering through more curtain calls than I can remember. This was truly someone that America had grown to love, and I think this was when we first realized that."

Pat Lillie talks about Burnett-mania in terms usually reserved for phenomena like Elvis Presley. "An hour and a half after the show in Pittsburgh, we left the theater on our way to the limo, not expecting anybody to be outside waiting for us. When we opened the backstage door, a wave of people suddenly began moving toward us, just wanting to touch and talk to Carol. Somehow, they trapped Chrissy up against a brick wall. As I was pushing Carol into the limousine, she was shrieking, 'Get Chrissy in here! Help Christine!' It was a very panicky moment of two different emotions. On one hand, we thought they were all going to kill us. On the other, we were amazed at how much Carol meant to them.

"Once we were inside the limo, the fans started jumping up on top of it, knocking on the windows and on the windshield and screaming how much they loved the show. They were absolutely maniacal, and we were totally shaken by it all; it was quite frightening."

But despite the prevailing hysteria, Carol never shied away from her public. On the contrary, for an hour or so after every show she would autograph postcards and photographs for fans in a backstage area. She sat behind a card table as a line of ticket buyers filed by and shook her hand and took photos of her. "The fans that mobbed us at every stop were usually the ones who couldn't squeeze into the backstage area during the sixty-minute time limit," Lillie remembers. "So that made them even more anxious. It was impossible to accommodate everybody."

Lillie recalls another remarkable tour incident. They were in Kansas City, and Carol had volunteered to visit a handicapped-children's hospital. Lillie said that she was squeamish about accompanying Carol, "because whenever I see the little children in those hospitals, I start to cry. I just can't bear it," she says. "But Carol insisted. 'Now, c'mon, Pat,' she scolded me, 'I am just as scared as you are. But we *have* to do this....'"

The two women were escorted into a large gathering room in the hospital. Around the perimeter of the room were crippled children in wheelchairs and braces and on crutches.

"When we finally got inside, I just sidled up against a back wall," Pat says sadly. "But Carol walked straight into the center of the room, and as she did, all of the youngsters began to scream and applaud. 'Hi, kids! How ya' doing!' she said very cheerfully."

On the other side of the room stood a four-year-old blond child with deep blue eyes. His legs were wrapped in steel braces, and when he walked he was forced to use little crutches. Awkwardly, but ever so persistently, he started toward Carol. As he reached the middle of the room, the other children quieted down and watched. Some of his little friends began to coax him on. When the boy was six inches in front of the visitor, he dropped his crutches and extended his arms up toward her, crying, "Carol! Carol!" Her eyes filled with tears, and she scooped the tot up into her arms. The two dissolved into each other.

But it wasn't all heavy drama and hard work on that tour; they also had plenty of fun. On many evenings, Carol and the cast members were so energized after a performance, they were not able to fall asleep. So, instead, they would play "dirty charades" into the early morning hours. Irwin Kostal never participated in this funny pastime, but his visiting brother once did, at Carol's invitation. "He came out of the hotel suite with his face beet-red and laughing like a madman," Kostal remembers with a mischievous grin. "It was nothing like what he expected. It was quite risqué."

Carol Burnett was now a hot property. Whether or not Joe Hamilton and Bob Banner planned it to happen, the summer tour certainly served to validate Carol as a popular attraction. Upon learning of her success on the road with the public, and given her Emmy-award-winning recent history on TV, all three television networks were now anxious to sign her to long-term deals. It wasn't unusual back in the fifties and sixties for the networks to sign entertainers to contracts that guaranteed them television security for years. For instance, in 1949 CBS contracted Jack Benny for fifteen years, and subsequently signed Lucille Ball, Phil Silvers, and Jackie Gleason to long-term deals. Probably the most publicized TV deal was one NBC made with Milton Berle in 1951—for thirty years!

"There are just so many top TV stars," CBS-TV vice-president Mike Dann once said, "so it's essential that you put them under exclusive contract. You may lose out if one doesn't work for awhile, but the loss is negligible compared to one starring in a hit show for somebody else."

By the time Carol wound up her tour in Las Vegas, the networks were bidding for her services so intensely that they'd sent deal makers and vice-presidents to meet with her at different stops along the way. In August, *The New York Times* reported that NBC vice-president Mort Werner wanted to sign Carol to star in a television series, but that she had turned him down, saying, "I don't think I have had the experience to be the star of a weekly TV program. I really want to do something on Broadway."

Her interest was still in the theater, but the tide of her career had definitely turned toward television. She was able to command a lot of money in TV, and that was difficult to ignore.

"All of the other offers were good, but not quite as good as CBS's, because with that one, *she* had control over what she did, not the network," recalls Joe Hamilton, who had become quite influential in Carol's decision making by this point. "It was pretty much unheard of to give an artist of Carol's stature back then such complete autonomy.

"CBS met with us on the tour and presented a contract to Carol that really wasn't good enough to me, or to Carol or her business managers. They changed it and brought us a terrific offer in Vegas. According to the new deal, Carol would have five years to make up her mind as to whether she wanted to do a variety show or a comedy series. In that five years, she would do specials. After the five-year period, if she couldn't make up her mind, they would make it up for her. We knew that would never happen.

"In Vegas, I remember sitting in the corner of the hotel room trying to be unobtrusive while listening to them give the details of the deal to Carol and her business managers. Every now and then, I would ask a question or bring up a point that would piss everybody off. I guess they sort of looked at me as an interloper. But the points got across, and she finally got what she should have gotten."

She signed the deal in Vegas; *The New York Times* made the announcement on August 29, 1962. Carol would be paid a million dollars, one hundred thousand dollars a year for the next ten years, for making one special a year and two guest appearances, and also four appearances on the flagging Garry Moore series in the 1962/63 season. The first special would air on February 24, 1963.

The future looked bright, but there were still some complications ahead.

Joe Hamilton is handsomely sharp-featured, blue-eyed, tall, and very charming. His demeanor sometimes seems a bit distant, aloof. Actually, he is quite shy, even introspective. Also, he is very conservative; his staff used to call him "Paul Prude." Hamilton is a reformed alcoholic.

At first, Carol was awed by Joe; he wielded so much power on the set and seemed so intimidating that she did her best to stay out of his way. Unlike Don, he wasn't outgoing and exciting and easy to get to know. He didn't say much to her at first, and she wasn't sure that he even liked her.

Hamilton is a strong-willed Irish Catholic who attended a parochial school in Los Angeles as a youngster. His father, also Joseph, was a tenor and organist at St. Vibiana's Cathedral in Los Angeles for thirty years. His mother, the former Marie Sullivan, raised six children—two boys and four girls. As a teenager, Joe was kicked out of eight high schools even though he was a good student. "I just was never real fond of people telling me what to do," he says.

After finally graduating, he joined the navy in 1946. For the next three years, he served as an aerial photographer. After the navy, Joe was accepted into the Los Angeles Conservatory of Music and Arts, where he learned to play just about all of the reed instruments. He joined a couple of singing groups, including the Merrymacs, in which he sang high tenor, and then the Skylarks quintet, in which he filled in all vocal parts.

The Skylarks were hired as back-up singers for Dinah Shore on her very prestigious *Chevy Show.* Eventually, Joe became interested in television production and left the vocal group. Soon, he was a writer for Dinah's show, and eventually Bob Banner made him music coordinator, and then associate producer. In November 1958, when Bob Banner and Associates took over production chores on *The Garry Moore Show,* Joe Hamilton became the youngest producer in television. He won his first Emmy for his work on the Moore show.

Joe has a vivid memory of his first encounter with Carol, mostly because it was a bit antagonistic. She was scheduled to appear on *The Chevy Show* in 1957. After rehearsal, Bob Banner told Joe that he would have to talk to Carol about cutting four minutes out of her routine because it was too long. Joe had just met her that day; it hardly seemed the best way to "break the ice."

"Carol, I'm afraid we're going to have to cut your material," he began carefully. "It's brilliantly written, but way too long."

"Oh, no!" she said, her voice rising. "We can't! It's fine as it is. I've worked too hard on this to cut it. And, anyway, it's musical, and you can't cut it as if it were a sketch. *It'll never work.*"

"Sure it will," Joe challenged her. He spread the musical lead sheet over a card table. "You just cut here," he said, indicating the end of a scene with his index finger. "And then cut here, cut *all* of this outta here, cut here, get *rid* of this part here, and end it right there."

"She looked at me as if I were from Mars," he remembers with a grin. "The nerve of this guy, to cut her material to shreds. She argued that it wouldn't work, and I argued that it would. I told her I'd give her an extra rehearsal with the orchestra so she could see for herself. She went along with it, but she didn't like it. It worked."

After her separation from Don, Carol was totally absorbed in her work. She began to wonder if she would ever again become involved with anyone romantically. The more successful she became, the more limited her options seemed to be in terms of finding a man who could deal with her popularity and demanding career. "I talked to her about the problems of being a star," Garry Moore has recalled. 'Don't louse up your love life,' I told her. 'Don't let some guy be Mr. Burnett.'"

Except for those first few baptism-by-fire weeks in New York, she had never been so alone. She didn't enjoy the freedom; she needed a close, loving relationship. Her depression about this was deepening and compounded by her constant state of work-related fatigue. Did she have a right to be unhappy when she was so successful professionally? she must have wondered. Still, when she was working *The Garry Moore Show,* as well as doing her radio show and all of her other career-related activities at the same time, there were moments when she could barely manage a smile to hide her despair.

One day, she was quieter than usual; when troubled, she usually retreats inside herself. Joe found her alone in a corner during a break, deep in thought. She looked perplexed. He put his arm around her and asked her what was wrong. Before she was able to answer, she broke down and started to cry.

Joe recognized the intensity of Carol's distress. He held her and comforted her until the sobbing ended. He was compassionate and suggested that perhaps she was taking her career too seriously, that she needed to relax more. Shortly after this, Carol decided to leave *The Garry Moore Show* and quit her radio program. She had already left *Once Upon a Mattress*.

Carol dealt with most people the same way. She plunged right in, exposed and vulnerable, ready to embrace immediately. That was her basic personality: She was totally trusting and openhearted. Her refreshing naiveté had always been appealing to the opposite sex, and was certainly part of Joe's fascination with her. "She doesn't know how important she's become," he said in 1962, "and in a way I think that's wonderful." Still, always the realist, Joe confided to friends that he feared Carol was in for some trouble. She was such an innocent, and so guileless, Joe was afraid she'd be used. How long could she survive in a show-business world fueled by ego and ambition?

Joe was different. He exercised more caution, he was practical—a feet-on-the-ground kind of guy. He had a keen survivor's instinct and, although always cordial, he was by nature suspicious of anyone new in his life. Once convinced of sincerity, though, his loyalty was guaranteed.

In many ways, Joe and Carol balanced each other: She would teach him to be more open, and he would teach her to be less gullible.

She was a public person; he was not. He dreaded cocktail parties as an ordeal; she accepted them as part of her lot in show business and learned to enjoy them. He loathed pressing crowds and sweaty handshakes and wondered how she managed it all. "That's show biz!" she'd say brightly. "It's all part of it. You gotta calm down, Joe."

Joe could see right through Carol's gregarious personality. It took a practiced eye to see the complex, layered reality beneath her outgoing exterior. It wasn't long before Joe recognized the fact that, in her own way, Carol was just as shy as he was. They were as much alike as they were different.

At first, he was an older—by seven years—and irreplaceable friend. He gave her love and approval. Soon, though, Joe was much more to Carol. What probably enhanced his appeal was that he could help ease the burden of responsibility she had for her career. He could supervise the details, the way he had in Vegas when she was deliberating over that million-dollar CBS deal, even though he would never actually be her business manager. Joe was able to support her career and ambitions without suppressing his own identity because he was already a success. He would never become "Mr. Burnett," as many felt Don had become.

"She may or may not remember this," Joe says, "but one evening before we were married, we were dining at the Four Seasons and she took out a pen and wrote on a napkin, 'You will always be the boss. Love, Carol.' And she dated it. I kept it in my wallet for about fifteen years," he adds, smiling.

"Joe has this strength," Carol told friends. "He's the kind of guy who can make all of the decisions and take on all of the responsibilities. That's so rare."

She also admired his closeness to his family. He had one brother and four sisters, happy parents, and the kind of well-adjusted family life she'd never known. One night his mother had Carol and Joe over to dinner. Marie Hamilton was very warm, generous, and loving and her graciousness so overwhelmed Carol that she actually cried.

When Joe's mother died in September 1968 she left behind forty grandchildren and eight great-grandchildren, a wonderful family of descendants.

Joe had been married since the age of nineteen, when he was just out of high school, and had eight children—five daughters and three sons. Separated about a year before he and Carol started dating, he had moved out of the home he and his wife shared, at first living in a Manhattan hotel room and eventually settling into an apartment on Columbus Circle. The fact that Carol was still technically married herself made the situation all the more complicated. She was not ashamed of her romance with Joe Hamilton, but she knew that for the time being it would be best to be discreet.

To many of her friends, this relationship seemed like a sword of Damocles threatening Carol's career. How would her public cope with this? Back in the early sixties, divorce was certainly not as common or as widely accepted as it is today, especially among Roman Catholics like Joe's family. And when the media got hold of the story, the fact that Joe and his wife had eight children would surely overshadow the fact that the Hamiltons had been separated well before Joe and Carol had started dating. A Burnett-Hamilton romance would certainly be fodder for gossip columnists.

Pat Lillie remembers: "It was a very beautiful, wonderful fairy-tale romance. Carol's friends all shared the belief that it's not wrong to fall in love with a man just because he has eight children. She didn't break up the marriage, but obviously there were problems ahead. When we were on the summer tour, Joe joined us for opening nights in each of the cities we were in. Carol and I talked about the relationship often. 'Eventually,' I warned her, 'this can of beans is going to open up. What are you going to say, what are you going to do?'

"Carol responded very matter-of-factly, 'I am going to tell the truth, pure and simple. That's all.'"

When Carol and Joe first fell in love, their lives weren't very complicated: They had the same schedules, both had even temperaments. As much as possible, they handled their daily routines calmly and rationally; they promised each other that they would try not to complicate their careers with emotional melodrama. "It's just our work," Carol would say. "Our everyday jobs."

When she was with Don Saroyan, Carol had a lot of theater-related fun. But with Joe, most of their favorite times were relaxing, quieter moments away from the world of show business. They would talk about how maddening their day at the studio had been, and how wonderful it would be when they'd be able to spend extended time together away from it all. Over private dinners, they would share confidences, and they soon discovered a mutual problem: They both found it extremely difficult to express feelings of pain and insecurity.

At first, the relationship between Joe and Carol developed without public notice. "We were not hiding it," Pat Lillie says. "We were just protecting it until things could be resolved."

The media had hitherto made little of Carol's private life. The public perceived her as someone who couldn't even get a date, let alone be in love, and she perpetuated that image of herself in press interviews. "I sit home alone every night in my pajamas and eat frozen dinners," she said when she appeared on David Susskind's *Open End* panel show. "On Tuesdays, it's spaghetti, and on Wednesdays I send out to the delicatessen."

Ironically, just at the time her relationship with Joe was blossoming, Carol's infatuation with Richard Chamberlain became misinterpreted and a story in the New York *World Telegram and Sun* touted the "budding romance," calling it, "the most unlikely romantic development of the year."

The article said that the fact that she worked for CBS and he for NBC was "a drawback to the romance." In reality, Carol and Richard were friends but nothing more. Carol and Joe evidently didn't mind the diversion the feature supplied. Indeed, in retrospect, it appears that the story was probably planted by Carol's well-meaning public-relations representative to divert any snooping press people from what could be a real story.

But Dorothy Kilgallen, who worked for the *Telegram and Sun*'s chief competitor, the *Journal American,* didn't believe in the Burnett/Chamberlain romance for a minute. She smelled a scoop, and made it her business to get to the bottom of Carol's private life. She discovered the truth in no time. "Carol and Richard are about as much in love as Martha Raye and Rock Hudson," she wrote in her August 29, 1962, column. "Carol's real sweetie is a handsome television executive, separated from his wife and many children, just waiting for the popular comedienne to get her divorce."

Carol was in Las Vegas performing when that brief column item hit the newsstands. (She was breaking Frank Sinatra's attendance record at the Sands. "He didn't mind," she joked. "He's one of the owners.") Joe was in New York, and when Kilgallen's report was brought to his attention he knew immediately that she wouldn't be discreet about his identity for much longer. The news was about to break, that was obvious. The question now was simply how to handle it when it happened.

Dorothy Kilgallen attempted to reach Carol at the Sands. Somehow, she managed to get Marty Allen involved as an intermediary between herself and the Burnett camp. "She threatened that if she didn't get a full exclusive story, she would write something miserable," says a friend of Carol's. "Don't quote me on that; her ghost will surely come back and haunt me.

"Carol didn't know what to do. Marty said, 'Give the interview,' but I think Joe had expressed doubt and was against her talking to Kilgallen," the friend remembers. "Dorothy Kilgallen worked for CBS-TV also, as a regular on *What's My Line?* CBS felt a strong obligation to Carol and Joe, and there was some talk

that Kilgallen might be persuaded by the network to lay off
Carol. The network was still courting Carol to sign that long-
term contract, and was eager to cultivate good relations. Also,
they would have liked for Carol to remain as uncontroversial as
possible at this time. But Kilgallen wasn't easy to discourage
when she was sniffing out a lead."

There were some people in Carol's camp who wondered if it
wouldn't be better to leak the story to a less controversial columnist. Kilgallen had a reputation as quite the sensationalist. "But
trying to find a columnist who would handle this story with tact
was like asking sharks to diplomatically organize a salmon dinner," says an observer. "One reporter was as bad as the next."

Pat Lillie picks up the story: "After we finished a show, at
around two in the morning, Carol and I sat in the lounge sipping
Stinger Mists, trying to decide whether or not to give Dorothy
Kilgallen an exclusive interview. She said very deliberately, 'I am
not going to make this a big problem. Joe and I have not done
anything wrong. I'm giving her the story because if I don't, who
knows *what* she'll print.'" She called Joe and told him of her decision; he went along with it reluctantly and decided also to talk to
Kilgallen.

It's characteristic of Carol, and has always been the way she's
handled any controversy in her life, to disclose the truth of a
potentially difficult situation before the media has an opportunity to distort the facts. In this straightforward, honest manner,
she would control so-called "gossip" pertaining to her private life
quite a few times in the next twenty years.

Carol called Dorothy Kilgallen the next morning and gave
her a frank and very upbeat interview. The article ran as a front-
page story in the August 31, 1962, issue of the *Journal,* with the
screaming red banner headline CAROL BURNETT IS IN LOVE WITH
A WONDERFUL GUY. The story was treated with all of the import of
a national news event; it was syndicated in newspapers all over
the country, including the Las Vegas *Sun.*

"America's favorite comedienne, Carol Burnett, is in love
with a wonderful guy," Kilgallen wrote, "and they expect to be
married 'when everything is straightened out.' The lucky fellow
is Joseph H. Hamilton, producer-director of the Garry Moore
TV show. From Las Vegas, Carol told me on the telephone, 'I'm
madly in love with him.' In New York, Joe said, 'The feeling is
mutual.'"

Kilgallen's article mentioned that Joe had approached his wife, the former Gloria Hartley, about a divorce, "and hoped it would not be too long before they come to an amicable agreement that would make it possible for him to marry Carol." She acknowledged the Hamilton children as ranging in age from thirteen to a year and a half, quoted an anonymous friend as saying that despite Joe's and Carol's discretion, "they might as well have sent up rockets saying 'we love each other' their romance was so obvious."

Considering the way she might have handled such a controversial situation, Kilgallen was quite generous in her report. She credited Joe's "encouragement and imagination" for helping to boost Carol's career "even though she has so much talent she would have made it big eventually.

"Carol is about as un-phony and normally blueberry pie as you can get and still stay in show business," she wrote. "She answers her own phone, and I'd bet money that she could make her own curtains."

It was fairly obvious that Kilgallen had been enchanted with Carol's honesty and was thrilled to be able to break this story. Carol handled the situation with great aplomb, and her charm completely won over Kilgallen. The gossip columnist even attempted to "protect" Carol by not mentioning in her article that Carol and Don were still legally married. Carol had set up residency in Las Vegas to obtain her divorce from Don, but the marriage wouldn't be officially over until September 25, 1962.

Don was in San Diego when Kilgallen's "exclusive" broke. Al Light, who had played piano for Don and Carol when they were "discovered" at that party in La Jolla, organized a summer-stock theater in San Diego and hired Don to perform; finally, he was working as an actor, and happier than he had been in a long time. Later, he went on to manage road tours for comics Rowan and Martin, and worked as part of the production team for *Rowan and Martin's Laugh-In* when that show aired on NBC in 1968.

"I had known Joe," he said, "because he'd been by our apartment at times. I thought it was a shame that Carol was drawing all of that criticism, going with a guy in a relationship that caused so many personal problems. Knowing her, I could imagine how sensitive she probably was to all of that. But people don't fall in love with other people always by choice...."

(Ironically enough, at around this time Don began dating Joe's sister Kipp Hamilton. "I used to joke with her that I was only seeing her waiting for the family reunion," he laughs. "We had fun, but that didn't last very long." In 1972, ten years after his divorce from Carol, Don married former stage actress Grace Rainer [DeWitts]. The two are still happily married today, with three daughters. Saroyan has given up his show-business aspirations and works a regular "sensible" job. About ten years after Don married Grace, she and Carol met in an elevator of the Wyndham Hotel in Manhattan. "You don't know me," Grace told Carol, "but we have something in common." Carol was perplexed until the woman added, "I'm married to Don Saroyan." They had a good laugh, and then, as they parted company, Carol said very graciously, "You are married to one of the most wonderful men in the world.")

Carol had considered the possible aftereffects of her interview with Dorothy Kilgallen, and decided that whatever the result, it was best to come out with the truth. Still, when the article was published and she actually saw it in black and white, she had to wonder if she'd done the right thing. "God, I hope they will understand..." she told friends with tears in her eyes. She was referring to Nanny, Chrissy, and the rest of her family, not to mention Joe's.

"I didn't want to say anything, but I don't see how we can hide something like this," she said. "Now that the cat is out of the bag, I guess it's just as well."

She didn't know it then, but she was in for one of the most difficult periods of her life.

12

"I don't plan to branch out in a regular TV series myself. Even if somebody came up with a smashing 'Carol Burnett Show,' I wouldn't do it. The last thing I want to do is shove myself down people's throats every week...."
—Carol Burnett to
The Saturday Evening Post,
1962

FOR THE NEXT YEAR, CAROL BURNETT WOULD BE FEELING HER way along, trying to decide just where she fit into the world of show business, how she could grow in her career and be happy doing it. She would have some false starts and also face some mean-minded criticism. That, combined with her personal problems, would make this time very trying for her.

Despite her very lucrative television deal, she still preferred stage work to TV. If she was to be a TV star, she would make her choices carefully. She was clear about what she would not do. For instance, she wouldn't do a TV series, especially one in which she'd play a regular role. "They'd probably name me Gertrude or Agnes, and that's all I'd be forever," she said.

She added, "I've been offered commercials, but I'll never do them unless I'm starving in the streets. You get identified as a car salesman or a soap salesman. It confuses fantasy with reality. I don't like it. You can make a bundle, but I'm not interested."

When theatrical producers Jule Styne and Lester Osterman approached Carol with a starring role in a Broadway play, she welcomed the opportunity. The show was called *The Unfair Sex,* and was based on Nina Farewell's 1953 book of the same name. Carol would portray the owner of a school in which she teaches girls about the "unfair sex"—men. Her motto is simple: "Marriage is the ultimate goal." (Nanny would have been proud.)

The play had not yet been adapted to the stage and a lyricist had not yet been hired when Carol made her decision. The only guarantee was that Jule Styne would compose the music, and that was enough for Carol. She said at the time that if Neil Simon was available, she'd like for him to adapt *The Unfair Sex* for the theater. Simon's *Come Blow Your Horn* had opened the year before on Broadway to critical acclaim.

It seemed like a good idea, but in the end it would never get off the ground (despite the fact that on October 10, 1962, *The New York Times* ran a major story on Carol's role in *The Unfair Sex).*

Carol was being offered a number of scripts, but probably the most interesting was one called *The Luckiest People,* based on the life of Fanny Brice. Jerome Robbins was director and choreographer of the David Merrick-Ray Stark attraction. Film producer Stark, who was Brice's son-in-law, had been trying to mount a Broadway musical based on her life after he hadn't been able to interest any Hollywood motion-picture studio in the story.

More than a couple of actresses were under consideration for the Fanny Brice role. First, Stark selected Mary Martin, but after lyricist Bob Merrill played her the songs, she decided that she didn't want anything to do with the show. Next, Stark approached Anne Bancroft, even though she seemed all wrong for the part. Bancroft agreed. She *was* all wrong. They asked Kaye Ballard to essay the role, but her schedule wouldn't permit her to take the job. In Jule Styne's autobiography, *Jule,* he wrote that Eydie Gorme was approached to star in the play, but that she wouldn't do it unless husband Steve Lawrence could appear as her love interest, Nicky Arnstein. Despite Lawrence's critical success on Broadway in *What Makes Sammy Run?* Styne didn't think of Lawrence as a musical-comedy performer.

"I remember the day the show's choreographer, Jerry Robbins, came over to talk to Carol about it," Joe Hamilton recalls. "I wasn't there at the time, but she told me that she loved the book. In fact, I still have the original script. By the time we got it, it was called *My Man.* It was a very funny libretto, but it had a lot of Jewish humor in it. And Carol never could carry off Jewish humor."

"It was flattering to be considered," Carol has said. "I gave it a lot of thought. It could be a huge hit. But I got to thinking about how it would be done. If the show concentrated on the dramatic events in Miss Brice's life, they needed a dramatic actress. If it dealt mostly with her as a performer, then they needed someone else who could work the way she did. I don't think I do. I ruled myself out."

Joe Hamilton says: "She told Jerry, 'You gotta look into a girl named Barbra Streisand.' We had seen Streisand do an interview with David Susskind, and she was kind of nutty. 'What you need is a nice Jewish girl like that,' Carol told him."

Tipped off by Carol, Jerry Robbins and Ray Stark discovered Barbra Streisand at the Bon Soir nightclub and cast her in the show. It was retitled *Funny Girl,* and the rest is history. "But Barbra doesn't admit to the fact that it was all Carol's idea," Joe Hamilton says with a grin. "And, of course, neither does Carol."

January 1962 began with the surprising announcement by *Variety* that Carol had been signed to costar in the Paramount film *Who's Been Sleeping in My Bed?* starring Dean Martin and Elizabeth Montgomery. When Carol was added to the cast, it was with the understanding that she would have an "Introducing" credit.

With a story by Jack Rose, the movie was to be directed by Daniel Mann, an odd choice since he was best known for his dramatic work in movies. This was one of those outrageous farces that Dean Martin excelled in.

The silly plot doesn't merit examination; suffice it to say that Martin played a doctor with a great sexual appetite, Montgomery his put-upon girl friend, and Burnett his well-meaning, flat-chested, man-chasing secretary, Stella Irving. Carol's biggest scene was a mock bump-and-grind strip. (The fifty extras were instructed beforehand to look as if they'd smelled something bad when Carol started taking off her clothing. "That wasn't a strip," she said later. "It was a fungus.")

Since Jack Rose found Carol "the funniest girl since Fanny Brice, bar none," it was decided to fatten her role in the film. So six of some of the worst scenes in the history of comedy were added, all featuring poor Carol.

When she was filming it, Carol was thrilled to be doing a major motion picture and joked that she should have tried this "movie stuff" earlier. "To think they poured thirty-five million into *Cleopatra* for Elizabeth Taylor when they could have had me for twenty-nine, ninety-five," she quipped.

"The movie was the hardest work I ever did," Carol has remarked, just a bit tongue-in-cheek. "You never know what you're doing. You get up at 6AM, challenge the make-up man for an hour or two, then you're on the set at 9 but don't start working until just before lunch break. After lunch, you do a three-minute scene and then it's time to go home."

Her friends were disappointed that the film Carol had chosen for her first movie was turning out so badly: the word was out before *Who's Been Sleeping in My Bed?* was even completed that it was a turkey. Upon its release, Carol would be more than a bit embarrassed by it.

In February 1963, *TV Guide* reporter Edith Efron wrote one of the more disturbing articles about Carol that had been published to date. Efron attempted to shoot holes in Carol's wholesome image by asking the suspicious question, "What is Carol Burnett *really* like?"

"Those who deal closely with her claim that her 'blueberry pie' normality is illusory," Efron wrote. "Her eager dedication to her career seems to be an iron wall that cuts her off from most of reality.... No one has ever heard Carol Burnett converse in a sustained fashion on any subject which does not relate in some way to the entertainment field."

Efron quoted Garry Moore as having said, "I don't believe we've talked more than two pages worth of anything but show business since I've known her." (Later, Garry would deny having made that statement.)

Efron also quoted Moore's analysis of Carol's comedy and, as he put it, "this making herself look ugly."

"According to a certain theory, it's this feeling of feminine inadequacy that drives women to become comics," Garry told Efron. "Carol lacks confidence. She is unsure of herself as a person." ("Yes, I did say that," Garry admitted, "because it was true and we all knew it.")

A CBS official who asked for anonymity added, "She's a pleasant, non-abrasive personality. No strong opinions on anything but her work. Off stage, she's a dullish girl."

Efron sniped, "It's not surprising that her romantic life has been troubled," and then went into detail about the turmoil surrounding Carol's relationship with Joe Hamilton.

"What did I *do* to deserve that article?" Carol sobbed to a friend when she read it. "It is *so* unfair. And Garry would never have said those things about me!"

"If anything, maybe she was developing a bit more backbone where that kind of stuff was concerned," Joe Hamilton observes. "But only a bit. When people said mean things about Carol, she'd pretty much shrivel up. She'd lie awake and feel awful all night long."

Carol was still stinging from the *TV Guide* feature when her first TV special for CBS aired on Sunday, February 24, 1963, and received fairly poor reviews. On *Carol and Company*, Carol's guests were Robert Preston and the comedy team of Allen and Rossi. Jack Gould of *The New York Times* preferred Preston to Burnett and wrote that "he walked off with whatever honors the evening allowed."

Gould also predicted trouble for Carol. In examining a counterpoint duet between her and Preston, he observed, "A harbinger of the difficulties that lie ahead for Burnett is that she was almost completely overshadowed throughout the number. Miss Burnett has a knack for mugging and vocal calisthenics, but on this occasion there was little of the sense of intuitive timing that is the stamp of the comedienne." (*"Ouch,"* Joe Hamilton said wryly when the review was read to him. "That hurt!")

Curiously, most critics preferred Carol's singing "Nobody" from her nightclub act to any of the comedy in the program.

It had been a rough month, and she wasn't feeling very optimistic by the time it was over. "It's scary to go on your own," she said. "I was coddled and protected, but there aren't many Garry Moores around. Most people in show business don't give a damn about you."

If there was a press backlash against Carol Burnett at this time, it was about to get worse.

In March, Carol told columnist Earl Wilson that she and Joe were going to stop seeing each other. "They felt the bad publicity was hurting his children and her sister," said Wilson. "But Joe was not so definite. He said he was hoping to obtain a divorce, that his wife had refused, but that if she relented he was not certain of the future."

"It was a tough time," says a friend of Carol's. "She was heartbroken that things were going so badly. But then, suddenly, it all turned around and Gloria decided that she would give Joe the divorce. They had reached a settlement that she was happy with, and she filed the papers. 'It's been very difficult,' Carol said at the time. 'This thing has gone on so long.' Gloria maintained custody of the children, but Joe had more than reasonable visitation rights."

On Saturday, May 4, 1963, Carol and Joe left New York on a flight headed to El Paso, Texas, and then on to Juárez, Mexico, where they would be married. Chrissy, now eighteen years old, went along as a witness to the ceremony. After their wedding, en route to their Hawaiian honeymoon (Chrissy went back to the East Coast), Carol and Joe stopped off at the Los Angeles airport and were besieged by photographers. There, they made the official announcement that they'd been married. "I am now Mrs. Joe Hamilton," Carol said, overjoyed, if not also a bit relieved.

"That's when it hit the fan," remembers Pat Lillie.

As soon as Carol and Joe were married, Joe's ex-wife and other members of his family began granting interviews in hopes of casting aspersions on the union. Earl Wilson wrote of a "rebellion against Carol by the sisters and mother of Joe Hamilton" in The New York Post. "The family is adamant against Joe's marriage to Carol," volunteered Joe's youngest sister, Kipp Hamilton, who was a regular contributor of articles to Catholic Digest. "Gloria is our family. We adore Joe, we love Gloria. We think Carol is a very talented performer, but this is family not show business. I can never accept her as my sister-in-law."

Kipp was also a television and theater actress at the time (she played opposite Robert Stack in Good Morning, Miss Dove, and with Burt Lancaster and Audrey Hepburn in The Unforgiven). She was married to the director of The Garry Moore Show, Dave Geisel.

In another interview, she said, "I simply refuse to see Carol. She's very nice; she's always been wonderful to me. But I have a sister-in-law in Gloria; a sister couldn't be closer to me. It would be very confusing if we had to divide our loyalty and love. If Carol's as sensitive as I think, she'll be hurt. But I'd rather hurt her than Gloria."

"We're a big family, and very close, so I guess it'll take a while for them to get used to it," Joe said to Earl Wilson by telephone from the Hawaiian Village Hotel.

"I am hardly the home-breaker type," Carol added.

"That's right. I initiated the whole thing," Joe concluded.

Carol told Wilson that she hadn't even met the whole family and that she hoped they would give her the opportunity to know them.

Worse than his sister's remarks were the emotion-wrought interviews Joe's ex-wife granted from the fifteen-room mansion Hamilton had purchased for her and the children in the affluent suburb of Scarsdale, north of Manhattan. Her comments to writer George Carpozi painted a fairly one-sided, rather damaging portrait of Carol as a home-wrecker. The former Mrs. Hamilton was described as a "pretty, petite ninety-pound blonde, elegantly trim and stylish and with a stark resemblance to Marilyn Monroe." She was understandably hurt that her fifteen-year marriage had ended; she was bitter at the time, and her words were cutting.

"Carol was deeply hurt by all of it," Joe Hamilton says. "The fact that the stories were absolutely untrue didn't help any. My marriage was dead before Carol even appeared on the scene."

"Once and for all, Carol Burnett did not break up Joe Hamilton's marriage," Pat Lillie insists. "Joe had been separated from Gloria several times before he started seeing Carol. Nobody wanted to believe that at the time because it was more sensational to believe the worst: A vixen comes in and breaks up a man's marriage and his family of eight children. But it simply was not true."

"Almost overnight, stock in Carol Burnett began to tumble," wrote Nora Ephron in *Ladies' Home Journal.*

Ephron was nevertheless one of the press people who supported Carol during this troubling time. "The uncertainties involved in her choice of a man to fall in love with, and the sorrow that their plans were built on the pain of others, have been an almost crushing private burden to her this winter," she wrote. "For...she is nice. She really is."

As controversy swirled around her, Carol tried to keep her sanity. "What's so awful about all of this," she said at the time, "is that I'd hate to hurt one child. But eight?"

She wouldn't say much more than that to the media. "I won't talk about it because of Joe's children and my sister," she said bluntly. "Oh, I know your private life isn't your own, and you have to realize that if you're going to be in show business. But why must they write such awful things?"

The controversy over Carol's relationship with Joe would surface every now and then in press interviews throughout their twenty-year marriage. Mostly, Carol refused to discuss the matter. "When you dredge things up, everything seems to be uglier than it was," she said in one interview (1968). "Things are great with Joe's kids now, and I wouldn't want to say anything to spoil it. I'd just as soon forget the whole subject."

Eighteen years after her marriage to Joe, Carol would admit, "The connection between us was absolutely instantaneous. Joe is...sexy. What can I tell you?"

The reporter asked what Carol would do if she discovered that Joe was seeing another woman. Her response was, "I'd sit him down and say, 'Listen, Joe, do you want to be with her all the time?' And if he said 'yes,' I'd say, 'Joe, *do* it.' Because I love him. And I believe that if you truly love someone, you want him to be happy. And if *you're* not making him happy, then you're glad for him to find somebody who will."

After the marriage, Carol and Joe moved into Carol's large Seventy-second Street apartment. They discussed tentative plans to buy a house in Connecticut, but meanwhile, it was back to work.

In late May 1963, Carol found the theatrical property she'd been looking for, a Jule Styne musical from a story by Betty Comden and Adolph Green called *A Girl to Remember.* The book, about a girl mistakenly caught up in a thirties Broadway-style extravaganza, sounded like a lot of fun, and Carol loved the songs. When George Abbott was brought in as director, Carol immediately agreed to do the play. With her name on the contract, the producers were able to secure a substantial three-hundred-thousand-dollar investment from ABC-Paramount. (ABC-Paramount invested $1 million in three Lester Osterman productions: *High Spirits,* Sammy Fain's *Something More,* and *A Girl to Remember*—all three of which were destined for problems that would cause the conglomerate to reassess its future theatrical investments.)

In June, theaters were booked for trial runs in New Haven and Boston for *A Girl to Remember,* and then it would be on to

Broadway for a November 23 opening at the Mark Hellinger Theatre.

"I'll be in the same dressing room that Julie Andrews had when she was doing *My Fair Lady,*" Carol enthused to friends. "I hope it's as good for me...."

The outlook for *A Girl to Remember* seemed hopeful, but then Carol discovered that she was pregnant. She was thrilled about having her first child, but now the show would have to wait, because the baby was due in February. Carol told the disappointed producers that she would be available for rehearsals as early as March, and that the play could then open in May. Though they didn't know it at the time, this snafu was just the tip of an iceberg of problems that were to plague this show.

Ever anxious to taint Carol's "good girl" image, some members of the media speculated about the exact circumstances of Carol's pregnancy. New York *World Telegram and Sun* columnist Frank Farrell claimed that the delivery date for the baby would actually be "around Christmas time." He assured his readers that Carol's condition was "evident weeks ago, though she and Hamilton have been married scarcely a month."

"My goodness," Carol told a reporter for *Newsweek.* "I guess I should have gone to *him* instead of to a doctor."

Meanwhile, Lester Osterman tried to pick up the pieces of *A Girl to Remember.* "We had the biggest advance sale that had ever happened up until that date in the American theater," he recalls. "Then we had to postpone the play and give back all of that money. All I remember was sitting on the floor with my general manager and my accountant while sending back something like a million dollars in checks. Yes, I remember that well," he says, laughing. "Also, we had to pay twenty-thousand-dollars to the Mark Hellinger Theatre for two weeks' rental of the theater, as well as payments to the other theaters we had reserved. We also had to pay the actors who'd been hired, for the time they'd set aside to do the show. And there were other production expenses. So we were losing money, and the show hadn't even opened yet."

In some respects, the delay was welcome. Jule Styne was preoccupied with severe financial problems at this time because of poor investments and tax problems. Also, Styne was confronted by another set of problems regarding Barbra Streisand. Streisand wasn't scheduled to open in his *Funny Girl* until March 1964, but, says a friend, "Jule was already tearing his hair out over her. Streisand's demands over who she would and would not work with on the stage drove him nuts. Carol's delay wasn't a problem for Jule...it was welcome."

On June 24, 1963, Carol opened a two-week engagement at the Dallas State Fair Theatre in the title role of *Calamity Jane*. The performances were test runs for Carol's second CBS-TV special, a taped presentation based on the 1953 Doris Day film, which Carol claimed to have seen "at least sixty-five times." She could recite almost every word of dialogue before they went into rehearsal. Writer Phil Shuken and Joe Hamilton revised the show constantly during its fourteen performances, trying to hone it for the television taping.

During the engagement of *Calamity Jane* in Dallas, Nanny joined Carol for a brief vacation. She basked in the glow of Carol's limelight. "Yes, I'm the reason Carol always tugs on her left ear," she proudly told the *Lawton Constitution* reporter who covered the *Calamity Jane* opening. "It's all because of me."

During the second week in July 1963, *Calamity Jane* was taped in playlike fashion, in black and white, with simple props and set design. The show couldn't compare to the lavish Doris Day movie, but Carol was believable and often funny as the ugly-duckling pistol-packing cowgirl who learns to be a woman the hard way, by falling in love (with Wild Bill Hickok, played by Art Lund).

Carol had a wonderful time doing the show in front of a live audience. Most observers felt, though, that she was robbed of a big moment, the "Secret Love" finale, when it was decided that she and Lund should perform the number as a duet. In the film, Doris Day sang the Academy-Award-winning song in a lilting, coy fashion. Carol belted it out in big voice and was then joined by Lund. The effect was anticlimactic.

The commercials were almost more memorable than the November 12 evening broadcast, which preempted *The Garry Moore Show.* In one advertisement, announcer George Fenneman was seen teaching an Indian the joys of Lipton tea. Finally convinced, the Indian decided at the end of the demonstration, "Me sooner Lipton." "Me, too," Fenneman concluded.

Carol's bad-luck streak with the media continued when *Calamity Jane* was greeted with a general thumbs-down from the critics. "There is a decided lack of originality about this show," panned *Daily Variety*. "Carol Burnett is an energetic entertainer, but ninety minutes of elaborate mugging and goofy guffaws gets pretty monotonous."

An article in *TV Guide* at this time did nothing to help Carol's public-relations image. Someone had the misguided idea of featuring her as a model of "at-home clothing" in four most unusual and uncomfortable Bill Blass designs. In the photographs, she was seen reclining on two pedestals and looking extremely awkward, wearing a brown wig, her mouth upturned in an odd smirk.

The backlash continued. An article in *Life* magazine made Carol seem more than a bit foolish when it came to handling financial matters. The writer said that she never paid attention to the amount of money she made, and at the end of the month she stuffed all of her statements in manila envelopes and into a bureau drawer without so much as a glance. "Which, I think, was probably true," Joe Hamilton says. "She used to tell me that she had worried so much about money when she was growing up, she wasn't going to worry about it when she was finally making some."

"She put together her summertime revue with such blithe disregard for economics, she soon found everybody on the show was making money except for her," wrote Ernest Haveman in the feature.

"Not true," Bob Banner claims. "First of all, she didn't put together the revue, we did, and secondly, we would never have allowed her not to make money on it. It was just the writer's conception of Carol as a know-nothing. More bad press where we were concerned."

Despite this bad press, Carol remained in good spirits because of the excitement of being pregnant. She went into labor on Saturday, December 5. She was taken to St. Clare's Hospital in New York, where Carrie Louise Hamilton was born.

"I was the first one other than Joe and Carol to see Carrie Louise," Pat Lillie says with a grin. "I came to the hospital with Joe the day after she was born and gave Carol a special present —a rubber pillow covered in sequins that spelled out 'OUCH!' "

Carol relished her new role as a mother and spent most of the next few months pampering Carrie. Things were going well, but then Carol's film debut came back to haunt her. She and Joe went to see *Who's Been Sleeping in My Bed?* at the Victoria 72nd Street Playhouse, and, as she had suspected all along, she was terrible in it.

"I should have been given the award for 'Worst Performance Ever Given in Movies by an Actress,'" she said. "I was confused, bored and I missed the audience. Nothing was spontaneous. If CBS ever shows it on their late show, I'll break my contract," she threatened, only half jokingly.

The movie was released to ambivalent reviews.

"It's so awful, it shouldn't have been shot but rather sliced and served with stuffing and cranberry sauce," wrote one critic.

"[She] utilizes her clowning and mugging abilities to advantage in a part that needs all the help she can give it," declared *Variety.* "Done with admirable restraint and the best kind of suggestiveness is a bit in which she is forced into doing a striptease number."

"Carol hates that movie with a passion," Pat Lillie says. "She doesn't even like to bring it up in conversation."

"I don't think of it as a bad career move," Joe Hamilton notes. "She had to start somewhere if she wanted to be in films. But Carol was sort of stunned by how bad she was in it. After that, she lost her enthusiasm for movies, which was probably just as well."

A couple of years later, Carol's costar in the film, Elizabeth Montgomery, was seated in Carol's TV studio audience with her husband, *Bewitched* director William Asher. "Guess what!" Montgomery asked Carol during the show's warm-up spot. "They showed our movie on an airplane we were on recently. And there were eight walkouts!"

During rehearsals for *A Girl to Remember,* George Abbott, working on his 104th play, and the producers changed the title, first to *The Idol of Millions* and then to *Fade Out–Fade In* to avoid three-way confusion among their shows *The Girl Who Came to Supper* and *Funny Girl.* Carol didn't mind; she said that she wasn't too thrilled with the original title anyway. "Wouldn't that have left the door open for critics to write, 'A girl to remember is a girl to forget'?" she asked, just a bit pessimistically.

Rehearsals for the show began on Monday, March 23, 1964, at the Mark Hellinger Theatre on West Fifty-first Street. The show would open on April 18 in New Haven, and then go on to

Boston on April 28 for four weeks before the Broadway opening
at the Mark Hellinger on May 26.

In the musical *Fade Out-Fade In*, Carol played Hope Springfield, described in Comden and Green's libretto as "modestly at-
tired, gawkingly charming and always a little self-deprecatingly
embarrassed. She is far from ugly, but exactly the opposite of
Hollywood oomph and glamour."

The show, a broad satire lampooning the gaudy experience
of the 1930's, was really old-hat in many ways *(Once in a Lifetime*
used the same premise and to better purpose.) But the songs,
costumes, and performances brought the show to life as far as
many observers were concerned.

"Even though it wasn't destined to be the biggest musical of
all time, it was quite a spectacular show," recalls Bill Hargate, who
assisted in designing costumes for *Fade Out-Fade In*. "In fact, it
was probably one of the last of the big Broadway-style musicals of
that era. It was very heavily costumed, and we all agreed that
Carol was wonderful. But when we saw the reviews in New
Haven, we knew we were in trouble. They were terrible."

One critic called the show "an antiquated book, a literary
chestnut, indeed," when it opened at the Shubert Theatre in
New Haven, and added, "there is considerable polishing yet to be
accomplished."

Joe Hamilton accompanied Carol to the pre-Broadway
tryouts in Connecticut and in Boston. The couple also brought
along seventeen-week-old Carrie Louise and a nurse to take care
of her when Carol was onstage.

At first, Joe decided to keep his opinion about the musical to
himself. "*Fade Out* was like every other musical when it opened
out of town—it was in trouble. But even *My Fair Lady* was in
trouble in out-of-town tryouts, so that was no surprise. Whenever
Carol was doing a show with another producer, I would purposely reserve my opinions because I knew how mad I got when
stars who had producer-husbands would try to interfere in my
shows.

"But I thought to myself after seeing Carol in *Fade Out*,
'Jeez, this really needs a hell of a lot of work.' It was a show that I
don't think she really ever enjoyed much. There were a couple of
moments that were hysterical, but the rest of it was mediocre. I
didn't think the show was good for her, and maybe she wasn't
particularly good for the show. But in those out-of-town tryouts,

things were so tense already, I am sure I never discussed these feelings with Carol. It would have been bad timing. . . . I kept my nose out of it."

Carol didn't need Joe's input. She knew the show was in trouble. It's been said by people close to the show that Carol felt that the problems with it were as much in its staging as in its score. "I think she had some artistic differences with Mr. Abbott when they were out-of-town," producer Lester Osterman recalls. "He was directing it one way, and she wanted to do things that she was more comfortable with. I don't know who was right or wrong.

"What finally came out onstage, without being any *Gone With the Wind*, worked. I don't think it was the greatest script I ever read, or the greatest score," Osterman concludes. "But Carol, Dick Patterson, Lou Jacobi, and the rest made it work; a funny, stupid kind of play that would probably be a smash today. She was at the height of her popularity, and we were thrilled to have her in the show."

Carol had hoped to convince the producers that the material was weak, that major changes were needed, new songs if possible. She wanted the Broadway opening delayed.

But Lester Osterman and Jule Styne had planned to open the show in New York during the World's Fair of 1964. Canceling it now would mean a major loss in possible revenue, and they had already lost a great deal of money when the show was postponed the first time. Plus, if there were any problems with the show, perhaps the producers felt they were being ironed out judging by the reviews in Boston when the musical played the Colonial Theatre. "Carol is just great and she's found herself a good show that will run as long as she wants to be in it which should be practically forever," said the *Boston Herald* write-up.

George Abbott recalls: "I never take out-of-town problems very seriously, and I didn't with *Fade Out-Fade In*. I told the cast, 'If it fails, it fails. There's no sense in going to the wailing wall and hitting your head against it. Just do your best. . . .' But I knew it wasn't the greatest vehicle for Carol or for anyone else involved. Still, we were committed to it. 'God help us,' I said to myself in New Haven."

Divine intervention or not, the next stop was Broadway.

13

"You know me, the little girl with the funny face who always wanted to be a Broadway star. Not any more. Television is so much more exciting than any other medium. I'll take TV."
—Carol Burnett
to Cecil Smith
Los Angeles Times,
September 4, 1964

TUESDAY EVENING, MAY 26, 1964. *FADE OUT-FADE IN* OPENED AT the Mark Hellinger Theatre on Broadway. A gala opening-night party for the cast was held at the Grand Ballroom of Delmonico's on Park Avenue.

This marked the fourth major production with music written by Jule Styne—the man who gave Broadway the music for *Gypsy, Bells Are Ringing, Gentlemen Prefer Blondes,* and dozens more—to open in New York in a four-month period: Styne's *Funny Girl* had debuted on March 26 at the Winter Garden to morning-after accolades that hailed Barbra Streisand as the Broadway "find" of the season; *What a Way to Go,* a Shirley Mac-Laine film for which Styne provided the score, was playing in theaters around Manhattan and across the country; "Wonder World," a World's Fair attraction in New York, was using eleven of his songs. Styne was coproducer as well as the composer of *Fade Out-Fade In*.

Despite his much-publicized tax woes and indebtedness, Styne seemed to be at a professional peak. Still, the opening of *Fade Out-Fade In* did not meet all expectations. "We only had half the advance ticket sales we had before we postponed the show," coproducer Lester Osterman recalls. "But still, the show opened successfully and was selling out, making between eleven thousand and eighteen thousand dollars a week, which in those days was a lot of money. We were satisfied."

They had good reason to be. With a gross of nearly ninety thousand dollars for its opening week, *Fade Out* broke the house record at the Mark Hellinger (which housed *My Fair Lady),* and at the same time became the highest-grossing show in town.

Nevertheless, Carol was allegedly still unhappy and wanted revisions. At this time, Jule Styne had his hands full with the Barbra Streisand vehicle *Funny Girl.* Since *Fade Out* was holding its own, he was reluctant to devote any attention to revisions. Carol was disappointed. Says Bob Wright, a Carol Burnett confidant: "She was unhappy because she couldn't get the producer's attention; she still felt her show was weak. But she had a contract and intended to honor it."

Styne, Abbott, Burnett, and most of the others associated with *Fade Out-Fade In* have the misconception that the play was given terrible reviews. Styne himself has said, "The Burnett show was a project that wisdom should have sent to the shelf." But actually reviews for the show were mostly positive in New York, and the reaction to Carol was overwhelming.

In *The New York Times,* Howard Taubman wrote that the play "spreads enough good cheer to suggest that it will be around for quite a while." Of Carol, he wrote, "There is no exhausting this girl's amiable zest or genial comedic impudence.... When she is on stage, the show is easy to take...."

The *Journal American*'s John McClain wrote, "...the magnificent madness of Miss Burnett, and the ubiquitous pace and precision of Ole Massa Abbott's staging, boots the show home a winner. It seems an assured smash."

Variety proclaimed: "It should be a hit for Broadway and the road, has the makings of a lively picture and is a potential item for stock. (*Variety* also praised Carol as being "practically a show in herself.")

Recalls Bob Wright: "Carol *was Fade Out-Fade In* and, in my opinion, some animosity slowly started building on the producers' side because they weren't getting any attention for their show. Carol was overshadowing them and the play. There were ego clashes early on."

Despite whatever was festering behind the scenes, *Fade Out-Fade In* seemed off to a good start, even though there were some unusual early mishaps. The day after the play opened, during hectic preparation for a Wednesday matinee, Carol forgot to put on a chemise under the dress that gets ripped off by the fans in the Chinese Theatre scene. She realized her blunder when it was too late to do anything about it, so when the actors tore off her clothes she was left standing on the Broadway stage in her everyday underwear. Panicking, she shrieked and threw herself to the stage floor. The audience cheered wildly, thinking it was all part of the show. The next day, the cast printed up a phony newspaper with the headline: BUBBLES BURNETT BARES ALL AT SIZZLING MATINEE.

By the beginning of June, ABC Records, which had cofinanced the show, issued the original-cast recording of *Fade Out-Fade In*. Also, to help promote the show, Carol recorded a wonderful album of Jule Styne standards for Decca called "Let Me Entertain You." The album, with orchestra conducted by Harry Zimmerman, included songs such as "Everything's Coming Up Roses," "Just in Time," and Carol's *Once Upon a Mattress* audition piece, "Everybody Loves to Take a Bow."

Carol's third CBS-TV special aired on Wednesday, June 3, 1964. Bob Banner and Associates decided to take the Broadway production of *Once Upon a Mattress* and tape it as a TV event, with the original cast and a few added attractions like Elliott Gould as the Jester. Joe Layton choreographed the show and codirected it with Dave Geisel. Joe Hamilton produced.

Carol and Joe were very disappointed with the network's decision to broadcast the program in black and white instead of in color; black and white now seemed passé to them. But the network didn't want to invest in a color broadcast.

When the show aired, in Garry Moore's time slot, it was the first time an actress starring in a current Broadway show was seen on national television performing another Broadway production. Critical reaction to the TV version of *Mattress* ranged from mediocre to poor. *Daily Variety* reported, "The vehicle is too flimsy to sustain interest...just a fair piece of froth."

By the end of June, Carol was decidedly ambivalent about *Fade Out-Fade In*. She told friends that she might have made a mistake when she committed to a two-year contract, that the musical was still not up to her expectations and was even frustrating to do. Though the theater was such a prestigious medium and had always been her dream, the novelty of reciting the same words and singing the same songs every night was wearing thin, especially since she wasn't happy with the material. Doing this show eight times a week was becoming a grind. Joe was negotiating a new television series with CBS-TV, and he wanted her to be a part of it. Could she do both? Or would that be pushing her endurance? she wondered.

In an interview with *The New York Times* that appeared on June 7, 1964, she seemed to be suggesting that if *Fade Out-Fade In* closed, she wouldn't be devastated by its failure. "I'm a fatalist," she observed. "The world does not revolve around me or my career or, in this case, this musical. It looks as though the show will run a long, long time, but if it doesn't, it's been an exciting experience."

"It's always a bad sign," notes one observer, "when the star of a major show begins hinting that maybe the show can continue without her, that it does not really revolve around her. If an entertainer wants to be considered indispensable to a production, she doesn't suggest otherwise. Barbra Streisand never would have, where *Funny Girl* was concerned. But, of course, there was a big difference between *Fade Out-Fade In* and *Funny Girl*."

On July 10, 1964, coming home after a Friday-evening performance, Carol was involved in a taxicab accident. Carol's driver was forced to brake suddenly in order to avoid a collision. The cab screeched to a halt; Carol was thrown forward. When she got home, she began experiencing some pain in her neck. It seemed like a classic case of whiplash.

The next morning, the pain was so severe, she called in sick. One of her understudies, Carolyn Kemp, filled in for both of the day's performances. The audience rebelled against the unexpected switch with a mad rush to the box office for $11,000 in ticket refunds.

Carol's personal physician, Dr. William Zahm, discovered that she had aggravated a herniated disc in her neck, an injury she'd sustained years earlier while doing a pratfall. This, combined with whiplash, was causing extreme pressure on her spine. "She has an extra vertebra in her neck," Joe Hamilton says of Carol. "That's why her neck is so long. Somehow, I think that was involved as well."

The doctor put Carol in a neck brace (she hated it and called it a "horse collar") and suggested that she quit *Fade Out-Fade In* and take a much-needed rest. Carol thought it over for a few days, but decided against leaving the show.

"I didn't want to go," she said, "because I didn't want to hang up the cast and the producers. I had said that the musical didn't revolve around me, but, still the audiences were asking for their money back when I wasn't there. I knew I had to go back."

She said later, after a performance, "Sometimes I feel like I look like a monster to the audience. I'm bent over and I can't straighten out. But if they want me that way, they'll get me."

"I remember that Carol felt terrible about not being able to go on," recalls stand-in Mitzie Welch. "I saw her in great pain. She went on as long as she possibly could, and did not hold back on her performances even though she was hurting."

At the end of July, matters were complicated when Carol had to have minor surgery in her doctor's office for a postmotherhood condition. She went to Bermuda for a week to recuperate. Carolyn Kemp and Mitzie Welch understudied for her. Osterman then decided to try to replace Carol until she could return. He tried to persuade Sheila MacRae to take over the role; she turned him down. Finally, Jule Styne contacted Betty Hutton, whose name went up on the marquee.

George Abbott recalls: "I didn't think it was a good idea. She didn't have Carol's naiveté. As much as I like Betty, she is not a Carol Burnett type. But we needed a star, and she was a star."

Hutton was having emotional and physical problems at the time, and many felt that Styne had offered her the role as a gesture of kindness. She arrived in New York on July 15 and took over as Hope Springfield, with little rehearsal, on Monday evening, July 27.

Unfortunately, as it turned out, casting Betty Hutton in the Carol Burnett role was a disaster. Not only wasn't she adequate in the part, no one wanted to see her do it. "Ticket sales for the eight performances collapsed as if the box office was quarantined," reported *Variety*. "It's the biggest star-replacement box-office slump in Broadway history."

"Sales took a nose dive from eighty-five-thousand dollars to something like twenty-thousand dollars a week," remembers Lester Osterman. "It was a terrible error in judgment."

Don Crichton, a dancer in the show, remembers: "Betty was very nervous and never really learned the role well. She was frantic about it. Sometimes she would fall out of character and talk to the audience. I felt terrible for her, and after it was all over I got a twenty-eight-page letter from her about the experience. She was devastated by it, and very sorry."

"One of her woman fans had come 700 miles just to see Carol Burnett," a box-office employee reported to a New York newspaper. "She burst into tears in the lobby when I told her that Miss Burnett would not appear. This is a one-woman Carol Burnett show."

Carol returned to the show on August 3 even though Lester Osterman's doctor suggested she take two more weeks off to recuperate from her dual ailments. Ticket sales boomed again, up to over ten thousand dollars at the box office Carol's first night back (as compared to four thousand dollars the show made on Betty's last night). But by now she was very disenchanted with the demands of being a theater star. She felt sick and needed time off, but she couldn't get it. It began to color her perception of Broadway business, and she spoke about it in negative terms to a newspaper reporter. "There's just no magic in it," she said. "Television has the magic. Boy, how I missed that tube. And I didn't know it until I got away from it. . . ."

By the end of the summer, Carol had agreed to star in a new CBS-TV series called *The Entertainers*. Repertory entertainment —a tradition in the theater—was new to television and had been an experiment on Tuesday nights with an NBC series starring actor Richard Boone; the same cast of actors played different roles every week. Bob Banner and Joe Hamilton thought this concept would work well in variety entertainment, and suggested the idea to CBS.

CBS was anxious to have Carol star in a weekly series, and at first they wanted to call it *The Carol Burnett Show*. She vetoed that idea. The timing was all wrong, and she was certain she couldn't handle her own show while committed to working on Broadway. Perhaps the wiser decision would have been to bow out of the series completely, but instead it was decided that she would share hosting duties with comedian Bob Newhart and singer Caterina Valente.

To most observers, it didn't seem like Carol could possibly juggle the TV series, even with her diminished participation, and her Broadway show. There seemed to be only one way out, but it would cost money. Nonetheless, Carol decided to make her move. Lester Osterman doesn't like talking about the ensuing negotiations, but he reluctantly replays the day Carol asked him to come to her and Joe's nineteenth-floor apartment on Seventy-second Street and Second Avenue to have a drink.

After some small talk, they got down to business.

Carol began cautiously. "Lester, exactly how much money is involved in this play?" she asked.

Osterman wasn't sure what she was getting at. "The capitalization is about three hundred thousand dollars," he answered, a puzzled look on his face.

Carol paused. "You know, I haven't been well," she said. "I'm really tired, Lester. Joe and I have talked about the possibility of my pulling out of the show. Would you take that amount for me to withdraw?"

"Three hundred thousand dollars!" Osterman exclaimed. "Carol, you're *crazy*! Where the hell are you going to get that much money? You're only making, what? Eighty-six hundred a week doing the show."

"Well, this is extremely important to me," Carol answered very deliberately. "I'm willing to pay to get out of the show. I think that's the only fair way to do it. In fact, my offer is five hundred thousand."

Lester grimaced. He was at a loss for words. "Gee, Carol, I don't know just how to evaluate this," he answered. All I can do is report your offer back to Jule [Styne], Betty [Comden] and Adolph [Green], and ABC-Paramount. I'll get back to you on it."

"Well, what do you think?" Carol urged. "I mean, how do you *feel* about this?"

"To tell you the truth, Carol," he responded, "I don't think I've ever heard of this being done before. But if you want out of the show, I'll relay the message. Your offer is almost double the initial capitalization. That seems more than fair. Are you absolutely sure about this?"

"Yes, I am," Carol said with determination.

Lester Osterman today recalls: "The discussion was very friendly. I believe Carol said at one point that she would be able to get the money from CBS; she had that big deal with the network. She definitely wanted out of the show. She never expressed anything particularly negative about it to me, just that she did not want to continue with it."

Osterman went to his partners with Carol's request. He said that ABC-Paramount agreed with him that they should accept

Carol's offer. "Jule Styne said, 'Do whatever you want,'" he remembers. "But authors Betty Comden and Adolph Green, who
were also partners in the play, felt that the show was making all
of this money and that it showed no inclination of slowing down,
and that it could be worth a lot of future money. They said they
wouldn't go for it.

"You know, I don't think this is very intelligent," Lester Osterman remembers telling Comden and Green. "Accept Carol's
offer."

Comden and Green refused, saying that too much of Carol's
offer would have to go to pay off cast members who had run-of-
the-play contracts. After expenses, they claimed, they still
wouldn't get their investments back.

Osterman went back to Carol and told her that her offer had
been rejected. He did not identify exactly which of the parties
turned it down, just that she had to continue with the show.
There was a lot at stake, not just box-office revenue but the future of the actors, crew, and theater employees.

"She was bitterly disappointed," says a friend, "but she decided
that she would bite the bullet and just stick with the show. Joe
was angrier about it than Carol; he thought that if she wanted a
release, she should have been given one for that kind of money."

Unfortunately, Carol's secret plan was somehow leaked to
the press. Mike Connoly reported in the *World Telegram* on September 8, 1964, "Carol Burnett offered the producers of her
Broadway musical the fantastic sum of $500 thousand to release
her from the show. Carol claims it's one of those 'or else' emer-
gencies. Meaning she just can't continue shooting her new TV
series, "The Entertainers," on the side in addition to having any
kind of home life with her husband and their child. She must
really mean it, a whole half million dollars worth." His report was
verified by *The New York Times*.

Carol's offer was certainly more than generous. Richard
Burton was released from *Camelot* in September 1962 by paying
only fifty thousand dollars to the show's producers. He wanted to
leave the production in order to go to Hollywood and star as
Marc Antony opposite Elizabeth Taylor in *Cleopatra*. Similarly,
for a mere thirty-five thousand dollars, David Merrick let Anthony Quinn out of *Becket* in 1960 so that he could film *Barabbas*
in Rome. At around this time, Elizabeth Ashley managed to get
out of *Barefoot in the Park* for only thirty-five thousand dollars,

money which she had to borrow, so that she could continue her then-blossoming film career.

This isn't to say that such situations are always pleasant and amicable. They usually are not. Most entertainers aren't able to leave their shows until their contracts expire. Barbra Streisand and Carol Channing never missed a performance of *Funny Girl* and *Hello, Dolly!* respectively, even though both had expressed an eagerness to move on to other projects. (Streisand was absolutely bored to death with her show after the first six months.)

On Friday, September 25, 1964, the first segment of *The Entertainers* was telecast. Much to Joe and Carol's chagrin, CBS would only allow the show to be taped in black and white. The Hamiltons still weren't able to convince CBS that color television was the wave of the future. The show was taped an hour before telecast to achieve the spontaneity of a live performance. This meant that Carol would have to perform in the series and then run across the street to the Mark Hellinger for her 8:30 curtain. *The Entertainers* would air from 8:30 to 9:30, simultaneously with her Broadway performance. The next day, Saturday, she was expected to do a matinee show and an evening performance at the Mark Hellinger. Of course, rehearsals for *The Entertainers*, and for changes in *Fade Out-Fade In*, were daily. She also had a heavy schedule of press interviews, photo sessions, and other business commitments.

How could she carry this work load? "That's just the point," she told writer Robert Wahls. "I don't want to disappoint anyone. I have signed my contracts. I am an adult and I'll have to try to go through with them. There's no way out."

If anything, the problem with *The Entertainers* was that there was too little of Carol Burnett and too much of everyone else. There were three hosts, and Jack Burns, Dom DeLuise, Ruth Buzzi, and John Davidson all made their first TV appearances on the show, not to mention guest stars and a troupe of dancers. On the first show, Carol appeared in a brief opening sketch, made an introduction, and wasn't seen again until the second half hour.

In the ratings game, *The Entertainers* was beaten by *The Addams Family* on ABC, and by Bob Hope's *Chrysler Theatre* on NBC.

Daily Variety called the show "an unwieldy smorgasbord" and predicted its quick demise.

On Monday night, October 12, Carol's neck injury flared up and she missed another performance of *Fade Out-Fade In*. Mitzie Welch substituted. By now, Carol had missed fifteen performances. Of a capacity gross of $11,500, refunds amounted to more than half ($6,500) when Welch performed.

"It was a nightmare," Mitzie recalls. "A terrific experience for me, if I was the type who didn't mind losing any self-esteem I might have had. I would be standing backstage ready to go on, when they would announce that the role of Hope Springfield was to be played by Mitzie Welch. I could then hear the entire audience moan, drop their programs in the aisles, and storm out of the theater."

"Carol was totally exhausted by this time," Don Crichton remembers. "She was very ill. I was with her in the apartment once, and she just broke down. 'What am I going to do?' she cried. 'I can't even get to the theater, how can I perform?'"

She talked it over with Joe; the course of action seemed obvious. The next day, she announced that she was dropping out of *Fade Out-Fade In* and suspending all of her other activities, including *The Entertainers*, after Friday's theater performance and TV taping. She would check into the Hospital for Joint Diseases on Tuesday, October 19, for an indefinite period of time. Her doctors decided to place her in traction for as long as it would take to treat the problem with her cervical vertebrae.

"I was very worried about her health," Joe Hamilton remembers. "To me, that was more important than the show, than the producers, than anything else. It was very personal, and sometimes personal matters interfere with business, but that's just the way it goes."

Where *The Entertainers* was concerned, Bob Banner and Associates was pressured by sponsors because without Carol Burnett, there really was no show. "When they would announce that Carol Burnett would not be performing, there was always a big pall over the audience," one fan of the show remembers. "People from out of town would wait for tickets...they didn't come to see Caterina Valente."

"Yes, we will try to get a replacement," Lester Osterman said unhappily to the press when asked about the future of *Fade Out-Fade In*. "Or maybe close until she recovers to fulfill the remainder of her year's contract with us, which expires in January 1966 [nineteen months away]."

Even though Carol's representatives stated that she was in traction six hours a day, Lester Osterman, Betty Comden, Adolph Green, and Jule Styne didn't believe she was as sick as everyone in Carol's entourage was saying she was. ("I did what I could to stay out of it," George Abbott said later. "My job with the show was over.") The four partners instructed their attorney, Herrick K. Lindstrom, to do whatever was necessary to force Carol to continue in the play. So on the morning of Wednesday, October 21, a hearing was held before Justice Samuel Hofstadter to enjoin CBS from airing *The Entertainers*. If Carol couldn't appear on Broadway, she should not be permitted to appear on television, even if those appearances had been taped in advance, Osterman and Styne argued.

Also, they approached Actors' Equity and asked the counsel to inform Carol of her contractual obligations to the show and to the 130 people it employed. A hearing was scheduled for November 20.

"Joe was infuriated by all of this," says a friend of his. "He thought their actions were contemptible. The producers dared to impugn his wife's motives, showed none of the paternalistic concern for Carol's health he thought they should have. And, also, any appearance Carol made on *The Entertainers* was brief and more a courtesy to the sponsors than anything else. At first, Carol was amazed, then confused and hurt."

It must have been a public-relations ploy, and an unfortunate one at that, dreamed up by somebody in Carol's camp, to have her photographed in her bed at the Hospital for Joint Diseases, in traction and looking pitiful while watching herself in a taped segment on TV in *The Entertainers*. The photo ran in all of the New York papers on October 24, 1964, and smacked of exploitation.

Also, it could be argued that her appearances on *The Entertainers* at this time were the result of very poor judgment. They only served to exacerbate an already tense situation between Carol and her theatrical producers. When Carol made two appearances on *The Entertainers* from her hospital bed while recovering from what the producers told the press was "an alleged injury," the cameos served to engender more hostility.

When the judge finally ruled on *The Entertainers* case, he

ruled in Carol's favor but reserved his decision on future episodes of the series. The irony of this judicial business was that the ratings proved that no one was watching *The Entertainers* anyway.

By now, Carol had missed twenty-six shows since the play opened: Carolyn Kemp did seven, Betty Hutton eight, and Mitzie Welch eleven. Welch was continuing in the role. Insurance had been obtained by the producers to protect their investment whenever Carol could not appear (the producers were to receive twenty-five hundred dollars for every show she missed starting with the fourth one) but that amount didn't come close to compensating them for their terrific losses at the box office whenever anyone filled in for Carol.

Carol was in the hospital until Sunday morning, November 8, when she was released and told that she must receive further treatment at home. The next day, the producers of *Fade Out-Fade In* posted their closing notices and said that they hoped to reopen when Carol could return to the show. They had no choice—the show had made only $18,090 that week, this compared to the $64,344 it had made the last week Carol appeared.

Bitter about what was happening to *Fade Out-Fade In*, the producers showed no mercy in wording their closing memo to the entertainers and crew members. The notice, posted backstage at the Mark Hellinger for all to see, proclaimed:

> Due to the failure of Carol Burnett to appear and to her not informing us as to the date of her return, the show is forced to close. We wish to thank each and every one of you for your hard work, cooperation and understanding, both before and during the crisis we found ourselves in. We sincerely hope you will all rejoin the cast when we reopen. This notice is without prejudice and with full reservation and without waiver of any and all rights of management against Carol Burnett.

Two days later, Carol posted her own memo backstage in the same place, on the call-board.

Carol's notice of November 11, 1964, read:

> Dear Gang,
>   Just wanted to let you know how sorry I am about the whole mess.
>   Someday when it is all over, I'd like to tell all of you and

the public about the producers and their play. What I want you to know is that I did try to hang on, even when Doctor Lippman—the doctor Lester Osterman recommended to me—told me last September that I would risk serious injury if I didn't cease all activity.

As things stand now, I have no idea when the doctors are going to let me work again, which, by the way, is why I could not let our producers know.

I've even been told this neck problem may have to be taken care of surgically as a last resort if it does not respond favorably to the treatments I am now receiving.

In any case, I want to express my sorrow and thanks to all of you and to Mitzie who did such a great job during my absence.

I love you all. Thanks for everything. And I hope we can someday work together under happier and healthier circumstances.

> Love,
> Carol

When Lester Osterman and Jule Styne heard that Carol had narrated a special feature from her home for *The Entertainers* called "The Beatles in America," they sent her an acrimonious telegram demanding to know when she would return to their show. Carol responded with a hand-written reply on yellow stationery dated Tuesday, November 17, 1964:

Dear Lester and Jule:

In answer to your telegram of November 13, I have no idea when, if ever, I can return to the type of physical activity I was doing before I went into the hospital—simply because the doctors themselves do not know.

I am sorry I got sick. I am sorry the play had to close because I was sick. I am sorry you don't think I am sick.

Enclosed are the doctor's statements.

I hope when you read them you realize how unfair you have been.

You both know I kept going on in *Fade Out-Fade In* even when Doctor Lippman, the doctor Lester sent me to, told me I would require hospitalization to treat this injury. You both know I did the show on several occasions with my back and neck medically frozen—and at times taped. You both know Lester once even asked me to do the show in a neck

brace, saying I could cut anything out of the show I wanted
...just so long as I showed up. This would have been as
unfair to the paying audience as it would have been to me.

I have been told that I may someday have to undergo
surgery if I do not respond favorably to the treatment I am
receiving. That, gentlemen, is scary!

I narrated a film last week, for about 11 minutes, while
in my apartment on my couch while in a neck brace. How
you can equate this with two and a half hours of strenuous
performing on stage, eight times a week, is beyond me.
Again, I am sorry I got sick—and I am sorry you are mad at
me for it.

Carol
P.S. Please excuse the stationery. It's all I have in the
house.

Had she failed her public? Was she doing the right thing in
refusing to go on with the show? She felt that she should somehow dedicate herself to making amends, but at the same time she
didn't think she should be held culpable for making her health
her first priority. Questions of self-doubt kept her awake at
night.

"So what do we do now?" a dismayed Carol wondered to her
husband one morning. "God! When will this all end?"

"Are you going to just let them drag your good name
through the mud, Carol?" Joe responded. ("I had had it up to
here," he remembers years later, "but it wasn't my place to come
out swinging; it was hers.")

"No. I think it's time to start fighting," she decided.

Up until this time, Carol had dealt with her feelings about
her producers and their play in a remarkably patient and diplo-
matic manner. For months now, she'd felt that she'd been publicly humiliated by false accusations and by slurs on her honesty
and integrity. She appeared to have taken the criticism without
even wincing, even though she confided to friends that she was
crushed.

"I think the whole bunch of 'em really took some unfair
shots at her," Joe Hamilton recalls. "It was unkind and damaging."

But by now, the consensus among industry observers was
that Carol was faking her injury in order to get out of a show she
didn't enjoy. Those unfortunate appearances on *The Entertainers*

aside, and with proverbial hindsight being 20/20, Carol's biggest mistake was in publicly voicing her dissatisfaction with theater life. She'd certainly chosen a bad time to begin expressing a preference for television work.

The unsuccessful attempt to buy her freedom after the car accident was fair business. Unfortunately, when the fact that she was turned down was leaked to the press, an obvious conclusion was that she wasn't satisfied and would now go to major extremes to get out of this quandary.

Her friends offered unstinting support. "It was all a matter of unfortunate coincidence and circumstance," Bob Wright says in Carol's defense.

But to many observers, circumstances seemed to have conspired too coincidentally; the weight of public opinion was shifting against Carol. Her days of silent disdain had to be over. "I guess a woman can't be a star unless she's not only intelligent but half made of steel," she told her friends. On November 25, 1964, she filed her own charges with Actors' Equity. In a press conference held at the Hamiltons' apartment, Carol lashed out at her producers. She charged that Osterman and Styne were trying to "destroy me as a performer" by "attacking my personal and professional integrity."

Wearing a lemon-yellow turtleneck sweater over her neck brace, Carol distributed to the press photocopies of her written complaint to Equity, which said in part, "As a member of Equity, I earnestly request Equity to protect my name. I ask Equity to take whatever steps may be appropriate to prevent the producer from inflicting further injury against me and from damaging other actors in the future."

At first, she was stiff and tentative in front of the skeptical reporters, but soon Carol was detonated like a grenade. "I'm mad at all of them," she said angrily.

Some members of the East Coast media contingent went slack-jawed when Carol asked that Lester Osterman and Jule Styne be "deprived of their right to act as producers in the theater." They were harassing her to get "a money settlement," Carol charged. And then, in a curiously naive observation that probably weakened her case, she added that "the show has closed through no fault of my own."

She said that Osterman and Styne wanted her to pay off the huge production costs of the show so that ABC-Paramount could at least get its initial three-hundred-thousand-dollar investment back. Carol called the maneuver "an out-and-out power play."

"At first, she was willing to buy her way out peacefully," said one friend. "But now it had gone too far. Now, she said she wouldn't give them, to use her words, 'one single penny.'"

"I am fighting back," Carol told the reporters, who had dogged her for months and were never really satisfied until now. "I don't like to fight. But I'm fighting so that they won't do this to anyone else.

"I would call a truce if an agreement could be reached with some degree of reasonableness—but I don't think these people are capable of reasoning. They are unfair. I think they want money."

Instead of the invidious effect most people expected Carol's words to have on her bosses, Osterman and Styne expressed only tacit dismay. "All we have ever asked of Carol was to return to the show when she recovers from her illness," they said in a prepared statement.

While all of this melodrama was happening on Broadway, Carol's TV series, *The Entertainers*, was sinking fast.

Carol returned to the cast of *The Entertainers* in January 1965. She and the cast rehearsed atop New York's Park Sheraton Hotel for an episode featuring Metropolitan Opera star Eileen Farrell. Carol had been out of action for ten weeks, and was very nervous about the Friday taping.

"Her physical activity was now extremely limited," associate producer Bob Wright remembers. "We had production meetings with the writers and choreographer and told them, 'No more physical comedy, no falling out of windows, no pratfalls. Only verbal comedy.' She wore that neck brace for a long time."

"The doctor told me that I may have to go under the knife," Carol told a friend. "He wasn't kidding, either. He wasn't just saying that to help me get out of my contract with *Fade Out-Fade In* as the producers seem to think I'm trying to do."

By now, *The Entertainers* was known among critics as "TV's Hard Luck Show." (*TV Guide* called it "a videoland disaster area.") Joe Hamilton and Bob Banner hoped that interest in the repertory format would grow, but it never did. The show failed to find an audience (or maybe it found them and they didn't want it).

Banner and Hamilton had decided that one way to garner

attention for the show was to capitalize on the then-burgeoning sixties' rock explosion by featuring rock-and-roll acts on the program. The ratings increased slightly, but now the studio audience was a younger one, and this aggravated one of the stars of the show, Bob Newhart. He said that the people watching were from a generation that did not understand his humor, so he quit the show. "Who needs it!" he said, disgusted with the whole thing.

Making matters worse, Caterina Valente had committed to a concert tour, and now she was forced to tape her *Entertainers* spots in advance. There were other changes in the cast lineup as well.

So by the time Carol came back to work, the show was a patchwork quilt of prerecorded and live-on-tape sketches, with hosts and substitute hosts trying to make sense of it all. *The Entertainers* was moved to Saturday nights at 9:00 P.M., but, wrote one critic, "there is no camaraderie between the hosts and guests— these people act as if they don't even know they're on the same show."

Carol grimaced when she read what critics thought of the program in its new time slot; she had pretty much reconciled herself to the inevitable. "You're always hoping for a smash hit, and this wasn't it," she said at the time.

Finally, Actors' Equity held their many hearings on the case of *Fade Out-Fade In.* "We went in front of a jury of our peers," Osterman remembers. "She hired Gus Dickien, a major political lawyer. I used my attorney, the famous arbitrator Theodore Kheel. We had these two high-powered attorneys battling it out as if it were a murder trial.

"The trial itself was very time-consuming, and it went on for weeks," he adds. "Actress Blanche Yurka was foreman of the jury, and she was about eighty years old at the time. One day, I looked into the jury box and she was sitting there sound asleep, snoring. And I had to ask myself, 'What am I *doing* here, this is so ridiculous.'

"We won the trial completely. And for Equity to go against one of their own was, to put it mildly, surprising. They told her to come back to the show."

The rest of Lester Osterman's recollection suggests that there is more to this story than anyone, other than Carol and perhaps Joe, really knows. "I refuse to gossip about Carol," he says, "but she had a very personal reason for wanting to be free of the show, and it had nothing to do with the show. She told me the reason that day when she made the offer to buy her way out."

Osterman's comments also suggest that perhaps the producers had an underlying sympathy for Carol's predicament, even during the trial. "The real reason she wanted out was not revealed in court," Osterman says. "She's a nice lady who just got trapped with her own personal life."

A friend of Carol's adds, "Carol told me that she signed on to do the show before she was married, and, of course, before she had the baby. She said that had she known what was going to happen in her life, that she was going to have a family, she never would have committed to the stage for such a long period of time."

Pat Lillie attempts to shed more light on the situation: "In my opinion, perhaps the show separated her from Joe and his work more than they really wanted. I'm not sure, but maybe part of it all was that she and Joe wanted to work together now that they were married.

"But I know she wasn't faking her injury," Lillie concludes. "To this day, she still has neck problems stemming back to that time. If Carol wanted to get out of that show, she was a big-enough star at that time to stand up and quit and then take the breach-of-contract suit and call it a day."

So now Carol's energies would again have to be split between the theater and television, and she was still ailing. She was totally dismayed. How it had all happened was beyond her, she told friends. Life was sweeter when she saw Chrissy married to actor Will "Sugarfoot" Hutchins. Her sister was happy; that was important. And then, on January 27, 1965, Carol started the new year by promising Equity and her producers, "I will do my utmost to perform in the show."

But Joe Hamilton angrily denounced Equity's decision, saying, "It's a pretty sad commentary when they tell you a show cannot survive without its star. That sure doesn't say much about the show." (It's interesting to note that even *Funny Girl* continued to have a profitable run after Barbra Streisand left the show and was replaced by Lainie Kazan.)

Fade Out-Fade In was scheduled to reopen on February 15, and the producers reportedly invested another one hundred thousand dollars—fifty thousand dollars from ABC-Paramount and the other half from Osterman, personally—into restructuring the show with new sets, songs, and costumes for Carol, who had, by now, lost a great deal of weight. Jack Cassidy would not be in the cast because of other commitments; he would be replaced by Dick Shawn.

It's always difficult to gauge the effect of unfavorable publicity on an entertainer's public, but the New York theatergoers' ambivalence about Carol was apparent when *Fade Out-Fade In* reopened at the Mark Hellinger on the fifteenth. By now, most people were not sure who would be performing in the lead role, Carol or one of her understudies. The top ticket price was $9.90, and on reopening night—attended by celebrities such as Lauren Bacall, Phil Silvers, and Jane Withers—sales were very low. The box office was little more than $3,000—this compared to an $11,821 full house. Or, as Lester Osterman put it, "We had lost all of our momentum, and now we were losing our shirts."

Meanwhile, CBS canceled *The Entertainers*. The last episode aired on Saturday, March 27, 1965, "and we all let out a sigh of relief," recalls Bob Banner.

"I was glad *The Entertainers* bombed," Lester Osterman said at the time. "I thought it might bring Carol to her senses and make her realize that she had a winner in *Fade Out-Fade In* and that she'd stick to it."

About a week later, on the evening of Thursday, April 8, Carol became ill while she and Joe were having dinner before that night's performance at the Mark Hellinger.

"Look, Carol, you obviously can't go on tonight," he told her.

"Oh, no!" she said. "Here we go again, Joe! I have to go on. It's just not worth the aggravation of what will happen if I don't."

"To hell with that," Joe decided. "I'm your husband, and you're staying home." He sent Carol to bed.

Joe called the theater and told Osterman that Carol seemed to have a virus and that she would be seeing her doctor, Alexander Berk, in the morning. Meanwhile, they'd have to make do until they got the doctor's report.

The producers were exasperated. There was nothing left to do but to call in Carolyn Kemp to replace Carol and then wait to see what was going to happen next. Five days later, on April 13, the verdict was in: Carol was seven and a half weeks pregnant. She wouldn't be able to continue with the show in this state and in her already weakened condition. Carol said she wondered if she could at least work until July, but her doctor advised her against it. He told her to quit the show, so she did.

Of course, Osterman, Styne, Comden, and Green were unnerved by Carol's latest bombshell. "They really forced her to go back into the show," Joe Hamilton says, "and then, when she became pregnant, they said that she was doing that on purpose to get back out, which, of course, was ludicrous."

Perhaps the producers could have found a way to make her continue working in *Fade Out-Fade In*, but by this time everyone was so disgusted with the situation, no one pressed any legal action. The producers claimed that they'd already lost half a million dollars on this debacle.

Carolyn Kemp finished out the week, and on Saturday evening, April 17, 1965, *Fade Out-Fade In* faded out once and for all.

It had certainly not been a good year. Because of all the problems and controversies swirling around Carol, her future in the New York theater looked hopeless, and after she'd worked so hard for recognition there. It's true that she wasn't sure that she enjoyed being a theater star as much as she thought she would, but, still, it had been her passion, a lifelong absorption, and now it was over.

"Broadway wouldn't touch her after all of that," Joe Hamilton remembers grimly. "We realized that she wouldn't be able to do anything in New York for a long time. Today, the public doesn't even know what the hell *Fade Out-Fade In* was. But people in the theater, they remember it well. They have never forgotten...." (To date, Carol has not appeared on Broadway again.)

At this point, there were more important matters at hand than Carol's profession. If she were to have a healthy child, she knew that she would have to take special precautions because of her already weakened physical state and emotional condition. Carol spoke of having a baby boy this time; she was grateful that she could actually be pregnant again after all that had happened. The pregnancy seemed like a ray of hope in an otherwise very dark year.

But on the evening of April 29, Carol complained of stomach pains. She was rushed to Doctor's Hospital in New York.

There, she lost the baby.

14

"You were created by TV. Television is growing, and you should grow with it. Do a series, Carol. Stop being such a chicken. . . ."

—Lucille Ball to Carol
Burnett, 1965

IN OCTOBER 1965, THE HAMILTONS MOVED TO THE WEST COAST BE-cause they felt that they were too removed from Hollywood, where motion pictures and television production were centered. The couple bought an opulent, two-story, fourteen-room Tudor-style Beverly Hills mansion. The house, once owned by Betty Grable and Harry James, was furnished, and Carol had to admit that sleeping in Grable's bed was giving her a "complex"; the Hamiltons refurnished the home. The house's impressive history was always an interesting subject of conversation. "At midnight, a man comes through here blowing a trumpet through a tissue," Carol joked.

For Carol, finally owning a home was a thrill, as she had not lived in one since she was a child in San Antonio.

Along with a Beverly Hills address came servants, maids, and all of the other accoutrements of wealth. At first, it was diffi-cult for Carol to adjust to such luxury. When guests would come to dinner and she would have to ring a bell to summon a servant, she couldn't do it without a flustered remark.

She ended the year on the concert trail, breaking in a new show in Lake Tahoe before heading to the Sands in Las Vegas, where she opened on December 8 to decent reviews.

They had no sooner got settled in Los Angeles when Joe was hired by NBC to produce a new variety show in New York starring Sammy Davis, Jr. For the next few months, he and Carol would be commuting between coasts.

On February 14, 1966, Carol, Lucille Ball, and Zero Mostel went into rehearsals for Carol's fifth television special, *Carol + 2*.

The first time Carol met Lucille Ball was backstage at the Phoenix Theatre on May 12, 1959, the night after *Once Upon a Mattress* opened. Ball came backstage to tell Burnett how much she enjoyed her performance, and Carol was, to say the least, awed. She tried to put on a mask of self-confidence, but she didn't fool Lucy. Lucy knew right away that Carol was nervous about meeting her.

"If there's ever anything I can do for you, kid," Lucy told her (and she still calls her "the kid" today), "just let me know."

When the network was planning Carol's TV special, they gave her a list of possible female guests for the show. When she asked why Lucy wasn't included on the list, someone told her, "Lucille Ball *has* specials; she doesn't appear on them."

Carol desperately wanted Lucy for the show, so she disregarded the network's edict and called her personally. Lucy agreed.

The special represented the first time Carol starred in a show taped on the West Coast. She loved working on the CBS TV City soundstage, Studio 33, where Red Skelton taped his show. She'd appeared there in the past when Garry Moore's show had come to Los Angeles to tape a couple of segments. The layout provided the studio audience with a close view of the stage and the performers with an unobstructed view of the audience. Even today, Carol insists on taping her shows in Studio 33.

Carol + 2, produced by Joe Hamilton for Bob Banner's production company, aired on March 22, 1966, to terrific critical reaction.

Meanwhile, Sammy Davis's series was canceled, and Joe Hamilton settled back into the Beverly Hills homestead with Carol. On May 25, 1966, they announced that they were expecting another baby. (A daughter, Jody Ann, was born on January 18, 1967.)

In August, Carol made her first concert appearance in Los Angeles with an engagement at the Greek Theatre. And then, in October, she hosted another TV special, this one called *Carol and Company,* with Rock Hudson, Frank Gorshin, and Ken Berry.

Time was ticking away on Carol's contract with the network, and now an important career decision had to be made. Mike Dann, vice-president in charge of programming for CBS Television, expressed his dismay over the *Carol and Company* special, insisting his network take better advantage of Carol's many talents. At this same time, according to Carol's exclusive contract, she had to either come up with a concept for a series, or she would have to star in whatever vehicle the network proposed.

CBS wanted her to do a situation comedy. But Carol knew that she didn't want to spend every week trying to develop what she called "a goofy Cousin Clara type." Mentor Lucy, however, saw nothing wrong with that, and she loved the idea of "passing the torch" to Carol. "Do a sitcom," Lucy told her, "and you'll never have to work for the rest of your life."

But Carol wasn't sure that she could handle the responsibilities of weekly television as smoothly as Lucy had since 1951. "She is really a much stronger person than I am," Carol told friends. "I'm very wishy-washy. I'll take direction and let people have their way. Lucy, on the other hand, knows exactly what she wants to do and takes no nonsense. If a someone writes an unfunny line, she'll say it outright: 'That's the worst line I've ever heard.' "

Carol secretly wanted to follow in Garry Moore's footsteps, host her own variety show so she could play an assortment of characters and have a wide selection of guests every week. Joe agreed with her. She also stipulated that she wanted to do the show from Studio 33.

She still had reservations. She had never been the center of attention on any of her specials (it was always *Julie and...* or *... + 2* or *...and Company),* and she didn't have confidence that the public would tune in every week just to see her. "After all," she told Joe, "look what happened to *The Entertainers!"*

"But that was different," Joe argued. "You weren't even there half the time...there was a lot of bad press, the show was wrong, the format didn't work...."

"I know. I *know*!" Carol moaned. "But what if I fail?"

"You won't fail!" Joe reassured her.

On October 12, 1966, CBS made the announcement: In a year, Carol Burnett would headline her own variety show.

Only one woman had ever met the long-term challenge of hosting a weekly hour-long variety show: Dinah Shore. But *The Carol Burnett Show* would go on to become one of the most unlikely success stories in television history. Not only would the original series win nearly two dozen Emmy awards, it would go on to enjoy multigenerational success in years of syndicated reruns.

For the six months leading up to the start of rehearsals in August, Joe Hamilton put together a concept for the show. Carol's contribution was based on personal experience. She realized that one of the reasons for the success of *The Garry Moore Show* was that he cleverly surrounded himself with a repertory company of players with whom an audience could develop a relationship. Because of her theatrical background, as well as her insecurity about starring in her own vehicle, this sort of "group spirit" appeals to Carol: She's always thought of herself as a performer rather than as "the star."

So the search for a repertory company was on.

Many observers of comedy would argue that being a so-called "second banana" is one of the toughest jobs in the field. The capable "second banana" must be talented enough to complement the "first banana," the star of the show, but not so funny that he overshadows that performer. A consummate second banana must be willing to dim his own ego so that someone else's can shine. It's often a thankless, discouraging line of work, or, as one of the greats at it, Don Knotts, once said, "If every second banana who's ever delivered a straight line is honest with himself, he's gotta admit that somewhere along the line, he wished he could be top banana. Otherwise, he's a liar."

There have been some second bananas who have achieved almost as much fame and success as the people they have supported. Carol Burnett is a good example. She never really seemed like a second banana on *The Garry Moore Show,* even though that's precisely what she was. She was destined for greater accomplishments, regardless of what fate had in store for Garry. But most entertainers in her position have difficulty sustaining careers after their top banana begins a decline. That's because the public can never identify what it is the second banana excels at—in order to be good at his work, he must be "best" at everything from dialects and accents to physical comedy and schtick. He has no real personality, he's just very funny. The best thing he can do is latch on to a new top banana.

Harvey Korman is the quintessential second banana. Harvey was born on February 15, 1927, in Chicago. In 1946, after a year and a half as a seaman in the navy, he enrolled at the Goodman School of Drama at the Chicago Art Institute. Korman wanted to become a classical actor: He specialized in the title role in Shakespeare's *Hamlet,* and never for a moment considered a career in comedy. After four valuable years of training in Chicago with contemporaries like Shelley Berman, Karl Malden, and Geraldine Page, he headed for Broadway, where he hoped to become a "...legitimate actor. That was my goal," he says wistfully. "My dream...the stage...Broadway. I prayed that Brooks Atkinson wouldn't die before I got there." Harvey landed a few acting jobs before he found himself selling candy bars in Radio City Music Hall with Dom DeLuise.

After returning to Chicago to do theater work, he would go to Hollywood twenty times in the next few years, hoping to find steady work as an actor. He never did. He toiled as a food checker and a cashier in between sporadic acting jobs that only served to whet his appetite for more. At one point he played Hamlet in community theater and, though his portrayal generated some interest from the movie studios, it garnered no work because, as he puts it, "big-shot producers came out expecting to find a young blond Adonis and, instead, found a kind of balding, aging Jew."

In between visits to the West Coast, he went back to New York again and was cast in the play *Uncle Willie,* but he was fired while the production was in out-of-town tryouts. "I got canned just around Christmas," he recalls. "I remember having my Christmas meal in a Waldorf cafeteria. And then later, standing at the window of my hotel room up about twelve stories, a bottle of bourbon in my hand, and I looked at the snow and thought, *'What* the hell is there to live for?' I really thought about..." He cuts his sentence short and sighs.

In 1960, Korman was in Chicago acting a supporting role in a play called *Mr. and Mrs.,* written by Sherwood Schwartz, who happened to be Red Skelton's head writer. The play, like Skelton's variety series, was produced by Cecil Barker and directed by Seymour Berns. Berns was impressed with Korman, and suggested that he return to Hollywood for more auditions. Harvey married model Donna Ehlert that September and then moved to Los Angeles. He was immediately hired for a few appearances on Skelton's show. "But for one reason or another, Red didn't want to work with me anymore," he recalls. "I don't know why. I can only speculate that he somehow felt threatened. It wasn't because I was bad; it was only because I was good."

After Korman endured two more lean years with a few bit parts on *The Donna Reed Show* and *Hazel*, Seymour Berns recommended him to Perry Lafferty, producer of *The Danny Kaye Show*. It was 1963, and Korman was about to give up acting and move back to Chicago. "I was thirty-six years old," he recalls, "and facing a lot of family pressure to do something with my life. Whereas they used to tell me, 'Go and become a doctor,' now they were saying, 'Go be a pharmacist, you're too old to become a doctor now.'"

For the next four seasons, Korman made an impressive name for himself as Danny Kaye's second banana, playing everything from Nazi prison-camp commandants to Mexican banditos and British spies. "I emerged on that show slowly, laboriously," he says.

But because both Harvey and Danny were moody and volatile personalities, theirs was a love-hate professional and personal relationship. "He was an enormously talented guy," says Korman of the late comic actor, "but very difficult to work with. Most of the people on the show were pretty unhappy. He was very demanding. It's not often that he was ever pleased with anything."

Maggie Scott, script girl for Kaye's show, recalls with a smile, "Harvey and Danny used to play baseball, just throwing the ball back and forth. One day they got into a fight, and Harvey, like a little kid, shouted out very emotionally, 'I'll show you! *I'm never gonna play ball with you again, Danny!'* They were like children, pals, friends but enemies."

When Kaye's series was canceled in 1967, Harvey was, as he puts it, "devastated, because I was sure I would never work again." As it turned out, he wouldn't be out of a job for very long. At the time of Kaye's cancellation, Carol and Joe were searching for "a Harvey Korman type," they said, to play opposite Carol. They auditioned over fifty actors, people like Bernie Kopell (who at the time was playing Siegfried, the German-accented leader of KAOS on *Get Smart,* and then went on to play Marlo Thomas's next-door neighbor on *That Girl* and Doc on *The Love Boat*). They even interviewed the actor who played the robot in *Lost in Space,* Donald May. But a "Harvey Korman type" did not emerge among the bunch.

"If he's available, why don't we just get Harvey Korman?" Carol suggested one day.

The chemistry between Carol and Harvey was extraordinary from the start; they would go on to become one of the most inspired pairings in comedy history. But, still, a certain frustration would always be a burning part of Harvey Korman. "If I have any ambition," he said during the Burnett show's early days, "it's for my own show, and more money, and more power...."

One of the gimmicks that never failed to work for Carol on *The Garry Moore Show* was exploitation of her homely "can't-get-a-guy-to-save-my-skin" image. Whenever a handsome guest star would appear on Garry's show, there would be the inevitable scene in which a flabbergasted Carol would swoon over the good-looking personality, all the while knowing that he was "too good" for her and wouldn't give her a second look. Comfortable with this form of self-deprecation, Carol decided that she'd like to have a heartthrob on her show so that she could play off of him in this manner. So in April 1967, an "open call" was announced in the Hollywood trade papers for a "Rock Hudson type." They weren't looking for an announcer; rather, they were looking for an actor to portray an announcer and also do some minor sketch work.

Arnie Rosen, a veteran comedy writer who, with Nat Hiken, created the Sergeant Bilko character for Phil Silvers and had also written for *The Garry Moore Show,* was hired as head writer for Carol's show. He wrote a sample of the kind of banter in which he thought Carol and the announcer should indulge, and gave it to her and Joe on April 4. In the script, Rosen described the announcer, John Smith, as "tall, broad-shouldered and darkly handsome."

About one hundred actors auditioned, but none seemed "darkly handsome" enough.

The next-to-the-last audition was scheduled for thirty-one-year-old Lyle Waggoner. Waggoner, raised in St. Louis, moved to Hollywood in 1965 with his wife of four years. The former door-to-door encyclopedia salesman went to the West Coast hoping for a career in show business; he was ambitious if not also a bit on the naive side. On his first day in the city, he looked in the Yellow Pages under "Actor" and found nothing. "Then I looked under Movies, Films, anything, and started making phone calls," he remembers.

Eventually, he enrolled in a new-talent program at MGM

and then was signed as a Twentieth Century Fox contract player. Lyle, 6'4", weighed about 190 pounds at the time, and auditioned for the title role in the *Batman* series.

Waggoner remembers the day his agent sent him to meet Joe Hamilton at CBS, Monday, April 17, 1967: "His secretary walked me through the offices, past all of the other secretaries, who gawked at me, and then in to see Joe. Joe and I hit it off, and then I was walked out and past the secretaries again, all of whom turned to stare at me. I found out later that this is how they auditioned all the guys who tried out for the part—the secretaries were the ones giving the thumbs-up or thumbs-down. If you had half a brain, Joe was satisfied. You had to get a good reaction from the secretaries to pass the real test. Evidently, I got a good reaction," he laughs.

A few days later, Lyle was called back to meet Carol and was a bit late for his appointment. "I found the rehearsal hall, threw the door open, and rushed inside," he recalls. "They were all waiting for me, sitting around a table. When Carol saw me, she jumped up out of her seat, screamed, and fell on the floor pretending a dead faint. I took that as my cue, and scooped her up in my arms and said something very gallant. It made her laugh. I had the job."

Carol has always believed that the best comedy is somehow related to real, honest life—that the whole point of great comedy is to be able to assimilate personal experiences. The way she "kidnapped" her kid sister and then raised her might not have seemed particularly funny as it was happening, given the circumstances. But as time went on, Carol couldn't help but recognize the comedic possibilities of a situation in which older sister and her nice-guy husband raise a rebellious adolescent girl. Chrissy was happily married by 1967 to actor Will Hutchins. Everything had worked out for the best...and now it was time for some laughs.

At one point, when CBS was trying to entice Carol into starring in a sitcom, Joe Hamilton proposed the idea of taking this part of Carol's background and lending it to that format. It was a good idea that might have worked. (Twenty years later, Pam Dawber made a moderate success of this basic concept with *My Sister Sam.*) Now that Carol insisted on a variety show, she and Joe decided to use the kid-sister premise as material for a recurring sketch to be called "Carol and Sis." Always one to plan ahead, though, Joe told the media that if the variety format was unsuccessful, "Carol and Sis" might still be expanded into a sitcom starring his wife.

Many girls were auditioned for the part of Carol's sister, like actresses Deborah Walley (hired that same season to play Eve Arden's daughter in *The Mothers-in-Law*), Joyce Bulifant (who went on to become Murray's wife on *The Mary Tyler Moore Show*), and even former "Mouseketeer" Sherri Alberoni. Later, Carol would joke that her real sister, Christine, called and asked for the part, "but I had to tell her that she just wasn't the type."

At this time, a seventeen-year-old cheerleader from the Los Angeles suburb of Inglewood named Vicki Lawrence was trying to plan her future. She would go to college, she decided, to become a dental hygienist, "a nice, clean profession," she once remarked. "You buy a few uniforms and never have to worry about what to wear in the morning."

But her mother wanted her to be in show business. It was an ambition she'd held for her daughter for years: She'd enrolled the girl in classes for ballet, tap, and modern dance; she'd paid for music lessons so that Vicki could learn to play every instrument from piano to bass, drums and trumpet. So Vicki was at a crossroads.

She did enjoy writing letters to celebrities and living vicariously through their lives via fan magazines. One day her mother suggested that she write to Carol Burnett and tell her how much she resembled her. It was true. Vicki actually looked as if she could have been Carol's sister. (Once, she starred in a production of *Macbeth* in high school and a review mentioned that "Lady Macbeth looks exactly like Carol Burnett." When she did an impression of Carol in a talent show, she brought the house down.) Though she couldn't have known it at the time, she even made pronouncements that sounded like Carol. "I hate my mouth," she would complain to her girl friends. "Please, God! I need a chin!"

She wrote the letter, asking Carol for advice about show business, and enclosed a photo of herself that she'd clipped from a local newspaper article about her participation in the upcoming Fireman's Ball; she was a contestant for the coveted award of "Miss Fireball." She mailed the letter off to CBS.

Carol received it and was amazed by how much Vicki resembled her. Since they were casting the part of her sister in the show, Carol decided to get a closer look at the girl.

A few days later, the phone rang in Vicki's home. Her mother answered; it was Carol calling. "It's Carol...*Carol Burnett!* Pick up the phone, Vicki!"

Vicki got on the line. "Look, Marsha," she began impatiently. "Would you please stop playing jokes on me? I know this is you..."

Carol assured Vicki that it wasn't her friend Marsha. She explained to the astonished teenager that she'd been impressed with her letter and picture, and that she would be coming to see her in the "Miss Fireball" contest. "But I'm very pregnant," Carol told her. "So, please, don't tell anyone that I'll be there. I don't want to be seen like this. Just save me two seats in the back row. I won't bother you that night, but I'll call you in a couple of days to discuss your career."

"What career?" Vicki managed to ask.

"We'll talk," Carol answered, and with that she hung up.

The night of the contest, Carol did show up as promised. She wore a huge red coat and had her hair wrapped in a turban, "looking like a giant red blimp," Vicki recalls with a laugh. The host of the show was so amazed to spot Carol in the audience, he excitedly introduced her. So much for her anonymity. When Vicki won the title, Carol was coaxed up to the stage to crown her.

A short while later, Vicki got a job in the singing group the Young Americans, and made an appearance with them on *The Andy Williams Show.* Someone called Carol from New York and told her that he'd just seen a girl on the TV who was her "double." Laughing, she explained that she'd already met the teenager. "It was as if we were destined to get together, one way or the other," Carol said.

A few days later, Carol gave birth to her second child, Jody. Vicki and her boyfriend went to the hospital to bring flowers for Carol, which they planned to leave with the nurse. But the nurse was so certain Vicki was Carol's sister, she quickly ushered her in to see her. They talked; Carol said she'd be back in touch.

Based on her appearance, it was fairly obvious that Vicki Lawrence was the best choice for the role of the kid sister. Four months later, when she read for the part, on Wednesday, April 19, her extreme lack of experience and self-confidence was the most memorable thing about her. "I was a very shy person," she once told a reporter. "I didn't trust my instincts or opinions on anything." She thought of herself as "slightly better than average." "Capable but colorless," is how Harvey Korman described her.

It had been narrowed down to two actresses: Vicki and a young woman named Heather North. North didn't look like Carol, but she could act, so that was a point in her favor.

Both girls were hired to appear in test tapings of the show that would be sent to the network affiliates. Two shows would be taped, and the winner would be decided upon by the reaction to her performance of the studio audience. "I talked CBS into that by telling them I felt it would be an important piece of casting," Joe Hamilton remembers, "and worth it to have the two audiences in. Plus, we needed something on tape to show sponsors, who didn't really know what Carol was going to do...."

On Friday evening, July 21, 1967, Carol and her new cast made the thirty minute test tape at CBS-TV, sponsored by Sanka Coffee and Winston cigarettes. There were no guests; just the Carol Burnett "family." This test taping and the first season of the series were directed by Clark Jones, who had directed *The Sammy Davis Jr. Show* for Joe Hamilton. Jones didn't want to move to the West Coast, and only agreed to work on Carol's show for the first season as a personal favor to Joe Hamilton. (The next ten years of Carol's series would be directed by Dave Powers, who started his career as a cue-card boy at CBS and went on to become an Emmy-award-winning director.)

"I have a very vivid memory of our first gathering in the rehearsal hall," says Harvey Korman, who had never worked with Carol before. "Carol gave a short speech that said, in effect, I really want one thing for us—I want us all to be happy and to get along with one another.

"The reason for that, I think, was because most of the crew members were CBS employees who had worked on Danny Kaye's show before Carol's. There was some animosity on Danny's part, I believe, about the fact that his guys were still working. He felt that because his show was canceled, none of us should work again. I think she sensed how unhappy many of us had been with Danny. She didn't want that negativity hanging in the air, so she dispelled it immediately. We knew right then that this show would be different."

Roger Beatty was stage manager for Carol's show during the first year, and he went on to become assistant director and writer of most of the "Carol and Sis" sketches. He recalls: "Carol made it a point to learn and memorize everyone's name in that first week, from the big shots at CBS all the way down to the key grips. And then, when she walked down the hall, all you heard was 'Hi, Ed!,' 'Hi, Frank!' Believe me, when a big star knows the name of the guy who sweeps up, well, that does wonders for everyone's morale. And there was never any 'Miss Burnett' stuff with her either; everyone called her 'Carol.' I worked for Red Skelton for eight years, and he didn't know my name until the fifth."

The test taping.

First, a promotional "teaser" tape was produced using a *What's My Line?* format with moderator and four panelists.

"Mystery guest, will you enter and sign in, please," the moderator announced. Carol "signed in" on the blackboard in front of the blindfolded panelists.

"Are you the star of a hit motion picture?" the first panelist asked.

"No," Carol answered in a trick voice.

"Are you in a hit Broadway play?"

"No," Carol answered again.

"Do you currently have a hit record?" the next panelist asked.

"No."

"Oh. Are you Carol Burnett?" asked the fourth panelist.

The show began. Carol was introduced by Lyle and, in a brief monologue, explained how difficult it was for her to host a show ("It's not because I'm awkward or frightened," she said, "it's because I'm awkward *and* frightened.") She then brought out Waggoner for the weak-kneed-ugly-duckling-star-meets-handsome-hunk-announcer bit. "To think," she concluded, "we almost hired Harry Von Zell."

(Arnie Rosen's vision of the interplay between Carol and Lyle was amazingly well planned—they used the exact script he had written back in April for "John Smith," just substituting

Lyle's name throughout. In coming weeks, Carol would bring Lyle out for silly reasons, like asking him to help her with a snap on her dress just so that she could melt at his touch, or proudly introduce him to a female costar and then act distraught and dejected when the guest began flirting with him. Rosen realized immediately that the possibilities for this kind of interplay with Lyle were limited. On August 16, he sent an "urgent memorandum" to all of the show's writers: "We are in *desperate* need for "Oh, Lyle, would you come out here for a moment?" bits for Carol. Any ideas? *Help!!!*")

The test taping continued. Carol introduced Harvey, and the two managed a quick dialogue about nothing in particular before he set up the "Carol and Sis" sketch. "She had been married for only a year," he explained to the studio audience, "when suddenly there was the patter of not-so-little feet—her teenage sister Christine came to live with her. Carol has hundreds of 'Bringing Up Sister' stories," he finished, "and we hope you enjoy the first one."

In the sketch, Carol and Harvey played what would become recurring roles as Carol and Roger Bradford, a bland middle-class couple raising Carol's sister, Chrissy (no explanation was ever given as to why Chrissy lived with them). In the first "Carol and Sis" sketch, Chrissy invited an official from the college she hoped to attend home to meet her guardians. The heavy-bosomed, well-dressed, stern woman was played by character-actress Reta Shaw.

As it turned out, the visit was poorly timed because Roger had just given Carol a sleeping pill to help her rest. Carol would have to meet "Mrs. Welles" in her dazed state; she couldn't stay awake, which was the running gag throughout the sketch. (She ends up falling asleep on the woman's bosom with her thumb in her mouth.) At the end of the sketch, Carol is knocked out by a swinging kitchen door. (Every "Carol and Sis" sketch ended with either her or Harvey being hit in the head by that kitchen door.)

After that segment, Carol showed the studio audience a tape of her first Garry Moore appearance when she performed the "Singers" routine, and then she performed part of that routine live.

The show concluded with Carol, Harvey, and Lyle on stage, Lyle saying, "We hope you'll be with us for the first Carol Burnett show, Monday, September eleventh, at ten o'clock." Harvey then introduced "the young lady who played Carol's sister." During the first taping, he brought out Heather North to a mediocre reception, and at the second taping he introduced Vicki Lawrence to just about the same level of excitement.

They hired Lawrence anyway because, as Joe puts it, "She looked more like Carol than Carol did, so we figured we'd give her a shot. Carol, really, was pretty insistent that Vicki be given the job. She saw something there. Believe me, none of the rest of us did."

The CBS network wasn't very excited about the test tape; they simply felt it wasn't funny. But, because of Carol's contract with them, the brass had to commit to the series. Still, there was some hedging. They asked if it would be possible to do the show in thirty minutes instead of a full hour. And then they wondered if they could commit to a half-season of thirteen shows instead of a full twenty-six-week season. Joe Hamilton insisted that Carol be given the full hour *and* the full season. "They're just trying to cut down the risk factor," he told the production staff. "Well, it ain't gonna work...."

Executive producer Bob Banner wasn't worried. "I have never done a new show where the network was confident of success," he says. "I understood the apprehension in Carol's case, given that *The Entertainers* didn't work and Carol was as much known for her illnesses at this point as she was for her comedy. 'What if she couldn't make a taping,' they wondered, and 'what if she gets sick and what if this and that...'"

Forty of the two hundred CBS network affiliates decided not to air the show; the network decided to try to keep that information from Carol so as not to add to her distress. But she couldn't help sensing the pervasive lack of confidence in her new endeavor, and that, combined with her own insecurities, made her certain that *The Carol Burnett Show* would fail.

And as if all of that weren't enough, Carol also felt a deep sense of responsibility toward the people who had relocated to the West Coast to work on the show; many of her coworkers from Garry Moore's show were also part of the huge crew. They had husbands, wives, and children, and had had to uproot their families and relocate to the other side of the country. Most put their homes up for rent so that, in case the worst happened, they'd have a place to go back to. But, still, Carol couldn't help thinking of the inconvenience all of this was causing.

The writers on staff were making nine hundred dollars a week. One New York-based writer, Bart Andrews, recalls the first time the writing staff met with Carol on the second floor of the CBS building on Beverly Boulevard in Hollywood. They were all seated at a long conference table while discussing sketch possibilities with Joe Hamilton when there was a knock on the door. Carol walked in.

"She looked like a young, fresh-faced kid, even though she was thirty-three," Andrews remembers. "She came in tentatively, as if she didn't really belong. Joe said, 'Let me stop and introduce my wife and your boss, Carol Burnett.' There was a smattering of applause. By her reaction, you knew right away that she didn't like Joe calling her the boss."

"I hate to say this," Carol began apologetically, "but I don't think we'll be here beyond Christmastime. I just have that gut feeling."

It wasn't exactly the morale builder Joe had hoped she'd deliver. Carol stayed for ten minutes, chatting with the writers, and then left.

On the first actual show taped, Carol's guests were Mike Douglas and Lynn Redgrave. This would become the third program to air. It wasn't the strongest script, and, ironically enough, the best part of the proceedings wasn't even taped.

Carol decided that she wanted to do a question-and-answer segment, as an "audience warm-up." Garry Moore had always done this type of free-wheeling banter with his fans while she watched from backstage. Eventually, Garry would bring her out to meet the audience, and Carol enjoyed the give-and-take rapport so much, she added a "Questions and Answers" routine to her nightclub act.

So on the first taping, before the cameras began rolling, Carol came out to polite applause and began fielding questions. The kinds of laughs she got here were different from the laughs she got in the sketches that followed, because the audience was laughing with Carol, not at her. They were responding naturally to her candid, warm personality. Joe Hamilton, Bob Banner, their director, Clark Jones, and everyone else on the crew agreed that this had been the best part of the show. The only problem was that, like Garry Moore's sessions, it hadn't been taped.

That evening, Joe told Carol what they'd decided. "Carol,

we've got to have 'Questions and Answers' as part of the show."

She looked at him as if he'd stepped on a puppy. "We can't do that! The only reason it works is because I know that the camera *isn't* rolling. I can't do it, Joe," Carol complained.

"But you've *got* to do it, Carol," Joe replied. "The audience is going to have to focus on someone; the success of a variety show depends on the *personality* of the host."

"I'm a comedienne, a performer, not a personality," she insisted. "We'll have good guests. People will tune in to see them."

Joe was unrelenting. "It doesn't even matter who the guests are, who the writers or producers are, the audience wants to see the hostess, and this is the perfect way to showcase you. You're great at this, Carol!"

Carol listened carefully, but she didn't like what she was hearing. "It's time you were yourself... everything depends on it," Joe concluded.

Carol reluctantly agreed that she would allow them to tape "Questions and Answers," but made certain that all understood that she was still extremely nervous about the idea; she didn't offer any guarantees that she'd be good at it. But when Bob Banner told her they were going to use the spot in the beginning of the show instead of in the middle, where Garry usually did it, she was all but frantic.

Banner laughs at the memory. "Between Joe and me, she was really badgered into the 'Questions and Answers' concept. We harped on it for about a week, until finally, being the professional she is, she said, 'Fine, if it's what we have to do, we'll do it.'"

The next week, they taped two "Questions and Answers" sessions, one that would be edited into the previous week's show and one for the current week.

Without a doubt, Carol's "Questions and Answers," as simple a device as the segment was, became one of the keys to the series' eventual success. The format gave her the opportunity to relate to the public in a simple, unaffected way that was genuine and totally winning. She was always honest in her answers, and funny as well, proving that she didn't need her script pages to make an audience laugh. In all of the years of Questions and Answers, Carol never used one cue card or script. It was the only time in the program, besides those moments when she was persuaded to sing out of character, that Carol was totally herself.

Sometimes in this segment, Joe and the crew would try to pull practical jokes on her. Once, they put a man in a gorilla suit and sent him out onto the stage to interrupt the proceedings. "She was absolutely frightened to death," Joe says, laughing at the memory. "Later on, we said, 'Christ! Maybe we shouldn't have done that. She could've had a heart attack right there on the stage.' It was a funny bit, but we cut it from the show."

"Let's turn up the lights and see if you all have anything you'd like to ask?" Carol would always say at the start of every taping. Each week, about twenty minutes of questions and answers would be taped and then edited down to the few that would be broadcast. Carol knew that there were certain questions she'd always be asked ("How did you get your show?" "Where are you from?") and so she had stock answers ready, because these wouldn't be used on the air. On every show, she was asked to do her famous "Tarzan" yell; she always complied. "You gotta give 'em what they want," she joked.

The best questions were the most bizarre. Once a woman asked about the kind of wax being used on the stage floor. Carol brought the prop man up to help with the answer. Another week, Carol had a cold and was trying to pump some adrenaline into her system by extending the Q-and-A session about fifteen minutes. A woman in the back, who apparently couldn't have been more bored, stood up and politely asked, "Carol, when are you gonna get to the acting part of the show?" Another week, a voice from the back of the theater asked, "Who was the best actor you've ever worked with?" "Harvey Korman," she quickly answered. It was Harvey who'd asked the question. Once, in 1970, then-Governor of California Ronald Reagan joined Carol to field questions from her studio audience.

"When Carol went through her *All My Children* addiction and all of the rehearsal scheduling had to be done around that soap," recalls script girl Maggie Scott, "she used to love telling the audience about the current plot during 'Questions and Answers.' We in the crew would just sit in the booth and watch the clock tick along while she'd excitedly go through this whole convoluted story.

"Well, at this time, we used to make it a practice to shoot her down and criticize her during 'Questions and Answers,' all in fun. Of course, we knew she couldn't hear a word we were saying. She'd just see our mouths move in the booth and wonder what we were talking about. Once, she went and got a tiny little headset with no wires, and then had it keyed into our booth. That Friday night, she started this *All My Children* thing again in front of the audience. I said in a huff, 'Is she gonna tell that *goddamn story* again?' And Carol responded, 'That's right Maggie, I'm gonna tell that *goddamn story* again!' "

September 11, 1967, 10:00 P.M., CBS-TV. *The Carol Burnett Show* made its television premiere. The episode was taped just a week earlier, with guest star Jim "Gomer Pyle" Nabors (a close family friend and godfather to Carol's daughter Jody). Nabors went on to be the first guest of every season.

Carol had terrific lead-in programming that the network hoped would guarantee her a large audience: *Gunsmoke* at 7:30, *The Lucy Show* at 8:30, Andy Griffith and *Family Affair* at 9:00 and 9:30. (Meanwhile, whether or not the intent was to sabotage, torture or exploit, ABC chose that same week to air Carol's first film, *Who's Been Sleeping in My Bed?* Judith Crist called it "a tasteless complication about sex" in that week's *TV Guide*, and the movie aired two days after Carol's CBS debut.)

On her first show, Carol walked out onto the stage in a garish orange miniskirt, her hair flaming-red and cropped short. She was obviously scared, but the awkwardness was somehow touching. Years later, when she looked at tapes of this evening, she would gasp at her appearance and demeanor.

During the repartee with the audience, she was amazed that someone actually asked about the *Stanley* series. Then, in a refreshingly unusual moment, the result of nervous chatter, she talked about the programming on rival networks and how disappointed she was that she'd now have to miss the shows.

Animated charwoman graphics officially opened the show with the now-familiar music, entitled "Carol's Theme" ("I'm so glad we had this time together..."), written by Joe Hamilton.

The first sketch was to be a recurring bit, Harvey Korman as F. Lee Korman interviewing a celebrity on the program *VIP*. "This is more than just a television show," Korman announced proudly. "It's an invasion of privacy." That week, the subject was "Shirley Dimple" (Carol as Shirley Temple, caught in a time warp, an adult in childhood clothing and curls). It wasn't very funny.

Jim Nabors sang Dusty Springfield's "You Don't Have to Say You Love Me"... in Italian.

A sketch called "The Ski Lodge" featured Carol and Jim as two misfit skiers who meet on a vacation. "Last year, I broke my arm in two places," she said wearily. "Denver and Chicago."

She signed the cast on his right leg, "Roses are red, violets are blue, I'm anemic, how about you?"

After a break, Burnett and Nabors performed a very lengthy duet of Broadway show tunes that only served to slow down the show's pace. When polished, though, this type of medley with guest stars, as well as the evolving Broadway musical-style revues, would become vital to the show's uniqueness.

The "Carol and Sis" sketch was mediocre; Roger (Harvey, making his second and last appearance in the hour) complaining that Chrissy (Vicki) doesn't get out of the house enough, and then fixing her up with a blind date. Vicki, who amazingly enough, looked then much like Carol's daughter Carrie looks today, had about five lines in the sketch. She had no stage presence whatsoever; she sulked throughout the entire scene. (On the first day of rehearsal, Vicki had to walk through a doorway and throw down a book. She did so, and director Clark Jones asked her, "Vicki, is that the way you walk through a door and throw down a book?" She nodded. "Boy, do we have a lot of work to do," he said with a sigh.)

Probably the best segment of the show was Carol's Charwoman mime in a discotheque fantasy and then her ballad rendition of the Seekers' hit "Georgy Girl."

At the end of the program, as it would become her custom, she sang the first verse of her classic theme:

> I'm so glad we had this time together
> Just to have a laugh or sing a song.
> Seems we just get started and before you know it,
> Comes the time we have to say so long.

The guests, and for this show the regulars, signed Carol's scrapbook as the credits rolled. That scrapbook bit was perfectly calculated genius as well; the implication was that not only was the audience in awe of Carol's guests, so, it appeared, was Carol (and sometimes she really was!). The perception was that the woman on the screen was very much like the woman you might meet on the street. She was a friend; she might make a good houseguest once a week.

It wasn't a great show. Early ratings were lamentable, and most critics didn't expect that the series would last more than a single season. CBS's reaction was guarded; the network had committed to giving, or at least appeared to be giving, the show a fair chance. CBS received 141 fan letters for the program the week it aired, not counting 75 fan letters to Carol. Vicki got five letters, Lyle got four, and Harvey three.

After the premiere, Joe Hamilton went to Manhattan to meet with CBS programmer Mike Dann. Behind Dann's desk was a bulletin board with the network's complete lineup for the coming months. In Carol's time slot, in January, there was a question mark.

After a forty-five-minute meeting, Joe asked nonchalantly, "Oh, by the way, Mike, what's taking Carol's place in January?"

"What do you mean by that, Joe?" Dann asked innocently. "We're *sure* Carol will still be on the air."

"Then how come you have a question mark in her time slot?" Joe asked suspiciously. Dann blanched; he'd forgotten to cover up the network's prognosis.

At one point, Carol called some of the forty CBS affiliate representatives who were lukewarm about her series and asked them to please lend their support. As always in the past, when she needed to, Carol never shied away from dealing with the network bosses. "Frankly, Carol," one told her, "we love you, but we don't think your show has a chance."

The guest lineup that first year was a strong one that included Liza Minnelli and Sid Caesar (on the second show), Eddie Albert and Jonathan Winters (on the third), and Lucille Ball, Tim Conway, Imogene Coca, Diahann Carroll, and Richard Chamberlain on subsequent episodes. By November, all forty holdout stations were airing the show, though not at the times the network prescribed (in New Orleans, the program was seen at midnight). After the first year, the series was renewed, but just barely.

They went into their second year running scared, but again with a solid lineup of stars such as Carol Channing, Ella Fitzgerald, Lana Turner, Betty Grable, Martha Raye, and Sid Caesar. Garry Moore and Durward Kirby were also guests on two shows. (Also that year, on August 14, 1968, Carol had another baby, Erin Kate.)

When the network moved the show to Wednesday evenings

at 8:00 P.M. in September 1971, it still existed in relative obscurity. It wouldn't be until December 1972 when *The Carol Burnett Show* was moved to 10:00 P.M. Saturday nights as part of the now legendary CBS comedy block *(All in the Family, M*A*S*H, The Mary Tyler Moore Show,* and *The Bob Newhart Show)* that it would find its audience and become one of the most praised and successful variety shows in television history.

15

IN THE BEGINNING, JOE AND CAROL ESTABLISHED THE GROUND rules. Joe was the boss; Carol was the star. Wisely, he never interfered with his wife's creativity; he provided an environment in which she could do her work without strain and tension. One of the reasons Carol enjoyed such a warm relationship with the crew and her costars was probably because she remained a peer; she stayed on their level. If anyone had a problem or a dispute, it didn't fall into her lap. It was in the best interests of the show that Carol not be involved in backstage politics. For instance, Joe believed that if Carol and any member of her cast were to have become embroiled in a contract dispute, it would surely have interfered with the on-screen rapport that meant so much to the show's success.

"Joe is smarter than I am," Carol would simply say.

"It was Joe's show, and Carol was the lead actress on it," Lyle Waggoner contends. "She stayed out of the business end. Smart gal. Though I must say that we used to joke and wonder if, at night, when she and Joe were in bed, Carol didn't say, 'Now listen, Joe, this is what I want you to do tomorrow...'"

Joe Hamilton maintains, "Carol was never interested in business. In fact, we had the same business manager for years. His partner insisted that his clients come in quarterly so that he could explain their finances and investments to them. It was all numbers to Carol; she hated going. After the first couple of meetings, she told me she wasn't going anymore. So for the next eighteen years, I took care of it.

"Where the show was concerned, it was also her decision not to be involved in its business, and a wise decision at that. She always deferred to me. It may have happened that someone would try to go around me and to her, thinking she was an easier

255

target, but I don't think anyone was ever successful at that.

"We tried to maintain a happy atmosphere as much as possible. I never had an argument leave my office. I had stars, agents, managers, and writers all tear at each other in this office," he says, motioning to the chairs in front of his desk. "But never once was it not resolved before the office cleared."

In the beginning, Joe recalls, it was difficult for him and Carol to leave the business end of the show at the studio. It was such an important part of their lives together, how could they just abandon it all when the day was over? "That first year, we took a lot of it home," he says. "Mostly because we were so worried about the show. But then, after we were a hit, we made a conscious effort to leave as much of it at the studio as we could, as impossible as that was. Inevitably, I would read her her lines on Tuesday nights before the first run-through. We'd go out to dinner and discuss the sketches. The show wasn't a burden, it was an important facet of our lives together. The first season and the last were the years the series was probably always on our minds at home, because both years were crucial.

"But we had personal responsibilities as well. Carol always had the easiest work schedule in show business, and she made sure that never changed. It was ten to five for her except on the two nights we prerecorded music and then taped. She was always there for the kids, always the best mother.

"I can't say we never went home at the end of the day ticked off with each other because of something that happened at the set. But that sort of thing was infrequent. We didn't play husband-and-wife at the studio, or we would never have gotten a single sketch done. It was always performer and producer, except when Carol wanted to borrow my office to watch *All My Children* and I wanted to have a business meeting at the same time," he laughs. "*Then* it was husband-and-wife time...."

There are many memorable sketches associated with *The Carol Burnett Show.* The ones that were broadcast are strong examples of the kinds of material acceptable to Carol and Joe. But the ones that didn't make it on the air give good insight into some of the creative decisions being made behind the scenes.

For example, all references to the military draft or the war in Vietnam were hastily excised from all rough drafts during the years the war raged.

Once, in 1968, a "Carol and Sis" sketch revolved around Carol getting accidentally inebriated. The word "drunk" was immediately removed from the script and replaced with "smashed." Apparently, the writers were sensitive to Carol's family background.

Always, if a sketch was offensive to any living person, or to any racial or ethnic group, Carol would not do it.

For instance, in 1967 a *VIP* sketch was written that had Harvey Korman—as F. Lee Korman—interviewing John Lennon (Lyle Waggoner) and "that painter of great sensitivity and producer of great dirty movies," Yoko Ono. The couple was interviewed in the bedroom of their English Tudor mansion, while sitting in their bed. Carol was supposed to use a broken Japanese accent in her portrayal of a dim-witted Yoko Ono.

The Arnie Rosen script included this comic dialogue:

HARVEY
Yoko, everyone says that John is
very much in love with you. How
does he show it?

CAROL
He buy me things, and never once
mention Pearl Harbor.

HARVEY
Did you ever have a fight?

CAROL
Only about Okinawa.

HARVEY
John, it's said you are worth
millions. What are you going to
do with all that money?

LYLE
A few more million and I'll be
able to get Yoko's teeth fixed.

HARVEY
Yoko, why did you marry John?

CAROL
All Beatles, they look alike to me.

> **HARVEY**
> You don't seem to like that name,
> Yoko. Do you?
>
> **CAROL**
> To tell you the truth, it bug me.
>
> **HARVEY**
> It's an unusual name. What does it
> mean?
>
> **CAROL**
> Japanese for Shirley.

"Pretty funny, but Carol will never go for this," Joe scrawled on Rosen's script. "Let's cut and replace with a duet."

VIP was usually a sore spot in planning the show, because Carol and Joe were always very concerned about offending high-profile people and conventional dogma. Sometimes celebrity names were changed "to protect the innocent." In one, Carol played Ethel Kennedy but, at the last minute, the writers changed the name to Ethel Kidaday. "Isn't it true that your husband, Robert, wears his hair long to appeal to younger voters?" Korman asked. "Oh, I don't mind the long hair," Carol responded as Ethel. "What gets me is that darn surfboard in the bathtub." The sketch was eventually cut from the show.

Throughout TV history, producers and stars have had creative battles with conservative network censors over controversial material. Carol was always fairly sensitive to her audience, and the writers usually tried to censor themselves. If a sketch was ever questionable, Carol would remark to Joe, "I don't think Fred and Marge are going to like this." Fred and Marge were an imaginary couple Carol and Joe invented to typify the tastes and opinions of middle-class America. Fred and Marge didn't like risqué humor from Carol; they set the guidelines for the show. Also, they disapproved when a sketch seemed condescending. "Watch it! Don't play down to Fred and Marge." Paradoxically, Fred and Marge also understood the technical end of television production; they knew when Carol was lip-synching a song, when she wasn't singing live, when the camera was somewhere it shouldn't be.

Carol paid close attention to the climate of the fan mail, and someone was actually paid to tabulate opinions based on that mail. (For the first year, it was Carol's cousin Janice Vance.)

Still, despite their concern, no one would ever accuse Carol's writers of being prudish. Sometimes the most intriguing comedy seems to fall between good taste and racy humor. Each week, a representative from the CBS Program Practices Department would examine the scripts and decide what could be broadcast and what couldn't be.

There were ways to get around the Program Practices people. What the writers used to do was slip in a number of thoughts and words that they *knew* would not get past the censors, and then barter dialogue that they never intended to use for lines that were somewhat questionable.

A good example of this kind of trade-off comes from a script of the recurring parody of soap operas called *As the Stomach Turns*. In this particular episode, Nanette Fabray played the neighbor of the always-troubled star of the show, Marion, played by Carol. Fabray's character was addicted to prescription pills, and Marion was supposed to talk some sense into her over tea. There were numerous references to habit-forming drugs, so in order to get those past the censor, the writers threw in extra "problems" that they knew would never be acceptable:

As the sketch opens, the doorbell rings. Fabray goes to the door and opens it to find the handsome pharmacy delivery boy, Steve (Lyle). "Here's your order," he says to her helpfully. "Some uppers, some downers, and some Dippity-Do."

Carol sizes up the good-looking hunk and sidles over to him. "Steve," she purrs, "do you make *all* the deliveries in this neighborhood?"

"Why, yes, ma'am, I do."

She whispers in his ear, "See you in half an hour with a little vaginal jelly." And then she winks at him.

[Here there was a note on the script from Arnie Rosen: "Joe, this could be changed to 'See you in a half an hour with a box of Q-Tips.'"]

As he leaves, Carol pops a pill in her mouth.

"And what are *you* taking a pill for?" Nanette asks her friend suspiciously.

Looking toward the door with a lovesick expression on her face, Carol says, "Birth control."

Obviously, the chances of anything like that getting on the air in 1968 were slim, and the possibility of Carol actually doing it was nil. The references to "vaginal jelly" and "birth control" were all deleted, traded in for the references to drugs in other parts of the script.

Carol and Joe's favorite story about the censors involves their ninth show, taped on October 28, 1967, with guests Nanette Fabray and Sonny and Cher. On this episode, the "VIP" segment featured Carol as a nudist explaining the three requirements for joining a nudist camp: "A high intelligence, good moral character...and twenty/twenty vision."

Joe Hamilton remembers: "We had Carol standing behind a picket fence, one board across her top and one across her middle so as to appear naked. Harvey asked her what nudists do on Saturday nights and she responded, 'Well, we dance.' Then, he asked, 'Well, *how* do nudists dance?'

"Obviously, there were about a thousand possible answers to that question. But we immediately discarded all of the suggestive ones and decided to have Carol reply, '*Very* carefully.' That was in good taste, I thought, and funny.

"When he read it, the censor came up to me and said, 'No way, Joe. You can't use that line. It's too dirty.'

"'Look, I'll use any line you give me that makes sense,' I told him. 'We're not changing the question. You just come up with the answer.'

"So he went back up to his office and worked this problem out with his staff. Later, he came back into my office with this answer: 'Cheek to cheek.'"

Laughing, Joe remembers telling the censor, "That's a lot dirtier than what we'd even planned. It's funny as hell."

Occasionally, Carol and CBS's Program Practices Department would disagree on a matter that didn't involve her show. For example, in 1969, Julie Andrews asked her to endorse a social movement called People for Peace, which Julie and many other celebrities were spearheading. When Carol appeared on *The Merv Griffin Show,* then a CBS late-night talk show, she held up the People for Peace armband and appealed to viewers to send letters to Mrs. Martin Luther King (who in turn would forward them to President Nixon) saying they were praying for peace. The network deleted her fifteen-second speech from the broadcast, saying that such a display was against their policy. Her lips were moving, but there was no sound.

"I want a copy of your so-called policy," Carol demanded of one executive. "I want to see *where* it says we shouldn't be praying for peace." Carol personally called Robert D. Woods, president of the network, and complained. "I felt like an absolute jerk when I saw what they did," she said. "It made it seem as if I said something dirty, or un-American."

The next couple of years would see major changes behind the scenes. Arnie Rosen, Carol's talented head writer and producer for the first five seasons, became tragically ill with a kidney disease and eventually died. At first, he was replaced by a staff headed up by Buzz Kohan and Bill Angelos; then, veteran writer/producer Ed Simmons was recruited. Simmons, who had cut his teeth in 1950's TV with partner Norman Lear as a comedy writer for Dean Martin and Jerry Lewis, stayed with Carol's show for the remaining five years of its run.

Vicki Lawrence had become a comic revelation. When she started with the show, she was a novice with little obvious ability. She blended into the scenery. "I know Vicki, and I don't know Vicki," Harvey Korman once said to *TV Guide*. "Deep down she's probably very ambitious, but she's so insecure. What do we do with her?"

Artie Malvin, who was the show's special-material writer, recalls, "We were all very skeptical of her. We didn't know what the heck to make of her. She could perform adequately, but there was no magic. Most of us said, 'There must be somebody better.' But Carol obviously had greater intuition than any of us."

In the beginning, Vicki would say her few lines in the "Carol and Sis" sketch and spend the rest of the time in a corner doing needlepoint.

"I think at one point Carol decided it wasn't fair to just have this girl say, 'Bye, I'm going to Marsha's' at the beginning of every 'Carol and Sis' routine and then disappear for the rest of it," Maggie Scott says. "Carol believed she could do more, and she told the writers to start developing material for Vicki. If she didn't feel Vicki had done enough in a sketch, she'd pull herself out of a scene and make them replace her with Vicki.

Once, the cast was doing a Marx Brothers finale with Vicki playing the silent Harpo. Everyone else had lines, but, of course, Harpo did not. Vicki rehearsed the routine a couple of times, and then, in front of the entire crew, dancers, and cast, she naively blurted out in frustration, "But I just don't understand why I don't have any lines here!" Everyone laughed and she was terribly embarrassed; her feelings were hurt.

What's fascinating about Lawrence is that she was a lot brighter than most people realized; she had an innate talent for sketch comedy, just as Carol had suspected all along. Vicki was a creative sponge—she retained everything she observed in Studio 33 and blossomed by association.

"She became one of the best character actresses in the business," Artie Malvin estimates. For a brief time, she was even a recording star (her "The Night the Lights Went Out in Georgia" was a number-one hit in 1974. It was written by Bobby Russell, to whom Vicki once said she was married "for about ten minutes." In 1974, she married her current husband, Al Schultz, who was makeup director for *The Carol Burnett Show*).

Vicki went on to win an Emmy as Best Supporting Actress in a Musical Variety Series (1976), and in her acceptance speech she said, "I can't think of anyone I'd rather look like than Carol Burnett."

Though she once credited Carol with "every wonderful thing that's happened to me in my adult life," she does not enjoy giving interviews to discuss their friendship, or her association with the series. "Her feelings about those subjects are really the only things reporters want to know about Vicki Lawrence," says one of her confidantes, "and she's sick of talking about them. Carol would feel the same way if the only questions people ever asked her were regarding her feelings about Garry Moore and *The Garry Moore Show.*"

Harvey Korman was still not particularly content, despite his success with *The Carol Burnett Show.* Sometimes his frustration was reflected in his comments to the press, such as this one: "Carol has been quoted as saying that if I left her, she'd cut her wrists," he said in June 1969. "But her husband Joe told me quite confidentially that the cuts would not be fatal and could be covered up by small bandages."

Lyle Waggoner left the show after the seventh season, when his initial contract expired. Though it happened so gradually most people didn't seem to notice, Lyle had come a long way in terms of acting ability and was no longer only "the announcer." He had become a featured player in sketches and proved to be quite capable. But, still, he was difficult to cast because he wasn't a character type; he was just a good-looking guy who was best playing handsome police officers, doctors, and plastic movie stars.

Today, Lyle says that he didn't see much of a future for himself as an actor on Carol's show, or in syndication, where money could be made on the series after it ended its network run. No variety show in TV history had ever been syndicated, and, says Waggoner, he wanted to appear on something that would have a financial payoff beyond its initial run. (Two years later, he landed a job as Steve Trevor, Lynda Carter's boyfriend on *Wonder Woman*. It ran three years and went into syndication.)

"I also left the show because they were not good payers," he says frankly. "Joe Hamilton was a very good businessman, and he got Vicki and me for nothing. We had no negotiating power. Harvey, on the other hand, had lots. After seven years on the show, I was making about twenty-two hundred dollars a week." (Today, Waggoner still receives royalties from the reruns, but only from the last two years he was connected with the show, since the first five years are not in syndication.)

"None of us was happy with the amount of money we were being paid. It was a source of aggravation, always. But we were happy as hell to be on a show with Carol," he concludes.

"Lyle was hired to be an announcer, a good-looking hunk," Joe Hamilton explains pragmatically. "The salary for that was not very high. When we started using him more, we gave him a bigger increase in salary than what he should have gotten. But it still wasn't up to what he thought it should be. And to be honest, there are just too many 'Lyle Waggoners' in this town.... I could have hired ten of them and paid them half as much as I paid Lyle and they all would've been thrilled to death."

Lyle has to agree with Joe Hamilton. "Joe could have gotten rid of me, and Vicki, too, at any time along the way and it wouldn't have hurt the ratings much."

Waggoner recalls that at the beginning of his seventh season he told Joe Hamilton that it would be his last. "I was hoping he'd say, 'Look, we really want you to stay, what's the problem? Can we give you a little more money?' He never did."

"I think the gimmick wore out with Lyle," observes associate producer Bob Wright. "It was truly a one-joke gimmick we couldn't keep up. Lyle as an eight-by-ten glossy, hired for his looks. His talent was limited, and I don't mean that derogatorily. He just wasn't a Harvey or Tim [Conway]. We didn't fight his leaving because we just felt it was best. He left, more or less, on his own...."

It probably didn't do much for Lyle's image as a serious art-ist when he appeared in a nude-photo layout in the first issue of *Playgirl* magazine. Waggoner's photos were discreet, but rein-forced his beefcake image in the minds of those who thought of him as nothing more than a pinup.

Apparently, there was some bitterness surrounding Lyle's departure. "I didn't *mean* to upset the applecart or hurt people's feelings, but the word was that I had," he says. "They weren't happy about my leaving, but you know what? Nobody ever told me that during the year they knew would be my last."

"Mostly, I think Joe just felt that Lyle was being ungrateful by asking for so much more money than he was probably worth at the time," says a friend. "He felt he should have been more of a team player."

Waggoner did his last season without ever discussing the matter with Carol, out of respect for the fact that all business matters were dealt with by her husband. His departure was un-ceremonious; he says that there was no acknowledgment of his last show from the cast or crew. In fact, he doesn't even re-member the last taping.

In retrospect, Lyle Waggoner was undervalued. Reruns re-veal that Waggoner became a competent, reasonably versatile foil, much more than a mere "poster boy." But, still, when he left the show he was not missed, by either cast or audience. He never came back for a guest appearance, and was rarely mentioned.

(One of the few times Lyle's name was ever brought up again was in an ad-lib from Harvey during one of the *As the Stomach Turns* sketches. Dressed in drag as the buxom Mother Marcus, he was explaining to Carol that he—er, she—was a spiritual me-dium. "I communicate with the dearly departed," Harvey said, and then, after a moment of concentration, "I think Lyle Wag-goner is coming in." Pause. "Oh, false alarm." (Carol sat next to Harvey, shaking with suppressed laughter. She retaliated, though, by suddenly reaching over and tweaking one of his fal-sies.)

"I walked out of there, and that was it," Lyle says sadly. "I didn't see or hear from any of those people again, except for Vicki's husband, Al Schultz, who is a buddy. But that's the nature of this business," he rationalizes. "It was a job, and when I fin-ished it, that was that. 'When you finish a show, you're on your own, pal,' that's what I learned . . ." His voice trails off.

Lyle Waggoner has displayed great business savvy in recent years, and today he owns a successful company called Starwagons, which specializes in renting motor homes to television and movie studios for use as trailers for makeup and dressing.

It's not unusual for actors to be unhappy with their salaries. In a *People* magazine interview dated March 21, 1983, Vicki Lawrence called Joe "a tough negotiator." In order to stay friendly with Carol, she said, they never discussed business. "I wasn't in the position to ask for anything, so I got the shaft," she was quoted as having said. She said that after five years on the show, she was making eight hundred dollars a week. Later, when Joe wanted her for a spinoff of the "Eunice" sketches, which became *Mama's Family,* she noted, "I played hard to get—I *was* hard to get and received a good deal. I'm finally learning how to act like a star."

"I had to talk to CBS three years in a row to convince them to let me keep Vicki on the show," Joe Hamilton explains. "They wanted to pull her off. But Carol felt very strongly that Vicki had potential, which, of course, she did. Still, for the first five years, she wasn't worth much more than what she was making, let's face it. When she became more valuable, her salary increased."

Of all the salary headaches Joe Hamilton faced, though, the ones involving Harvey Korman were the most complex and emotional. Korman's were complicated by the fact that he was beginning to feel great frustration in his work as second banana, and was also having marital problems. "Everyone was always very friendly and cooperative on that set," he says with a mischievous grin. "I was the only one who was, well, a pain in the ass. I never had any problem from the people on the show . . . all of my problems were internal.

"My biggest gripe with *The Carol Burnett Show* was that I never felt I was paid enough money," he says, echoing his costars' sentiments. "I always felt that I was worth more. I felt, and still feel, that I was a costar of that show, even though I know Carol would not agree with me on that. The writers wrote for both of us . . . for me and Carol.

"My agent had to keep reminding me, 'This is *not The Harvey Korman Show,* or *The Harvey and Carol Show.'*"

"I love Harvey, and he knows that, but he can be such a jerk," Joe Hamilton counters. "He used to quit the show at the end of every season. He and his agent were absolutely irrational, in my opinion. Carol and I never took a salary increase in eleven years. We were the only ones who didn't. Of course, we got profits after the third year, but our salary stayed the same."

At the beginning of the sixth year, Hamilton remembers, he was having an especially difficult time with Harvey's contract negotiations. Exasperated, he turned the matter over to the network, "and I told them, 'Look, you guys deal with Harvey and his agent. I won't do it anymore. I don't care if the guy gets two hundred thousand dollars a year, he'll be getting it from CBS and not from me.' I never again dealt with Harvey on money. But to this day, he still thinks I was screwing him, that I was personally underpaying him."

"Harvey was always a lot of fun, but an unusual personality because he was an angry man on the inside," Lyle Waggoner observes. "He loved to complain. He was at his happiest when he thought things were going wrong. In fact," Waggoner laughs, "it made us feel good to be around him because he always made us feel we were a lot better off than he was. For seven years, though, I marveled at his phenomenal imagination and creativity. His ability to perform in anything awed me."

There is certainly no disputing the fact that Harvey Korman is one of the most talented comedic figures of the last fifty years. A writer once noted that he could "make Dante giggle in the ninth circle of hell." Over the course of his ten years on the show, Korman played virtually every type of character imaginable; his rapport with Carol was memorable.

The Carol Burnett Show is probably best remembered for its brilliant satires on movie classics. These sketches always offered a wide range of appeal—nostalgia for the fans who enjoyed Hollywood's Golden Era, movie camp for the younger viewers.

The cast spoofed dozens of Hollywood classics (once they even did an hour-long parody of *The Dolly Sisters* called "The Doily Sisters," with Carol playing the Betty Grable character and Vicki the June Haver part). In some parts the sketch mirrored the film almost word for word. Three of the most memorable pieces were takeoffs on *Love Story, Mildred Pierce,* and *Gone With the Wind.*

The *Love Story* parody, "Lovely Story," aired February 1, 1971, as part of a show that starred Rita Hayworth and impressionist Jim Bailey. Harvey played the Ryan O'Neal role, Oliver

Harvard; and Carol the Ali MacGraw part, Ginny Caballeru Wo-jowoski DeFuccio. (MacGraw loved the sketch, but O'Neal told friends he thought it was "cruel.") They are college students and lovers from totally different social backgrounds; he's a struggling preppy, she an upwardly mobile socialite.

In the sketch, the future looks bright. Right after their wedding, they receive a telegram with the news that Oliver has just been appointed Chief Justice of the Supreme Court.

                    CAROL
It's only a beginning, but you're
on your way.

                    HARVEY
Darling, just think, now we have
everything. I have you, you have
me, we have the new job, all the
money we want . . . we'll have a
future of unlimited joy and
happiness.

(CAROL COUGHS, TWO QUICK
COUGHS.)

                    HARVEY
Uh-oh.

(WITH A MELODRAMATIC
FLOURISH, HARVEY LIFTS HER AND
TAKES HER TO BED. LYLE
SUDDENLY APPEARS AS A DOCTOR
AND, AFTER EXAMINING CAROL, HE
TELLS HARVEY THE DEVASTATING
NEWS: SHE HAS ONLY FIVE MINUTES
TO LIVE.)

                    HARVEY
              (FORCING JOVIALITY)
Well, honey, there's nothing to
worry about. How about
something to eat?

                    CAROL
Oh, yes, I'd love a four-minute egg.

> **HARVEY**
> Uh, no dear, that's cutting it a
> little close.

In "Mildred Fierce" Carol portrayed the long-suffering Joan Crawford character in the forties-style black wig, thick eyebrows, and with exaggerated shoulder pads in all of her costumes. "I almost couldn't get her to wear the eyebrows we designed," Bob Mackie laughs. "'Oh, my God, these are so awful,' she told me."

Harvey played her two-timing lover, Monty Slick, and Vicki her insolent, spoiled daughter, Veda.

In order to support her child, martyr Mildred takes a job as a waitress, to her daughter's extreme embarrassment. Soon she is able to finance her own business, but she hopes Veda will never discover her terrible secret. One day, Veda drags out a huge poster she found on the side of the road. It's of Mildred in her waitress outfit, affecting a homey pose, one hand on her hip, her other arm extended, palm up, and motioning to the words on the sign: 500 FEET TO MILDRED'S FAT BURGERS. STOP IN AND PUT ON THE FEEDBAG...

"Not only are you a waitress, but you've got this hideous picture to prove it," Vicki squeals.

"Gee, I don't know," Carol says thoughtfully. "I think it's kinda swell.... (She stands next to the poster and reenacts the pose.)

"I figured out, if I could save all my tips, I could buy a restaurant of my own," she says, seeking her daughter's approval. "And so I did, and now, Veda, I own the whole chain. I *am* Mildred's Fat Burgers."

She pulls her daughter close and tries to hug her, but Veda is repulsed. "Take your hands off me, you sleazy, greasy person," she says. With that, she slaps her mother on the face.

Carol does a double take, and then, in her best cutesy Shirley Temple voice, she says, "I know a *wittle* girl who got up on the wrong side of the bed this morning."

Later in the sketch, the "irresponsible lecherous playboy" Monty Slick comes into Mildred's life, and Veda, always on the lookout for the glamorous life and a handsome, rich boyfriend, begs her mother to marry him.

"...without loving him? Veda, is that forthright?"

Vicki shoots Carol a disgusted, bored look. "Mother, forth-right does *not* buy Ferraris."

Mildred agrees to marry Monty, but the moment she embraces him, he begins kissing her flirtatious daughter behind her back. Soon, Veda and "Stepdaddy" are having an affair. Later, Monty confesses his indiscretion to Mildred as gently as he can. "Yes, it's true, Mildred," he says. "I'm sick of you *and* the smell of Crisco."

"All right," Mildred decides bravely as she leaves the room. *"I don't need a brick to fall on my head."* (Three bricks fall on her head.)

But Monty won't marry Veda, and so she pulls out a pistol and shoots him. Then she asks her mother to take the blame. Mildred hesitates. Veda whines, "All I have ever asked you for in my life is to cover up *one lousy little murder.*"

Mildred agrees, but puts her foot down—Veda definitely may not attend the prom. "Kids, they sure keep you hoppin'," Carol says to the camera with motherly resignation.

"Joan Crawford called me after that sketch aired," Carol once recalled in *TV Guide.* "She was hysterically funny. First she complained that we gave the 'Mildred Fierce' sketch more production than Warner Bros. gave her entire film. Then she pointed out that my shoulder pads were bigger and better than hers...."

In "Went With the Wind," Harvey played Captain Rhatt Butler, Tim Conway was Brashly, and Vicki Lawrence essayed the screeching Sissy in an on-target exaggeration of the Butterfly McQueen role. Carol played the ever-suffering, put-upon Miss Starlet. ("If I gotta make *tuna casseroles*—and go without my grits —this war won't get to me.") Guest Dinah Shore portrayed Southern belle Melody.

The sketch was written by Rick Hawkins and Liz Sage, both in their early twenties at the time and both staff members for only about a month. Carol wasn't certain that the parody would work. "So many people have done *Gone With the Wind,*" she said. "Even *we* did it a few years ago," she told head writer Ed Simmons. But since the epic was scheduled for television broadcast in a few weeks, Carol decided that the sketch might be topical. "Let's give them a shot at it," she said. "The worst that can happen is we don't use it." It turned out to be one of the most popular—if not *the* most popular—of the show's many movie take-offs.

When the Yankees steal her clothes and she realizes that Rhatt Butler is on his way over, Starlet dashes upstairs clutching the drapes from Tara's living-room window. Moments later, she comes sauntering down the stairs in an improbable new outfit: The curtain rod, balanced on her shoulders, drips with yellow brocade and fringed green curtains. On her head, she wears a towering matching brocaded headpiece.

"That . . . that gown is *gorgeous*," Harvey sputters.

Carol poses, trying to appear insouciant. "Thank you. I saw it in the window and I just couldn't resist it."

(Her descent down the stairs in that outfit is probably the most memorable moment in the show's history.)

"We did a lot of comedy, but I never heard laughs like I did when she came down the stairs in that getup," says Bob Mackie. "The audience saw her take the drapes upstairs, but nobody knew what she was going to do with them. It wasn't written that way, it just evolved. I didn't come up with the idea of having her wear the drapes until the day before taping. We didn't even have time to do a proper fitting.

"When she was at top of the stairs, out of the audience's view, the change had to happen very quickly. The dresser and I pulled this big thing on Carol, all of this heavy velvet drapery, and the way we were pulling and tugging, we were afraid she'd topple backward down the steps. Finally, it was time. She walked down the stairs in that getup, and the people screamed and laughed so long they had to stop taping. I was standing backstage wondering what was going on, because I couldn't see the action. I was afraid that she accidentally fell down the stairs under the weight of that heavy outfit, and that the audience thought it was all part of the sketch," he laughs. "I knew her entrance would be funny, but not *that* funny."

In the seventies, it became rather in vogue to be satirized on *The Carol Burnett Show*. Some of Carol's impersonations over the years were hilarious; there were many, but her best were impressions of Carmen Miranda, Mae West, Julie Andrews (as Mary Poppins), Doris Day, Cher, and Dinah Shore as host of her talk show in 1971 ("Hi y'all," she gushed in a Southern drawl. "Oooh-wee, have we got a show lined up for you. I'm going to show you how to sauté a possum and construct an extra wing on your little old plantation with used Dippity-Doo jars.")

Guests usually felt comfortable while rehearsing and taping the show. This was mostly because their comfort was always considered the top priority. "Our prime consideration on every taping was, Is the guest happy?" says Joe.

Carol did everything possible to make the guests' appearances on the show easy, right down to telling her special-material writers to give her the tough harmony parts in medleys so that the guest could breeze through the easier melody line and not have to work twice as hard.

Some great legends appeared over the years.

When Carol did a takeoff of the movie *Gilda*, the late Rita Hayworth was so impressed that she sent a telegram lauding Carol and saying that she should have done the original. Carol called and asked Rita to appear on the program and, with the stipulation that she not have to wear sexy clothing, she agreed. On the show that aired January 22, 1971, Rita's *Gilda* and Carol's "Golda" were shown to the audience, and the pair also did a pantomime routine as charwomen.

Rita was terrified in front of the live audience when she was to tape a sketch with Carol and Harvey. Her memory, as a result of the early stages of Alzheimer's disease, was failing, and many on the crew feared she might forget her lines. At one point in the sketch, Carol, as a star-struck waitress, was singing "Put the Blame on Mame" to customer Hayworth. Carol tossed back her head, and her wig "accidentally" fell off. The audiences howled, and with that Hayworth finally relaxed and completed the sketch beautifully.

"I have always believed Carol did that on purpose," Maggie Scott says. "Her wigs never fell off by accident. No way! She did that to loosen things up for Rita, even though to this day she won't admit it."

When Gloria Swanson appeared, recalls Scott, "she came with so many suitcases of health food, there was no room in the dressing room for her. But she worked so hard, you could tell she was from the old school where work really mattered." Swanson also played a charwoman character with Carol.

Gloria had written a letter to Carol complimenting her on her bizarre "Nora Desmond" character, a spoof of Swanson's Norma Desmond role in the 1950 film *Sunset Boulevard*. Carol's aging, slightly senile, and drunken former silent-screen star Nora always believed she was on the verge of a comeback. She would trip down the stairs, eyelashes askew, cheeks sucked in, and then torment her bald-headed and infinitely loyal butler, Max (Harvey Korman).

Carol responded to Gloria's letter by inviting her to appear on the show. "Gloria and the dancers did a routine," staff writer Gene Perret laughs, "and we couldn't help but joke that they should have made a dress with handles for her. Every time she had to move somewhere, the guy dancers would come out and carry her across the stage."

When Joanne Woodward taped an appearance, husband Paul Newman watched her from the producer's booth. "He was saying, 'Jesus, I could never do that. How do these people do this?'" Ed Simmons remembers. "We shook hands afterward; he apologized because his hands were soaking wet. That's how nervous he was about the prospect of his wife working with Carol live before an audience—and without benefit of a dozen retakes like they do in movies."

Lana Turner made an appearance. Recalls lead dancer Don Crichton: "I did a waltz with her. She was fragile, absolutely scared to death of the number. Every day, we'd all wait for her to arrive to see what she was going to wear. She arrived the first day of rehearsal in a white turban, white coat, and white dress; she came to the set every day wearing a fabulous fur."

"When we booked Ben Vereen, he was almost like a throwaway guest," writer Gene Perret remembers. "We couldn't get anybody else that week, so we got Ben Vereen. But then, about a week before the first rehearsal, *Roots* aired, and received the highest rating in TV history. All of a sudden, the guy is a major star, and we didn't feel the comedy was good enough. 'These sketches won't *do* for Ben Vereen!' Carol said, horrified. 'We can't give Ben Vereen *this!*'

"When Tommy Smothers appeared, he was a helluva nice guy, but we knew from what we'd heard that he could never remember his 'mark' in a sketch—where to go and where to stand when he said his lines. So the sketch we wrote for him had him in a hospital bed the entire time. And everybody walked around the bed and spoke to him while he lay there. We knew how to play it safe when we had to."

Telly Savalas made an appearance and was supposed to play

Nanny (now a spry seventy-nine years old), Carol (thirty-one), and director George Abbott (seventy-eight) backstage after the opening-night performance of *Fade Out-Fade In* at the Mark Hellinger Theatre, May 26, 1964 *AP/Wide World*

Carol, in neck brace and suffering from injuries sustained in a taxicab accident, and her husband, Joe, leaving The Hospital for Joint Diseases in New York, November 8, 1964. The next day, the producers were forced to close down *Fade Out-Fade In*. "I am sorry you don't think I am sick," Carol told them. "I hope you realize how unfair you have been." *Neal Peters Collection*

Carol was co-host of the short-lived CBS series *The Entertainers*, which *TV Guide* dubbed "TV's Hard Luck Show." She returned to the cast in early 1965 after being out of action for ten weeks due to her accident. Here, the January 16 show (left to right): Dom DeLuise, Ruth Buzzi, John Davidson, Caterina Valente, Carol, Chita Rivera, and Boris Karloff. *Pat Lillie Whelan Collection*

The first publicity photo of Carol (thirty-four) with her *Carol Burnett Show* leading men, Harvey Korman (forty) and Lyle Waggoner (thirty-one), April 1967 *Groove Tube Photos*

Vicki Lawrence, who turned eighteen a month before this photo was taken in April 1967, was hired to play Carol's sister because the two looked so much alike. At first, Vicki didn't appear to be very talented, but Carol had an instinct about her ability, and she was right! In a few years, Lawrence won an Emmy for her work. "You might say Carol took me to her bosom. Such as it was," Vicki deadpans. *Groove Tube Photos*

Lyle Waggoner was hired because he turned the heads of the women who worked in Carol's office. "The secretaries were the ones giving the thumbs-up or thumbs-down to the guys who auditioned," he recalls. Waggoner played the part of the handsome announcer over whom Carol would swoon weekly. *Groove Tube Photos*

ANNOUNCER (V.O.)

Ladies and gentlemen ... Miss Carol Burnett.

CAROL:

Hi. Welcome to our show. I, er .. Say,
can I be honest with you right from the
start? One of the hardest things in the
world for me to do is stand here and make
the little speeches that the hostess of a
show is supposed to make. It's not because
I'm awkward or frightened. It's because I'm
awkward and frightened. I mean I feel like
such a goof (GOES STIFF AND WIDE-EYED WITH
STAGEFRIGHT)....

Good evening, ladies and gentlemen, I'm
Carol Barnett, Burnett! (NORMAL) So why
torture you and myself? What we did was very
simple. We hired an announcer to help me with
introductions and things. We interviewed dozens
of men and I hired the one with the most pleasant
voice. I'd like you to meet him. His name is
John Smith. John, would you come out for a moment?
(JOHN ENTERS. HE IS TALL, BROAD SHOULDERED AND
DARKLY HANDSOME.)

JOHN:

Yes, Carol?

CAROL:

I just wanted the audience to meet you, John, and
for you to ... Oh, God! (SHE GOES WEAK-KNEED AND
LIMP AND SAGS AGAINST HIM)

A page from the preliminary script of the first episode of *The Carol Burnett Show,* as written by veteran comedy writer Arnie Rosen. Note that the role of the hunk announcer was conceived months before Lyle Waggoner was hired. The script was used almost exactly as shown here, with the exception of Lyle's name having been substituted for "John Smith." *Joe Hamilton Productions*

                    CAROL

... Now I'd like you to meet another young man

who, I'm happy to say, will also be a permanent

member of our cast. His name is as familiar to

you as it is to me. Say hello to...

(SHE GOES BLANK)

                    HARVEY (O.S.)

Harvey!

                    CAROL

Harvey Kornman.

(HARVEY ENTERS)

(APPLAUSE)

(THEY KISS)

                    HARVEY

Well?

                    CAROL

Well what?

                    HARVEY

Aren't you going to swoon or anything?

                    CAROL

Why?

                    HARVEY

Well, I watched you and Lyle and I thought if

I came out and kissed you, you'd fall down.

                    CAROL

Have you been eating onions again?

                    HARVEY

Forget it.

Another page from the first script, on which Carol introduces Harvey Korman for the first time *Joe Hamilton Productions*

                    (HARVEY AND LYLE JOIN CAROL ON STAGE)
                              CAROL
                    Well, that's it for tonight, folks. We er,
                    er...
                              LYLE
                    (STEPPING IN) We hope you'll be with us for
                    the first Carol Burnett show Monday, September
                    11th at 10 O'clock.
                              CAROL
                    (WHO HAS BEEN WATCHING HIM ADORINGLY)
                    If I don't melt first.
                              HARVEY
                    And we'd like to introduce the young lady
                    who played Carol's sister in our sketch
                    tonight -- Heather North... Vicki Lawrence.
                    (GIRL ENTERS)
                    (APPLAUSE)
                              CAROL
                    Goodnight now, and thank you. You've been
                    a pleasure.

                    (MUSIC: THEME)

A page from a test-taping of Carol's show in which actresses Heather North and Vicki Lawrence both played Carol's sister in front of two separate audiences. Lawrence won the role based on the crowd's reception to her performance. *Joe Hamilton Productions*

Harvey tries to keep Carol—who has just taken sleeping pills—awake during the test-taping of a "Carol and Sis" sketch called "Sleepless Beauty" on July 21, 1967. Korman won four Emmys during his ten years on the show. *Groove Tube Photos*

Jim Nabors, thirty-four, was the premiere guest on *The Carol Burnett Show* when it debuted on September 11, 1967. He went on to appear as the first guest of every season. *Groove Tube Photos*

Here's an odd publicity photo for Carol's first season. The CBS-TV security guard seems to be telling Carol to get lost. *Groove Tube Photos*

Carol and Ethel Merman, who was always one of her idols, rehearse a show-tune medley for the Burnett show taped on February 21, 1969. *Groove Tube Photos*

Carol as Nora Desmond—a takeoff on Gloria Swanson's character from Paramount's *Sunset Boulevard*. Swanson so enjoyed the characterization that she complimented Carol in a letter in 1972. Flattered, Carol asked Swanson to appear on the show as a guest. Steve Lawrence, also pictured, was a regular guest and one of Carol's favorite sketch comedians. *Groove Tube Photos*

Carol successfully spoofed the personalities of many celebrities, and here she is as Doris Day sometime during the 1969–70 season. Doris's son, Terry Melcher, thought that the send-up was cruel and he complained about it. *Groove Tube Photos*

One of the most popular sketches was a takeoff on *Gone With the Wind,* called "Went With the Wind," in October 1976. Carol played Starlett O'Hara, Vicki played Sissy—in a wonderful Butterfly McQueen impression—and Dinah Shore played Southern belle Melody. The sketch got the biggest laugh in the show's history when Carol paraded down the staircase wearing a curtain rod. *Neal Peters Collection*

In the summer of 1977, Carol was directed by Robert Altman in *A Wedding,* which was filmed in Lake Bluff, Illinois. She committed to making the movie before she had even seen a script because, as she put it, "I don't care what the movie is about...I just have to work with Altman." The film was released to mixed reviews in September 1978. *Love Child Enterprises*

Carol invited Dick Van Dyke to join the cast of her series when Harvey Korman left after the tenth season. But the program's writers didn't quite know what to do with Van Dyke, and he was uncomfortable with the variety show's weekly grind. He quit the series after a few months. *Love Child/Rydell Collection*

Carol fields questions from the audience—a popular weekly tradition—on the final episode of *The Carol Burnett Show,* taped on March 17, 1978. Though Carol was putting on a happy face, her heart was breaking. At this time, her fourteen-year-old daughter Carrie was addicted to drugs. *Neal Peters Collection*

Vicki as Mrs. Tudball, Carol as Wanda Wiggins, and Tim Conway as Mr. Bernie Tudball laugh it up during a break in taping the last show. Mr. Tudball's constant frustrations concerning his dippy secretary Mrs. Wiggins—who he claimed graduated from "The Secretarial School for the Idle"—made for many funny moments. Conway won four Emmys during his years on the Burnett show. *Neal Peters Collection*

Craig Richard Nelson as a psychiatrist, Carol as Eunice Higgins, and Vicki as Mama in a shouting-match sketch from the last segment of *The Carol Burnett Show.* Carol says that the tragic Eunice—whom she played in thirty-two sketches—was her most challenging character. *Neal Peters Collection*

Carol's charwoman character is probably her most identifiable, but she didn't always enjoy doing it and felt that the bit was overused. This was the last time she played the role on her series. Carol decided to end the show after 11 years, 286 episodes, and 22 Emmy awards. *Neal Peters Collection*

In 1979, Carol starred in the television movie *Friendly Fire*, about a family's struggle to determine how their son was killed in Vietnam. Here, Carol and director David Greene share a warm moment. *Steven Brinberg Collection*

The emotional turmoil Carol was experiencing at this time because of Carrie's drug addiction gave her greater insight into the role of Peg Mullen in *Friendly Fire*. In a scene from the film, she tries to deal with the senseless death of her son. *Love Child Enterprises*

Carol with Ned Beatty in a publicity still—a photo they both hated—for *Friendly Fire*. "It looks like something right out of a movie from the thirties," Carol observed. "I call this pose 'expression number forty-two.'" *Steven Brinberg Collection*

In March 1979, Carol starred in Robert Altman's *H.E.A.L.T.H.* For this scene she was required to dive into a pool. Carol had been afraid of diving ever since her days at Hollywood High when she leaped off the board and sneezed just before she hit the water. "Working with Bob is one way of conquering old fears," Carol joked. *Love Child Enterprises*

In July 1981, Carol played the boozing and scheming Miss Hannigan in the film version of *Annie*. (Bette Midler had also been considered for the role.) The film opened at Radio City Music Hall the following May. *Love Child Enterprises*

By the summer of 1986, Carol had completed her memoirs and been inducted into the Television Academy Hall of Fame. Here she is in costume as Charlotte Kensington, widowed matriarch of a failing raisin dynasty in the five-part television comedy hit *Fresno. Groove Tube Photos*

Carol Burnett today
Love Child Enterprises

a sketch with Harvey where they were two businessmen talking about an account, but in such a way that it appeared they were talking about a romantic involvement between them. Savalas didn't like the gay overtones of the sketch and didn't want to do it, but he eventually decided to go ahead with it anyway. During taping, when he said the first line, the audience howled. "You could see the change come over him," said one of the writers. "His eyes sparked as if to say, 'Hey, this is funny! I'm not even a comedian, and these people are laughing at me.'"

"Steve Lawrence was probably our favorite," Joe Hamilton says. "He appeared countless times, and became a great sketch artist. He starred with Carol in a parody of *The Postman Always Rings Twice,* and I also remember he was Bogart to Carol's Katharine Hepburn in *The African Queen* takeoff." ("I will *repel* your fleshy cravings," Carol, with that great Hepburn quiver in her voice, warned him.)

"One day we had a time problem and had to cut four minutes from the show. 'Hey, cut my song!' he said. I told him, 'Steve, you're a singer, that's why we pay you.' He said, 'Yeah, but the comedy is so much better. If I had to choose between being a comic and a singer, I'd be a comic.'"

In all the years of *The Carol Burnett Show,* there was a problem with only one guest. Paul Williams was booked, and when he received the sketch material in advance, he approved of it. Carol's attitude had always been that if a guest was uncomfortable early in the week, change the material; Williams seemed satisfied, so no changes were made. But then, the day before they were scheduled to go before audience and cameras, he sent a wire to Carol saying he was uncomfortable with the comedy and didn't want to do the show. Most people connected to the show felt that Williams's behavior was unforgivable. "He should have expressed his dissatisfaction earlier in the week, when it was still possible to do something about it," says Ed Simmons, "instead of leaving us in a desperate situation."

The show went on without him. Dick Patterson, a good friend who had starred with Carol in *Fade Out-Fade In* and was a recurring bit player on the show, filled in for Williams in the sketches. At the end of the show, the whole cast was on stage in tuxedos and gowns getting ready to tape their final bows when Carol stopped the proceedings. "We can't do this without Dick," she told Joe. "Somebody, please get Dick into a tux. He has to be up here with us." There was an expensive ten-minute delay, but, said Carol to a friend, "it was worth it."

Although one of the most exciting segments of any *Carol Burnett Show* was when Carol would join her costars or special guests in song, Carol has never thought of herself as a singer. "If I had to sing for a living, I'd be selling apples in the street," she likes to say. But Joe Hamilton, and many of her fans, believe that she is one of the most underrated vocalists in the business, "and that's because she underrates herself," says Joe.

Recalling her success singing "Meantime" on the *Julie and Carol at Carnegie Hall* special, Joe continued to encourage Carol to sing straight, not in character. When her series became popular, the network received a lot of mail asking why Carol didn't sing more, especially since the year the show debuted, RCA released a terrific album of songs by Carol called *Carol Sings*. "We had to drag her in [to] the studio for that one," Joe laughs. "We'd make a tape and say, 'Sounds good, let's play it back,' and Carol would dash off to the ladies' room so she wouldn't have to hear it." (Another album, called *Together Again for the First Time*, was recorded in 1969 for Tetragammaton Records, and teamed Carol with Martha Raye; in 1971 Carol recorded an album for Columbia, *If I Could Write a Song*.)

Maybe one reason Carol was insecure about singing on the program was because once, she had performed a ballad and was very proud of it, only to receive a telegram the day after it was broadcast from one of the most respected singers in show business. "Stick to comedy," he suggested. That hurt; she believed he was right, and she never forgot it.

"When I have to sing a solo, all I do is think about that spot and it unnerves me so much that it louses up the rest of the show for me," Carol has explained. "If they say, here's Carol in a pretty dress with her hair combed and she's going to sing, I freeze up." She was most comfortable singing the songs in character, like the Charwoman spots when she, as the cleaning woman, would sit on her pail and sing an affecting "I coulda' been a contenda" type of ballad. But even those became a grind after a while.

Harry Zimmerman, the original musical director of the show, remarks, "We had her singing 'For Once in My Life,' and she performed brilliantly, with a big, enthusiastic voice, while sitting at the edge of the stage. She had on a frilly dress and looked gorgeous. She hit her final note, sustained wonderfully, and the audience cheered. Then, to cap it, she fell back on her elbows, crossed her eyes, and made a funny face. It wasn't the moment we'd hoped for...."

Artie Malvin, special-material writer for the show for the entire eleven years, recalls: "I began trying to think of ways to make Carol comfortable. We built a homey set with clown pictures on the wall, because she likes pictures of clowns, and came up with the idea of her sitting on a staircase, answering a letter from a fan with an anecdote that went into an appropriate ballad. She was game. As it turned out, she was terrific in the spot for a few weeks. One day, she came to me and said it was driving her right up the wall. She put her foot down and said, 'Look, I tried it. I hate the spot. Please, let's not do it anymore.' We didn't." (Carol called it "the diabetes spot" because it was so "sweet.")

Insecure as she may have been, she was nonetheless supremely proficient. "I have worked with almost every important performer in the business from Sinatra on down. Carol Burnett and Bing Crosby were, in my eyes, the two quickest studies I've ever worked with," says Malvin. "And as brilliant as Bing was with music, he had a lot of trouble with harmony. Carol didn't." Malvin speaks of the time in October 1970 when Carol played all three Andrews sisters in a takeoff of *Hollywood Canteen*. Instead of lip-synching to a record, she spent many hours in the studio recording each Andrews sister's harmony part herself.

Carol was very definite about the kind of music she would and would not sing on the show. She wasn't at all interested in rock and roll, as one might expect. She concentrated on Broadway music and standards: Jule Styne, Rodgers and Hart, Gershwin. Artie Malvin and Peter Matz say they pushed for contemporary acts to interest a younger audience, but the only pop acts that appeared were entertainers who could handle theater music as well as their own hits, artists like Cher, Dionne Warwick, and the Pointer Sister.

When Artie Malvin did try to introduce contemporary material, Carol was usually not eager to perform it. Once they did a routine based on the then-new musical *Hair*, with which Carol was not yet familiar. She tentatively began reading the lyrics to the song "Aquarius" on rehearsal day. Then she walked over to Joe and whispered in his ear, "Jeez, you know, Artie usually writes such great stuff. But this is *awful!* Why'd he write this?"

The interesting paradox of Carol's insecurity as a singer is that she doesn't mind, and in fact thrives on, singing with another performer. Contrary to what one might think, she was never intimidated by singing complicated medleys with some of the most adept vocalists, like Bing Crosby, Perry Como, Ella Fitzgerald, Mel Torme, and Eydie Gorme, with whom Carol did some of her best and most memorable singing. "It's not that she's insecure about her voice, I don't think, as much as she just doesn't like to be onstage alone as Carol Burnett, talking *or* singing," Ken Welch observes.

Joe Hamilton disagrees. "Carol never really had confidence in her voice; she never thought she was that good a singer. She told me, 'I can sing Broadway songs, but that's it.' I said, 'No, you can sing any song that's written.' A lot of us felt that way."

"I just feel that people have a right to expect a voice like Eydie Gorme's or Barbra Streisand's. They are *singers*," Carol has insisted.

Artie Malvin remembers the day in February 1969 when Ethel Merman, Carol's longtime idol, was to tape a medley with her. "Ethel warned me in advance that she'd have to have the material early," he says, "so I sent over a cassette a couple of days in advance. On Saturday, she calls me on the phone, and in this big, brassy Merman voice, she nervously screams at me, 'The *goddamn* tape came out of the cassette...*goddamn contraption*!' She was a wreck. "You know what, Artie, I'm not gonna be able to read those *goddamn cue cards* either; I'm too *goddamn nearsighted.'*

"I thought we were in big trouble. But on Monday she arrived with the whole 'goddamn' medley absolutely memorized. Carol came in, and she, too, had it memorized. My office, which had a piano in it, was about eight feet by eight feet. The pianist started playing, and they started singing. When Merman opened her mouth in this room, the volume came out as if she were projecting from the stage of the Imperial Theatre. Carol was singing, too, and she's got a big voice. Still, I walked over to her and put my ear up to her mouth as she sang because, I swear to God," he laughs, "you could not hear one sound she was making."

Despite her background in musical comedy, Carol doesn't know how to read music. She isn't alone; some of the most brilliant vocalists in music history don't know an A-flat from a flat tire. She got through eleven years of special musical material and complex counterpart medleys by developing an ingenious system she calls "squiggles." "It was a notation system not a single one of us understood," musical director Peter Matz says with a grin. "But it worked. She had these 'squiggles' on the cue cards, arrows, circles, twists and turns on every word to indicate the highs and lows of the melody. How she matched harmony parts with these scribbles was always beyond me...."

"I watched Carol teach her method to Eydie Gorme, the consummate singer," Irwin Kostal remarks. "Eydie, who can't read music either, caught on right away. The system was too confusing for the unfortunate bunch of us who could [read music]."

Once an observer watched as Julie Andrews, who can read music, copied all of Carol's "squiggles" onto her lead sheets for a medley they were doing together. Carol patiently explained each and every little curve while Julie scribbled all over the paper. "Why, Julie?" he wondered. "Why are you doing that?"

As Carol pretended not to listen, Julie explained with that very proper accent, "Well, you see, I simply wouldn't *dream* of making a fool of her...."

16

By 1972, *THE CAROL BURNETT SHOW* HAD BEEN ON THE AIR FOR five relatively successful years. Carol was on a magical roll; she had earned numerous awards and citations in recognition of her work, and had even appeared on the cover of *Life* magazine. She was one of television comedy's few active female geniuses, and, as such, was tremendously popular and well liked; over the years, she'd forged a truly inspiring bond between performer and audience. As one writer has stated about Carol, "When she comes out to say good night, you momentarily sense that you're not just looking at an entertainer—you're looking into the face of a human being. The show's endurance said much about the irrefutable power of television at its best: People loved Carol Burnett. They seemed especially to love the way much of her humor seemed to focus on everyday inanities. They felt her comedy spoke to them.

In July 1971, Carol taped another television special with Julie Andrews, this one called *Julie and Carol at Lincoln Center.* It aired the following December. That same month, Carol also appeared in a television revival of *Once Upon a Mattress* for CBS. Production cost was six hundred thousand dollars, this compared to the budget of the first special ten years earlier—ninety-one thousand dollars.

While Carol was rehearsing for the *Mattress* revival, she got a phone call from Walter Matthau. The two had met a couple of times at parties, and Carol had told him that she'd enjoyed his work in films, but they were not close friends. At first, when she got the message, she assumed he was calling to ask for a charitable contribution or a donation to a political campaign. "That's the only time a movie star calls a television performer," she joked. She returned the phone call.

"Do you still love me, Carol?" he asked.

"More than ever."

"Wanna work with me?" he wondered.

"Is the pope Catholic?" she answered. "Am I crazy? Of course I do. When?"

That evening, Matthau, Jennings Lang from Universal, writer/producer Julius Epstein, and director Martin Ritt joined Carol and Joe at their home. The men presented the Hamiltons with the script to a film called *Pete + Tillie − Stevie* (eventually retitled *Pete 'n' Tillie,* with Stevie's name changed to Robbie in the story), based on a novella titled *Witch's Milk* by Peter De Vries, inspired by the tragic death of his son from leukemia. The script was about a crudely witty and irrepressibly cheerful market researcher, Pete Seltzer, who meets Tillie Schlaine, a good-hearted, conservative "loser" who's determined not to become a spinster. They discover each other on a blind date at a party arranged by Tillie's matchmaking friend Gertrude. After dating for six months, they marry and have a son, Robbie. Pete and Robbie have an ideal father/son relationship; but then, at the age of nine, the boy dies of cancer. The remainder of the script deals with the pair separating as a result of the tragedy.

"I read it and laughed and cried and loved it," Carol told film critic Charles Champlin later. "And then I said, 'Why me?'"

For years, Carol had been reading movie scripts, hoping to find a vehicle she could use to stretch her talent. Despite the disappointment of her first film experience, *Who's Been Sleeping in My Bed?*, she still wanted to star in a major motion picture. It seemed the natural progression for her as an artist to take a risk now and then. Joe wasn't as enthusiastic as Carol was about this ambition.

"Frankly, my personal opinion from the start was that Carol would be in over her head with *Pete 'n' Tillie,*" he says. "But I understood that she wanted to challenge herself, and I agreed with her that she should. I had two very long lunches with the director and writer, Ritt and Epstein, because they were having second thoughts, I believe, and were very concerned. 'Do you think she can handle this role?' was the first thing they asked.

"'I can't answer for Carol as a talent,' I told them. 'Her talent speaks for itself. After all of these years, I should hope that it would. I think she should stretch, but whether or not this is the right vehicle or the right time, I don't know.'

"I can't read movie scripts the way I can read television scripts," Joe admits, "but my gut reaction was that it would be just a little too much of a stretch for her. I might have expressed that, but Carol has a mind of her own. When it was time to start work, it was her first big film to speak of, so we were very excited."

As soon as *The Carol Burnett Show* ended its sixth season in mid-June, Carol began production on *Pete 'n' Tillie*.

Walter Matthau said of his experiences on the set with Carol, "We're a couple of movie clowns. We worked overtime to make each other laugh. I wouldn't have dreamed of trying some of the pranks I pulled on Carol with some of my other leading ladies, like Streisand or Ingrid Bergman or Maureen Stapleton. But with Carol, it was a show-business compulsion to break her up every chance I got."

The characters Carol and Walter played sparred through a series of dates in the film before finally consummating their courtship by making love. Walter, seen from the back, then celebrated the event by playing ragtime piano in the nude.

"I didn't know how she would play the seduction scene in the film," he told a reporter. "I knew she wouldn't be nude—that's not Carol—but that there would have to be a suggestion of nudity. Well, I thought it would be a body stocking. Comes the moment for Carol to arrive from her dressing room. I, personally, am getting goose bumps from my lack of clothing. Carol, I see, is wearing a covering robe. We get ready to do the scene. I remove her robe and do a double take. She has been fitted with an enormous bra stuffed with bean bags...."

Later, when they did the scene, Carol said she was so nervous and shy, she wore two bras and two slips. "When I slipped into bed with Walter, he looked me over in that very unsubtle way of his and asked me, 'Warm enough?'"

As much as she enjoyed working with Walter Matthau, filming *Pete 'n' Tillie* was a frustrating experience for Carol. First of all, she had to play "straight man" to Matthau, and she hadn't had time to become totally comfortable with that role. But, worse, she simply did not understand her character. "I can't figure out why the hell Pete even calls her up for another date," she told friends. "Tillie is such a pain."

To her, Pete's interest in Tillie—and the subsequent romance—seemed improbable. Matthau's character was so charming and had such a natural sense of humor, she felt that perhaps Tillie should be more of a spontaneous person herself, someone able to appreciate Pete's personality instead of a stone-faced bore. "How can a great guy like Pete fall in love with such a drip?" she kept wondering to herself.

Still, when she was on the set, Carol was afraid to ask too many questions about her character or about the plot line; instead, she elected to stay out of the way, playing Scrabble in the corner while the scenes were being set up.

Throughout the shooting, she had the nagging feeling that she was playing the role "too close to the vest. I'm too scared to come out and give the character any personality," she lamented. "I want her to be more dimensional, but I'm not sure how to do it without *overdoing* it. 'Walter Matthau and Carol Burnett meet on a blind date.' People are going to think, 'sketch time!' If I so much as move an eyebrow, I feel, people are going to expect me to do a pratfall."

Martin Ritt was also concerned that Carol might instinctively resort to slapstick, and, says one observer, "he sat on Carol most of the time, warned her to be careful, and maybe even intimidated her a bit. Movie directors used to scare the hell out of Carol. She wanted to please so much, she was afraid to go out on a limb in front of Ritt."

Carol wanted desperately to do a credible acting job, and she felt that the only way she could accurately monitor herself would be to look at the "dailies" (movie jargon for the footage of film shot that day). She felt experienced enough to be able to pinpoint what, if anything, her performance lacked. But Martin Ritt, best known at that time for directing the television movie *Sounder,* would not allow any of the actors access to the dailies, because he felt that viewing them would be intimidating. It might affect the "naturalness" of their performances.

Ritt was only trying to protect Carol from her own vast insecurities. "If she sees herself as Tillie, she'll be so confounded she won't know what to do with her performance," he explained to one of his associates. "She's not going to like what she sees, so what's the point?"

Carol disagreed with Ritt's reasoning. "But I've seen myself so many times on television, I won't go into a catatonic state," she argued with him. "I can change some things if I know what I'm doing. I think it'll be to my advantage and maybe to the movie's if I'm allowed to see my work."

She lost the argument.

"I guess I'll just have to play it safe," she decided. "I won't give the role too much. Maybe I won't be exciting, but at least I'll be safe. What choice do I have?"

In television, Carol became accustomed to an efficient, quick pace. But filming *Pete 'n' Tillie* reacquainted her with the slow art of film-making, where most of the day is spent setting up for five-minute scenes. "What's taking so long?" she kept asking herself. "What are these people doing? All of this backstage drama over one little scene," she told friends. "I have never played so much Scrabble in my whole life."

When the movie was finally released in December 1972, most critics had to agree that Carol's apprehensions were mirrored in her performance, that all of her suspicions about her work were, unfortunately, accurate. Her characterization of Tillie was far from well defined, her performance wooden. When she saw herself on the screen, she cringed. If there was one thing she'd learned about working in comedy, it was, above all, to be human. In *Pete 'n' Tillie,* she didn't feel that she was, as she put it, "human enough."

During one very crucial part of the film, after her son dies, Tillie walks into the backyard and delivers an antireligious diatribe, cursing God. "You bastard! You bloody butcher!" she screams. No sooner had she finished the speech when her voice was heard again on the soundtrack saying, "Later, I could hardly believe that was me." It was as if the studio executives were nervous about blasphemy coming from one of America's sweethearts.

"That totally ruins the effect," Carol said when she saw the movie. "But what could I do?" she defended herself. "The script came to me that way. I wasn't about to go in and attack the powers that be at Universal."

"*Pete 'n' Tillie* is a buttoned-up movie," wrote popular film critic Pauline Kael when it opened. "And I'd trade it in for the stripping act Carol Burnett did nine years ago in *Who's Been Sleeping in My Bed?* The two of them [Burnett and Matthau] could have been great together if she'd let herself go. For Carol Burnett to be so staid on the screen is a form of deprivation for the audience, like Barbra Streisand's not singing in recent movies."

Joe Hamilton has to agree. "I don't think Carol fulfilled the expectations and the wants of the public," he says in retrospect. "It spilled a little over the boundaries of what I, as a fan, would expect of her."

Kael felt that Carol was "dull." Carol agreed, and wrote the critic a letter saying so. "She really nailed me in a way I can learn from."

Interestingly, some critics who are just as respected as Pauline Kael had a totally different perspective on the film, and on Carol's performance. Charles Champlin of the *Los Angeles Times* gave the movie a rave review, and of Carol, he wrote, "She is playing against her image, and she is extremely affecting, revealing an intelligence and a womanliness which her comedy may not deny but does not celebrate either."

Pete 'n' Tillie was not a failure; it was one of the twenty top-grossing films released that year. Julius Epstein was nominated for an Academy Award for his screenplay, and Geraldine Page, who played Tillie's matchmaking friend, was nominated in the Supporting Actress category.

"It'll probably take me about ten years to know what I think about *Pete 'n' Tillie*," Carol observed after all was said and done. "By then I'll be able to go and watch it at a drive-in in Pomona, and throw up intelligently.

"Doing a movie is like being pregnant. You've waited that terrible long wait to see if it's ugly. And if it's ugly, it will rise to haunt you late at night on television. I know. I've got a couple that haunt me."

But even after *Pete 'n' Tillie*, Carol still had not learned all of the necessary lessons about film-making as they applied to her. She would repeat many of the same mistakes two years later, when she appeared in Billy Wilder's remake of *The Front Page*, the third screen version of the 1929 stage classic by Charles Mac-Arthur and Ben Hecht.

Set in the press room of the Criminal Court Building in the Chicago of the 1920's, *The Front Page* revolved around the lives of reporter Hildy Johnson (Jack Lemmon) and his crafty editor, Walter Burns (Walter Matthau). Carol played Mollie Malloy, a prostitute involved with a radical who was sentenced to death.

Carol took the role because she wanted to appear with

Matthau again, and also because of the rare opportunity to work with Jack Lemmon and Billy Wilder. "How often does a chance like this come along for an actress?" she exclaimed. All told, she worked on the set for about two weeks. (She donated her salary to charity.)

From her first day on the set, Carol was uncomfortable; she didn't feel that she was doing a very good job, and was too embarrassed to ask Wilder to either fire her or tell her what she was doing wrong. "I was completely out of my element," she remembered later.

She believed that repressing her great emotional depth ruined her characterization of Tillie Schlaine in *Pete 'n' Tillie*. And now she feared she was about to repeat that mistake with her latest role. Mollie was a complex personality, a "floozy" not unlike the many "floozies" she'd played so well in sketches. But in sketches, she was open in her performance; here, she was a closed book before she even began—and only because she was intimidated and confused.

Filming the movie was another frustrating, agonizing experience. Throughout, Carol never knew exactly what her scene, or anyone else's, was about, because all were shot out of sequence. Worse yet, even individual scenes were filmed in segments, so there was no opportunity to build to any emotional peak. "She just wanted to get everybody in a room together for about thirty minutes and say, 'Okay, now let's rehearse this damn thing,'" says a friend. "But she had to respect the frantic, sort of disjointed way Wilder works.

"Also, Matthau, Lemmon, and Wilder were great buddies and had this male-bonding kind of rapport. I think that perhaps Carol didn't feel that she fit in . . . she felt like an outsider."

But Carol never voiced any dissatisfaction on the set; she just quietly did her job and tried to remain unobtrusive. "She used to come back and say, 'They called me in at six A.M., but they didn't use me until eleven at night. I sat and sat,'" Vicki Lawrence recalls. "Can you *imagine* treating a star of her stature that way? Carol was so . . . so *naive*."

"I stayed out of it," Joe Hamilton says. "Carol was her own boss when it came to the films. I voiced opinions now and then, but I certainly wouldn't go down to the set and cause any kind of scene. That wasn't my place. I'm a television producer, and I don't expect movie producers to come to my set and tell me what to do . . . so I extend that same courtesy. In the movies, Carol paid her dues, yes, indeed."

In the end, though, *The Front Page* didn't make much of an impression on Carol's public, or on her career. Now and then, it resurfaces, a skeleton in Carol's movie closet. Once, she and Joe were en route to a vacation and, much to her dismay, *The Front Page* was being screened on the airplane. She told friends, "I was a captive audience unless I wanted to jump out over Omaha." For most of the movie, she cringed and hid under her coat; Joe felt bad for her.

After the film, Carol borrowed the stewardess's microphone and announced over the public-address system, "Ladies and gentlemen, this is Carol Burnett. I didn't know that this movie was going to be shown on this flight, and I would sincerely like to apologize to each and every one of you." The stunned passengers applauded, and the sound of their laughter made her feel much better.

"I felt so cleansed," she said later with a smile.

"Actually, I enjoyed the movie. I just didn't enjoy that woman I played who kept running in and out of it . . . the one who never stopped yelling."

If Carol learned anything from her movie experiences, she learned to start trusting her instincts, that asking questions is, in fact, permitted when you are the so-called "star." But the passive way she handled herself on those film sets was much like the way she'd handled herself on her series. She trusted Joe, her husband and producer, and the writing staff and the rest of the crew implicitly. Rarely did she interfere with their work, or argue with their points of view. On Fridays, she would get her script for the next week, and then she'd breathe life into the comedy and into the characters, asking few, if any, questions about the show. It seemed to work.

But now, Carol began wanting to probe into creative aspects of her series that, before, had not concerned her. This wouldn't be easy for her.

"I felt that awful double standard of a woman being assertive and therefore masculine," she explained. "When a man is assertive, he's a great guy. If a woman says, 'I don't like that; I don't want that,' they think she's emasculating everyone and they have names for women like that."

But then, as she explained to interviewer Tom Burke in 1972, "I woke up one morning and thought, I haven't the *slightest* idea of how the show is put together behind the scenes, and we've been on the air all of this time. I'd been lazy, so I decided to start toning my mind."

Today, Joe Hamilton says, "What happened is that she started to ask questions, the answers to which had been covered in production meetings that she hadn't attended. That was irritating to me. Also, she was growing as an artist and there were things she wanted to say, to get across, but by the time she brought these things to our attention it was too late to do anything about them. This was frustrating to her. One day, I said, 'Look, Carol, you have got to start coming into at least one production meeting a week. I'd like to pick your brain. You're funny. You have funny ideas. Plus, if we're planning something that you don't like, you should have the opportunity to veto it before it's too late.'

"Carol's mind is very fertile," Joe continues. "She's never locked into something. It's never in stone with Carol, and that's why she became so valuable."

At first, she kept quiet at the meetings, afraid to voice her views. She was reluctant to say things like, "It's not a good idea." Instead, she would say apologetically, "I don't think I'd be good doing it." But eventually, she began speaking up and contributing thoughts and concepts. It made the writers' work much easier, even though this new involvement took most people completely by surprise.

"When Carol got more involved, even Joe backed off," Jack Van Stralen, head of special effects at CBS, remembers. "He had great influence on her in the beginning, but not later. It was confusing to everyone, because it didn't fit the pattern she and Joe had established on the set. All of a sudden, what she said was important, whereas before she never said a word."

"My *mind* has no gender," she said at the time, "and the show is named after *me*."

"Carol was always pretty gentle," Gene Perret notes. "If she didn't like a sketch, she was honest and straightforward about it, and sensible. Not like a lot of other comedians, who charge the comedy writer with trying to ruin the career. 'Why are you doing this to me?' they scream. You have an off day and suddenly you're working for the Communists."

Perret remembers one sketch that was based on Carol's ideas. It was a parody on the no-frills airline concept, and in it Tim Conway portrayed the hapless economy customer. The rug in the airplane cabin went down the center aisle through first class and cut off just before his seat. He didn't have a seat belt, they tied him in with rope. At one point, Carol, the stewardess, announced, "Now we're going to explain the safety precautions. In case of emergency..." She proceeded to whisper the instructions into the ear of each passenger so that Tim couldn't hear them. There was turbulence during the flight, but only Tim's seat was affected—it rocked and pitched in every direction while the others remained steady and secure. At the end of the sketch, Tim was ejected to his destination.

Perhaps a reason for Carol's involvement in her show was that during this time, she also began to become more involved in the feminist movement. "We're still a very big minority," she told *Good Housekeeping*. "I'm getting very ticked off when men say a woman's place is in the kitchen. Why should it be?" Carol said that she very much respected women who make their points of view known but are still proud of their femininity, "women who manage careers as well as a man, and are still feminine, like Lucille Ball."

At this time, one of the writers had put together a sketch about women's lib where Carol was to play Gloria Steinem on a talk show explaining the movement to the host, played by Lyle. As she did this, a mouse would run across the floor. Carol was supposed to jump up on her chair, scream for help, and proclaim her fear of mice. Then all of the buried clichés were to come out, triggered by that phobia. She was supposed to start babbling, "Oh, I need a *man,* and I need *kids,* and a *home*!"

Everything about this went against Carol's new convictions. She thought the sketch was in poor taste and that the ending was a "cop-out." "Lyle is in the sketch, too," she complained to Joe. "Why not let *him* jump on a chair, too? Men can be just as scared as women. Look at the man in *1984,* his great fear was rats."

Joe didn't agree.

"I hate arguing and friction," Carol asserted. "There's no excuse for insisting on your way when you have some of the best writers in the business. But dammit, Joe, that ending *does* make me mad. It's unfair to women, and I am *not* going to do it."

"Carol, you're letting these women's lib notions interfere with your comedy," Joe warned her.

Today, Joe laughs at the memory. "Oh, yes, we had quite a row over that," he admits. "She became strong-minded and stubborn about certain things she didn't think were funny, that she disapproved of on principle and wouldn't do. When she went into the women's lib movement, she did it with both feet and both hands. But there is a lot of rich comedy material about women's lib, not putting it down but satirizing it as you would anything else in life. So, yes, Carol killed some very fertile comedy material because she was overboard on the movement.

"We had one sketch that did air with Harvey and Lyle as construction workers arguing over a job, and Carol as the new coworker who finishes the work behind their backs as the men argue and bicker like two clichéd women. At the end of the sketch, she pulls off her overalls and has on a miniskirt underneath. Then the guys take her out for a drink, proving she was still very much an attractive woman even though she could do a 'man's job.'"

Another sketch had an ardent feminist applying for a job and, while waiting for the boss, mercilessly criticizing a stranger (Harvey Korman) for extending simple courtesies such as opening a door for her, or picking up her dropped briefcase. "You sexist pig!" she called him. "Every time you do that it reminds me of fifty years of oppression!"

As it turned out, Harvey was the man with whom she had an appointment, her potential employer. Carol was very uneasy about the sketch and decided not to do it. Jean Stapleton was the guest that week. "If Jean wants to do it, that's fine," Carol said. Stapleton did the sketch.

"Maybe I'm just older," Carol observed in 1975, "or maybe it just took me this long to decide what I feel or say might be important to somebody else. I always used to be so afraid I would hurt someone, and I never wanted to make an enemy—both on the show and in real life. Now I find it's easy and good for you simply to say *no*. I should have tried it sooner."

"But as talented as Carol was on that show, she often did not know her limitations," her director Dave Powers notes. "She thought she was more limited than she really was. And if you gave her total freedom, you wouldn't get the performance from her that she was capable of. So we still had to push her when she would resist material."

One of the decisions Carol made was to cut down on bosom jokes. "We've had enough of them," she told Joe. "Sometimes we've gotten too risqué. If it's a clever kind of risqué joke, I don't mind. But, otherwise, no way..."

This isn't to say that every decision Carol made became gospel. Joe Hamilton was still the executive producer; he and Carol had a give-and-take relationship. Sometimes she won; sometimes he did. Once, she and Vicki were doing a sketch about two women in a singles' bar sniping at the other women present. Carol had the line "Her stretch marks glow in the dark," which Joe said he thought was "gross."

"But I love that line," she insisted. "It's bitchy, but the kind of thing one woman would say about another."

"Carol, it's disgusting."

The line was cut.

Carol's devotion to feminism was the subject of friendly debates between her and Joe for years: "Yesterday he asked me, 'You really think a woman should work and the man should stay home, just because she might be able to earn more money than he can?' I said, 'If she is *better* qualified than he is, yes.' He just stared.

"I'm teaching the kids, too," Carol said. "Erin Kate says, 'I want to be a nurse' and I say, 'Nooo, a doctor.' And Joe *stares*. Carrie will say, 'I'm going to be a stewardess,' and I tell her, 'No, *pilot*.' And he explodes. He asks, 'You would *really* ride in an airliner flown by a *woman*?'"

Joe had always reinforced feelings of adequacy in Carol. But now that she was "finding herself," she didn't need quite as much prompting and encouragement from him. Now that she was cutting to the quick of some of her problems, she didn't want anyone camouflaging the areas on which she was working.

She would say, "I'm awfully dumb about movies," and Joe would counter, "Carol, you are *not* dumb."

"But, Joe, I *am*. I *need* to work on that."

Joe would compliment her on her dancing. "You're a natural dancer, you just don't know it."

"You know what?" she'd shoot back. "That's a lot of bull..."

Pronouncements to the contrary, Carol still had a long way to go before she could be considered totally self-confident. There was still that paradoxical "shrinking violet" side to her. Her friends remember the time in 1975 when she met one of her idols, Cary Grant, who Harvey had told her was a fan, at a cocktail party. She tried to hide in a corner and said she wanted to go home. When Joe asked why, she told him, "If he's a fan of the show, I don't want him to meet me, because that will spoil everything."

As she was going for her coat, someone tapped her on the shoulder. She turned around, and it was Cary Grant. "Hello, how do you do, Carol Burnett," he said very congenially as she stood there gawking at him. "It's so nice to meet you. I watch the show."

She was at a loss for words. "You . . . you . . ." she stammered. "You are a real credit to your profession," she said stiffly. He thanked her and they parted.

"Oh, Joe, how could I have said that?" she moaned on the way home. "Never in my life have I ever said that to anyone. I'm so embarrassed. . . ."

Throughout her years hosting *The Carol Burnett Show,* Carol still managed to find time to work in the theater—not on Broadway, however, but in Los Angeles. Back in May 1971, she and George Kennedy starred in Neil Simon's *Plaza Suite* at the Huntington Hartford Theatre in Los Angeles. It was the first time Carol had appeared on the stage since the *Fade Out-Fade In* debacle, and this was a nonsinging role, costarring in a three-act play with someone who'd never appeared on the stage before. Both actor and actress were nervous and expressed as much in their press interviews at the time, but the show was a success and the reviews positive.

In June 1973, Carol and Rock Hudson appeared in *I Do! I Do!* at the same theater. Gower Champion, who directed the musical on Broadway, also directed this version. A year later, Burnett and Hudson took the show on a successful eight-city tour. Rock, like George Kennedy, had never appeared professionally onstage before, and was praised for his willingness to be such a good sport. Carol, of course, was in her element before the live, receptive audience. To her, the satisfaction of being able to grow in a role and develop a character was a welcome relief after so many years of quick sketches and slapstick humor.

In March 1974, Carol starred with Alan Alda in a TV adaptation of Bob Randall's Broadway play *6 RMS RIV VU,* produced by Joe Hamilton and codirected by Alda and Clark Jones, who directed the first year of Carol's series. Carol and Alan played two married people who had an accidental meeting in a vacant apartment each had gone to look at for possible occupancy by their families. When they were drawn together and forced to fight the attraction, the results were pretty much what one might expect from an extended *Carol Burnett Show* sketch.

The show was done in three acts in front of an audience, and Carol said at the time, "It's one of the most favorite things I've done. I got tremendous satisfaction as a performer, on a par with the Julie and Carol shows, as far as having a terrific time." More than anything, Alda taught Carol a great deal about how to handle serious, poignant dramatic moments. "He shares what he knows with such generosity," she said later.

Ironically enough, Alan Alda was raised in the same area in which Carol was brought up. The two discovered in conversation that Alan, who'd had infantile paralysis as a youngster, used to lie in bed and listen to the neighborhood children playing in the nearby field. Carol was one of those children.

The Carol Burnett Show was a well-oiled machine, with sketch writers, special-material writers, and technical people constantly working on one show while planning ahead for the future, sometimes as many as eleven shows in advance.

A typical work week for Carol:

Monday. First, there would be a script meeting to go over any potential problems with the show that was to be taped on Friday. Recalls producer and head writer Ed Simmons, "Carol would be in on all of these preliminary meetings. And then, later on, Tim. Never Harvey. We wouldn't let him in. I was told by Joe right from the start, 'We all love and understand Harvey, we know how very valuable he is, but he does not come to meetings to discuss material. He hates everything, doesn't have the sense of humor of a gnat, and depresses everyone at the meeting.'"

After going over the script, the cast and guests would retreat to a rehearsal hall downstairs.

While the cast rehearsed, the writers made the changes that had been requested at the morning meeting and continued working on sketch ideas for future shows. Meanwhile, Bob Mackie and his staff, who had spent the weekend going over designs and choosing fabrics, were sewing this week's costumes for the stars, guests, dancers, extras, and anyone else on camera. Also at this time, the music department—Peter Matz, Ken and Mitzie Welch, and Artie Malvin—would meet about the numbers for the show that would be taped in two weeks.

Tuesday. "At 10:00 A.M. we had one of our most important meetings of the week," Simmons remembers. "I would go in with a batch of sketches for future shows for Carol to see, sketches that I'd selected from all the ones submitted by the writers. Since Carol did not go to the writers' meetings, this was her first crack at these scripts. Some stayed in for next week's show, some were junked, some would have to have a different ending. By Thursday, the entire script for next week had to be finished and mimeographed so that the cast could have it when they left the studio Friday evening.

"It was always a little hard to figure Carol during these meetings," says Simmons. "You never knew what would strike her fancy, and that could be intimidating. You had to remember that this was a woman who had seen and done it all. You had to forget that nothing really sounded new to her, and just hope that you could present a strong case. Her main concern was always, 'Well, what does Vicki do?' 'Harvey won't like this, will he?' 'Where does Tim come in?' Once, by accident, we laid out an entire show and forgot to include Tim Conway in any of it...and he was the guest that week."

Wednesday. Assuming there were no major problems, there would be a complete run-through of the current week's show at 3:30 P.M. "The cast would bust their guts to do the best possible job," Simmons says, "in front of forty crew members, writers, and everyone else involved—none of whom ever laughed. It was a tough audience." One guest star, Pat Carroll, used to call these run-throughs "the Nuremberg Trials." It was always difficult for the guests to have to perform before all of those glum, analytical faces in the windowless rehearsal hall that resembled a school gym.

Also, Bob Mackie would fit everyone in their costumes. Peter Matz would analyze the musical numbers performed at the run-through with just piano and drums, and then finish up orchestrations for the week. That night, and into the next day, he would be, as he put it, "orchestrating feverishly."

After the run-through, Joe, Carol, Ed Simmons, and the writers went into Joe's office to go over any notes that had been made. "One of Carol's main concerns at this point was the studio audience's comfort," Simmons says. "She would want to rearrange the show, saying, 'If I did this I could get into that costume faster, and then they won't have to wait so long between sketches.' She played to those three hundred people as if it were a Broadway show every Friday night, and that's why the audience was always so enthusiastic. If it meant rerouting to satisfy their needs, she'd want to do that. In the end, it satisfied the larger viewing audience.

"She was also concerned about sound effects. The more real they were, the better the laugh, she would say. She hated slide whistles to denote falling out a window, or drums to signify getting hit in the stomach. She wanted real body sounds, real clunks on the head. . . ."

From this point on, everyone was committed to doing the show as scripted with no further changes. "Rarely were there any problems, but we had to have a final meeting out of protocol," Simmons says. "I'd turn to Carol and say, well, what do you think? She'd say, 'I think I'd like to know how you guys are with paper airplanes.' Suddenly, we're all making paper airplanes and throwing them at each other, because we knew the show was in good shape. . . ."

Thursday. This was "camera blocking" day, the most tedious day of the week, where director Dave Powers would meticulously work with the cast to find the right camera angles for the sketches and musical numbers. Also, the music and any vocals that called for it were prerecorded.

Friday. At around 11:30 A.M., there was another camera-blocking rehearsal to fine-tune the show, "a start-and-stop rehearsal," as they called it. Sometimes a line or two still wasn't working; Carol would call upstairs for a new one, and the writers would scramble to come up with something better. Then someone would send the joke down, and it would be inserted into everyone's script.

That night, there would be two tapings, a dress taping and a final taping, with a production meeting between the two. "You can never tell with an audience," Simmons says. "Sometimes the dress would go right down the tube after we thought we had a great show. Never did Carol or Joe blame any of us. It was always, 'Gee, cold audience tonight. I guess they had to wait too long in line to get into the studio.'"

Throughout the week, scenic designers, choreographers, special-effects and props experts and all kinds of network people would weave in and out of the schedule.

After the second taping at 7:30, the cast and crew left the studio, with scripts in hand for next week. Usually, Carol, Joe, the costars, and many of the crew members would go to a restaurant and celebrate the end of another work week.

"Carol and Joe's absolute calm made the work possible; their aura of confidence filtered down to everyone else," Peter Matz observes. "Yes, there were times when we'd say, 'Jesus, we'll never make it.' Afterward, we'd all sit in the City Slicker Bar across the street from CBS and lament about how much better the show could have been...but there was always another shot at it next week, always fertile ground where you could stretch on the next show."

"Even though the show was ambitious, there was never that panic pressure you get on a lot of shows," director Dave Powers says. "Nobody ever really yelled. It probably all stemmed from her and her energy; she had a calming effect on everyone. In these kinds of shows, the lead comes from the star. If she's pleasant, everyone's pleasant. If she's a bitch, everyone's bitchy."

Only once did a sketch make it all the way through the week and then fall completely apart at taping. It happened in the tenth year: Tim Conway was playing an elderly mobster getting ready to sell out to another underworld figure and retire from the business. Steve Lawrence played a gangster, and Carol his gun moll. Tim's character died before the transaction could take place. Carol and Steve's job was to make it appear that he was still alive until after the deal was struck, by moving his arms and nodding his head. Carol hated the sketch from the start, but Joe was sure it would work. In front of the audience, the sketch got no laughs at all; they simply didn't understand the premise. At one point, Tim was to fall head first into potato-chip dip. As soon as he did, Joe went out onto the stage, stood in the center with his arms folded across his chest and said simply, "Stop doing this!"

Carol ripped off her wig, ran to Joe, and embraced him. Then she turned to the audience and exclaimed, "Thank God! He just saved our marriage!"

It was a funny moment to everyone but Gene Perret and Bill Richmond, the sketch's writers. "We felt lousy about it. I didn't take it well," says Perret. "I knew Joe had waited until the point when Tim fell into the dip so the sketch could end with a laugh. Then they were telling the audience how badly it was written; Bill and I were sitting in the booth saying, 'C'mon, guys, this just isn't fair.'"

(They never let Joe forget that night. Years later, Hamilton had a mild heart attack at the wedding of one of his sons. When he was in the hospital, he got a get-well card from Gene Perret and his partner with the message "Stop doing this!")

"There are many times when I'll rehearse all week thinking that maybe the sketch isn't for me," Carol once noted. "I can't find the *key* to it. There has to be an element of truth even when you throw a pie—a thought behind your face that makes it funnier when you connect.

"But then at the last minute, I find out how I'll be dressed, or I put on the wig or the make up, and suddenly a voice comes out of me or a walk develops or an attitude. And I think, Gee, I *am* talented. That thrills me to death. I go into the second floor bathroom at the studio, and I lock myself in a cubicle. Then I start talking and practicing over and over until the voice sounds right. Once I was trying to do an old lady's cackle for a long time in there. When I walked out, there were three old women staring at me as if I'd gone crackers."

Carol credits designer Bob Mackie as having helped to inspire many of her characterizations. Mackie started his career as a sketch artist for Edith Head and Jean Louis before being hired as an assistant designer on Judy Garland's CBS variety series. He quickly became a hot property as a result of his flamboyant designs for female entertainers such as Diana Ross, Cher, Mitzi Gaynor, and others. In his office, he has a framed, autographed photo of Carol with the inscription "To Bob, Thanks again for weekly miracles. Love, love, love, Carol."

Mackie designed Carol's wardrobe for the entire eleven years, and at one point he was also designing costumes for Cher's series, taped across the hall at Television City. He says that Carol and Cher had almost exactly the same measurements; in fact, some of Carol's old costumes were used in sketches on the Cher program.

"But Carol was very intimidated about looking attractive,

glamorous, or pretty," he recalls. "It always made her nervous. If she looked grander than she thought she was, she'd always do something terrible, like wipe her nose or clear her throat, or worse, cross her eyes. We never discussed it, but you knew she didn't think she was very attractive; she wasn't Loretta Young. So I did what I could to make it comfortable for her. I designed clothes for the Questions and Answers that were kind of casual even though they were formal. Everything had to have pockets so that she had a place to put her hands."

Very often, when Mackie got his script on Friday evening, he found that there weren't exact descriptions of the characters. Sometimes it was obvious: A hooker is a hooker. But sometimes a role fell into a gray area. A good example is Mrs. (Wanda) Wiggins, the secretary Carol played opposite Tim Conway's Mr. (Bernie) Tudball. The sketch idea, about a dippy secretary who frustrates her boss because she can't figure out how to use the office intercom, was a concept that Conway himself came up with.

Mackie says that the original characterization for Mrs. Wiggins was as an old gray-haired lady. But Carol had done any number of old ladies (and at one point the Grey Panthers criticized the show for "presenting the worst...view of older citizens"). Mackie came up with the idea of the clichéd secretary in her thirties who spends all of her time looking very busy but never files anything but her nails; she's always primping and getting ready for that after-work cocktail party. Carol came up with the dippy, empty-headed voice, and Wanda Wiggins, one of the dumbest people on earth, was born. "Mrs. a-Wiggins, where didja get your brain from? The Spiegel catalogue?" Mr. Tudball would ask her with his weird Swedish accent. "Sounds like you went to the Secretarial School for the Idle."

Mackie gave Carol a blond, seventies, Farrah Fawcett-style wig to wear, and then designed her black skirt to be so tight she couldn't help but squeeze her knees together and push her rump out when she walked. In one sketch, Conway studied her stroll across the office and retorted, "That's a novel idea, walking around and pointing to places you've already been."

And what happened if she couldn't get a "handle" on the character, if the sketch was just not that funny?

Carol has always maintained that being a writer for a variety show is one of the toughest assignments in television. "It's a thankless, impossible job to come up with ideas week after week —new concepts, new characters, new sketches. To have to set it up, 'score' and give it a good blackout. Four or five of those every week, it's impossible."

With typical candor, she once said, "Let's face it, they can't all be gems. So my approach is to commit to it and approach it as if it's the best sketch ever written, even though you know damn well it's the worst. You try to snow not only the audience, but yourself. Sometimes it works and you can really get away with it. Other times, you're glad when it's over and you move on...."

17

ABOUT THE EIGHTH YEAR OF THE SHOW, TENSION ON THE SET was unusually thick. Harvey Korman had become increasingly difficult. He was having emotional problems at the time that had nothing to do with the show but inevitably affected his temperament. "I was immature," he explains. "I was in therapy. I was chasing women. The marriage was flawed and, in turn, I was a flawed father. [Korman had two children by that marriage.] Then, everything came apart when my wife left me." Harvey turned to *est* training, and he said that its theories helped him a great deal; others claim that they only made him more headstrong, gloomy, and defensive.

Korman was frustrated with his role on the show, and never felt duly recognized. He had won three Emmy awards; but he was bitter—and rightly so, many people may feel, about the ceremony surrounding the second award, because the academy didn't feel obligated to make the presentation on the live telecast; rather, they wanted to give it to him at a luncheon. Korman boycotted the luncheon, and Joe Hamilton accepted the award for him.

Once during "Questions and Answers," on a particularly grueling week, a member of the audience asked, "What is Harvey Korman *really* like?"

Carol had to bite her lip. "Well," she began cautiously, "he's just the same happy-go-lucky character he is on TV." The crew broke up.

That week, Carol had a plaque made and placed it on Harvey's dressing-room door. It said MR. HAPPY GO LUCKY.

"Carol would usually be able to kid Harvey out of his moods," Joe recalls with a smile. "She'd rib him that things can't be as bad as he thought they were, that the script was funnier

314

than he believed it was. She'd get him out of it most of the time, except for one particular time when he almost ruined a show. That, to her, was the final straw.

"Harvey had been a pain for about four shows, and, after one of them, Carol really felt that his attitude had damaged the work. It was one thing to be a private pain in the ass, but when it interfered with the show, we all tried to draw the line.

"After the show, I went back to her dressing room. The door was locked. I knocked and told her it was me. 'I'll be finished in a minute, Joe,' she said.

"Ten minutes later, I went back, and she told me that she'd had Harvey in there, that she had told him off. 'He'd better be whistling down the halls from now on,' she said, 'because, damm-it, Joe, I don't want to see that grumpy face around here any-more.'

"She really let him have it," Joe says proudly. "I mean, she *really* did. She even threatened that she was going to call Harvey's agent and maybe even have him taken off the show. Well, this was a new Carol to me. I had to stop and digest it. All I could say was, 'Gee, Carol, that's the first time you've done that in all of these years. It's probably about time. I'm sure you made quite an impression on the guy.'"

Then, later, Joe thought about the legal ramifications of what Carol had done, and he warned her, "Be very careful when you do that, because you can get us in a lot of trouble. You don't know the contracts. I do."

"I don't care, Joe," she insisted. "I had to get that off my chest."

"To my knowledge, that's the only time she ever did any-thing like that," Joe concludes.

Today, Harvey, who says that he did not resent his second-banana status, has to admit, "As much as I felt like I was a costar, Carol was the one who did the Questions and Answers, she was the one who did the medleys with Eydie [Gorme], she had the solo comedy bits. It was *her* show. The fact is that without *The Carol Burnett Show*, there might not have been a Harvey Korman; but without Harvey Korman, there would still be a *Carol Burnett Show*. I can accept that today, but not back then. Back then, it was extremely frustrating."

Things took a turn for the better for everyone when Tim Conway was signed on as a regular.

"The minute Tim showed up, everyone began to laugh again," Carol told writer Leo Janos in 1976. "It's not that he's the funniest man on *television*, he's also the funniest man alive. One week into the season, we knew it was going to be great again."

Conway was born in Willoughby, Ohio; he graduated from Chagrin Falls High School in Ohio and spent two years in the army. After his discharge, he joined a television station in Cleveland as a writer-director, and soon became a comic. During a visit to Cleveland in 1961, Rose Marie, from *The Dick Van Dyke Show*, discovered Conway hosting a late-night movie show. She arranged an audition for him on *The Steve Allen Show*, and Conway was hired on as a regular. He married that year (he eventually had four sons and a daughter) and, in 1962, he was cast as the hare-brained Ensign Parker in ABC's *McHale's Navy*.

Harvey Korman notes of Tim, "He is innately funny, the type of guy who you'll be in a room with and then suddenly notice that he's gone. Then you'll look out the window, and there he is hanging down from the roof looking in at you. That's actually happened.

"He's tough to get to know," Korman continues, "because you have to dig through a lot of schtick to get to his soul. But once you find it, you realize it was worth the search. He's one of the good guys."

In Tim, Harvey found a confidant, a buddy on the set; they became close friends. "Tim and I were so miserable during most of our years together on that show," he explained. "We were both going through divorces. We both had secret lives; you might say we were naughty boys at times. There was a lot of turmoil, confusion, and pain. Those sketches were like a catharsis."

"Harvey, of course, is a sick man, and should obviously seek professional help," Conway says, deadpan. "Seriously, though," he adds, "I do think you're always funnier in a more depressed state. We were at our funniest, I think, because we were just able to say the hell with all the crap in our personal lives, let's get dressed up as frogs.

"I think a turning point was the day Harvey had this real serious problem and we were discussing it in his dressing room. As we were trying to find a solution to this heavy emotional dilemma, we caught a glimpse of each other in the mirror. I was wearing a chicken suit, and he was dressed as an Avon Lady."

Most viewers wondered if those many times Harvey and Tim

couldn't get through a sketch for all of the stifled laughter were legitimate. In fact, the cast and crew were so certain Tim would crack Harvey, they had a standard one-dollar pool, betting on how early in the sketch Korman would crumble. Conway says he planned in advance many of the shenanigans he pulled to break up Harvey, without, of course, telling his victim. Harvey did the same. Often they would involve the technical crew, when props were concerned, and swear their accomplices to secrecy. A sketch would be rehearsed one way, and then done another way in front of the audience. Basically, Tim Conway performed for his co-stars, and he says, "I felt that if I could break *them* up, certainly I could break up the audiences at home."

"Harvey was a real target for me," Conway admits, "and the minute I would look him in the eye, it was over for him. Often, he would plan something to crack me up on the air and it wouldn't work. I'd just stare at him as if to say, 'What a jerk,' then he would end up being the one to crack, not me. I loved to see the pain in his face."

Tim says that Carol was more difficult to catch off-guard. "She never believed in breaking what is called that fourth wall, meaning she didn't like to come out of character. Once in a great while, I could break her up. She wasn't easy to torture though, because, for the most part, she was very serious about being funny."

Writer Gene Perret says that Conway's ad-libs were "a plus and a minus. They could be deadly because Tim has a sense of humor that is very 'inside.' A lot of times we would be laughing at Tim because he was doing something he shouldn't be doing—and the reason he shouldn't have been doing it was because the people at home wouldn't know what the hell was going on."

Producer Ed Simmons comments, "There was a running joke on the show: Never give Tim Conway an entrance. Have him in the scene from the start. Because if you give him an entrance, it'll take him ten minutes to get through the door. Sometimes I think we gave him a bit too much freedom. Tim would stray so much, you'd forget what was happening in the sketch. But Carol and Joe let him have his freedom because when it worked, it *really* worked."

Toward the last couple years of the show, Carol was looking for more than a quick laugh in a funny sketch. She was inspired by the long movie satires they'd done, and was certain that the viewing audience's attention span was longer than had been thought by network programmers. Also, she wanted to make a statement with her comedy. As she explained in 1976, "I'm not as fond as I used to be of sketches that don't have anything to say. Not that I'm a big message deliverer. But I now like to find sketches that have more of a point-of-view. It used to be okay to take pratfalls and fall out of windows for no reason, but not anymore."

Of all the characters Carol has played through the years, she has said that her favorite is Eunice Higgins, the crass Southern housewife whose life with her dim-witted lummox of a husband and domineering mother provided some inspired tragi-comedy in thirty-two memorable sketches.

"Eunice" was written by Dick Clair and Jenna McMahon. Originally, Vicki was to portray Eunice, and Carol was Mama. Soon after rehearsals started, they decided to switch roles in order to have more fun with them. Harvey Korman played Eunice's husband, Ed. Because the writers and cast enjoyed the "Eunice" concept, and because audience reaction was strong, Carol, Harvey, and Vicki began reprising the roles and developing them.

If there is a fine line between horror and humor, the "Eunice" sketches crossed that line more than frequently. One critic put it best when he described the obnoxious characters as "a kitchen stewpot of malcontents and dopes, viciously raking one another over the coals, then making up only to start screeching again. It's so repulsive, it's wonderful."

The "Eunice" characters were originally written as being from the Midwest. Carol and company developed the Southern accents among themselves. "We wrote Eunice as a thoughtless woman," Dick Clair said, "but Carol put vulnerability into her."

"Don't start with me, Mama!" Eunice, always on the verge of a breakdown, would scream. "I am trying to hang on to my poise with *every fiber of my being*."

Eunice is one of those people who, in her view, could have had a better life, a career in show business, if only everyone else in her family hadn't interfered. "Eunice knows there a big world out there, but she believes she can never touch it because of her lack of opportunity and her fear of going out into it," Carol once explained. Or, as Eunice put it in one of the sketches, "I do everything for everybody, and everybody treats me like dirt."

Eunice sabotaged her own life every step of the way with negative thinking and selfishness, the typical loser syndrome. Also, she seems to believe that her unhappiness gives her license to be unkind to everyone around her.

Carol was brilliant at this portrayal, and it could be argued that she identified with the complexities of Eunice's character. If she hadn't been so determined to change her circumstances when she was younger, to make some of her "pipedreams" come true, Carol might have become a Eunice herself—a self-destructive, mean-minded, sad Eunice. Or maybe not. Still, the imagination behind the characterization must lie in the possibilities.

Bob Mackie dressed Carol as Eunice in a tacky, faded floral-print dress (always the same outfit in every sketch), white platform shoes, and her hair in a permanent permanent. Carol would stick her jaw out obstinately and pop her eyes in outrage, yet she was never truly ugly, just pitiable. She has said that she patterned Eunice after her mother, and the stressful relationship between Eunice and Mama certainly bears a strong resemblance to the tension between Louise and Nanny. "That's your fourth beer today," Mama would nag Eunice. "And I've needed *every one of em!*" Eunice would shoot back.

In one sketch, Eunice, Mama, and Ed went to a classy restaurant for a night on the town. But it's an evening of humiliation for poor Eunice when simpleton Ed orders a burger and fries ("Sky's the limit," he enthuses) and Mama steals the toilet paper from the ladies' room (shades of Nanny!). "When will I *ever* be able to associate with *human beings?*" an exasperated Eunice wonders.

Once, Eunice, Mama, and Ed had to go to the local school to visit their two sons' schoolteacher, played by Maggie Smith. The boys were incorrigible. The script revealed Eunice in her most small-minded moment. Carol has recalled, "I remember I read it and said, 'Oh, boy, this is sad. This is so...so...sad. I said to Vicki, Harvey, and Maggie, 'Just for fun, in rehearsal, let's play it straight.' And the result was devastating. ("I wasn't meant to have boys," Eunice whined to the teacher. "I *hate* those little no-neck monsters. When it was another boy, I wanted to *die!*")

Probably no "Eunice" sketch was more moving than the one in which Eunice seized the opportunity to go to Hollywood and meet her destiny on *The Gong Show:*

In the family living room, she insists that Ed and Mama listen as she practices her song. "Feelin's who-*a* who-*a* who-*a*, Feelin's," she whinnies before delivering the prized speech she wrote to prove her great sensitivity and depth: "Yes, there are so *many* good feelin's," she says melodramatically. "Like the ones I get watching the dawn come up and caress the deep purple walls of Raytown's Feed and Grain Emporium...."

But Ed decides that the song is dull; it needs to be shorter and peppier. "*You think Peggy Lee got to be a star by singing short and peppy songs?*" Eunice demands in her piercing Southern screech. "For your information, I have a class act, and they only gong the bad acts, they only gong the goofball acts, *they do not gong a class act.*"

Soon, she and her delusions are off to Hollywood.

Backstage before the show, when Eunice is most nervous and vulnerable, Mama calls to complain that the kids won't eat her macaroni and cheese. She wants to know when Eunice is going to forget this silly nonsense and come back home.

"*I am never coming home!*" she explodes. "I am going straight to the top. I am gonna have me a big house with a swimming pool and, if necessary, I'm going to hire me a bodyguard and a lawyer to *keep the two of you off my property....*"

Showtime. Eunice walks out onto the stage wearing a homemade sequined, ankle-length gown that fits her like a glove filled with water. A costume-jewelry tiara sits delicately on her head. Her face is caked with so much stage makeup, she looks deathly ill. But this is her big chance; finally, she is doing something about her life, and now everything will be different...better.

Self-consciously, she sings her song as the celebrity panel—Jamie Farr, Jaye P. Morgan, and Allen Ludden—watches. But she's so off-key, so awful, it's heartbreaking. The sound of the gong shatters her dreams.

As she stands in her fantasy spotlight, all of America laughs at her. Her eyes fill with tears, but she refuses to cry. The image freezes and shrinks into nothingness.

The role of tight-jawed, self-righteous, and defensive Mama (Thelma Harper) made Vicki Lawrence a star. It's astonishing how Vicki made that sour-faced, crotchety character come alive with nothing but body padding, a gray wig, and spectacles.

Producer Ed Simmons recalls the first day Vicki became Mama. "When she came into the rehearsal hall, Vicki was wearing a tight T-shirt with no bra; a young, beautiful, full-figured girl," he remembers. "Suddenly, she set her jaw, changed her expression and attitude, her voice, and this old woman emerged. Right away, we were caught up in this character, and we hadn't even designed a wig for her yet. To me, *that's* acting."

"It was as if she was possessed," cocreator Jenna McMahon has said. "She never needed makeup to look old. She just *was* old."

"She blew us all away," said Carol. "The first time she did it, flies could have flown in our mouths as we stood watching. I felt like Mama Rose in *Gypsy*, the ultimate stage mother. I was so proud."

Vicki has said that the reason she never wore aging makeup was because "Carol didn't believe in keeping the audiences waiting in between sketches. There was no time for anything elaborate. It turned out to be best..."

"As much as Carol loved doing the 'Eunice' sketches, that's how much I hated them," Harvey Korman says. "I hated my character of Ed Higgins because I hate portraying someone who's more stupid than I am. I didn't know how to approach it. I was lost. When I would see it in the week's script, I'd cringe and say to myself, 'Oh, no! Another bad week.' I loved watching them, they were so brilliantly written, but I just wished I didn't have to be in them."

Harvey had good reason to dislike the part, says producer Ed Simmons. "The bottom line is that it was a lousy role," Simmons remarks. "He was always getting dumped on by those awful women. It was the dullest role of the three, but Harvey managed to infuse it with something; he made it interesting to me...."

Joe Hamilton recalls having some problems with the network's Program Practices Department over some of the language in the "Eunice" sketches. "The *hells* and *damns*," he says with a grin, "gave us a lot of headaches. But that's how those characters talk. They weren't being obscene, they were just talking. We went through this controversy with the censors about how *All in the Family* had X number of *hells* and X number of *damns,* and if they did, why couldn't we? 'Because they're a sitcom, and you're a variety show,' they told us.

"So, as always, we would make trade-offs. We'd write in, say, twenty-seven *hells* and *damns* knowing full well that the censors would want to take out about eighteen of them. Then we sat down to serious negotiation: 'Okay, I'll give you four *hells* and three *damns,* if you let me have one *hell* here and two *damns* there.' That always worked," he laughs.

In 1982, Clair and McMahon wrote a three-act, ninety-minute stage play called *Eunice,* which was taped as a TV special in front of a live audience. It was directed by Harvey Korman and Roger Beatty. The show aired in March, and Vicki subsequently won an Emmy nomination. Shortly afterward, Thelma Harper was resurrected for prime time in a new sitcom, produced by Joe Hamilton, starring Vicki and Ken Berry, as her son Vinton, and titled *Mama's Family.* Carol made a few guest-star appearances as Eunice, and Harvey directed some of the early episodes. At his suggestion, Mama became less unreasonable, much more a genuine, vulnerable person than a hard-nosed caricature.

Throughout the years Carol's series aired, there was always much talk of the "cruelty" behind her comedy. Mostly, it was a highbrow theory that never amounted to much more than confusing rhetoric. Comedy is always elusive when it comes to definition, and especially if regarded in too somber a light. Granted, anyone who digs deep enough will probably find some element of wickedness in most displays of wit, but in Carol's case it was never sinister.

A woman gets hit by a pie, or slips on a banana—some people consider that wicked, and some, like Carol, just think of it as funny. When Carol did a sickeningly sweet parody of Doris Day, Day's son Terry Melcher found it quite cruel and complained about it; most other people (and probably even Day herself, given her background in comedy) found it to be rather amusing and on-the-mark satire. When Eunice finally gets her "just desserts," some viewers found her punishment heartless because the character is such a pitiful soul. Others thought of Eunice as a temperamental shrew. They were happy to see her get hers.

"In a very basic sense, comedy is very negative and cruel," Tim Conway observes. "It's 'She's so fat that...' and 'He's so dopey that...' It's probably the cruelest of all forms of drama. It can be pretty degrading sometimes."

In 1972, Harold Brodkey of *Esquire* magazine attempted to write a very long analysis of the "savagery" behind Carol's comedy. Both Carol and Joe consented to be interviewed for the feature, and both were completely baffled by Brodkey's line of questioning. Carol wasn't very comfortable, so she put up a barrier. In turn, the writer made her, and her husband, seem more than a little superficial. "Silliest damn interview I ever did," Joe said years later. "When I read it, I didn't even know who I was reading about," Carol added. (In retrospect, it's interesting that Carol allowed the writer so many hours of her time, considering some of the rather insulting questions he posed. "Do you think you're stupid?" he asked at one point.)

"It's not savagery, it's sweeter than savagery," Arnie Rosen tried to explain in a separate interview with Brodkey. "Maybe Carol would be uncomfortable to think along these lines, but we know pretty well that the basis of all humor is cruelty."

Rosen, who died before "Eunice" was even conceived, was Carol's head writer for five years, and so he probably understood her and her comedy better than most people. In analyzing Carol's earlier work, he also pinpointed possible reasons why she was so brilliant at identifying and playing the fury that motivated a character like Eunice Higgins, a woman just trying to hang on with "every fiber of my being."

"I think a lot of Carol's comedy is survival-oriented," Rosen observed in 1972. "You take a woman like that, a girl with the childhood she had—*no one* ever thought she was a beauty—there's going to be that survival instinct or there's going to be nothing. You take a woman who never shows temper, and who knows what outlet there is for it in her work? I don't say she does this. Maybe she doesn't do it consciously. . . .

"We're never obviously cruel, never obviously biased. Some say it's savage," he concluded. "I don't think that's the word. But when we find a target, maybe there is a little of the feeling of seek and destroy. . . ."

By 1975, as her show entered its ninth season, Carol had the nagging feeling that the sketches, with the exception of "Eunice," were repeating themselves.

Says writer Gene Perret: "We got into this thing with Carol where she wanted to have sketches that had 'meaning.' It got to the point where we were so busy trying to find 'meaning,' we were forgetting about 'funny.' I understood Carol's feelings—she was tired of doing broad comedy just for the sake of a laugh. She would come to us and say, 'Well, guys, it's just a sketch. It's just funny.' Our comment back was, 'Hey, that's what made the show what it is. You can't lose sight of the fact that you gotta be funny.'"

Carol was looking for challenging options beyond the kind of sketch work that was beginning to bore her. On March 6, 1975, she starred in George Furth's ninety-minute television adaptation of his Broadway play *Twigs,* a comedy-drama of suburbia in which she played three sisters and their aging mother. ("As the tree is bent, so grow the twigs," Furth wrote.) Sada Thompson won accolades for the 1971 Broadway play for her portrayal of the four characters. It was demanding work for Carol: The four roles were complex, emotional, and challenging. Joe Hamilton produced, Alan Arkin and Clark Jones directed.

Carol was said to be deeply unhappy with *Twigs,* with her performances, and with the way the show translated to television. Again, she felt that she'd probably gotten herself in over her head.

Meanwhile, there was concern on the *Carol Burnett Show* set. It looked like Harvey might not be back for the tenth season. If he were to leave the cast, it didn't seem likely that the show could survive. "Harvey Korman used to quit at the end of every season for more money, but he was always back," Ed Simmons says with a grin. "At the end of the ninth year, I was certain he was finished. During hiatus, I was sitting at my typewriter, and Harvey came stumbling in. He said, 'Well, I guess you talked to Joe and you know I'm back.' And I breathed a sigh of relief and said, 'You know what, Harvey? You are probably the biggest ass I have ever met in my life.' Then I got up from behind my desk and went over and kissed him on the cheek and said, 'But thank *God,* you're *our* ass.'"

The year flew by, and then, in March 1976, Carol taped another TV special, *Sills and Burnett at the Met,* with Beverly Sills at the Metropolitan Opera House. "I believe another Julie and Carol special was being planned," recalls the show's writer, Ken Welch, "and then Julie had to cancel. Carol thought teaming with Shirley MacLaine would be fun, but she had just been on the show the previous season. I thought Carol should be teamed with someone who would not be a normal guest on the show... someone like Beverly Sills."

It seemed an unlikely combination, "Opera Royalty Meets Queen of Comedy," and there was some trepidation on Beverly's part. Negotiations with Sills were on and off for weeks until, finally, Carol intervened. "I thought the whole thing was canceled," Ken Welch says, "but then Carol decided that she really wanted to work with Beverly, and so she called her personally and cut through all of that red tape. Carol will do that. She'll go through the proper channels, and if she isn't satisfied she'll take the bull by the horns...."

In an interview, Beverly Sills spoke about Carol and Joe: "Joe loves Carol's humor. He laughs just as loud as I do. She trusts his taste implicitly, which isn't to say that she doesn't sometimes fight his decisions. Also, Joe was as anxious to protect me in the show as he was to protect Carol. Everything had to be as perfect for me as it was for her."

"Do me a favor," Carol asked Beverly the night before the taping. "Pray for rain. It rained when Julie and I did Carnegie Hall, and there was thunder and lightning when we did Lincoln Center. It rained opening night for *Mattress*, on the night of my first Garry Moore show, and first show of my series. It's got to rain tomorrow for luck...."

The morning of the taping, there was a blizzard. The traffic commissioner declared a snow emergency for New York City. And Carol and Beverly had a wonderful time at the Met. The show finally aired on November 25, 1976.

The rehearsals were marred for Carol, though, when Joe Hamilton's secretary called her on the phone and read to her an item from the March 2, 1976, issue of *The National Enquirer,* with the bold headline CAROL BURNETT AND HENRY K IN ROW. The sixty-six-word gossip item said that a "boisterous" Carol had had a "loud argument" with Henry Kissinger. It also implied, to Carol's way of thinking, that she was drunk.

Carol and Joe had indeed recently been in Washington, for a performance before President Jimmy Carter and the prime minister of Israel. Carol had, in fact, said hello to Kissinger in a restaurant.

"My God! If what they wrote were true, wouldn't it have made headlines?" she asked the friend who read the item to her.

The full impact of the article hit Carol as she was walking across a street in New York on her way to rehearsal for the Sills/Burnett special. "Yo, Carol!" a cabby yelled at her. "I hear you really let Henry Kissinger have it! I didn't know you liked to get into fights! Way to go!"

"I was so mortified by that, I started to cry," Carol recalled later. "When I got to work, Beverly asked me what was the matter. I was absolutely at sixes and sevens...I wasn't really able to be myself at the rehearsal."

"How can they say that about me?" Carol asked Joe angrily. "They're trying to make people think I was drunk! That I am a loud, irresponsible drunk.

"Well, they're not going to get away with it,"she concluded. "I'm suing. That's all there is to it. I'm going to sue. And *that's* a wrap!" (She was using an industry term for concluding a scene.)

This wasn't the first time Carol had sued a publication for printing a falsehood. Back in 1971, *Inside TV* and *Movie World* gossip magazines published stories that declared that Carol would condone the use of marijuana by her children. She was infuriated by the inaccurate reports, and sued each magazine for $2 million. But later, she decided that the tedium of the suit wasn't worth the aggravation; both matters were settled out of court.

But that wouldn't be the case this time. Carol made good on her promise when she returned to Los Angeles after the *Sills and Burnett* taping. On April 8, 1976, while in rehearsals for her upcoming Las Vegas nightclub act with Tim Conway and the Pointer Sisters, she filed a $10 million libel suit against *The National Enquirer.* The case would drag on in the courts for the next few years...but to a very interesting, controversial, and landmark conclusion.

18

AFTER HER NINTH YEAR ON THE AIR, CAROL AND JOE MOVED into their new $2 million home in Beverly Hills; the house had two tennis courts and an Olympic-sized pool. *McCall's* called the home "a tangible payoff of nine seasons of network television" and said that the staircase "is the grandest staircase this side of Buckingham Palace" and the living room "is surely the most enormous living room in Beverly Hills, a community that prides itself on enormous living rooms."

It was said that Carol became concerned over the lack of privacy and security where she and Joe used to live. Tourists felt free to knock on her door without giving it a second thought because she was, after all, "our Carol." They would find her address by buying what Carol called "those damn movie-star maps. I do not know why those crooks are allowed to peddle them," she told an interviewer.

Once, a man rang the Hamiltons' doorbell at three o'clock in the morning to say hello to Carol; he was new in town and just thought he'd drop by. Another time, one of Joe's kids found a midwestern family sitting in her kitchen waiting for her to come down to breakfast. They had already gone through the kitchen cabinets. "Oh, we're just looking around," the man said. "Carol won't mind. We came all the way from Ohio!"

When they moved out, Carol and Joe hosted a black-tie, engraved-invitation garage sale, raising almost fifteen thousand dollars, and then donated it all to the Salk Institute for Cancer Research. They sold paintings, furniture, and, as Carol put it, "all kinds of crap," to their celebrity friends. "A lot of those things were Christmas presents we gave to Carol and Joe," Tim Conway quipped. "But since they were given to us by somebody else, it evened things out."

Joe was not eager to move, especially when he found out how much building a new home would cost. "I discovered," he said, "that when a couple builds a home, the divorce rate is about twenty-five percent; the separation rate is nearly forty percent. I didn't understand it then, but I do now. My God," he laughed, "that woman has driven me crazy. I'm as frustrated as she is by all of the delays and hassles that come with building. But it's as if she thinks *I'm* the builder."

But Carol found it difficult to contain her enthusiasm for the new home, not to mention her impatience to move onto it. She said that she thought of the experience as "a whole new chapter" for her and the family. "Just say I'm a very lucky human being," she told a reporter. "I adore my family and my job. I have a house with a front yard and a back yard."

Don Rickles lived in the quiet neighborhood where Carol and Joe were building the new home. One day, the caustic comic said to Carol, "Thanks a whole helluva lot for moving onto our street and bringing all of those damned tourist buses with you. Big-shot television star ruins neighborhood."

"Well, Don," Carol responded with phony sarcasm, "I guess the tourist buses had no reason to drive through this neighborhood . . . until now."

After Carol's sister, Chrissy, was divorced and raising a child on her own, she found herself living in an apartment she didn't like. Knowing this, Carol called one day and told Chrissy that she was thinking about buying a small house as an investment. She asked Chrissy to try to find one for her. Chrissy did. When the deal was closed, Joe and Carol handed Chrissy the deed—with the house in Chrissy's name.

(The first social event held in Carol's new home was the marriage of her sister to Fritz Frauchiger on July 4, 1976. The ceremony took place in the center of a circle of flowers in the Hamilton garden.)

At forty-two, Carol was estimated, in 1976, to be one of the highest-paid working women in the country; her annual earnings were said to be over $1 million. The media spoke of her "wonderful" life with three young daughters and a devoted husband. By now, she had a deserved reputation as being one of the nicest people in show business.

Writer Leo Janos interviewed her about her newfound spiritual enlightenment, daily meditation rituals, and the twice-a-week yoga classes at her home attended by such friends as Maggie Smith, Paul Newman, and Joanne Woodward. "For years I was like most everyone else, reaching for the brass ring on life's merry-go-round," Carol told him. "And like everyone else, I was mistakenly reaching *out*. The real quest takes place inside ourselves. I'm spending my time now reaching *in*."

Reluctantly, because she said she didn't want to sound "kooky," Carol spoke of her favorite book, *The Initiate,* which describes a British writer's conversations with a mystic of power and insight. "The trip I'm on is one that I have to take alone," she said. "Joe, for example, isn't really interested. But even if he was, this is something I have to do by myself and for myself."

Carol had completely forsaken "junk food," and was now eating only fruits, vegetables, dairy products, and other healthy foods. "Whatever she's doing, it certainly agrees with her," Harvey said at the time. "It's disgusting the way she glows with health."

Meanwhile, her show, now in its tenth season, was still in a rut. "When they did something she loved, she really got off on it," comments a friend of Carol's. "She still had great enthusiasm for the fun, meaningful material, but when they were doing something she didn't like, it was tough. Once I asked her, 'Why did you do that awful sketch?' and she said, 'Because we'd have come up ten minutes short if we didn't.'"

Harvey Korman's unhappiness over the material, combined with general frustrations that had mounted over the years in terms of his position on the show, hastened his decision. At the end of the season, he announced his intention to leave the cast once and for all, and this time he was not bluffing.

Ironically, considering all the years of angst, Harvey's departure was cut-and-dried, quick and simple. Joe Hamilton had called Harvey's lawyer at the end of the previous season to say that he was negotiating the contracts for the show's regulars, and to suggest that the attorney and Harvey go to CBS and make their deal. Harvey's lawyer told Joe that Korman would not be returning.

Hamilton recalls: "The attorney said, 'I told Harvey to come back, but he doesn't want to. He feels he's getting screwed and that's that.'

"I said, 'Hey, you know what he's making. You name me any

other second banana in this town making that kind of money.'

"So then I called Harvey to wish him luck. He told me he had this deal at ABC. I told him that if he needed me, just call. And that was the end of that.

"Harvey was making a helluva lot of money," Hamilton insists. "Most second bananas were making between thirty-five-hundred-dollars and nine thousand dollars a week back then. I really don't remember what Harvey's salary was, but I know it was over fifteen thousand dollars a week, which, at that time, was a star's salary. Carol herself was making only seventy-five hundred dollars a week in salary, though we had other percentages."

It was said that Carol was quite crestfallen by this turn of events. But, still, she would not get involved. "It was a tough situation," says director Dave Powers, "and when negotiations broke down, she was personally upset. She hated discord, it was awkward for her. I think she felt rather powerless about it all. . . ."

"There's a very private Carol that she'd rarely reveal," Ed Simmons observes, "and how she really felt about Harvey's leaving is anybody's guess."

Joe Hamilton says, "Obviously, Carol and I were disappointed. But I have to be frank and say that there was also a bit of relief, knowing that we weren't going to have to go through all of that drama and aggravation for another season. But the guy was brilliant and still is. Carol would miss him . . . a lot."

Another friend of Carol's speaks more to the point. "Carol had lost any patience she'd had with Harvey," she says. "There was a spiritual side of Carol at that time that made her feel very fortunate and grateful for her lot in life, and she couldn't understand why Harvey didn't feel the same way. 'Why is it that he always wants more, more, *more*?' she used to ask. 'How come he's never satisfied?' She decided not to interfere, to let him go off and pursue whatever it was that might finally make him happy."

Harvey Korman was offered a contract by ABC that he said he couldn't resist; it was to give him the opportunity to be a top banana on his own show. Korman was the latest in a string of performers who had been lured from other networks by ABC-TV program-director Fred Silverman, including Redd Foxx, Nancy Walker, Perry Como, and Barbara Walters. (Silverman was CBS's program director prior to *his* switching to ABC in 1975.)

"There's only one Harvey Korman," Silverman said in a press conference in September 1976, "and we wanted him badly. He's a fantastic comedy actor and a major reason for the success of *The Carol Burnett Show.*"

Korman finally felt fully appreciated as a performer, and was eager to begin work with the new network. But, still, he had to admit to some reservations. He told *The New York Times* that even though he was "a contented slave" on Carol's show, his exodus "could turn out to be a colossal mistake. We had such a great staff on Carol's show. How am I going to get people that good for my show? And where am I ever going to find another Carol Burnett?" he asked.

"I know that Carol was upset with me," he says today. "But Carol..." He shakes his head and his words trail off. "It wasn't a situation between Carol and me. How could it have been, when the two of us never really did business together? Maybe it *would* have made more sense for the two of us to have done business. After all, we were the ones who had to deal with the consequences.

"This wasn't an easy decision to make," he adds. "Despite all of the problems, I felt very close to those people. We were such a part of each other's lives, and a lot of water had gone under the bridge...marriages, divorces, deaths. We were a family, as corny as that may sound."

Joe Hamilton had a theory about Harvey's leaving. He felt that Korman was still hurting over the breakup of his marriage, and now that he had ended one family relationship in his life, he was determined to end the other—"the Burnett family"—and start anew with a clean slate. "I thought that was a crock," Harvey laughs. "But now I gotta wonder if Joe didn't have a point."

The Harvey Korman Show aired on ABC in 1977; he played an out-of-work actor named Harvey Kavanaugh in the sitcom.

It lasted four weeks.

Korman went on to star in a number of series, none successful despite the fact that he is regarded as one of the finest comic actors of our time. Today, he manages to be realistic about his post-Burnett success—or lack of it—on television. "People used to tell me, 'Harvey, you can't star in a show. No one knows what a Harvey Korman is.' I'd shout, 'The hell with you!' As it turns out, they were right. The reason is that I'm a little too talented," he laughs. "I can do so much, no one knows what I do. Also, I don't have what's called personal vision. Give me a script and I'll make it great. But don't leave it to me to come up with concepts or organization, because I can't. Tim [Conway] is the same way.

"Tim and I peaked on the Burnett show," he observes pragmatically. "Carol and Vicki would go on to other successes. Tim and I work today, but not to compete with our Burnett pasts, just to have a good time."

(In 1977, 150 episodes of *The Carol Burnett Show* went into syndication under the banner *Carol Burnett and Friends*. It has reached more than 85 percent of the country's viewing audience during the past ten years, and still wins its time slot in most major markets. Twenty-five new episodes went into syndication in September 1987.)

Carol, Joe, and their three daughters planned to spend the summer of 1977 with Beverly Sills and her family at Martha's Vineyard. But then Carol had the opportunity to work with Robert Altman, and so she jumped at the chance.

Robert Altman is a greatly respected director, a maverick known for his avant-garde movie-making techniques; his film credits include *Buffalo Bill and the Indians, Three Women, McCabe and Mrs. Miller, The Long Goodbye, Thieves Like Us, Nashville*, and, most notably, *M*A*S*H*. He has been praised for his treatment of women in his films; many successful actresses made strong first impressions in his movies, among them Lily Tomlin, Sissy Spacek, Sally Kellerman, and Shelley Duvall.

"If you want to lose your fear of the camera," Lily Tomlin once advised Carol, "you must work with Bob Altman. He will make you totally comfortable. *No one* makes movies like this guy."

Carol still wanted to do something worthwhile in the cinema, so she put the word out through mutual friends that she'd be interested in working with Altman. Meanwhile, he was casting for his new film, *A Wedding*. He'd been interested in Dinah Shore for the part of the bride's mother, but when she didn't return his phone calls he began to wonder how Carol might fare in the role. He approached her agent with the idea, and Carol accepted without so much as taking a look at the script.

"How can you commit to making a movie if you haven't seen the script?" Joe wondered. "I just don't understand it!"

"Because I *have* to work with Robert Altman," Carol explained. "I don't care what the movie is about...I just have to work with Altman. I think I *need* to...."

"But don't you think you ought to find out a little more about this?" he pushed.

"No, Joe," she insisted. "I know enough."

"I dropped it then," Joe says, "because Carol was hooked. She knew that major actors would work for him without knowing what the hell they were going to do, and that was enough for her. He's a brilliant film-maker, and her mind was made up. A few years earlier, Carol would have been scared to death to do something like this, go into a project blindly."

But after Altman gave her an outline of what the film was about and told her who her costars would be, Carol began to have second thoughts as to whether she could actually handle the work. "I have been awful in *every damn movie* I've ever done," she told friends. "I just hate all of 'em. And now I am so scared to death of repeating those mistakes...."

"That's because you've been too scared to make a fool of yourself," her actor friend Anthony Hopkins told her one evening over dinner. "Just follow your gut instincts, and you'll be fine. Take some chances...."

Robert Altman says that he and Carol did not discuss in detail her apprehension about film-making. "But in talking to her I was able to glean that she was quite unhappy about her prior work," he remembers. "I had the feeling that she had overanticipated the film business, and then overcorrected what she thought were her big problems. Like a lot of other people, Carol thought that making movies was some kind of big deal. It isn't.

"Also, part of Carol's problem, if you can call it that, is that she's a good girl, not a troublemaker like many of her peers. Instead of questioning the way she was asked to work in the other films, she just went along with the restrictions because she felt she had to. So she was very limited, both by the people she was working with and by her own attitudes," he concludes. "I don't think she misused her film opportunities. I think the films misused her."

Robert Altman has an interesting way of producing and directing movies—he makes it all up as he goes along. There is usually no script, just a general outline of what's supposed to be taking place before the camera. He gives his actors total freedom to create their characters, and so their characterizations evolve during the course of filming. No one quite knows what's going to happen from one day to the next. To Carol, it all sounded suspiciously like television.

"Someone like Carol is just real meat for me, because I know I'm not just going to get a good performance, I'm going to get a lot of creativity beyond a performance level," Altman says. "I'm getting writing from her, and great input. People like that search out people like me—they have a lot to give, and I'm willing to take it."

One day, he called Carol and asked her how she felt about the name "Tulip." She liked it, and so it became her name in the film. He gave her a three-hole-punch blue notebook containing elaborate typed descriptions and background histories ("backstories," to use actors' lingo) to each of the forty-eight characters in the film. Also included were extensive graphs of family trees and detailed explanations as to how everyone was related from one generation to the next. There was also an outline of everything that happens to each character in every scene, as well as a summation of what's happening to everyone else, even the people off-camera. Most of this information was never revealed in the actual film; rather, it was for the sole purpose of giving the cast a framework upon which to build their characterizations.

For the character of Tulip Brenner, the married mother of the bride who is pursued by Mac Goddard, the groom's uncle, Altman wrote, "She met her husband Snooks [played by Paul Dooley] while working as a waitress at a truck stop Snooks would pull into on his truck runs. She is truly religious and romantic... Snooks is the only man she has ever been with... Her reaction to Mac Goddard's advances would be shock and disbelief."

Carol wrote on the bottom of the page in big, deliberate handwriting: "...Then Tulip goes for broke with Mac until her 'religion' stops her."

A Wedding is the complicated, disorderly story of what happens the day a young man and woman from disparate families— old money and new—are joined together by matrimony. The bulk of the film takes place after the lavish Episcopalian church wedding, at the reception held at the groom's family mansion in a North Shore suburb of Chicago. The cast included Desi Arnaz, Jr. (groom), Amy Striker (bride), Vittorio Gassman (the groom's Italian father), Mia Farrow (a teasing nymph), and Geraldine

Chaplin, Lauren Hutton, Nina Van Pallandt, Dina Merrill, and in Altman's words, "hundreds of others."

During the course of the proceedings, the characters reveal dark secrets and scandals involving everything from incest, nymphomania, and epilepsy to alcoholism and interracial love. There are no less than two dozen stories going on at the same time, told in a succession of short, emotional, and often funny vignettes. The movie is meant to be a farce on rituals and façades, but it was so esoteric that it went right over the heads of most observers.

Carol's character, Tulip, falls for the illusion of romance when six-foot-seven-inch Mac Goddard, played with great flair by zany Pat McCormick, engages her in a flirtation. The sight of the overbearing, clumsy, and lovesick McCormick clutching Carol to his huge chest is memorable. Carol's role was an interesting Southern-belle-type character who fights the taboo of passionate love at first sight with everything she's got. Her great "affair" is all innuendo, flirtation, and flattery.

Before the film went into production, Altman held a press conference in Chicago and, facing twenty reporters, stated, "The purpose of this press conference is to dispel rumors that this film stars Carol Burnett. It actually has forty-eight major parts." Then he read off the whole list, even snoring at places. ("The real purpose of the press conference was to make the film sound dull so no one would come snooping around the set," he said later.)

Filming the movie in Lake Bluff, about forty miles outside of Chicago, was an enjoyable summer experience for Carol; she took her three daughters with her. There was none of that alienation and bewilderment inherent in her other film ventures. *A Wedding* was shot in continuity rather than in disjointed pieces, so that made understanding the work much easier for her. Not only was she allowed to see the film's "dailies," Altman encouraged it.

When the movie was released in September 1978, it was to mixed reviews, mostly negative. It wasn't a huge financial success, but Carol's instincts about working with Altman were on the mark. With him, she had definitely grown as an actress; she was finally released from her fright of film-making. Pauline Kael, who panned her in *Pete 'n' Tillie,* praised her performance in *A Wedding:* "[She] is more relaxed about acting for the big screen than she has been before, and she shows her gift—the quick pure looks her face can shoot out, those precisely overdone emotions of happy surprise, helpless heat, second thoughts. Carol Burnett brings out the insanity within sane people better than anybody..."

After the movie, it was back to work on *The Carol Burnett Show.* Replacing Harvey Korman would not be easy, but, says producer Ed Simmons, "There were no thoughts of panic. We still had Carol, Vicki, and Tim, a pretty good ball team."

But Carol and Joe put themselves in a very difficult, if not impossible, situation when they hired Dick Van Dyke to fill the vacated spot. Dick was anything but a "second banana," and Carol recognized this by making it clear that Van Dyke had costar status on the show. In fact, some of her friends say that she wanted to retitle the show *The Carol Burnett-Dick Van Dyke Show,* but CBS wouldn't allow it. (It was reported by the *New York Post* that Van Dyke was making five thousand dollars a week salary more than Carol—this not including Carol's ownership percentage of the show.) All of this is surprising, considering that in show business a star does not usually offer to share billing with another star.

"Carol leaned over backwards to make sure Dick was not treated like a second banana," producer Ed Simmons remembers. "He was not treated like Harvey, who, I believe, shared an office with Lyle for most of those years. Dick had a huge office of his own and was given 'star treatment.' Joe and Carol told me to discuss all sketches and clear all ideas with Dick. But Dick was a reticent type; he would say yes when he meant no. He was trying to be accommodating, I knew that. He was scared to death, I think."

Carol and Dick had known each other for twenty years, back to the days when both received the *Theatre World* Newcomer Awards for their Broadway debuts. They had appeared briefly together on *The Garry Moore Show,* and then, in April 1977, they costarred in the Bernard Slade play *Same Time Next Year* at the Huntington Hartford Theatre in Los Angeles.

Van Dyke had entered a crucial phase in his life and career. In 1974, he made the surprise announcement that he was a reformed alcoholic, and in the fall of 1977, he was the star of an NBC series, *Van Dyke and Company,* which lasted only twelve weeks. The day that show was canceled, Van Dyke was, ironically, taping a guest spot on Carol's program. He'd heard that Harvey was leaving the series and asked him, "How can you go? Boy, if I had this job, I'd stay forever."

Despite fairly obvious evidence that seemed to indicate that Van Dyke was brought into the fold out of mutual desperation—his to be back on television and Carol's to save her series—Carol deflected any such suggestion. "I don't care what anybody says about the reasons Dick and I are getting together, or about his career or mine," she said testily in an interview. "All I know is that we work together better than any two people and it's a very exciting proposition. It's going to give the show a whole new lease on life and be fun—and for me, that's all that counts."

"It doesn't matter to me what people speculate," Dick added. "What I want to do, at this point in my life, is to do what I want to do and enjoy it. I can't think of anything more enjoyable than working with Carol. Besides, our instincts are alike. We're almost a one-man show."

Most people involved with the program seemed to feel that the addition of Van Dyke to the cast was the natural solution to any problems created by Harvey's absence. "After Harvey left, we thought we had it made with Dick Van Dyke," said script girl Maggie Scott. "I heard some of the crew joke about it, saying, 'Harvey's gone, but who cares? We got Van Dyke!' But then you could see all of that peter out after the first week."

The odds were stacked against Van Dyke's fitting in from the very beginning. As talented as he was, he couldn't adjust to the fast pace of production everyone else on the show was by now accustomed to. "He couldn't learn his script as fast as the rest of them," Scott observes. "I think it started to give him a complex. He'd still be hanging on to his script on Wednesdays and Thursdays, long after everyone else had memorized it."

"Dick was like a fish out of water, as much as we love him," Joe Hamilton agrees.

Also, Dick wasn't as versatile as Harvey. He couldn't really do accents, he wasn't as much a character actor. Other guest stars had to play the Kormanlike characters. "There were many times when we'd sit in the booth and say, 'Christ, imagine what Harvey would have done with this part,'" says Ed Simmons.

"Harvey was more than a sketch actor, he was an actor who would get *into* sketches. The reason he was never a first banana was because he was never dominant over the characters he played; he *became* those characters," observes associate producer Bob Wright. "But Dick was a first banana in every sense of the word because he had a dominant personality. In other words, if you put a funny wig on Harvey, he was a character; if you put one on Dick, he was Dick in a funny wig."

Gene Perret spoke of the difficulty the writers had in coming up with suitable material for Dick without sacrificing Carol's obvious preeminence on the show. "We didn't know what to do with Dick in terms of status. And Carol understood this. She knew that she was dealing with an equivalent, yet he wasn't really equal because it was her show, and not theirs. We couldn't give him too little, because he was a major star, yet we couldn't give him too much, because it was Carol's show."

Dick's life-style became even more complicated when he moved his family back to Arizona. Prior to this, they were living in a house in Coronado, California; he'd rented a two-bedroom apartment in Hollywood and was commuting on weekends back to his family. But now he had to fly to Phoenix on weekends and then back to Hollywood on Monday. Perhaps if he had enjoyed the work, the grind would have been worthwhile. He didn't.

It's interesting that Carol made the same observation about Dick that many of her colleagues have made about her. "He does have a guard up," she confided to friends. "He's friendly and open...but there is a reserve about him. It probably has to do with this business—it's a hard business."

By November 1977, Dick was finished. "We came back from Thanksgiving vacation, and he was gone," says one crew member.

"I am really sorry to lose him," Carol said. But she wasn't interested in trying to find anyone else. From this point on, Harvey's spot on the show was filled by guest stars such as Ken Berry and Rock Hudson.

"Carol walked into my office one day and she said, 'Ed, Dick's off the show,'" Ed Simmons recalls. "She looked very tired, very distressed. It hadn't been a good couple of months. 'I have to make it clear,' she said, 'that this has nothing to do with the sketches. Please, tell the gang it has nothing to do with them, Dick was just miserable and he wanted out.' She was afraid that this blow would be demoralizing to my staff at a time when we all sensed we were in deep shit."

As she told Ed Simmons, Carol wasn't unhappy with the

writing on the show, as much as she was bored by it. She told friends that she didn't think she could do another restaurant sketch as long as she lived. "And how many movie salutes can you do?" she asked. "We must've saluted Harry Warren twenty times!"

"It wasn't that we ran out of ideas," says Gene Perret. "It was that we'd run out of ideas Carol would buy. Again, we were back to her wanting to make a statement.

"She's right, the show got tired. If you have a sketch that makes a statement and is still funny, that's terrific, but rare. Once you go for the statement and forget about the funny, you get a tired show."

The problems on *The Carol Burnett Show* were exacerbated by the success of the new ABC entry, *The Love Boat*, which had been airing opposite Carol on Saturday evenings since September 1977. *The Love Boat* was closely patterned by ABC after its successful *Love, American Style* series (1969–74), dealing each week with new comedic stories about romance featuring different stars in each episode.

For the first time since Carol had occupied that time slot, she was being seriously challenged in the ratings. Even though her show was still winning Emmy awards, it was obvious that not as many people were tuning in. To Carol, the worst possible ending to the last eleven years of hard work would be cancellation. She wouldn't allow that to happen.

"That's it. It's over," she told Joe.

Carol's mind was made up by Christmas, but only a few close friends knew of her decision. The time had come. She was going to end the show.

"Carol wanted to play it this way," Bob Wright explains. "She wanted to wait until we were renewed, and then say 'Thank you very much, but I will not return.' She needed that knowledge that they wanted her. A lot of us tried to talk her out of it, Joe and me included. 'We gotta make it a dozen years, Carol,' we told her. 'You can't stop at eleven.'"

Carol explained to friends, "I just don't want some network executive to knock on my door one day, step in and yell, 'Hey! *Stop this! This has gotten out of hand!*'"

When Carol's show sank to a shocking fifty-eighth among all network shows in the ratings in December, CBS moved the show to Sunday evenings at 10:00 P.M., where it joined the comedy block of *All in the Family* and *Alice*. It seemed to some observers that the network was giving Carol's program one last fighting chance by moving it out of the *Love Boat* battlefield.

"Look, it's their store," Carol told the *Los Angeles Herald-Examiner* in January 1978. "They could just as easily have canceled us as move us to another night. I'm pleased with the way the network has treated us. I have no gripes."

When asked if she was disappointed by the low ratings, Carol's response was, "Disappointment implies high expectations and that I didn't have. When I heard about *Love Boat*, I said this will be a hit.

"I wouldn't be devastated if my show ended; there are other things I want to do," Carol said, priming her public for her decision. "The only thing I would miss is working with the people here at CBS. Some of them I've known since 1960. But I won't fight it when the time comes to go."

It's interesting that after the show was moved to Sundays, it soared to number nine in the Nielsens. But that did not change Carol's mind.

In the next few weeks, Carol began telling her staff and co-stars of her decision. She, Joe, Roger Beatty, Tim Conway, and their wives were dining at Le Dome in Hollywood when Carol broke the news to them. "We're not going to do the show next year," Carol told her startled friends. "I just feel that eleven years is enough..." and she started going into her reasons.

The scene played out like a sketch from her show. Tim Conway's French onion soup was scorching hot, but—trying to act nonchalant and unaffected by Carol's news—he very methodically took in one steaming teaspoon after another. "Fine, that makes sense, Carol," he said quickly as he proceeded to burn his tongue.

She started to cry. "I just...well, I just..."

It was obvious to everyone that this was one of the most difficult decisions she'd ever made.

"Listen, hey, Carol, my God, don't worry about it...." Tim said, trying to reassure her as he guzzled glasses of cold water. "We understand..."

Carol excused herself and went to the ladies' room.

Once she was gone, Tim turned to Joe and shifted his stance. "Joe, it's quite obvious to me that your wife has gone crazy. She should be in a mental home," he said. "Now, I want you to get her back here, and let's all sign on for another four years. Okay? Fine."

Tim remembers: "We all made jokes about her mental lapse, that she'd get over it and we'd continue next year. But we knew ...We knew..."

"For me, the show ended in the tenth year when Harvey left," Vicki Lawrence said sadly in 1978. "I really missed him. I don't feel it's been as strong a show this year. There's been nothing that I've been proud of this year..."

"People flatter me and say that if I had stayed, the show might have continued," Harvey Korman comments. "I doubt it. Frankly, I was surprised that Carol didn't give it up after the tenth year. There wasn't much left."

No public announcement of Carol's decision was made at this time.

Just as she suspected, or at least hoped, her show was renewed by the network. "You're on for next year," Robert Daly, president of CBS, told Carol and Joe.

"Thanks, but no thanks," was Carol's quick response.

"Carol, you know what's going to happen now, don't you?" Joe asked. "We're going to take our attorney and business manager up to a meeting with Bob [Daly] and Bud [Grant, head of programming], and all they're gonna want to know is how much more money you want. Because this is what most stars do. They say they're quitting when actually they're wanting more money."

Just as Joe predicted, the CBS brass tried to offer Carol a financial inducement to return. "They couldn't believe it," Joe says, smiling. "The network offered us the moon to stay. But Carol insisted. 'No, the show has run its course,' she said. She wouldn't budge."

Ed Simmons remembers: "I was told, and I think it came from Joe, that she was offered an unprecedented three-year contract at a large raise, a larger show budget as well, if she would stay. CBS tried to clear all the decks for her. But her attitude was that a lot of money had already been made by all, and enough was enough."

The official announcement was made in February 1978. "We have asked Carol to reconsider her decision and return with her show for a twelfth year, but she has remained firm in her decision," said Robert Daly. "All of us at CBS look forward to the fact that she will continue to be seen on the network in major specials, and also to her return on a weekly series—the sooner the better."

"Another series?" Carol mused. "I'm never one to say never, but the way I feel now, I seriously doubt it.

"I am certainly not retiring from TV," she clarified. "It's just that after eleven years and two hundred eighty-six shows, including those that remain to be done this season, I want to be free for a while from the demands of a weekly show. Since going on the air we have done close to fifteen hundred comedy sketches and some five hundred musical numbers."

Carol was particularly sensitive about the industry's foregone conclusion that she had ended the show because of poor ratings. She bristled at the inference that if she hadn't quit, she would have been canceled. It hurt her pride; she admitted that she wasn't above that. When *TV Guide* published a report that credited "industry sources" with the information that "stiff competition from *The Love Boat*," had hastened her decision, Carol shot off an irate letter to the publication.

"Who are these industry sources who claim other reasons for my decision?" she wondered. "A clear-cut, honest, simple explanation seems to be unheard of in certain circles. I have never been a quitter or given up. If that were true, we wouldn't have gone this far. Quite simply, I feel we've 'done it' as far as a prime-time variety show with our format is concerned. A wonderful chapter for me has closed..."

After eleven years and twenty-two Emmy awards, the last *Carol Burnett Show* was taped on March 17, 1978. The two-hour retrospective with new sketches aired on March 29. Carol and Tim wrapped up the Mr. Tudball and Mrs. Wiggins series by having the characters move into new offices (at the end of the sketch, she accidentally locked him in the old one). Carol and Vicki ended the Eunice saga—Eunice went to a psychiatrist (played by Craig Richard Nelson), and Mama joined her. They rehashed old self-pitying history.

"If you had wanted a career in show business, don't you think you would have stayed in Lula Bell's tap-dance class for more 'n a week when you were ten?" Mama demanded.

"If you and Lula Bell woulda stopped ridiculing me every time I did a time-step," Eunice began, her voice rising, *"I'd be giving Mitzi Gaynor a run for her money today!"*

The frazzled psychiatrist tried to put all of this hostility into reasonable perspective: "You know, nobody really cares about

Lula Bell's tap class, or Mitzi Gaynor, anymore."

Jimmy Stewart, Carol's favorite actor, made a surprise visit singing "Ragtime Cowboy Joe." Carol reacted with sincere tears.

Highlights from past programs were shown, along with outtakes and clips of some of Carol's favorite duets. They put together a comical medley of Carol's "Tarzan" yells.

Tim, Carol, and Vicki introduced all of the bits and flashbacks. Somehow, the show seemed incomplete without Harvey Korman's presence, especially since some of the funniest bits involved him. Joe Hamilton says that they did not ask Harvey to come back for the show (but he was seen for a fleeting moment in a cameo, kissing Carol, dressed as the Charwoman, good-bye).

"The whole show was a terribly emotional experience for everybody," associate producer Bob Wright says. "There wasn't a dry eye in the control room. At the end, she said to us, 'Give me about three minutes.' But she wouldn't tell anybody what she was going to say or do."

Carol, in charwoman garb, sat on her bucket and delivered a moving, emotional, heartfelt speech about her reasons for leaving the program, and how much the last eleven years had meant to her. "This is an evening of mixed emotions for me," she said, her voice trembling with emotion. "Like graduation, it's a sad and happy time. It can't be possible that it was 1967 when Harvey, Vicki, Lyle, and I stepped on this stage for the first time. It does seem as if it were only yesterday."

Carol reiterated that "ratings do not have a thing to do with my decision. If they did, I would have called a halt to the proceedings a long time ago, because there've been many, many times when they've been a lot lower than they've been this season."

However, she admitted, she did feel it was "classier to leave before you're asked to. Quite simply, I'm no dummy," she said. "Now is the time to put it to bed."

She spoke of the "marriages and divorces and deaths and births" the crew and cast had experienced together. And she thanked the producers, writers, and crew.

"No one could feel more grateful than I am tonight for having had the opportunity to work with and learn from the brilliant talent of Harvey Korman, who has no creative limits," she observed. She also praised Vicki's growth as a comedic actress, and Tim Conway's genius and personality ("The fact that he's even nicer than he is talented is the best thing you could know about him.")

"On behalf of all of us, I want to thank you here tonight," she concluded, her eyes filling with tears, "and all of you who've been watching us, for making these years possible. You brought us together, and we're all so very grateful. I love you."

And then she sang "Carol's Theme" one last time. She struggled with it, determined not to break down, not to let her emotions overwhelm her. "I was never as proud of her," Joe recalls, "as I was when she gave that speech and then sang the song. To me, it was a golden moment."

> I'm so glad we had this time together
> 'Cause it makes me feel that I belong.
> Seems we just get started and before you know it,
> Comes the time we have to say so long.

After she finished, she tugged on her ear in recognition of Nanny. And then she turned around and walked into television history.

19

"I am no expert in drugs. I am no expert in being an addict. But I *am* an expert on being helpless, scared to death and without hope. I am an expert in being a parent who has gone through this..."

—Carol Burnett
to *People*, 1979

CAROL BURNETT'S WORLD SEEMED IDYLLIC. HER CAREER HAD been a fulfilling one, and now that the series was over, she sensed exciting new horizons ahead. She had a devoted husband with whom she shared not only a deeply personal relationship, but also a fascinating professional life. She was "Mom" to three beautiful children, who all seemed to be healthy, happy, and well adjusted to the circumstances of her celebrity. For instance, the night of the last show of her series, when Carol went to bed, she found a neatly printed note on her pillow from her nine-year-old daughter, Erin. It read: "Loved the show, Mommy. A real tearjerker."

Carol was respected and well liked among her peers and coworkers, known as one of the nicest, most giving women in her field. For years, not a shred of controversy had tainted her public persona. She had a charmed life.

"I think everything is okay. I think I'm a terrific mother, I adore my kids; they adore me, so far," Carol wrote for *McCall's* in 1977. "No major problems. No big communication gaps..."

But at around this time, Carol discovered that all was not as perfect at home as she had believed it to be. Her discovery might have had something to do with her decision to put *The Carol Burnett Show* to bed...or it might not have. She has never said. But her life did take a dramatic turn in 1977, and it would be two years before she would be able to rest easy once again.

Her daughter Carrie Louise was thirteen, and had just enrolled in the ninth grade at the Westlake School for Girls. Westlake was one of the most exclusive private schools in Los Angeles, with 647 girls from affluent families in attendance.

From the start, Carrie seemed to be having trouble at Westlake: Her grades, which had always been good, were slipping. Carol rationalized that it was because the school's curriculum was demanding. But she began to notice that the friends Carrie brought home were rowdy, undisciplined, and very spoiled. One day, much to Carol's dismay, she discovered that Carrie was smoking cigarettes. Carol reacted as many parents do at such a discovery—she punished the girl by having her bedroom phone disconnected. Then she and Joe made Carrie promise to stop smoking.

But Carrie's personality wasn't quite the same, and her parents knew that the change couldn't have been due to nicotine. She was sullen and disagreeable, not the friendly child Carol and Joe had raised. She was always fatigued, and moped around the house as if she hadn't been getting enough sleep. There were phone calls for her at odd times on the various house lines. Carol realized that something was very wrong, and she was determined to find out what it was.

"Against all of my convictions about the right to privacy, I started invading hers," Carol has confessed. "I began snooping around her room. I guess I wanted to prove to myself how wrong this gut feeling was. Instead I proved quite the opposite. I found weird scraps of writings. Senseless poems, stories and drawings. I found things I didn't even recognize...drug paraphernalia."

When she began eavesdropping on her daughter's telephone conversations, some of her worst fears were confirmed. Carrie was drinking beer, and from what her mother could glean from the one-sided conversations, she was apparently socializing with drug users. The thought of her innocent child keeping company with "that" element was terrifying to Carol. But soon it became clear that Carrie wasn't all that naive; at thirteen, she was smoking marijuana. "My reactions, in order, were shock, terror, disgust, hurt and anger," Carol has admitted. "Hell, was I angry."

In an article Carol wrote in 1980 about Carrie for *Ladies' Home Journal*, she remembered: "I felt as if I'd been kicked in the stomach. Not *my* kid...vivacious, pretty, a fine student, a sensational sense of humor, loving. At thirteen, she already had it all. Why would she *need* to use a mind-altering chemical?"

Carol and Joe tried to bring up their children to be as unaffected and unspoiled by Carol's success as possible. In raising the girls, it was always a matter of trying to strike a careful balance between generosity and frugality. Carol had had only the barest of essentials when she was growing up with Nanny, and now that her children had so many advantages, she couldn't help but think that the girls were a lot luckier than they realized. In press interviews, she would express exasperation that they didn't appreciate their unlimited fortune. "It's funny, you work and you want everything for the kids. Yet sometimes I want to take them and show them where I lived with Nanny," Carol said, "and I want to say, 'Look, you've got a bed and you've got a closet so keep it clean, *damn it!*'"

One night Erin, five at the time, announced that she'd given the matter careful consideration and had decided that she'd like to appear on her mother's series. "I'd like to start off in small parts, of course," she said demurely. At first, Carol had to smile at the girl's precocity, but when pushed, she responded with a resounding "No way!" She told the child, "My old lady didn't have a TV show of her own. You go out there and work for yours the way I did."

Carol really couldn't relate to her children's reality; they had always "had it good," and words like *Murphy bed* never entered their vocabulary. Her daughters probably became bored very quickly with Mother's lectures about how grateful they should be for their life-style—that would certainly not be unusual in parent/child relationships. "I wish I could show them how little they need to be really happy," Carol told a friend. As she said this, one of the girls stood behind her mother's back and rolled her eyes to affect boredom.

Once when Carol took Carrie with her on a trip to New York, she showed her the small one-room apartment over the Italian restaurant in which she and Don Saroyan had lived when they were first married. The proprietor said later that Carol broke down and cried at the sight of the apartment. "I wanted Carrie to see the place," she sobbed. "*I* wanted to see it... because this is where it all began for me. It all started here...all the *joy.*" One wonders if Carrie was impressed.

"Face it, there's *no way* the girls can appreciate what having my own room would have meant to me when I was their age," she decided later. "The values they come by, they're going to have to reach out a lot harder for than I did."

Carol hoped that she had discovered the truth about Carrie's drug problem in time. Joe had been through this before with two of the children from his previous marriage. He knew that he and Carol were in for a bitter battle of wits and wills, but even he didn't know then the extent of the melodrama about to unfold.

Joe and Carol sat down with their daughter and confronted her. "We've been going through your stuff, Carrie, and this is what we know..." They stated their case. Carrie was dismayed and embarrassed. With tears welling in her eyes, she tried to explain, "I've only been *experimenting*... like lots of other kids."

"Experimenting? My God, Carrie, what does that *mean?*" Carol asked. She was as much genuinely interested as she was horrified. Why would thirteen-year-olds need to "experiment" with drugs? Carol had never in her entire life so much as *touched* a marijuana cigarette, let alone smoked one.

"All the kids are doing it!" Carrie said, frustrated with her mother's lack of finesse in these matters. "I'm not hooked. I've got more sense than to get hooked...."

"*I'm not hooked!*" The words shook Carol to her foundation. How did this child even *know* the phrase? It seemed so foreign coming from her lips. Suddenly, Carol was becoming very frightened. She turned to Joe. He was speechless.

They spoke calmly to Carrie for a while, hoping to reassure her because they could see that she was obviously frightened of their reaction. If they could deal with this problem rationally, they thought, maybe they could avoid an emotional confrontation.

In raising her children, Carol had taken care never to let them see her upset. "If I was angry at one of them, I *never* yelled," she said later. "I'd go, 'Now let's sit down and discuss this,' all the while believing 'They're going to think I'm the best mother in the world.'

"Carrie, please promise us," Carol finally pleaded. "If you're at a party and all of the kids are using drugs..." Carol's voice trailed off; she shuddered at the suggestion.

"Call us, and we'll come to get you," Joe concluded. "We mean it, Carrie. Promise us."

"I promise," Carrie swore.

"And promise us that you'll stop this 'experimenting,'" Carol begged.

"I promise."

Mother, father, and daughter cried a little, hugged each other, and went to bed happy.

Carol and Joe were relieved. They thought they'd handled the problem rather well.

But in a few days, Carrie's behavior was even stranger than it had been before. Now, her speech was slurred. Her eyes were glazed, as if there was no spark of life behind them. When asked to explain, she insisted that she was not using drugs, that she was just tired from "all of this schoolwork."

Joe and Carol didn't know what to think. What if their daughter was lying to them and still "experimenting"? What would they do then? While they tried to figure out what was happening, they decided to "ground" Carrie for a month. She was permitted only to go to school and then come back home. When she was moody every day, excitable one instant and depressed the next, her parents thought it was because of the punishment—they didn't know it was because the girl was getting high on drugs while she was at school.

The tension was becoming almost unbearable. Joe and Carol were beginning to argue much more than they ever had in the past. There were times when Joe wanted to forget about the problems for a while and concentrate on something else, anything else. But Carol couldn't do that. Her child was in danger, and she could think of nothing else. Soon, Carol, Joe, and Carrie began seeing a professional therapist. But Carrie couldn't relate to the doctor. She saw him as an enemy. And he did nothing to help Carol and Joe communicate. "All of this is driving a wedge in our marriage," Carol lamented.

Meanwhile, they tried to keep these problems from their other two children, Jody (age eleven) and Erin (age ten). "But they know it all," Carol told friends sadly. "Our whole family is coming apart. And God help me, I don't know what to do!"

As the months passed, the problems got steadily worse. Carol's "raids" on Carrie's bedroom were becoming part of her daily routine. She was finding pills, Quaaludes, "uppers," and "downers." Once, she found small scraps of paper with references to cocaine. Nothing surprised her anymore.

Whenever Carrie would be confronted with something new that had been discovered in her room, she would claim that the drug was not hers, that school friends had left it.

"And, anyway, how *dare* you go through my things!" she screamed at her mother. "I can't have any privacy around here! You treat me like a *criminal*! I *hate* living here!"

"Tough!" Carol responded. "That's the way it's going to be from now on."

By the summer of 1978, Carrie was fourteen and had added "speed," Seconal, cocaine, and "mushrooms" to her list of habits. "My head was in one place, my legs in another," she later recalled. "After awhile you can't remember how many you've taken. First you take the drug, then it takes you."

With an empty, bored look in her eyes, Carrie would stare at her mother as Carol tried to tell her how worried she was, how much she loved her and wanted to help her. Carrie would refer to these discussions as "Mom's Lecture Number 1,274."

"I never felt so alone in my life," Carol remembered. "Joe was alone. Each member of our family was alone. And helpless."

Carol's career had to continue despite all of this domestic despair. But because she is such a private person, most people on the set of *The Carol Burnett Show* those last two seasons had no idea what was happening in the Hamilton household. Carol did not confide in her coworkers. As far as she was concerned, this was a very personal problem. She was determined to keep it at home and not bring it to the set with her.

"I never got an inkling of the problem," Carol's producer Ed Simmons says. "Nobody on the show did. If we had known, we all would have been heartbroken for her and Joe. We would have tried to help—even though there was probably nothing we could've done. Carol kept a so-called 'stiff upper lip' at the studio.

"You have to wonder, in retrospect, if what was happening at home was an influence on Carol's not wanting to continue with the show," Simmons muses. "When you have something like this tearing your guts out, it's hard to be funny, I would think."

Harvey Korman, who was finishing out his tenth season when the problems first began, says, "We would've all been there for Carol, but she wasn't willing to share. We wanted her to open up. We were hearing things...."

"As soon as the series was finished, we began making plans," says Bob Wright. "Carol said that she definitely wanted to keep working. Erma Bombeck was very big then, and Dick Clair and Jenna McMahon, who wrote *Eunice,* did a treatment on Bombeck's *The Grass Is Always Greener Over the Septic Tank.* Carol loved it and wanted to do it as a TV movie."

Septic Tank starred Carol Burnett and Charles Grodin as a New York couple, Dorothy and Jim Benson, who decide to forget the hassle of big-city life and move their family to what they think will be an easier existence in suburbia. "She's caught between fun and fertilizer," read the ad copy for the special.

(One of the Benson children was played by Eric Stoltz, who went on to movie fame years later in the film *Mask,* in which he played Cher's deformed son.)

Joe Hamilton produced the two-hour movie, which aired on October 25, 1978, to decent ratings but mixed reviews. Carol wasn't particularly happy about the way the movie turned out. She told friends she was more disappointed about the outcome for Erma Bombeck's sake than for her own.

In short order, Carol also filmed an updated TV adaptation of Laura Z. Hobson's novel *The Tenth Month.* In it, she portrayed a respected New York free-lance journalist, divorced and in her forties, who unexpectedly becomes pregnant out of wedlock. The baby's father is already married, with children. He—as well as her brother and her sister-in-law—thinks she should have an abortion. Though she doesn't want to abort the child, she fears the scandal of unwed motherhood. So she hides out in Spanish Harlem to await the arrival of the baby she has decided to have secretly and then adopt legally. In the end, she changes her mind; the child will know she is his mother.

The adaptation was written by Joan Tewkesbury (who'd written *Nashville*). When the story was originally conceived in the 1940's, the plot was interesting and evocative. But as a contemporary piece, given that it isn't such a scandal anymore for a single adult woman to have a baby, the movie seemed out of touch with the times. In the end, it was a rather dreary work that came at a dreary time in Carol's life.

Also at this point, she was beginning work on *Friendly Fire,* a made-for-TV movie in which she would star as the crusading mother of a soldier killed in Vietnam under mysterious circumstances. This would be a demanding, draining role, and would present itself at an already difficult time in Carol's life. She was also committed to Robert Altman's next motion picture, *H.E.A.L.T.H*, which was set to begin filming early the next year. So despite the drama unfolding at home, Carol was determined to continue working.

January 1979. Carol and Joe were still mystified as to what they should be doing about Carrie's drug dependency. Naively, they stopped Carrie's four-dollar-a-week allowance. "Maybe that will help," Carol offered halfheartedly. "I really don't know any-more...."

Carrie then began selling her possessions—clothes, jewelry, radios, records, anything she could find—to get money for drugs. (A counselor later estimated that Carrie spent $10,000 on drugs in 1978 and 1979.) Soon she was "dealing" narcotics at school, and established quite a little drug business for herself.

"I was generally wasted all the time," she would say years later. "I'd get loaded mainly in school, during free periods or lunches. We'd sneak off-campus and smoke marijuana and take Quaaludes. I remember one time there was a group of us at the water fountain in front of Mr. Reynolds [Nathan Reynolds, the school's headmaster] and we were taking pills while we were talk-ing to him. He didn't know what we were doing..."

When Joe Hamilton called Nathan Reynolds to complain that there was apparently a drug problem at Westlake, Reynolds's response was that he had expelled students from school when they were caught using drugs...but that he couldn't expel them if they weren't caught in the act. "And we certainly can't police the whole school," he added.

Carol and Joe later enrolled their youngest daughter, Erin, at Westlake, so they apparently still had confidence that the school was doing its best to monitor any drug problem on campus. But, still, they took special care in keeping track of Erin's friends and her whereabouts.

(Nathan Reynolds later maintained that drug use at Westlake was "minimal—almost nonexistent," even though Carrie claimed that "eighty percent of my school gets high." He said that the standards were so high for those who paid the annual $3,250 tuition to attend that any student with a drug problem would be spotted easily.)

"I was up to two grams of cocaine a day," Carrie confessed. "My grades dropped from the 90s to the 70s and a couple of teachers asked me about it but I was never confronted. I'd do coke in the bathroom and out in the parking lot. I spent every cent on it....

"Before I could do my homework or anything else, I was thinking about how I could get more dope," she'd later recall. "Anything. 'What are you selling? I'll take it.' Eventually, my day consisted of getting high before school, second period, fourth period, sixth, seventh and eighth, and then when I got home, before dinner and after dinner."

How did all of this happen? Carol and Joe really had no idea, and though they had only an inkling of how serious the problem was, they knew they had to find a solution. They soon realized that they couldn't trust the girls Carrie was bringing home from school. These fresh-faced youngsters in neatly pressed skirts and blouses were the enemy. At Carol's request, they were to leave their purses in the kitchen when they came to visit to ensure that they didn't smuggle drugs into Carrie's room. Sometimes, if he had enough evidence, Joe would call their parents to tell them that their children were drug users; most of the time, he said later, the parents would hang up on him. These were socially prominent, affluent people, and they were blind to the problem of drug abuse.

"Our daughter would never use drugs," one insulted woman told Joe before clicking him off the line.

"But, today, it's not a question of environment," Joe would say years later. "The only difference is that kids in better neighborhoods get better dope."

At night, when Carrie would finally fall asleep, Carol and Joe would toss, turn, and agonize the hours away, even though they knew they had a difficult workday ahead of them in the studio. Carol would get up in the middle of the night and check on Carrie. Was she still breathing? "My God! What if she stops breathing!"

Strangely, it didn't seem so long ago that Carol and her three little ones would say their prayers together and cuddle up in bed. On her way out of the room, Carol would purposely bump her head on the door, make a face, and walk into the wall. The girls would squeal with delight. It was all so simple.

Once, when Carrie was a little girl, she told a white lie, for which Carol spanked her. At bedtime, the child was still sniffling, so Carol went into her room, put her arms around Carrie, and talked about truth, character, and the importance of honesty. Carrie listened intently, never once taking her eyes off of Carol's face. As they spoke nose to nose for twenty minutes, Carrie seemed spellbound. "What a wonderful mother I'm being right now," Carol thought, as she smiled to herself and looked into her daughter's eyes. "I am *really* getting through to my child at this moment."

"Mommy?" Carrie began with an inquisitive look in her eyes.

"Yes...yes, baby. Do you have a question?" Carol knew that whatever answer she gave would be remembered by Carrie for the rest of her life.

"Mommy, how many teeth do you have?"

"Oh..."

She and Carrie certainly had some funny times together. One afternoon, Carol took her to lunch at the Palm Court of the plush Plaza Hotel in Manhattan. There was a long line for seating, but when the maître d' saw who she was, he took Carol's arm and led her and Carrie directly to a table. Carol was embarrassed, but her feet were tired, so she figured, What the hell...

After they'd eaten their meal, a distinguished-looking woman at the next table leaned over to Carol, and in a very nasty tone snapped, "We were here *before* you, but you were seated and served *first*. Now, how do you explain *that*?"

As her daughter watched, Carol glared at the woman levelly, and with mock indignation answered, "Because *I* am a first-rate hooker!"

Carrie was amazed; mother and daughter laughed about that for hours.

It seemed impossible that the years had passed so quickly, that everything had changed so much.

When Carrie was asleep, she still seemed like one of Mommy's fun-loving, precocious girls. But this "other person" she became when the sun came up was someone Carol didn't know, someone who terrorized her and treated her like an enemy. A mean-minded, selfish drug addict slept inside of young Carrie Hamilton, and there seemed to be nothing her mother could do about it.

How would Carol ever be able to turn on all comedy cylinders for a television special with Dolly Parton, *Dolly and Carol in Nashville?* She was to begin rehearsals for the show on December

28 for a January 10, 1979, taping before a live audience at Opry-
land. The program would air as a Valentine's Day special on February 14, 1979.

Joe Layton, whose friendship with Carol dates all the way
back to 1959 when he staged *Once Upon a Mattress*, produced the
Dolly and Carol special along with Ken and Mitzie Welch. He recalls that it wasn't a particularly enjoyable experience for anyone.

"I think maybe Carol needed to work to keep herself busy,"
he says. "I may be wrong, but I don't think that being in Nashville doing the show was a terribly happy time for her. She was
not quite the same; she was totally exhausted and drained. All of
the people around her were walking on eggshells...."

Carol had even begun to stutter, a result of her constant
nervousness.

"She tried to put up a good enough front," Layton continues. "Though she laughed and giggled, to those of us who'd
been on her sets for years, we knew that this particular atmosphere wasn't what it should've been. Carol's attitude was that
we're committed to this, let's be professional about it, get it done,
and wrap it up."

"People must carry on, whether they're in the public eye or
not," Carol would say. "You have to try to have a semblance of a
life. And you pray a lot."

There had to be a reason for Carrie's problem, but no one
could get to the root of it. Extreme peer pressure seemed to be
the logical culprit. Still, Carrie had once told Carol that she was
fighting for her own identity, that since her mother was a well-
known celebrity, she didn't feel significant; the only way she felt
she could "be my own person" was when she was high. Somehow,
to Carol and Joe, that excuse seemed much too convenient.

At one point, Carol retorted derisively to Carrie's claim,
"Gee, Carrie, your mom's a star. *Tough luck!* That's a cop-out, kid.
You were born into these circumstances, and it's up to you what
you do with them.... Look at Jane Fonda. She didn't use her
father as a cop-out. *She's her own person.*"

That little speech went right over Carrie's head.

"I'm compulsive and I'm an extremist," Carrie would explain years later. "I did have a big ego. I wanted to be Big Something. If I couldn't be the big wheel, at least I could be the big
dope fiend."

Two more doctors were consulted; neither of these consultations helped. "We would threaten, cajole, plead and negotiate," Carol said. "Joe would hit the ceiling, then I would. I would go in her room and she would start talking and make no sense. All I could do was cry. We were frightened to death of her."

Perhaps they should send her to school in Europe, they thought. Maybe she needed to be separated from her friends. That was one consideration. But what if she were to totally rebel and in defiance take twenty pills instead of just one? Carol and Joe felt they had to be careful; they didn't want Carrie to hate them. "But she already did," Carol said later. "Then one night she overdosed on some pills and we found her sitting in her robe on our driveway at five A.M."

They'd finally reached a breaking point. "Joe and I hit bottom," Carol remembered. "We were devastated, crying ourselves to sleep every night. Now I was beginning to hate Carrie. My own baby..."

Naturally, Carol was guilt-ridden at these feelings of resentment toward her daughter. She wondered how she could feel this way about her own flesh and blood. There seemed to be no end to the mysteries of this nightmare. In time, she would understand that it wasn't really Carrie she hated, but rather the drugs that were taking over her daughter.

There were times when she wished Carrie would have an accident and have to be in a body cast for months, anything to get her off the drugs. Those were the depths to which she'd sunk.

Her friends couldn't help but notice that Carol's face would darken whenever she spoke of Carrie; the glow of motherly pride in her eyes was all but gone. "She was ashamed of the girl," says one friend. "And she was ashamed of herself. She and Joe were distant toward each other. Her other daughters were scared, they didn't know what to do or who to turn to. All of the attention from their parents seemed focused on Carrie. They could never have fun together anymore; the family was all but wrecked."

To the outside world, it seemed as if Carol Burnett had it all. Only *she* knew the chilling truth. Her fame and money didn't matter, because her eldest daughter was addicted to drugs. Carol would gladly have traded in her wealth and success, all of those

People's Choice awards and Emmys, the TV series, anything at all, just for some kind of "cure" for Carrie.

How she must have envied women with close-knit families, with children whose gravest problems involved their complexions and grades. These were loved ones who shared with one another and did simple things together—like gathering in front of their television sets on Saturday nights to watch a funny lady sing about how glad she was to have "this time together." She elicited much laughter in households across America but, ironically, there was none in Carol's. In her household, there was mostly despair.

20

DURING THE TIME SHE WAS LIVING WHAT *PEOPLE* MAGAZINE would later label "Carol's Nightmare," Carol Burnett was working on a role for a TV movie that called for the kind of emotional reserve many people believed she wasn't capable of tapping. One has to wonder if the trauma of the real-life drama with her own child might actually have given her more depth as an actress to play the distraught mother of a boy killed in Vietnam.

Friendly Fire is the true story of Peg and Gene Mullen from La Porte City, Iowa, whose twenty-five-year-old son Michael goes off to fight in the Vietnam War in September 1969. After he is killed five months later, his parents' sorrow turns to bitterness and anger upon discovering that he has been denied the "honor" of dying in battle. He is listed as a "non-combat" casualty, not even a statistic of war, and hence not listed among its casualties by the Pentagon. "Why are they listed as non-battle casualties when they're just as dead as anybody else?" Mrs. Mullen asks.

As they pursue the truth surrounding their son's death, they are met with bureaucratic red tape, evasiveness, and, worst of all, lies. President Nixon sends them photocopies of his speeches on the war; Peg Mullen angrily returns them. She and her husband believe that the government has been conspiring all along to cover up the extent of U.S. losses in Vietnam.

In time, these wholesome, patriotic midwestern Americans —fourth-generation farmers and part of Nixon's prized so-called "Silent Majority"—actually become enemies of a government they had, before now, supported without question. Much to their shock and outrage, their phone is tapped and their mail censored. They are ostracized by friends and neighbors.

C.D.B. (Courty) Bryan, a writer for *The New Yorker*, became interested in their story and began to help in their crusade for the truth. As it turned out, Michael Mullen was apparently killed by accidentally misdirected American mortar fire, a tactical error in maneuvers—"friendly fire." Bryan was saddened but nevertheless satisfied by the explanation. However, the Mullens, by now radical antiwar activists, were not; they believed that there was more to the story.

Bryan's article about this series of events in the magazine was expanded into book form and critically praised as an important work about the Vietnam experience. By focusing on the Mullens' story, particularly on Gene and Peg Mullen's anguish, the book seemed to encompass the whole tragedy of the Vietnam War. (It was later estimated that there were over ten thousand non-battle deaths between 1961 and 1973, victims of so-called "friendly fire," whose deaths were usually not reported on the six o'clock news broadcasts.)

By 1978, five years had passed since March 1973, when the last U.S. troops left Vietnam, and producer Martin Starger was able to sell the idea for a TV movie about the Mullens' tragedy. (It should be noted that there had been other Vietnam-related movies on television prior to this, all of which were met with mixed reviews and even animosity. There were also related major motion pictures, most notably *Coming Home, The Deer Hunter,* and *Apocalypse Now.*)

Martin Starger and his Marble Arch Productions purchased the dramatic rights to Bryan's book for a three-hour ABC-TV movie. Fay Kanin was hired as coproducer and screenplay writer.

David Greene, Emmy Award-winning director from London (whose credits included *Rich Man, Poor Man,* the first legitimate network miniseries, *Roots,* and later *Fatal Vision*), was hired to direct *Friendly Fire.* Greene, who wasn't a big fan of Carol's and had rarely seen her series, somehow felt that she would be ideal for the role of Peg Mullen. "I had read about the terrible ordeal Carol went through as a youngster, with her parents and alcoholism, the way she raised her kid sister," he says. "My God, I thought, this woman must have great depth, great emotion for having gone through all of this. And I thought that if I could get her to link up with that emotion in her, I would have the actress for this role. My identification with Carol Burnett was not through her comedy, but through her background."

Greene says that when he approached ABC with the idea of casting Carol as Peg Mullen, he was met with "a barrage of opposition from everybody." They felt that as soon as Carol walked onto the screen, the public would think of her as a comedienne, and that association would destroy the film's credibility.

"They handed me a list of actresses they wanted for the part," Greene remembers, "and the chief actress they were really honing in on was a famous lady whose name I won't mention. She would have been acceptable in the role, but I wasn't excited about her because I felt I knew exactly what she would do."

ABC-TV programming chief Brandon Stoddard (who went to Yale with *Friendly Fire* author Bryan and once told him that his book was "far too threatening for television") recalls: "We thought of Joanne Woodward, Maureen Stapleton, Cloris Leachman. Donna Reed was very interested. We weren't sure which way to go. . . ."

Faye Kanin felt immediately that Carol would be perfect in the role. "I really had no doubts," she says. "Somehow, when one watched her work in the comedy sketches, there was always a sense of an accomplished craftswoman there, and there was also a sense of a dark emotional underbelly. You knew she had resources . . . she had depth, she understood and drew upon real human strengths and frailties."

Hoping to delay Greene and give him the opportunity to reconsider this "crazy" idea, the ABC brass suggested that he look at some of Carol's work and come back to them with some assurance other than "gut instinct" that Carol could be convincing in this role. He screened *Pete 'n' Tillie* and agreed with the critics who felt that Carol had totally negated herself as a performer by trying to be as unlike "Carol Burnett" as possible.

Greene then located a video tape of the final broadcast of *The Carol Burnett Show.* Nothing on the show impressed him in terms of drama until the end of the program, when Carol, in her charwoman garb, sat on the bucket and gave her impromptu speech. Riveted, he watched as she spoke of the sadness she felt about quitting the show, and how very much she had enjoyed working with, and would miss, her costars and crew.

"I could see that she was deeply moved, that she wanted to cry," David Greene says, "but that she knew she had so many minutes in which to make this speech. She would exert her discipline, she would not spray her emotion all over the screen, she would maintain control, be professional. As I watched her, I realized I was seeing Peg Mullen, a woman full of deep emotion, sadness, maybe a little anger, but she's damned if she's going to show it. I had my proof that Carol could do this."

The ABC executives decided to contact Carol, and when she received the script she was astonished that she'd been selected. "I kept looking at the name on the script," she said later, "to see if it was mine."

"When she first read the script, she told me about it, and I told her it sounded like a good idea," Joe Hamilton says. "Perhaps I was a bit reluctant, but any hesitation I might have had had no bearing on anything. I never stopped her from doing anything she believed in. I didn't get too involved in *Friendly Fire* because that was her baby ... I may have gone to one meeting, if that. When she accepted the role, I went to the set one day. Other than that, I didn't interfere."

"Carol was scared and she wanted to see me," David Greene remembers. "So I went to her and we talked for an hour or two. It was the first time I'd met her, and I found her to be a lovely, warm person who was a bit apprehensive about taking such a big step in her career. In the process of our talk, I reassured her and told her why I believed in her, and we decided to give it a shot." Ned Beatty was hired to play Gene Mullen, Dennis Erdman, Michael, and Timothy Hutton his brother, John. Sam Waterston played the role of the *New Yorker* journalist C.D.B. Bryan.

The television version of *Friendly Fire* was not welcomed by the Mullens, who pleaded with the author not to sell the rights. It's not uncommon for residents of the midwest to associate the word *Hollywood* with everything they consider crass and sleazy. The fact that the movie was being made at all, and that Carol Burnett had been unexpectedly cast as Peg, was, to the Mullens' way of thinking, exploitative. They also felt that the movie would open old wounds; they had put much of their pain behind them.

Also, Peg and Gene Mullen were upset about Bryan's book and charged that he had betrayed them by believing the government's story that there was no intentional cover-up of their son's death. They felt that Bryan had turned against them, and had distorted critical elements of their story. "He has me almost deranged," Peg Mullen said of the way the author depicted her in the book.

They did not wish to meet Carol, Ned Beatty, or any of the

other actors or crew. "We're not going to see it when it airs," they told the media.

The producers tried to build a relationship with the three surviving Mullen children by expressing their wish to make a strong statement about the Vietnam War. The producers hoped that Michael's siblings could convince their parents that the film could serve a positive purpose and make millions of viewers aware of what had happened to Michael Mullen.

Peg and Gene Mullen softened to the extent of offering the use of their farm for location shootings. But when David Greene felt that the actual farm was not visual enough for television, and had sets built that were—as he put it, "more traditionally American"—the Mullens were only more convinced that the film would not be realistic. It would be a while before their opinion of *Friendly Fire* would change.

Meanwhile, Carol couldn't help but be concerned that she was going to face the same kinds of problems with this TV film that she'd had with the cinema features she'd done. Her experience with Robert Altman had been more rewarding for her in terms of expressing herself as a dramatic actress, but *A Wedding* did have some comic overtones, and *Friendly Fire* had none.

The first scene shot was one in which Carol is seen driving to the post office to mail a box of canned grapefruit juice to her son in Vietnam. David Greene had chosen this particular scene to be her first since it had no dialogue and was not at all emotional. It was just a simple moment to ease Carol into her work.

"Action!" Greene shouted.

Carol started the car and drove up to the curb. She opened the door and started to get out with the package.

"Cut!"

She had stopped the car in the wrong place.

As they were setting up the scene again, the director went over to Carol, put his arm around her, and said, "You know, Carol, when that car stopped and you opened the door with the package in your hand, I suddenly had a great scenario play out in my mind. You could drop the package, trip over it, fall on your face, pick it up, and hit your head on the door...I saw at least five different schticks there."

Carol couldn't help but laugh. "You saw five? I saw twenty-five!" she said. "The car could've rolled backward without me, and then I'd chase it and try to get behind the wheel, and..."

The ice was broken, the unsaid spoken. Carol was, indeed, a comedienne at heart, and there was no need to forget that in order to do this role. "I had the lesson from *Pete 'n' Tillie* that we weren't going to get anywhere as long as we approached the role with the 'don't be Carol Burnett' attitude," David Greene says. "I wanted her to take a positive attitude rather than concentrate on who she wasn't supposed to be, a comic; concentrate on who she was in the film, a distraught and angry mother. After that day, there was no need to discuss her fears, or the fact that she was a comedic actress. We dealt with the business at hand."

There are many wonderful, gripping scenes in *Friendly Fire*. One of the most unforgettable is when the entire family accompanies Michael to the airport the day he leaves for Vietnam. His parents are touching in their awkwardness, unable to mask their deep concern. "An image of Carrie as an infant flashed through my head," Carol said when asked about her preparation for the scene. "The costume people had made this terrific mistake; they got Michael's hat just a little too big and it made him look as if he were twelve years old. That's when the image of Carrie came, when they first handed her to me. It sounds silly, but I licked her head. I didn't want to let her go. I wanted to hold on. The memory of that, and what I was doing in the scene with my 'son' just ripped me apart."

"Another fine scene is when Peg sees her boy lying in the casket and begins to tremble," David Greene remembers. "Carol's hands, her arms, her whole body just begins to shake, exactly as it had happened, according to Peg's memory. It was very moving. Peg was distressed because her son seemed so whole, complete. Virtually unmarked, he only had a small bullet wound in the back of his neck. 'Why couldn't he have been blown to bits so that I could believe he died in a war?' Carol said in the next scene."

"There weren't too many kidding-around sessions on the set," Carol recalled later. "It was simply because it was a real story about real lives, and we knew that there were people like the Mullens who were still living the pain.

"To this day, the Army has not given any real explanation," Carol said of Michael Mullen's death, "It seems to come down to: it wasn't anybody's fault. That's the way the movie ends; it leaves you hanging. That may not satisfy some people. It's real life; there aren't always answers."

It's not difficult to imagine that the emotional turmoil Carol was experiencing at this time with her daughter gave her greater insight as to how to handle the scenes in which she had to deal with the senseless death of her son. Whether she realized it or not, Carol must have been drawing from genuine courage, grief, and despair, from the extreme disappointment she felt at the way Carrie seemed to be squandering away her own life.

Carol easily related to Peg Mullen's focus on solving the mystery of her son's death, which was so obsessive that even on her daughter's wedding day, Peg couldn't concentrate on anything else. Peg's single-mindedness became, as much as anything else, a way to deal with losing her son.

It was exactly like that for Carol where Carrie was concerned: Carol's life and career had to go on, but nothing really mattered except her daughter's addiction to drugs. Sometimes, it seemed that the only way to deal with Carrie's problem was to dwell on it constantly, even at the expense of everything else in her personal life. Carol has even said that a "wedge" was driven into her marriage to Joe, because of the problems at home.

What's amazing is that, given the turbulence in Carol's personal life at the time, she was able to give to the role in *Friendly Fire* the concentration it required.

Working with Ned Beatty was probably a very important link to that concentration. Beatty is a trained actor with a great deal of emotional depth and the ability to express it all in films as diverse as *Nashville, Deliverance,* and *Superman.* He helped Carol set the tone for the drama as it unfolded. His character was the more emotional one, easily given to tears. Hers was very spiny, sharp, and stoical, courageous yet restrained. Unfortunately, Carol was not able to consult Peg Mullen. But it's difficult to believe that she could have been any more convincing, even if she'd had Mullen's cooperation.

Eventually, two of the three surviving Mullen children, Patricia (an attorney) and John (who was operating an agricultural-supply business at the time), came to the location in Stockton, California, where the movie was being filmed (Carol did no actual shooting in Iowa).   Fay Kanin recalls: "Carol was, of course, very nervous when she heard that they were flying out to watch. In the first break after a shot, David Greene and I introduced them to Carol. Carol and Pat embraced and burst into tears. I remember being fascinated that the first reaction would be tears. There was strong identification there."

Shortly before the movie aired, Peg Mullen wrote Fay Kanin a letter saying that she and Gene had finally come to terms with the film. Apparently, her children had convinced her of the film-makers' good intentions. "She said she could feel a rise of military in the country again," Kanin says. "She wanted the movie to be shown immediately, because she hoped it could be of help."

Friendly Fire aired on Sunday, April 22, 1979. Carol and Joe attended a screening in Washington for the secretary of the army and took Carrie with them.

Carol talked to a reporter from *The New York Times* about her decision to accept the role in *Friendly Fire*. "I love the British attitude toward actors with repertory companies that permit actors to perform all kinds of roles," she said. "In this country, the industry limits you. I prefer comedy, but there is no reason to put blinders on yourself. If you run scared all the time and play it safe—doing what is expected—how are you going to learn anything?"

In another interview, this one with *Washington Post* TV critic Tom Shales, she had to admit, "I was never outspoken politically because I felt I wasn't intelligent enough in that area to come out and start doing that. As a performer I was always nervous that, well, suppose I made a wrong choice and I might sway a couple of votes the wrong way. Then I would be responsible. I didn't want to use my show as a soap box."

It was tempting for the media to draw a correlation between Peg Mullen's political awareness and the changes taking place in Carol's own thinking at this time. In most interviews, Carol was asked about her interest in the women's movement, and she talked freely about her crusade for the passage of the Equal Rights Amendment. To her, she said, the issue was not a political one but rather a moral one.

Carol also talked of her eagerness to meet Phyllis Schlafly, who at the time vehemently opposed the ERA. "I might even pick up the check," she said. "I would ask her why she is doing this because evidently she is supposed to be intelligent, and an intelligent person *has* to be for equality. The ERA is not anti-family or pro-abortion and lesbianism. But the Schlaflys and such push these 'hot' buttons because they induce panic in the voters."

(While on the road campaigning for the ERA, Carol sent Faye Kanin a note saying, "I'm fighting to be heard. I'm getting all the feelings that Peg Mullen must have had." Later, she had to qualify: "You can't equate me with Peg because I did not lose a son, but I certainly felt a lot of frustration when I came up against some brick walls where the ERA was concerned.")

Carol said she wasn't concerned about what her crusading for the ERA might cost her in terms of audience favor. "The passage of the ERA is far more important than whether Carol Burnett is asked to do her Tarzan yell again," she said.

Friendly Fire was met with great critical acclaim and posted a huge Nielsen rating despite competition from CBS's popular family offerings *All in the Family* and *Alice.* The *Hollywood Reporter* review noted that Carol's performance "ranks easily among the finest acting revealed by any actress in any medium."

"Outside of the Burnett show, I think *Friendly Fire* was the best thing she's ever done," Joe Hamilton observed. "It was a big stretch, but unlike *Pete 'n' Tillie,* it was advertised as such. People didn't expect her to be funny; she satisfied the audience's expectations."

Publicly, Carol bristled at the obvious suggestion that *Friendly Fire* was a "stretch" for her as an artist, even though privately she must have known that this was true. "People ask me if I consider this a breakthrough," she said at the time. "When someone who is known for being comedic does something straight, it's always a 'big breakthrough' or 'a radical departure.' Why is it that no one ever says that if a straight actor does comedy? Are they presuming comedy is easier? In some ways, comedy is harder, and some actors can't master the timing."

"I did not set out to change my image," she insisted. "To me, that would have just been a B-movie plot."

Carol had to admit to close friends, however, that she did feel her character was depicted a bit too solemnly in the film. "I felt that Peg Mullen had more of a sense of humor than what was displayed on the screen," she admitted.

Fay Kanin and Peg and Gene Mullen had become friendly through telephone conversations and letters before the show aired. When Kanin was in Washington for the governmental screening of *Friendly Fire,* the first call she received after it aired was from Gene Mullen. "He said that he'd watched it all," she remembers. "Peg was in another room trying to avoid it, but couldn't help hearing the sounds of it. Soon they were watching it together. He said they loved it, though Peg couldn't watch it all in one viewing. They bought a video recorder for the airing, and she did watch it later. Then the press began calling on them, and they once again had a chance to express themselves; they had a second platform, about what had happened."

"We are still bitter," Peg Mullen told the media. "The anger will never leave. Nothing could make it leave."

"I thought I had cried for the last time quite some while back," Gene said. "But I cried as I watched the show."

Gene and Peg Mullen continued to be in touch by telephone and letter with Fay Kanin after the show aired. "When Gene died about a year ago [1985], I was very moved that Peg called me to say that he'd passed away just an hour after it had happened," says Kanin. "I thought it was wonderful that we'd gone from people who were antagonists in the beginning to this. I know I represented for them all of the people of *Friendly Fire*, and since we were among the ones first to hear that Gene had died, I felt we had become part of their family."

One humorous story that stands out in David Greene's memory unfolded on Carol's last day of *Friendly Fire* taping in Stockton. As she was wrapping her final emotional scene, a production technician whispered urgently in David Greene's ear, "Please, you gotta ask her to do her Tarzan yell when she's finished."

"I beg your pardon?" David Greene asked. "You want me to ask her to do *what*?"

"Her Tarzan yell, her *Tarzan yell*! She's *really* great at that. Ask her to do it."

Greene was perplexed; he hadn't even known Carol *did* a Tarzan yell. But by the time she'd finished the scene, his curiosity was piqued. It seemed an odd request to make after six weeks of intensely emotional work, but he couldn't resist.

"Carol...might I ask..." he began in his very proper British accent. "Would you honor us with your Tarzan yell?"

At first, she was utterly confused. She'd been Peg Mullen for so long, she'd almost forgotten about her famous Tarzan yell. Carol shrugged, and then she stood up and let out a bellow that shook the rafters.

"*CUT!*" David Greene commanded, leading the laughter.

21

WHEN CAROL, JOE, AND CARRIE RETURNED FROM THE WASH-
ington screening of *Friendly Fire,* in 1979, their relationship was about to take a crucial turn. One evening in May, Carrie
stormed through the house, slamming doors and going into a
tirade over having been grounded. Infuriated, Carol followed
her up the stairs and into Carrie's bedroom.

"You have *no right* to be mad at *us!*" she screamed at Carrie.
Carol was shaking now, too upset and distraught even to cry.
"*You're* responsible for putting yourself in this position. How *dare*
you be angry at us! We've been trying to help you, you...you
spoiled little brat! You'll never leave this room again, I promise you
that. We don't know how much more of this we can take," Carol
concluded, out of breath.

As she turned to leave, she added, "And you can put that in
your *goddamn bong* and smoke it!" Then she walked out, slamming the door behind her. Once out of the room, she burst into
uncontrollable sobs. She had rarely lit into Carrie like that, and it
was odd, because this incident wasn't any more exasperating than
countless others with her daughter had been.

Suddenly, Carol felt as if history was repeating itself. My
God, she thought to herself. I'm Mama. I'm becoming my own
mother! I'm out of control...totally out of control, like Mama!

Years later, Carrie would admit, "I'm sure it was like her past
coming back to haunt her. But every kid is rebellious," she explained. "Mom's parents were a little out there, so Mom was rebellious in that she was very straight. Since she was so straight, I
was a little out there...."

Though Carol felt nearly overwhelmed by all of this emotion, she realized that she couldn't totally give in to despair and

anger, not now. For her child's sake, she knew she had to remain strong and controlled.

Throughout the years of raising her children, Carol had always tried to stay in control. She valued a calm, orderly atmosphere because she had seen so much confusion and anger as a youngster. She didn't like to show her children negative emotions. Her daughters had never heard their parents argue or Carol swear.

"I wanted to be the Loretta Young, Irene Dunne version of the perfect mother," she confessed years later. "I tried never to let the kids even see me cry. I think they probably thought they were living with some kind of robot. I tended to go into a shell, which isn't healthy because you store up resentments to the point where the least little thing sets off a chain reaction."

But now she was beginning to think that she had protected the girls too much. Perhaps they needed to see the darker sides of their mother in order to understand that she, too, was human, that she, too, hurt. "The world isn't a pretty pastel bubble, and they should know that," she said later. "The kids should see me cry, and I should tell them *why* I'm crying so *they* can comfort *me*."

The Hamiltons' family physician, Dr. Paul Tobias, recommended a drug-rehabilitation program for Carrie located in Houston, Texas, where he'd once worked. It claimed a 70 percent recovery rate with the twenty-two thousand young drug addicts who'd undergone a program based in part on the methods used by Alcoholics Anonymous. Naturally, when Carol and Joe told Carrie they were sending her to this hospital, she was adamant that she would not go.

Carrie had big plans for the summer. She was looking forward to experimenting with LSD and determined that nothing get in her way. She and her friends had said that this was to be their "summer of love and acid."

"I'm not going to Texas. No way!" she decided to herself one afternoon. She packed a few things and ran away from home.

Carol and Joe were frantic when they discovered that Carrie was gone. "You think we'd be used to this by now," Carol cried. "But, Joe, so help me, I can *never* get used to this! What are we going to do now? Where has she gone?"

They waited anxiously for some word from their daughter, pacing the floors until well after midnight. And then, the phone rang. It was Carrie. She was with a friend; her parents picked her up.

Carol had never been so relieved to see her daughter. Carrie was safe, but, unfortunately, unchanged. "I hate you for forcing me to go there," she shouted at her mother. "You don't love me. You've *never* loved me! And I *hate* you! *I hate you both!*"

By now, Carol was used to Carrie's "hatred." She stared back at her daughter coldly.

"Fine. Hate me, then," Carol shot back. "I don't care, anymore, Carrie. *You're going!* I love you enough to let you hate me." Carol and Joe had made up their minds to use force if necessary to get Carrie to Houston.

Finally, thirty days of peace. Carrie would be in Deer Park General Hospital for a month, and for that one month's time, at least, Carol knew she could be sure that her daughter was under supervision and treatment.

By June 1979, all of the strain, work, and draining emotions had taken their toll on Carol. The last six months, marked by professional triumph with *Friendly Fire*, had also, she believed, been marked by personal failure with her daughter. "Carol was like the walking wounded," says a friend. "She was emotionally and physically whipped by months of anguish. She had almost bottomed out. When Carrie entered the hospital, we all thought it would be a time Carol could take to rest."

But during this period, someone had the odd idea of trying the television-variety format one more time, in just four episodes that would air during the summer of 1979. Most observers agreed that there was simply no need for such a television mini-series, and many of Carol's friends were confounded as to why she would add more heat to her pressure-cooker existence. Some members of Carol's circle suggest that she must have needed to continue working in order to hang on to whatever was left of her peace of mind.

The series was touted as a "reunion" of sorts once again teaming Carol with former co-stars Vicki Lawrence and Tim Conway. When CBS-TV decided not to air the program, ABC picked it up. Nevertheless, this show was taped in Studio 33 at CBS—Carol's favorite studio.

Most people don't remember the *Carol and Company* series. Carol wasn't quite the same during these proceedings; there was a distinct hollowness to her personality. She seemed to be working on overdrive; her appearance took on a strained pallor that had never been there before. She seemed painfully thin. And with others, while she wasn't exactly chilly, her customary warmth somehow seemed a bit forced.

"I think Carol had to tire of that constant image she felt she had to uphold," Jack Van Stralen, special-effects supervisor, notes. "God! That must be tough on somebody. She's a human being and she's got to get out her frustrations like anyone else, but she was always smiling and jolly. I saw her make an *effort* to be the old Carol despite everything that was happening. There just isn't a *person* like the one Carol was trying to be under those circumstances."

On the series, some major name performers appeared as guest stars—Alan Arkin, Sally Field, Cheryl Ladd. Despite the presence of these and other big "names," the series took a beating in the ratings game. It was time to move on.

"What I think the experience did for Carol was make her say, 'Yes, I did the right thing by putting the show to bed,'" her director Dave Powers said. "It was like 'You can't go home again.'"

Carrie was an angry, resistant fifteen-year-old girl in June 1979, when her father checked her into the Palmer Drug Abuse Program in Houston. Carol decided not to go to Texas with Joe and Carrie. She didn't want the others there to treat Carrie any differently because her mother was a television personality. Her daughter was known by the others in her group-therapy sessions simply as "Carrie from L.A." The program's founder, Bob Meehan, said that her anonymity was "probably the best thing that ever happened to her."

Carrie went through a detoxification program and began undergoing intensive therapy. In a couple of weeks, Joe flew back to Texas to see his daughter. She was obviously in better shape. He took her sisters along, and Jody and Erin agreed that Carrie seemed to be getting better. (Joe was inspired by Carrie's success and encouraged two of his children from his former marriage, Joe, twenty-seven, and Jenny, twenty, to join the Palmer Drug Abuse Program.)

Before the month was out, Carrie called her mother and asked if she would come to visit.

"I was both elated and scared," Carol remembered. "Would she scream at me? Would I crumble?"

On June 26, Carol went to Houston. The moment she saw Carrie, she knew that the girl was on the road to recovery. For the first time in years, Carol was able to look into her child's eyes and recognize Carrie's personality. "I hadn't seen *her* in there for a long time," she remembered later.

Carol couldn't help but stare. For a long minute, she peered into her daughter's clear, beautiful eyes. Carrie took her mother's face in her hands and brought her closer.

"Are you okay, baby?" Carol asked.

"I'm okay, really," Carrie answered, smiling. She placed an index finger on each of Carol's cheeks. Her thumbs rested under Carol's chin. "I can never thank you and Daddy enough. I love you both . . . so much."

"We love you, too," Carol responded. "Oh, God, we love you . . ."

And then Carrie wiped away her mother's tears.

Carrie decided she wanted to stay in Texas. She wasn't strong enough to come back to Los Angeles and face her friends and peers. So she lived at the home of her sponsor, enrolled in a public high school in Houston (along with forty other PDAP members), and went to several PDAP meetings a week.

Carrie was on her way to recovery, but the gossip about what was happening had by now got back to Carol. It had never been Carol's way to shrug and let people surmise what they liked about her personal life. She wanted to set the record straight about Carrie, and talked to Joe about going public with the truth.

"I am not going to have people gossiping about my daughter," she told him. "I want the story to come straight from us. At least they'll hear it the way it really happened."

In August 1979, Carol and Joe decided to make a public statement about what had happened to their family. Besides the fact that they didn't want Carrie's problems to be exploited and even exaggerated by the news media, Carol and Joe thought they could be helpful to others facing similar situations. Carrie agreed; one of the precepts of the PDAP is that the patient shares his or her experience with others who may benefit from the example.

"We were so happy about Carrie's recovery, we didn't want to sit back and be quiet about it," Carol said later. "We had to tell people our mistakes, how we attempted to negotiate and beg and plead and all of the things we did. We wanted to reach out to other parents and say, 'Look, if your kid had a brain tumor, you're not going to operate. What makes you think that because you're Mommy and Daddy you can deal with drug addiction?'"

For the next year or so, Carol, Joe and Carrie appeared on television programs and consented to magazine interviews to discuss Carrie's drug addiction. "Don't be afraid of your children," Carol said decisively. "Don't be afraid they will hate you; they already do. It's the chemical in them. They don't care about you. All they care about is getting high.

"If they are taking dope, we, as parents, must take immediate action. We won't buy any protests or excuses because a drug addict will look you right in the eye and lie. . . ."

Because Carol is a high-profile celebrity with such a galvanizing personality—someone who'd been welcomed into the homes of television viewers as a "friend" for years—the media coverage in which she and her daughter bared their souls was riveting. Carol has always epitomized qualities other people admire: determination, positive thinking, the art of being able to get through life with her sense of humor intact. So it wasn't difficult for her to be convincing and to persuade her audience to deal realistically with the drug problems facing contemporary youngsters and adolescents.

The press was, naturally, eager to take advantage of Carol's soul-baring honesty. Whenever a public figure willingly submits to such personal scrutiny, he or she can expect eager cooperation from the fourth estate. The media lapped up the controversy.

Carrie returned to her Los Angeles home in September for a visit. "Some of my friends are proud of me," she said at the time. "And some won't have anything to do with me anymore. It hurts to let go, but I won't associate with losers."

In October 1979, Carol, Joe, and Carrie appeared on a special edition of Dinah Shore's syndicated talk show, along with Bob Meehan (founder of the Palmer Drug Abuse program), Los Angeles psychiatrist Dr. William Rader, and an eighteen-year-old man who'd successfully gone through the program. In a remarkably self-assured and controlled way, Carol explained what had happened to Carrie, herself, and Joe over the last two years. Halfway through the show, Dinah introduced a young girl and her mother; the girl confessed that she was abusing drugs and, when encouraged by Carrie, she agreed to go to Houston to enter the program. It was an emotionally moving program that elicited hundreds of letters and phone calls of praise. It seemed that the Hamiltons' domestic problems were indeed making a difference in other people's lives.

Carol proceeded to raise money to establish a Los Angeles chapter of PDAP by sponsoring fund-raisers at her home, and she also started a campaign against the sale of drug paraphernalia in record stores and head shops. Of course, there were charges that Carol was exploiting her pain and misery and, worse yet, her daughter, for the sake of some very high-profile exposure. A CBS employee recalls, "It was like she was whining, 'My parents were alcoholics, now my kid takes drugs.' Frankly, I was offended."

It was difficult for Carol to become angry at those charges, or even to respond. She was tired of being mad; the last year had been the worst year of her life, filled with confusion and anger. Now that Carrie seemed to be close to fully recovered, Carol chose to ignore the accusations and continue with her personal campaign against drug abuse.

In December, Carrie celebrated her sixteenth birthday in Houston. In January 1980, she moved back home and began attending a new school. Her grades went up. Carrie was determined to "stay clean" and began to make new friends; most of her former friends—the "druggies"—she cut out of her life entirely.

The resolution of Carrie's problem also marked a personal reawakening for her mother. In dealing with her daughter's turmoil, Carol had finally begun to recognize facets of her own identity that had been buried under years of self-doubt and feelings of inadequacy. Much to her amazement, she did find the necessary resources to survive the situation with Carrie, which she had thought was too much to bear. When she reflected on the way she'd handled it all, she was almost as proud of herself as she was of Carrie.

Privately, for Carol, all of the misery had resulted in a very personal victory. She had once been vastly insecure, with almost no confidence in herself. She always *needed*. But that was all in the past. Now, she had a new self-image as someone efficient and strong, someone who could cope and conquer. She knew that from this point on, she would be able to deal with life's vicissitudes. In understanding that, she found hope and consolation.

Publicly, Carol Burnett had become a profile in courage by overcoming the shock and confusion surrounding her daughter's bout with drugs. It had been a terribly personal ordeal, but anyone interested was privy to the complicated details. Public recognition of her courage, combined with the political impact of *Friendly Fire*, saw the birth of a new Carol Burnett.

22

CAROL WAS ENTHUSIASTIC ABOUT HER RECENT SUCCESS IN A dramatic role, especially since she and Fay Kanin were nominated for Emmy awards for their work in *Friendly Fire*. (Both women lost in their respective categories, though David Greene walked away with a director's Emmy.) "Isn't it wonderful what a little experience and a lot of senility can do for one's perspective?" Carol commented in 1979. "Why, I can even watch myself on screen today without wanting to crawl under my seat, or up the aisle with a bag over my head...."

At about this time, actor Alan Alda approached Carol with a script he had written and planned to direct and star in, titled *The Four Seasons*.

A comedy/drama that chronicles the friendships of three New York couples during the seasonal courses of one year, *The Four Seasons* was set against the vacation backdrops of a spring retreat, a Caribbean vacation, a college during parents' weekend in the fall, and a winter ski resort. "Like the year, friendships also have seasons," Alda explained. By the time winter arrives, all three couples—one of whom divorces early on—have gone through emotional changes involving risk, envy, loyalty, and compassion, and conflict that is not really resolved so much as overlooked.

Alan Alda portrayed his character, attorney Jack Burroughs, as one of those "let's-get-it-all-out-in-the-open" kind of people. His gently reasoning voice was as irritating as it was sensible: He refused to allow a problem to lie dormant; it must be resolved, but beyond that, he must be convinced that *he* has done the resolving. Jack's wife, Kate, a *Fortune* magazine editor, was to be played by Carol.

Carol read the script and, because she and Alda were good

friends, felt at liberty to be honest about her feelings regarding
it. "You really don't know where these people are coming from,"
she told him. "And Kate, well, she's too perfect. There isn't really
anything here for me to play."

"I think there's a blandness about playing somebody who's
too good to be true," Carol explained later. "It's tough to make it
interesting. Somebody who's got a lot of problems gives you a lot
more to dig for."

"I patterned the character after Arlene," Alan explained to
Carol, referring to his wife.

"Well, don't you two ever have a fight?" Carol asked.

"You're right! We'll change it," Alda offered. "We'll make it
better. Something you can get into."

Carol suggested that an argumentative scene between her
and Alda be added to the script. As Alda envisioned her, Kate
was an extremely conscientious woman whose "goodness" meant
that she was usually taken for granted by her husband and
friends. After Carol and Alan reworked the script, the character
had depth in that she resented the complacency she engendered.
She realized that her competence allowed people not to think
about her existence.

The other couples in the movie were played by Len Cariou
and Sandy Dennis as the husband and wife whose marriage is on
the rocks (he pairs up with a blond stewardess played by Bess
Armstrong) and Jack Weston as a neurotic dentist and Rita Mo-
reno as his wife. The three couples, who have little in common,
don't seem to like each other very much and we're not told how
they became acquainted, yet they are somehow good friends just
the same.

Carol and cast had a fun time during the film's three-month
shoot in Vermont, North Carolina, Georgia, and the Virgin Islands. "There sure was a lot of eating on that set," Carol joked.
"Eight o'clock in the morning and we'd be eating. Chinese food,
over and over. I was ready to throw up, but Alan would keep on
eating. Even between takes. Plus, he doesn't gain weight," she
said, feigning exasperation. "I hate that man. He's rotten!"

They finished the movie in late May 1980, and awaited its
release.

Six months later, Carol went to San Francisco to begin work
on another unfortunate film venture, an offbeat comedy/drama
produced by Jay Weston, directed by David Lowell Rich, and ti-

tled *Chu Chu and the Philly Flash*. Alan Arkin and Burnett play
two lovable—and sometimes not so lovable—losers who become
embroiled in a weird espionage caper. Don Crichton choreographed a madcap Carmen Miranda-inspired song-and-dance
routine for Carol, whose character is also an outrageous street
performer. The movie's premise so stretched the imagination
that most critics couldn't remember the plot long enough to review the movie when it was finally released by Twentieth Century
Fox (in 1981).

Carrie was back on drugs.

"Oh, my God! Not *again*! We can't go through this again!"
Carol cried to Joe. "When will this finally be over?"

After all of the high-profile publicity, all of that tearful soul-
baring on Dinah Shore's show, the agony of detail for the *People*
magazine cover story, those countless proclamations of Carrie's
sobriety, the girl was still addicted to drugs.

"I thought our problems were over after Dinah," Carol told
friends. "The euphoria was like what I had experienced when
my dad told me he had stopped drinking. I was literally dancing
at home. I was on cloud nine."

Carrie's continuing addiction was a rude reawakening for
her mother, not to mention the rest of her family. This time, her
problems would be intensely private. Carol would only make one
statement about the situation to the media. "This is not unusual,"
she said pragmatically. "We know that Carrie is an addictive personality. She will need ongoing treatment." She tried to continue to handle this family crisis sensibly while her public watched,
but inside it was tearing her up. She and Joe were considering
moving to Hawaii with Erin and Jody; Carrie didn't want any
part of it.

"Carol was absolutely sick about that," says a friend. "What
made it worse was that Carrie wanted nothing to do with either
Carol or Joe. Apparently, she had cleaned herself up for her
parents—not for herself. She was out of touch; a lot of the time,
Carol and Joe didn't even know where she was. Carol had no
choice—from what she learned through the Palmer program,
she knew that she had to let her kid go. She was very careful not
to let the press know that Carrie had alienated herself from the
family. When asked, she would say that Carrie was living with
friends and cleaning herself up."

"I hit the streets," Carrie says in retrospect. "I went out again and got loaded and stoned for nearly a year and a half. I don't remember every place I lived, but they were the worst places you could think of. Sometimes I stayed with friends—usually boyfriends—anyone who would put me up."

"I simply won't give her any money," Carol told a close friend in late summer, 1980. "I will not approve of supporting her unless she does what I want her to do. We've told her that if she wants to return to school and study, then, fine, we're willing to pay for that. But other than that—forget it. If you haven't gone through it," Carol concluded solemnly, "you may think it sounds cold."

Carrie was on her own. Carol and Joe felt there was nothing they could do but let her know they would be there if she needed them. They would move to Hawaii as planned. In December 1980, they decided to move to a cliff-top condominium on Maui, and continue to maintain the home in Beverly Hills.

During visits over the years to friends like Jim Nabors who lived on the islands, the Hamiltons were seduced by the tranquil Hawaiian life-style. Their plan was to live in the condo on the island of Maui until they built a rustic "pole house" on five and a half acres of land they purchased from Jim Nabors at Hana, on the island's southern tip. Their condominium overlooked the island of Molokai: Every evening gave birth to a breathtaking sunset. "Each time I watch it, I think Charlton Heston is going to appear to deliver the ultimate message," Carol joked.

But, despite her optimistic demeanor, life on the island without Carrie was not easy for Carol. "I'm in such conflict over this move," she confided to one friend. "I feel like I'm turning my back on my daughter. Why can't she just throw herself into my arms? Why can't things be like they used to be?"

Erin and Jody Hamilton, now in the sixth and eighth grades, were enrolled in the Parker School on the Big Island. They commuted the thirty-minute flight home to Maui on weekends; during the week they stayed with Carol and Joe's friends Anita and Paul DeDomenico. Later, they were enrolled at Seabury Hall on Maui. Carol was happy to get the girls out of Beverly Hills. "I don't want my kids to be Guccied and Puccied to death," she said, only half joking.

It seemed the time had come to pare down. When Carol first started making money, she wanted the biggest house possible—

big enough so that all of Joe's children could visit and there would be enough room for them, and for Carol and Joe's girls as well. "I bought all kinds of *things* to make it perfect," she has admitted.

But then she realized how foolish all of that was. "We had a house big enough for everyone to be there but we were never all there at the same time," she confessed. "And now I don't need all of those *things* I acquired."

Beverly Hills just wasn't what it used to be, anyway, so it wouldn't be difficult to leave it behind. For the last few years, Carol had felt a melancholy longing for the Beverly Hills "Old Guard." When she and Joe attended an anniversary party for Jimmy and Gloria Stewart in 1980, she was reminded how transitory the "New Guard" really is. Cary Grant, Irene Dunne, Gregory Peck, Loretta Young, and other cinema legends socialized at the Stewarts' party. Turning to Joe, Carol said sadly, "You know, I don't think there will *ever* be people like this again in this town."

Everything was changing rather quickly. Carrie stayed in touch sporadically, but mostly she was out of the family picture. She had dropped out of school, much to her parents' dismay. She couldn't keep a job and was now living in a small apartment with a boyfriend. At five feet eight and a half, her weight would plummet to an emaciated eighty-five pounds.

Also, by now, Carol and Joe were leading largely separate lives. Whereas they had once shared every part of their day, now he had his work, she had hers. At night, there was little to discuss. Even more important, the days when Carol used to make statements like, "Joe's the boss, he knows more than I do," were gone. For the last ten years, she had proved that she could take charge of her own life. Friends now noted that Joe was spending more time in California than he was in Hawaii with Carol. The Hamiltons were obviously growing apart.

"I asked Joe about it privately, and his attitude was that Carol's place was in Hawaii and his was in Los Angeles. That they got along better if they were apart. If Carrie needed him, he would be in the city for her. She hardly ever called," says a friend of Joe's. "Part of the reason for the Hawaii residence must have been to put some space between Carol and Joe. I think it would be safe to say that by the end of 1980, there was a bit of trouble in paradise."

In Hawaii, Carol Burnett had time to think about her life and make some rather important decisions. "Some people don't want to take time to reflect—they have to keep everything on schedule or they get the guilts," she told a friend. "Not me. Not anymore.

"I can sit down and not feel guilty [in Hawaii]," she said. "I can look at the sunset and not feel that I should be doing something else. Hawaii takes away all my guilt."

On March 12, 1981, Carol's $10 million lawsuit against *The National Enquirer* finally made it into the courtroom. The proceedings would be very closely monitored by celebrities and media alike because it represented the first time in the *Enquirer*'s twenty-eight-year history that a libel case against it had reached the trial stage. The case evoked memories of Maureen O'Hara's 1957 libel lawsuit against *Confidential* magazine; her suit eventually helped to put that publication out of business.

Carol's case was considered a crucial test of the libel laws by a public figure. "The yellow journalists are taking the first amendment and making a mockery of it," she had said. At a two-day deposition, Carol was seen wearing two T-shirts. One said, "Never Underestimate the Power of a Woman," and the other "God, Love, and Truth Will Out."

The item in question was in the March 2, 1976, issue of the *Enquirer:*

> At a Washington restaurant, a boisterous Carol Burnett had
> a loud argument with another diner, Henry Kissinger. She
> traipsed around the place offering everyone a bite of her
> dessert. But Carol really raised eyebrows when she
> accidentally knocked a glass of wine over one diner—and
> started giggling instead of apologizing. The guy wasn't
> amused and "accidentally" spilled a glass of water over
> Carol's dress.

In its April 13, 1976, issue, *The National Enquirer* printed a retraction:

> An item in this column on March 2 erroneously reported
> that Carol Burnett had an argument with Henry Kissinger at
> a Washington restaurant and became boisterous, disturbing

other guests. We understand these events did not occur and
we are sorry for any embarrassment our report may have
caused Miss Burnett.

Because the retraction was not given the same high-profile
positioning in the tabloid as the original article, Carol called the
attempt at reconciliation "tantamount to being hit by a hit-and-
run driver and then having him send you a bouquet of crab grass
when you're in the hospital." *The National Enquirer* hoped to settle
out of court, but she refused.

By now, Carol was considered in Hollywood as something of
a leader among a group of ten celebrities who were also suing the
tabloid at that time for a total of $62.5 million. The other suits
involved cases filed against *The National Enquirer* by Linda Blatty,
wife of author William Peter Blatty; Rory Calhoun; Marty Ingels
and his wife, Shirley Jones; Ed McMahon; Phil Silvers; Rudy Val-
lee; David Parlour, former husband of Jane Powell; Paul Lynde;
and Dr. Max Shapiro, Elvis Presley's dentist.

In order to win her case, Carol, as a "public figure," had to
present "clear and convincing proof" that the tabloid either deliberately lied or recklessly disregarded the truth.

Carol would be in court every day of the two-week trial. (Joe
would not join her until the last day.) Her presence made the
case even more newsworthy—a television camera was positioned
in the courtroom and recorded most of the trial. Whenever Carol
would emerge, she would be met outside the door by blinding
lights and obtrusive minicams. As film crews walked backward in
front of her, and with microphones shoved into her face, Carol
would try to make her way down the hall while answering such
deft questions as "I take it after all this you're going through, you
think it's worth it?" The press would lead her right up to, but
thankfully not into, the ladies' room.

Some of the most interesting revelations during the trial related to the inner operations of *The National Enquirer*. It was revealed that the columnist whose name and photo appeared on
the item that prompted Carol's lawsuit did not, in fact, write the
column; it was written by an *Enquirer* editor who wasn't certain of
the story's accuracy.

Ironically enough, during the first week of the trial, Henry
Kissinger was in Los Angeles on other business. He told the press

that when he met Carol in the restaurant, she "acted in a perfect
ladylike fashion." Their meeting was, he said, "very brief and
very friendly. There was no commotion of any kind going on.
Miss Burnett spoke in a very civilized manner that suggested no
drinking at all." Kissinger, who submitted a sworn deposition to
that effect, did not appear in court.

Carol's musical arranger, Peter Matz, testified before the
five-woman, seven-man jury that he had dined with Carol and
Joe on the night in question. "Lew Wasserman was with Kissinger
and he and Joe are friendly," Matz said later. "So Wasserman
introduced Kissinger to Carol. She had never met him before
and was thrilled. Kissinger was charming and he said something
like, 'Are you having a good time in Washington?' and then I
think he said something like, 'Well, you wouldn't if you had my
job.' The whole thing lasted, I'd say, about one minute."

The *Enquirer* was represented by William Masterson, who
had prior experience with libel lawsuits, having represented
Newsweek, Associated Press, *The New York Times,* and the *Los Angeles Times*. He termed the item "a farcical, whimsical recounting
of the conduct for which Miss Burnett has been compensated
quite handsomely over the years."

Masterson added that the tabloid had a long history of publishing flattering stories about Carol. Before the trial, he said,
"even if, and I emphasize '*if*' the item were inaccurate . . . even
assuming the retraction was insufficient, what's the damage? The
evidence will show that this retraction was sufficient to set things
straight."

Carol's attorneys, E. D. Bronson and Barry Langberg, managed to locate the couple who had dined in the restaurant at an
adjoining table to Carol's. It was hoped that they could verify that
any food sharing was done sensibly, that Carol did not "traipse
around the place offering everyone a bite of her dessert." In
what had to be one of the more bizarre testimonies in judicial
history, the Washington, D.C., residents testified in great detail
about the civil manner in which they came to share their Baked
Alaska with Carol, and she her chocolate soufflé with them.

On Tuesday, March 17, a taut-faced Carol Burnett took the
witness stand. In an emotional testimony, she called the tabloid's
gossip column "disgusting" and "a pack of lies."

Counting each grievance on her fingers, she explained very

clearly and very deliberately, "It portrays me as being drunk, it portrays me as being rude, it portrays me as being uncaring, it portrays me as being physically abusive." She could feel the hurt rising within her all over again.

"Because it was in print, it will never, ever, not be a part of me," she continued. "When I'm dead and gone, it will be in my files—newspapers and libraries keep files—and my kids, my grandkids, and my great-grandkids can look it up. I really know that most people believe what they read—and that hurts."

Carol recalled that after she read the item she wondered how she would be able to speak publicly about the problems of alcoholism. "How am I going to have any credibility? They are going to think, 'Who does she think she is to tell me there is a cure? She runs around having fights with people and throws wine on them.' I felt awful." She said that she and Tim Conway had recently been in a restaurant together and that she was afraid to laugh at his jokes for fear of what the other diners would think of her.

When asked about her personal drinking habits, Carol said, "I drink wine with dinner. I drink an occasional sherry, and once in a while, if I'm on an airplane," she continued, with rising impatience, "I'll have a Bloody Mary."

She said she had "two, maybe three" glasses of wine that night at the Rive Gauche, that she was not intoxicated. She also talked a little about her parents' bouts with alcoholism and explained that it was because of her background that she was so sensitive about the article.

Under cross examination by Masterson, Carol acknowledged that she had often played drunk characters on her series. "But any time I ever did a drunk on my show, it was as a loser," she quickly clarified. "They were never portrayed in a glamorous light."

Masterson also pointed out that even though Carol said she was upset about the article, she did manage to complete the *Sills and Burnett at the Met* television special, which he said was described in Carol's press material as "one of the legendary Burnett specials." He also maintained that Carol had never seen any kind of doctor for her claimed emotional distress and mental anguish. He got Carol to agree that her career and income had suffered no damage after the item appeared, and she had to admit that it "might have been better."

"I challenge anyone to come up with a shred of evidence that the *Enquirer* had any intent to injure Miss Burnett," Masterson said in his closing remarks. "Nowhere in the item does it say that she was drunk, tipsy, feeling no pain, fractured, wasted, smashed, any of the universal words that are present in the English language to say that someone has overimbibed."

Carol's attorney E. D. Bronson reread the article and reiterated that practically every sentence in it was false.

The trial was over on Tuesday, March 24. There were three days of deliberation, days that Carol spent in a nearby hotel waiting for the verdict and playing Scrabble to pass the time. And then, on Thursday, much to her delight and amazement, Carol was awarded $1.6 million in damages. (A juror later noted that most of the deliberation was not over the *Enquirer*'s guilt but rather about a dollar figure to award Carol.)

In the dramatic conclusion to the two-week trial, the jury first found the tabloid liable for three hundred thousand dollars in general damages—when Carol heard this, she instinctively covered her mouth with her hand. When the jury handed down its decision that the tabloid pay Carol an additional $1.3 million in punitive damages, she gasped audibly. She broke into a broad smile, and then into tears as she leaned over and kissed Joe, who sat by her side. Later, she shook the hands of all of the jury members and thanked them individually.

Attorneys for the *Enquirer* argued that the verdict was an affront to the First Amendment, that the award was "excessive."

This decision was handed down in a climate of growing concern over the effects of large punitive damages on First Amendment rights of free speech. Carol's award was eventually cut to eight hundred thousand dollars. Most of the money went to pay the legal costs of the five-year-long battle. Carol donated one hundred thousand dollars to "The Carol Burnett Fund for Responsible Journalism" at the University of Hawaii, and another hundred thousand dollars to the Graduate Journalism Program at the University of California at Berkeley.

The National Enquirer further appealed the case, all the way to the Supreme Court. In July 1983, Carol's award was cut again —this time to two hundred thousand dollars. She was quite upset about this latest decision. "I don't think that's enough to deter them," she said. "I don't think they should get off like that." She considered going back to trial again to contest the reduced damages. But then she decided that she'd made her point about the *Enquirer*'s ethics.

Carol and the tabloid reached an out-of-court settlement in December 1984. Both parties agreed not to reveal the details of that settlement. "You can only assume that Carol got more than two hundred thousand dollars," said a representative.

"I don't know what the long-term effect of my victory is," Carol observed in 1986. "I think it has changed people's thinking about going after such publications if you can afford it. You can puncture that balloon if you are stubborn enough."

In May 1981, *The Four Seasons* was released to hostile reviews. Wrote Peter Rainer for the *Los Angeles Herald-Examiner*, "Alda's vision doesn't make any emotional sense. We come out of the film with the same question we had in the beginning: 'Why, oh *why*, don't these people take separate vacations...?' Burnett matches up well with Alda. They have the same figure and coif."

"As a director, Alda is no less subtle," wrote another critic. "When he wishes to make his meaning clear, he generally cuts to a close-up of Carol Burnett's wise, warm countenance as if to say, 'trust this woman.' Since everybody loves Carol Burnett, everybody is satisfied."

Most of the reviews did praise the actors' performances, and *The Four Seasons* became a tremendous hit. It grossed over $11 million in its first ten days. Eventually, it went on to net $50 million on a budget of less than $6 million.

It's interesting that a disagreement developed between Carol and Universal Studios when that film company decided to promote her as a potential Academy Award-winner for her work in *The Four Seasons*. It's a Hollywood ritual that movie studios pay for expensive advertisements in the trade papers to tout performers they feel should be awarded Oscars. Many times, the chosen stars are simply not deserving. But it's all part of Hollywood politics and image-making.

When an advertisement appeared in one of the Hollywood trade papers encouraging the Academy of Motion Pictures Arts and Sciences to consider Carol for an Oscar, she was dismayed, embarrassed, and extremely angry. "I considered it very misleading and a waste of money," she said of the studio's campaign. Though she said she felt her castmates gave wonderful performances, she termed her work in *The Four Seasons* "[O]kay. No gem. Certainly not Academy Award-caliber. If it had been I wouldn't have objected to the campaign.

"This whole Oscar thing can get so silly with everyone and their uncle taking out ads. I don't want to be part of it—unless I deserve it."

Columnist Marilyn Beck called this unlikely squabble between studio and star "a first in studio flackery." Universal withdrew plans for future advertisements.

Unfortunately, following *The Four Seasons* came the release of the truly disappointing *Chu Chu and the Philly Flash*. It was as if some mean-spirited person opened a closet, and another one of Carol's celluloid skeletons fell out at just the wrong time. But luckily, *Chu Chu* came and went with little fanfare or notice, and didn't diminish Carol's growing recognition as a serious actress.

"I'm in the autumn of my life," Carol told the *Los Angeles Times* in June 1981, in her first major interview since the victory against *The National Enquirer*. "I'm not the person I was five years ago. I'd no idea I was this strong."

The reporter noted that forty-seven-year-old Carol sat in the sunny garden at the Beverly Hills Hotel, lunching on a light salad and sipping white wine. "She looks tan, fit and less frail than she has in years," the article read. "She is a clear-eyed, practical, middle-aged woman with a sense of humor and an even stronger sense of herself."

In July 1981, Carol had the opportunity to appear in a major movie musical, something she'd always dreamed of doing. She liked to say that if she'd been around in the forties, she would have been playing Virginia O'Brien and Betty Garrett roles; or she would have been June Allyson's best friend. But by the 1980's, the movie musical was a lost art form. No one made them anymore, mostly because, sadly, few people wanted to see them.

Annie was inspired by Harold Grey's Depression-era comic strip "Little Orphan Annie," in which an irresistibly cute freckle-faced and red-mopped orphan is taken into the home of millionaire Daddy Warbucks for a week. Once there, she proceeds to spread good cheer and barrels of joy all around.

Annie, which debuted in April 1977 and went on to win seven Tonys—including Best Musical—had been one of the biggest musicals in Broadway history. All of the major Hollywood studios engaged in a bidding war for the film rights. In December 1977, David Begelman, then president of Columbia, bought the rights for a record price of $9 million. Begelman knew that this would be a risky undertaking; Hollywood history has it that Broadway musicals usually don't translate well to the big screen. (There have been exceptions: Carol Reed's *Oliver!* was a terrific stage show and even better movie.)

Carol knew going into this project that unless the result was something of *Gone With the Wind* proportions, the notices would probably be poor. But, still, she was interested in doing the film and playing Miss Hannigan, the boozing, scheming matriarch of a New York orphanage. In 1979, when Randal Kleiser (of *Grease* fame) was scheduled as the film's director, an announcement was made that Carol would be starring in it with Jack Nicholson. But by 1980, Ray Stark was the film's producer and John Huston was its director—an odd choice given the fact that the seventy-five-year-old Huston is best known for his work in dramas and in character studies. Nicholson was out and Albert Finney was co-starring as Daddy Warbucks. Also in the film were Aileen Quinn as the perpetually cute Annie, Ann Reinking, Bernadette Peters, and Geoffrey Holder.

The idea to use Carol Burnett in the film came from its executive producer, Joe Layton, a friend of Carol's dating back to her early days in New York. Layton, renowned for the magnificent ways in which he has staged concerts for "divas" such as Bette Midler, Cher, and Diana Ross, recalls, "It was a toss-up between Bette [Midler] playing the role and Carol. They were both approached. Bette, too, would have been wonderful, but she'd decided that she wanted to be a straight comedienne in her films, as opposed to a caricature. Carol loved the idea of playing this bizarre person. So the part was hers."

Carol was pleased that Layton thought of her and, she told reporters, happy that her transition from television to film was being so easily accepted by her peers. "I was able to cross over into film because I was very lucky in the scripts I was sent, and the people who called me," she told *American Film* magazine. "Goldie Hawn, who used to be a television person, has helped me enormously. So have Lily Tomlin and Alan Alda. The stigma isn't there so much now, but television is still the bastard of the industry. I get so mad at movie people. They call it 'cinema' or 'film.' It's just *movies!*"

In her bright orange fright-wig, matching smeared lipstick, and campy gypsy clothing, Carol flounces and bullies her way through the film in a broad, wonderfully comic portrayal. Hannigan is a woman so mean she refers to her charges as "my little pig droppings," so man-hungry she seduces every male in sight. One observer called Carol's characterization "a nightmare image of maternalism—the mother who would throw the baby out with the bath water." (It was said that John Huston told her, "Play the role soused and it'll really work.")

"She's sexually very aggressive, which people can take better in comedy than in straight drama," says screenwriter Carol Sobieski of Carol's portrayal. "She is redeemed at the end—not because I was told to do so because Miss Burnett is a big star, but because it didn't make dramatic sense to allow such a major character to disappear."

"What attracted me to Miss Hannigan was the chance to do something outrageous on film," Carol admitted, "to really cut loose the way I do in my TV sketches."

It's interesting that Dorothy Loudon, who replaced Carol on *The Garry Moore Show,* played the part of Hannigan on Broadway and won a Tony for her performance.

Filming this $42 million extravaganza (which went $15 million over budget) was a trying, not to mention expensive, experience. "There were all kinds of logistical problems," Joe Layton remembers laughing. "There was lavish costuming, elaborate sets, money, money, *money* was being spent like there was no tomorrow!

"Maybe it's because Carol and I go back so far to a time when we were both young and silly, or maybe it's because we are *still* young and silly, but I have to say that everything we did together on *Annie* we personally found quite hysterical," Layton adds. "I don't think we stopped laughing for a full minute the whole time we were working."

23

IT WAS SUMMER 1981, AND CAROL WAS AT THE BEVERLY HILLS house making plans to return to Hawaii. The phone rang in the living room; Carrie was on the line. She couldn't pay her rent, and she had nowhere else to turn.

"How much do you need, Carrie?" Carol asked, choking back tears.

There was silence.

"Carrie, are you still there?"

"Two hundred. I need two hundred dollars, Mom," Carrie answered. From the defeated tone of her voice, Carol knew that the girl hated to ask.

"Come to the house, Carrie. Come and get the money."

When Carrie got there, she says today in retrospect, "I was shanghaied into going for help. My mom knew I was dying and said, 'Screw it! I'm finally going to save my daughter.'"

For a moment, the old, lovable Carrie had resurfaced; she and her parents were getting along. But even though she was reaching out for help, she still wanted her independence. So she exploded when, on October 1, Carol and Joe checked her into CareUnit Hospital in Orange, California. The hospital is devoted to helping patients conquer drug addiction.

"Sure, just like last time," Carrie screamed at her parents; again, she felt they were betraying her. "I hate you for throwing me into this place! I can't wait for my birthday [in December]."

And then, in one breathless sentence, she warned them, *"Once I turn eighteen, I can do anything I want!"*

Carol considered her daughter's threat; it sent a chill through her.

Two months. If her daughter wasn't "clean" in two months, Carol knew that there would be nothing else she could do to

Carrie—no other rehabilitation program she could place her in —without the girl's consent. She prayed that sixty days in Care-Unit Hospital would put an end to the nightmare that most of her friends had assumed ended long ago.

In December, when Carol paid a visit to Carrie, the girl immediately noticed that there was something different about her mother. Carol seemed overwhelmed with exhaustion. It was as if Carol had resigned herself to accept what she couldn't change. Perhaps her resolve had finally been flattened by years of anxiety over this problem. "You'll soon be eighteen," Carol began slowly, very deliberately. "And, Carrie, when you turn eighteen, we won't be able to help you anymore. I don't know what else I can say to you, do for you. I love you...but what can I do?" Her voice trailed off.

Suddenly, Carrie realized what was happening. For the last couple of years, she had isolated herself from her family, but she had known in her heart that if anything dreadful happened she would not be held completely responsible—Mom and Dad would bail her out, would help her whether or not she said she wanted their assistance. Thank God, she felt, they were able to "force" her into rehabilitation programs because she was a minor. Oh, no! she now thought to herself. My corners won't be padded any longer. I am *really* going to be on my own.

Today, Carrie remembers, "Even when I was at my most screwed up and wanted to die more than anything else, I had moments of clarity when I wanted to do something—to somehow use my talents—to change the world. As I was lying in the hospital bed, I knew it was time to finally get off drugs. I had all of these romantic notions about being a junkie, and every one of them was wrong."

Soon afterward, Carrie was released from the hospital. She continued therapy with a psychologist she jokingly called "the dragon lady," who helped her understand "that I could still be a rebel, but that I didn't have to use drugs to be one."

Finally, it was over. There were no public declarations of her sobriety. Just as unceremoniously as it had begun five years earlier, by the end of 1981 the nightmare had ended.

Carol and Joe went into therapy sessions with the families of other patients. In these encounters, Carrie and other youngsters in trouble would confront their parents in soul-searching, and often very painful, group encounters. For Carol, this was quite embarrassing. At first, she was ashamed to show her emotions to so many total strangers. "I'm the recognizable one," she told Joe. "I'm the one who has been in these people's homes every week for eleven years. What will they think of me, of us?"

"She wasn't at all sure that this kind of therapy would work for her," said a friend of Carol's. "For someone so private, this was rather torturous. She couldn't help but feel that all of those people were staring at her, criticizing the way she raised her child."

But then, finally, Carol had to face the reality of the situation. "To hell with it," she decided. "This is my kid in trouble. It's time to open up and face it."

Today, Carrie Hamilton is fully recovered and has become a television actress of some acclaim. She regularly speaks to high-school students about the importance of saying no to drugs.

Carol is equally as vocal, from a mother's standpoint. "I've learned from drug programs and from the therapy our whole family had together that unless you tell your baby at birth, 'I am out to destroy you,' there's nothing to feel guilty about," she told a writer from *Ladies' Home Journal.* "Things go wrong because you're not the only one with your children all their lives. Once they get out in society amid peer-pressure . . . you pray, a lot."

Today, Carol and Carrie share a very close relationship; they are "best friends." Once, a psychologist suggested to Carol that she should treat her daughters as if they were outpatients from a mental hospital. After all, his reasoning was, at any other stage of life anyone who behaved as adolescents do would be locked up. But as Carol's girls got older, any generation gap between them and their mother narrowed. Carol and Carrie, in particular, found that they had a lot more in common than they had ever dreamed. "My relationship with Mom has blossomed because I no longer have anything to hide from her," Carrie now says.

And, now, Carol confides in Carrie about her troubles. They are peers; they double-date. In 1987, the two of them worked together on an episode of *Fame.* Carol played a cafeteria worker with show-business aspirations whom Reggie Wiggins, the rebellious student played by Carrie, took under her wing. Carrie said it was like "having my best friend with me for an entire week . . . when it was over I missed her terribly."

Later in the year, Carol and Carrie filmed a CBS-TV movie, *Hostage,* in Toronto. Carol played a wealthy, lonely Connecticut widow kidnapped by a disturbed and violent teenager, Carrie. In the end, kidnapper and hostage come to grips with their lives through their mutual ordeal.

Carol's agent recommended Carrie for the role. It was a difficult part; Carrie fretted that she would hurt her mother when filming the violent scenes in which she had to, as she put it, "throw her around a lot. I was terrified for her back," she said. "She was wearing this big brace. Oh, God, what if I hurt her? That was tough."

The movie received mixed reviews when it aired on Valentine's Day, 1988. Carrie showed the kind of great depth and potential as a dramatic actress that made her mother proud. That year, Carrie received kudos for her film debut in *Tokyo Pop*.

"We've seen it all, have been enemies and, now, buddies," Carol has said of her relationship with her eldest daughter. "I am so proud of what she's become, how hard she's worked. She did it herself, for herself. She used to ask, 'When will that awful time not be a part of me.' Someday it will not be a part of her at all; she will do something else that will be much more important."

Carrie has the final word in a feature for *Redbook* (November 1987): "Don't let anyone fool you: Drugs kill. And, looking back, I now realize that's what my mom was trying to tell me. But I was just too cut off from soul to notice."

At around this time, Carol finally got her chin.

She underwent a sliding horizontal osteotomy, a ninety-minute oral-surgical procedure to correct what her family used to call "the Burnett lower lip." The reason for the operation was not entirely cosmetic—Carol had been having headaches at the base of her skull, and a doctor suggested that if she had her bite corrected, the headaches might disappear.

Carol first learned of the operation when her daughter Jody balked at the prospect of wearing braces (both Carrie and Erin went through years of orthodontia—which, of course, Carol's parents could never afford for her). Jody's Honolulu orthodonist suggested the operation. He took X rays of both mother and daughter to determine whether the problem was hereditary; he discovered that Carol's "bite" was off and that she had a "weak" chin. "No kidding!" Carol laughed. "I had to pay for an X ray to learn *this*!"

Carol decided to have the operation—even though memories of a childhood dental visit still haunted her. When she was ten, a county welfare dentist had drilled and filled nine cavities of hers in a single session without benefit of Novocain. Since then, she's said, she's brushed her teeth ten times a day to avoid undergoing similar torture ever again.

After the operation, the headaches vanished—as did 14 pounds when Carol dropped from 124 pounds to 110 because she couldn't eat properly for two weeks—and four new millimeters of chin appeared. *People* magazine ran "Before" and "After" photographs a year and a half later, when Carol appeared on the Academy Awards presentation (1983) with Tom Selleck. She looked more beautiful and radiant. The difference was rather remarkable.

"Now, when it rains, I can feel it on my chin," she joked.

It's interesting that "both" of Carol's chins are on display in *Annie*. The film was finished before the operation, all except for Carol's "Easy Street" number with Bernadette Peters and Tim Curry, which had to be restaged by Joe Layton and refilmed after the surgery.

The year ended on a particularly sour note when Joe suffered a heart attack at the wedding of his son, John, to Marion McCarter at Loyola Marymount Chapel on Thursday, December 31, 1981. After insisting that the wedding continue, he was taken to Cedars Sinai Hospital.

This was the first time the press began to speculate about the state of Joe and Carol's marriage. Carol wasn't at the wedding. But whatever the state of their union by this time, she immediately flew in from Maui on Thursday to be by Joe's side, canceling a week of guest appearances on *All My Children*.

"Carol was absolutely frantic," says a friend. "She kept saying, 'Oh, God! Let him be okay!' They may not have been as happy in their marriage as they had once been, but they did still love each other. She couldn't bear the thought of losing Joe."

Eventually, Joe made a full recovery. "It was the best kind of heart attack," he said later. "It made me slow down and reconsider my priorities."

"Given the fact that Carol and Joe are so private, it's hard to say for certain, but I think Joe's heart attack made them both stop and think," says another source. "Life is too short not to enjoy it all. Joe was pretty much the same man he'd always been, but Carol had changed tremendously. She was so independent,

Joe hardly knew what to make of her. As much as she tried to please him, she knew she still had to remember to please herself. Joe felt quite left out...Most people felt that the marriage wouldn't survive very much longer."

In February 1982, Carol began work on another television movie of the week, *Life of the Party: The Story of Beatrice.* It was a chilling yet inspirational story, which many fans consider among Carol's finest works.

She portrayed a character named Beatrice O'Reilly, based on the story of Beatrice (pronounced Bee-AT-riss) Jorgenson, a former alcoholic who founded the first Los Angeles recovery house for female alcoholics. The two-hour drama costarred Lloyd Bridges.

Ken and Mitzie Welch, executive producers of the film, had for months been talking to Jorgenson about the possibility of a dramatic series based on Friendly House, the recovery home she'd started. Mitzi wanted Carol to meet Jorgenson because she felt the two would have a rapport in light of Carrie's problems and those of Carol's mom. Carol and Bea hit it off well; one thing led to another, and Carol became interested in doing Bea's life on TV.

During this time, ABC had been interested in having Carol star in a movie about drug abuse, broadly based on her experiences with Carrie. Carol wasn't interested in that idea, but she said she'd like to do a project based on Beatrice Jorgenson's story. ABC passed, and so Carol took the idea to CBS.

Carol spoke of Beatrice Jorgenson to writer Stephen Farber, for *The New York Times.* "She was a trailblazer. Thirty years ago it was very unusual to see a woman at an AA meeting. They were all closet drinkers and wouldn't dare venture forth to say 'I am an alcoholic.'"

"Bea was a real shit-kicker," remembers Elle Puritz, associate producer of the program. "Sober for thirty-seven years, she was from Texas, like Carol, and wore her charm on her sleeve. When she took to you, like she did to Carol, she *really* took to you."

Bea reminded Carol very much of her mother, Louise. Both had gregarious personalities ("My Mom could charm a bottle and get it to talk to her"). When Carol found out that Bea and Louise shared birthdays, she "got goose-bumps."

"Bea reminded Carol a lot of what her mother might have

been like if she could have stayed sober," says Elle Puritz. "And Carol was like a daughter to Bea. All she did was talk about Carol from the day she met her until the day she died. She would call and say [in a Southern drawl], 'Ma daughter Carol send me a duzen roses for ma birthday.' Or, 'Ma daughter Carol is coming over for lunch.' We would all gather around a very long dining table—me, Carol, Bea, and all of the girls staying at the house. We had wonderful meals together."

In playing the role of Beatrice, Carol was able to connect with and draw from her own painful memories and experiences. She hoped that this film would demonstrate to a large viewing audience that alcoholism is nothing to be ashamed of, that many people have been through it and have survived to lead happy, productive lives. The movie was also the realization of Beatrice Jorgenson's dream to encourage women to be more open about the disease, and to further the message of sobriety. The film made the last years of her life both fulfilling and exciting.

Elle Puritz has a special memory of Carol that did not relate to their work together on Beatrice, but speaks volumes for the way Carol relates to her public. In 1970, Elle, eighteen years old and living in Manhattan, was involved in an automobile accident and left bedridden for eight months. She went blind. Every Monday evening, she would listen to Carol's show; it was a happy respite for her from a grim time in her life. Elle felt a strong rapport with Carol and dictated a fan letter to Carol to her mother.

"I got a personal letter back from her," Elle recalls with tears in her eyes, "encouraging me in my strength, inspiring me in so many ways to survive what I was going through. It meant a lot to me that someone as busy as Carol Burnett would take the time to do this. We saved and treasured the letter.

"Eventually, I did get my sight back," she continues. "I moved to California, and in 1976 I found myself working as a production assistant for The Sonny and Cher Show across the hall from The Carol Burnett Show at Television City. I had my mother send me the letter Carol had written, and I brought it over to Carol and showed it to her. Years had passed, I was recovered, and our paths had finally crossed. We read the letter together, embraced, and cried."

Carol was praised by critics and fans for her performance in Beatrice when it aired in September 1982. But more important, she was satisfied with and proud of her work in the film. She felt that she'd done a convincing job, and that the movie made a strong, positive statement. She was finally beginning to have a confident sense of herself as a performer. She'd learned to be objective enough about her work to relate to the phrase "job well done."

After it was completed, Carol sent Elle Puritz a gift with an accompanying card:

> Dearest Elle,
> Got any more ideas?
> Love,
> Carol

When *Beatrice* was over, Carol was happy to retreat to her home in Hawaii. "This fall, I am not going to work," she promised. "I won't do anything unless Laurence Olivier or Katharine Hepburn calls."

Of course, she's made similar declarations in the past. Someone once suggested to her that she and Joe rent their beach house in California during the months they weren't living there.

"Heck, no," Carol said. "I will *not* rent that beach house unless it's to Laurence Olivier."

A few weeks later, the phone rang—Laurence Olivier, wanting to rent the beach house.

In April 1982, Robert Altman's *H.E.A.L.T.H.* was finally released. Carol had filmed the movie back in March 1979 at the Don CeSar Beach Resort Hotel in St. Petersburg, Florida, and it was originally scheduled for release during the 1980 presidential campaign. But because of problems both with the film and between Altman and Twentieth Century Fox, the movie was delayed. When it was released, it was only in limited engagements, and for the most part it went unnoticed.

There wasn't much of a cohesive story in *H.E.A.L.T.H.*, a surrealistic satire of the health-food industry and politics. The premise was, What happens when the delegates of H.E.A.L.T.H., a physical-fitness organization with political power, meet at a convention to choose a new president.

Lauren Bacall and Glenda Jackson also starred in the film. Dick Cavett played himself. Carol's character was Gloria Burbank, once the protein advisor to the United States, who had come to the convention as the U.S. president's personal observer.

"*H.E.A.L.T.H.* was considered a disaster in the industry; nobody understood it," Robert Altman admits. "It got bad reviews, if any reviews at all, so Carol didn't get accolades for her performance; nobody told her how improved she was. Yet she still believes it's a good movie. It takes a special person to be able to stick to that conviction when the rest of the world is telling her, 'Geez, that was pretty bad, Carol.'"

A month after *H.E.A.L.T.H.*, *Annie* opened at Radio City Music Hall (May 21), with one of the biggest publicity campaigns in recent memory, and to fairly poor reviews. Most critics felt that the film was much too garish and glitzy for its own good; the charm of the stage show was lost somewhere in the big budget.

Said one critic: "*Annie* has the same relationship to a great musical that lint has to stardust." Pauline Kael complained that the movie was too loud: "All of the little orphans seemed to have been trained by Ethel Merman!"

In the end, *Annie* earned back at the box office $37 million of the $42 million it cost to make. (But it eventually returned more than $80 million to Columbia, thanks to videocassette and foreign sales. Now, Ray Stark is planning a sequel.)

Though most of the movie's notices were poor, Carol's were terrific. Still, she felt bad about the film's lack of success. "I'm sorry about all the work everybody put into the movie," she said to *The New York Times* when asked to comment. "Any time a film fails it's a funny story to everybody but the people concerned. I guess the minute they bought the stage play for that much money, they were asking for big trouble."

During this time, Carol's life was particularly unsettled. She was helping to nurse Joe back to health, yet, for all intents and purposes, the marriage seemed to be over.

Carrie was on the road to a final recovery; Carol thanked God for that. But she somehow knew that her marriage couldn't be saved; she felt totally undirected now. "Sometimes I don't know where I'm going," she lamented to close friends. "Everything seems out of focus right now. So many things to consider..."

"Decisions had to be made, priorities had to be examined," remembers one of Carol's confidantes. "It was decided that Joe's health had to come first, and then after he was totally recovered they would decide what to do about the marriage. Everything was being done very methodically, one step at a time. Just like Carol. Still, it was difficult."

"I used to be wishy-washy, a real Charlie Brown," Carol said at this time. "I've learned that sometimes the surf has to come up and smash the rocks."

Though it had been coming for quite some time, it was still a shock to most of Carol and Joe's friends when, in October 1982, the Hamiltons decided on a trial separation. They'd taken the girls to Europe for a few weeks earlier in the summer—the first family vacation in years—and there they decided to make the separation official.

"There is no animosity between them and there are no plans for a divorce," Carol's publicist, Rick Ingersoll, said in a prepared statement. "There are also no third parties involved, no other woman in Joe's life nor man in Carol's.

"And while their children are certainly of the age when they can understand about such things, it isn't easy for them to deal with," Ingersoll added. "Carol and Joe are concerned about how they are taking it."

The plan was that Jody, fifteen, and Erin, thirteen, would live in the Hawaiian condo with Carol. Joe was to stay in the Beverly Hills home. Carrie, eighteen, was attending Pepperdine University in Malibu.

The separation was not marked by the kind of public emotional display that characterizes so many Hollywood marriages-gone-bad. "It was not a plate-throwing, emotional bust-up," says a friend. "It was more like the two of them had finally just run out of steam." In fact, publicly, Carol and Joe gave no reason for their decision. Friends have speculated that it was Carol who initiated the separation, but mostly there is mystery surrounding the breakup.

There had always been areas of incompatibility between Carol and Joe, but they managed to work them out—or at least they thought they had. "I'm far less outgoing than Carol," Joe once admitted. "In fact, I'm downright antisocial at times. I hate going to parties with a roomful of strangers. Hell, I never know what to say. I make terrible small talk. The whole thing is agony for me.

"Carol, of course, has no problem. Everyone comes up to her. But me . . . We went to one of those parties not long ago, and when we were driving home, I said to her, 'We have a problem. I had a miserable evening.' She said, 'Correction: *You* have a problem.' 'Nope,' I said, '*we* have a problem because I'm never going with you to one of these things again.'"

"Don't even ask me what happened between Carol and Joe," Pat Lillie warns, "because I have no idea. Carol and Joe made it clear by their silence that this was something to remain private. No one has ever said what happened."

"I never heard Carol say one word against Joe," Ed Simmons says, "nor have I ever heard Joe say one word against Carol. Ever."

Maggie Scott observes, "We all felt that they had the most perfect, storybook marriage. Now I have to wonder if that wasn't an additional pressure on them."

One of the only times Carol ever discussed some of the problems in her marriage was to Phyllis Battelle, a writer for *Ladies' Home Journal*. "For years, little things used to bother me," Carol said. "But I was too closed-mouthed, and so was Joe, because we both came from families where there was yelling and conflict. So I tended never to let it all out, and then I would see a sock on the floor and explode. Not because of the sock but because of all the things kept hidden, the time he was late and didn't call, the time he wouldn't talk.

"If Joe was preoccupied and didn't talk, I would take it personally, thinking I had done something wrong. I would be quiet, too, hoping that whatever it was would just go away."

Carol also mentioned Carrie's drug ordeal in connection with her failed marriage. "It became the all-consuming thing in our lives," she said. "There were times when I wanted to talk about it and Joe didn't; other times he wanted to talk and I was too exhausted."

But she made it clear that Carrie's problem did not cause an end to the marriage. "You can't blame something like this on someone else's problem. The problem was between Joe and me."

When the Variety Club honored Carol in a special presentation on November 21, Joe and Carol attended the taped-for-television gala together, sitting at a table with their daughters. They seemed particularly warm toward each other; at one point she tenderly kissed him on the cheek. "You have a lovely family," Lucille Ball commented to Carol.

But now when Carol and Joe were thrown into a work-related situation, there were problems. Carol had guested as Eunice Higgins on three episodes of *Mama's Family* (of which Joe was executive producer), but she wasn't expected to be back for more.

"There was serious tension on the set when Carol and Joe worked together during this time," says a spectator. "It wasn't that they argued; they *never* did in public. But there was a strain, and the atmosphere was cold. Carol, I noticed, was particularly argumentative about the scripts. There was one outburst about a script problem and everyone was visibly startled by it—"I would *prefer* to do it my way," she told someone in a very frosty tone—that wasn't at all like Carol. Joe was very quiet. So was everyone else. But you could feel the indignation in the air."

Nineteen eighty-two ended on a note of uncertainty. There were projects announced that would never materialize: another television special with Julie Andrews (*Julie and Carol in Rome*), and an HBO film with Marcello Mastroianni, *Time of the Cuckoo*. By now, most people felt that Carol and Joe would not reconcile. Only one thing was certain, said Carol at the time: "Whatever happens during this strange time will be for the best...I have a strong feeling about that."

Carol's first role after her separation from Joe seemed, to many observers, to hit very close to home. *Between Friends* is a thoughtful story about the unlikely friendship between two recently divorced middle-aged New England women. Carol, now fifty, starred opposite Elizabeth Taylor, fifty-one, as a plucky divorcee and nymphomaniac trying to find her way through middle age while coping with the problems of raising a rebellious teenage daughter.

The film, which was produced for Home Box Office, was offered to and rejected by all three networks. "Fifty-year-old women hardly *exist* on network television," noted one frustrated observer.

Carol and Liz became close friends while working in Toronto, where they filmed *Between Friends*. Their compatibility made the film that much more believable. They called each other E.T. and C.B. (still do); they watched soap operas together on their lunch breaks. Elizabeth refused to do an interview for *TV Guide* unless Carol, who was very protective of her, was at her side.

Mutual friends Roddy McDowall and Rock Hudson warned

the two women that they would have a difficult time working together without endlessly ribbing each other into hysterics and, apparently, they were right. Carol loved breaking Liz up; in one wintry scene in which she was to wear a full-length raccoon coat, she flipped up the back of the coat to reveal long underwear with the words "Blue Moon" inscribed on her bottom.

Carol would say of working with Liz, "If Nanny were alive to see this, it would've killed her!" Carol and Nanny had spent many an afternoon in the movie theaters watching child star Liz pout, laugh, and flash those baby-blue eyes on the big screen. Liz was everything the young Carol had dreamed of being: pretty, popular, rich, and famous. Despite the fact that Liz was so easy to relate to, the adult Carol still couldn't help but be awed by her presence. During a press conference to announce their teaming up for the film, photographers swarmed around Liz taking photographs, and Carol stood in the background with a camera, taking her own photos of Liz.

"What surprised me about the ladies when we were in rehearsal," recalls director Lou Antonio, "was Carol's sensitivity and Elizabeth's sense of humor. Carol grew up in comedy, and Elizabeth's strong suit has always been drama, yet I discovered that each of them has strengths in the other's territory. *Between Friends* reverses roles a bit—giving Liz a lot of laughs, Carol a lot of drama."

Antonio says that the only problem he had on the set was waiting in the morning while Liz applied her own makeup—she wouldn't use a makeup artist. "She's been doing that for thirty years," he laughs. "Nobody's going to change her, and I'd be a fool to try. Besides, look at the results!"

Carol as a nymphomaniac—and not in a comedy sketch— was a real stretch for her, not only in terms of her acting career but also in terms of her public image. She and her audience had certainly come a long way by accepting that she was, indeed, a fine-looking, desirable, and sexy woman, an equal in the film to her costar, who is renowned for her glamour and beauty. Back in the *Who's Been Sleeping in My Bed?* days, Carol would have portrayed Liz's loony, hopeless loser friend Gertrude, who tries to fix up Liz with a man she's not good enough to have for herself. Those days were over.

Still, despite her refreshing new self-confidence, Carol had to admit to friends she had a prudish side when it came to some of the sexier scenes with men in the film. She had lengthy talks with the writers and producers about these scenes. Though she hated to use the word, it sounded so artificial, she couldn't help herself: "I want them done *tastefully*."

One scene Carol had a bit of trouble accepting had her podiatrist lover sucking her toes in bed.

"I am *not* going to let this guy suck my toes and let it be seen by millions. *Period!*" she said decisively.

"Well, then, how are we going to do the scene, Carol?" director Lou Antonio asked.

"I don't know," Carol responded thoughtfully. "In the dark?"

In the end, they did it with a comical edge—they giggled throughout the scene. In making the scene funny, it became much less offensive to Carol, and she was no longer insecure about it.

The film was broadcast in September 1983 (right before Carol taped another TV special for CBS, this one with operatic tenor Placido Domingo, oddly entitled *Burnett Discovers Domingo*). Though the script was criticized as being too contrived, Carol and Liz received admirable reviews for their work.

During their time together in Canada, they talked about the subject of divorce in a press interview. "It's like a *petit mal,* a small death," said the experienced Taylor. "Real death is *grand mal.*"

Carol, who was still trying to sort out her feelings about her relationship with Joe, deliberated a moment and decided thoughtfully, "You grow out of pain, don't you think?" Liz agreed.

A half-smile played across Carol's face. "I take it one day at a time," she said of the estrangement. "Joe and I see each other a lot and talk on the phone every day. We all go through a series of little deaths in life, don't we?"

But Carol made it clear that her role in *Between Friends* had no bearing on her personal experiences with Joe. "I don't think of myself as Mary Catherine [Castelli, her character in the film]," she said. "Joe didn't walk out on me for another lady. Unlike the character I played, I have a great feeling of self-worth. There's a lot of hate and resentment in Mary Catherine," she concluded. "And in me, it's more . . . a sadness, a feeling of loss."

The divorce was very discreet and hardly publicized. Carol was of course, disappointed, but she couldn't help feeling that a marriage that lasted twenty years was not a failure. It was just over. Today, she is profoundly uncomfortable about publicly discussing the divorce. She simply feels that the details are nobody's business; that no one could learn anything from their experience. "Also, I respect Joe enough to allow him his privacy," she's explained tactfully. "There were no third parties involved on either side—and that's enough to say."

"The reason the marriage broke up is simply because she needed her independence," a friend of Carol's speculates. "The marriage no longer accommodated that need. The divorce was the consequence of the fact that Carol could no longer be Carol Hamilton...she was released from the marriage as Carol Burnett."

24

MAY 1984. ALONE IN A NEW YORK CITY HOTEL ROOM, CAROL WAS at a life crossroads when she became ill. She was tired and her bones ached; she hadn't felt so terrible in years. She crawled into bed and stayed there for days. Friends suggested she go to a hospital, but she refused. The hotel management sent up chicken soup.

She knew that her only physical ailment was a simple flu; but emotionally she faced the frightening prospect of personal evolution. Her marriage was over; Carrie and Jody were in college on the West Coast; Erin was also away at school and debating on whether or not to enroll in a Boston college. Carol hadn't been so alone since, perhaps, the first time she came to New York, those first few weeks at the Rehearsal Club before Don Saroyan blew into town and provided an emotional rescue.

She always held a special place in her heart for New York. This was where it had all happened for her, where she had started to realize her dreams. As she curled up in bed alone, she reflected on the past. Two marriages. Two divorces. Three children. Broadway. Television. Movies. She decided that she had good reason to be tired.

"It has taken so much energy out of Carol to perform and create all of these years, and still live her life," her longtime friend Don Crichton observes. "The public just doesn't realize the pressure she's been under for over twenty years. A star—and I probably shouldn't use the word because Carol hates it—of her caliber is still always on the block to deliver even though she has proved herself many times over. She has to have her moments alone to think. She has finally learned to like herself enough to be alone with herself. She *needs* those alone moments to recoup."

Carol stayed in bed or moped about for ten days before she

made the decision that she'd had enough. It was time to get on with her life despite the strong element of fear, a fear of not making the right moves, of disappointing herself with her personal choices and her audience with her professional choices. "But you just can't go to bed and stay there for the rest of your life," she decided.

"Once the Burnett show was over and the marriage had ended, Carol's independence and identity as a person had to soar to new heights," Bob Wright observes. "It wasn't as easy for her as she made it seem. Interviews with the press painted an easy transition. Divorce is never easy, let's face it. It was still tough on Carol. There was struggle, but also survival."

For the first time, Carol was on her own. Her new good looks—short-cropped brown hair, always a suntan, the "new" chin—had given her renewed confidence in herself. Even though the chin operation didn't turn out perfectly—it seemed to drag her mouth down a little lower on one side, making her face seem somehow less mobile than it once was—she was nevertheless pleased with the result.

By now, Carol had developed a high degree of flexibility that allowed her to move on, take risks, and live in the present. "I've got the wanderlust," she told friends enthusiastically. "I love to go, to do, experiment, experience, and then start something else again."

In the next year, Carol went about the business of making a new life for herself. She sold the condominium in Hawaii and, in September of 1984, moved to New York, into a two-bedroom apartment suite in the Wyndham Hotel (one large, brightly colored bedroom was reserved for any visiting daughter) that she called her "digs." It was a simpler, more circumscribed existence for Carol, who was now fifty-one. She enjoyed what she told friends was "the nice family feeling" of the Wyndham—"the wife of the elevator operator is the head of housekeeping," she said with a laugh.

"I had the big houses, the swimming pools, and now, this is a new life," she resolved. "I like where I am. It's orderly here, it's structured—and it's mine." (Carol also maintained a small condominium on the West Coast on Wilshire Boulevard.)

It seemed fitting that she begin life anew in Manhattan, a city where energy is always at peak level. "There's a great stirring here," she told friends. "I feel so stimulated now, so full of life."

For the first time in many years, she was also feeling totally at peace. She had grown extremely tired of the mix of public bravado and private despair—elation and depression—that had become the hallmark of her personality. Finally, there was pure satisfaction. She was almost childlike in her enjoyment of this new feeling.

Carol had never known such total freedom. For a woman who'd been as orderly as she'd been, she found the currently unsettled state of her life particularly intriguing. She turned her back on all of the rules and commandments that had made her the "perfect" mother, wife, and working woman. "Somebody once said, 'A lot of creativity comes out of not being too comfortable,'" she noted.

Now, she would only work and be "creative" when her mood swung in that direction. When she didn't feel like enveloping herself with the Manhattan bustle, she would live wherever her mood took her (even if that meant bunking with Jim Nabors in *his* Hawaiian home when she visited the islands).

She would also learn to be more aggressive in Manhattan, a city certainly not best suited to the meek and mild-mannered. No longer would she allow people to push in front of her in line at the supermarket; that was the "old" Carol. Now, she wouldn't allow a perfect stranger to come up to her table in a restaurant and literally push her fork down so that she could sign an autograph as had happened more than once to the "old" Carol.

Eleven suitcases accompanied her wherever she went, each one numbered with its contents clearly labeled (that orderly side of her couldn't help but creep through). One suitcase contained material for the book about her childhood that she had decided to write; it was her stability, her "home." She rented a typewriter until, much to her astonishment, she took what she called "a magnum leap" and learned to use a word processor.

It had been twenty-five years since Carol had made her New York theatrical debut in *Once Upon a Mattress* at the Phoenix Theatre. To celebrate the occasion, lyricist Marshall Barer wrote an imaginative article about his memories of the show, "1,000,000 Mattresses" for a theatrical magazine. He forwarded a copy of the article to Carol with a note expressing his idea to host a party to celebrate the show's silver anniversary. A spokesman for Carol assured Barer that she would call him, even though she and Marshall hadn't spoken to each other in twelve years.

"Oh, she'll *never* call..." Marshall recalls his cowriter, Mary Rodgers, as having said. "After all of this time! Never!"

Two days later, Barer found a cheerful message on his answering machine: "It's Carol! How've you been, Marshall? Give me a call!"

"I called immediately." Barer smiles. "I was wondering what she'd be like. We cackled and giggled on the phone like old times, and I sensed that she hadn't changed."

Marshall mentioned to Carol that he'd purchased a copy of a paperback biography of her from a local drugstore, and that the book had some troubling inaccuracies in it about *Once Upon a Mattress.* "Oh, I *never* read *those* things!" Carol responded quickly. "I just don't bother!"

"I'd love for us to get together," Marshall suggested hesitantly. He didn't want to appear too pushy.

"Wonderful!" Carol responded without missing a beat. "Let's do it! Pick me up tomorrow."

"I met her at the condominium she was staying at in Westwood," he recalls. "We drove to a restaurant there and giggled for two hours. It was as if no time had passed whatsoever from the days when we were trying to convince Mr. Abbott to use our special material for that second-act gap in *Mattress.* She hadn't changed; she looked even better, now that she'd had the surgery."

Carol and Marshall discussed plans for a gala celebration to commemorate *Once Upon a Mattress's* anniversary, and the black-tie party was held on Sunday, November 18, 1984, at the Rainbow Room in New York. There were over 150 guests, including many of the people who'd worked with Carol in the show and in other New York ventures. (Jule Styne, Adolph Green, and Betty Comden joined in the festivities, indicating that any animosity over *Fade Out-Fade In* had long since been dead and buried.)

In early 1985, Carol went to Paris to work with Robert Altman again in the hour-long drama he directed for Home Box Office titled *The Laundromat,* based on a one-act play by Pulitzer Prize-winning writer Marsha Norman. Amy Madigan costarred. It aired in April 1985.

"*The Laundromat* isn't even on my résumé," says Robert Altman of the program, which received little publicity, "and I would imagine not on hers, either."

The next year and a half would be quiet for Carol. An occasional guest appearance on television kept her in the public eye, but mostly she concentrated on writing her book and on developing a television special for ABC. She also decided that she couldn't proceed with her new life until she confronted, once and for all, her past.

"Sometimes if I'm driving through Hollywood, I feel pulled to that corner of Yucca and Wilcox," Carol had told friends.

She went back to the apartment in which she and Nanny lived, one last time on August 18, 1985. She had had so many disturbing dreams about that place over the years. "In some dreams, my mother is there, sometimes my grandmother," she once recalled. Carol would wake up sweating and repeating the last words she remembered from the dream: "But they told me you were dead...."

"Once there was a whole family in the kitchen taking a bath. But everything is always different," she said. "I knock on the door and the room has been redecorated—some of the walls knocked out, higher ceilings. Once there was a spiral staircase. Once, there was a decorator redoing the whole place. I could look out the window and see the ocean instead of the other apartment building butted up against it."

Many times, Carol would wake up crying. She was always trying to redo the past, and now it was time to accept it and move on.

For the price of one month's rent, the current tenants of 102 allowed Carol to spend an hour in the apartment with her tape recorder. She walked into the room, and froze. It hadn't changed much; the Murphy bed was gone and a shower curtain had been put up over the resulting hole in the wall. It appeared that the same dingy carpet covered the floor. The white tile in the kitchen—could it be the same tile? she wondered. The medicine cabinet in which Nanny used to keep her "hissy fit" medicines was gone, but the sink below it remained. The full-length mirror, the one Carol used to pose in front of and pretend she was Betty Grable, was no longer cracked; it had been fixed.

Carol needed only fifteen minutes in 102. A quarter-hour

was more than enough to reminisce. It was impossible to hold back the flood of memories and emotions.

She left weeping tears of sadness—for Jody and Louise, for Nanny—but there was a feeling of happiness, too, for having known and loved them all. Somehow, she knew she'd never have to go back. Apartment 102 would always be a part of her, wherever she was.

Carol credited noted author and playwright Peter Feibleman for inspiring her to write *One More Time*, her memoirs about her childhood. Feibleman is one of the five men Carol has dated since her divorce from Joe Hamilton. "'You should write this for your kids,'" Carol recalled Feibleman as saying. "'You've got a good story there. Write it, for heaven's sake!'"

"Write a page a day," he told her. "At the end of three hundred and sixty-five days, you'll have what is called a book."

Now, Peter Feibleman, who once coauthored a cookbook with Lillian Hellman, admits, "I didn't realize you don't go around saying things like that to Carol, because she'll do it. She had the kind of iron discipline and stick-to-itiveness to complete an assignment—so you better be careful what you assign."

"I was embarrassed about the thought of writing a book," Carol had to admit later. "It wasn't until ten months into the project that I was able to call it a book without stuttering."

At first, Carol spent entire days in her robe with a box of tissues nearby. The writing was painful, and all-consuming. At night, she was amazed to find herself dreaming of touching childhood experiences, of birthday parties and snippets of conversation. She would get up in the middle of the night to write down the names of people she hadn't thought of since she was a youngster; she says she couldn't get a good night's sleep unless she knew that a pad and pencil were at her bedside. Eventually, she put a tape recorder by her bed to capture her thoughts. The whole experience of doing the book was oddly exhilarating; never before had she been involved in anything so completely, so emotionally.

"In a scene I recall for the book—a tiny scene that won't matter to anyone—Nanny and Mama were arguing and I was doing water colors," Carol told Lawrence Christon of the *Los Angeles Times*. "I found me, at 52, touching the shoulder of Carol, at 14, saying, 'It's all right.' And now I wonder if at 14 I really felt that touch in some kind of reversal of time. I know it sounds like something from *The Twilight Zone* but I can't help but wonder, 'Did the me from the future touch me then? Is there something in me that knows in advance how things are going to turn out?' I never doubted that I could survive. I still don't."

After Carol finished the first one hundred pages, she showed Feibleman her work. It was a big step; she had never before revealed many of these memories to anyone. Feibleman was impressed with the poignancy of her words and helped Carol secure a deal for the book with Random House.

It wouldn't be until April 1986 that Carol felt comfortable enough with the script of her ABC television special to begin taping the show with guests Whoopi Goldberg, Carl Reiner, and Robin Williams. Another year would go by before the program would finally be broadcast.

On April 26, Carol celebrated her fifty-third birthday. UCLA, her alma mater, sponsored a party to honor her and to raise money for the college's performing-arts program. Six thousand people attended. For a twenty-five-dollar ticket price, the general public was seated in the upper reaches of the campus's Pauley Pavilion; celebrity guests paid five hundred dollars to sit in the front of the auditorium. Pierre Cossette produced the evening's festivities, which raised five hundred thousand dollars for UCLA.

Film clips of some of Carol's most memorable TV appearances (including her performance of "John Foster Dulles" on Ed Sullivan's program), and of her best-loved characters and sketches were shown to the audience. In addition to a video tribute from Ronald and Nancy Reagan, there were speeches and entertainment by Carol's celebrity friends. Julie Andrews joked of her first appearance with Carol on *The Garry Moore Show* ("She was very good...and *I* was superb"). Later an old videotape of a plump Liz Taylor was shown, after which a much thinner Liz in a formfitting spangled gown rose from her seat in the first row, took the microphone, and said of the clip, "Carol who *was* your fat friend?").

Carol's daughters, Carrie, Jody, and Erin, made a memorable appearance dressed as charwomen for a bump-and-grind song-and-dance number that was one of the biggest surprises of the evening for their mother. The girls managed to keep their performance a secret. Jody said that when she looked down from the stage, all she could see was Carol crying.

Carol was presented with the Distinguished Artist Circle Award from UCLA by the college's chancellor, Charles Young. She stood on the stage looking a bit self-conscious with her hands in her pockets and her head bowed, as Young praised her life and career. Afterward, the applause went on as though it would never stop. Bathed in the love and affection of so many longtime friends and fans, Carol was almost overcome with the joy she felt on this magical evening.

Pat Lillie was one of the coordinators of the program, which was chaired by Ginny Mancini (Henry Mancini's wife). She recalls: "The night of the event, Carol also had a cocktail and press party to attend. She was terrified of both. Still, today she is a very private, shy person, who becomes frightened when too much attention is paid to her. In that respect, she's a lot like the Carol I worked with on *The Garry Moore Show.*

"She kept wondering who would be at both functions, what she should do and say, how she should act—just trying to get the details straight. She's been to many of these in the past, but they're something she's never quite gotten used to."

Jim Nabors, Chrissy, and Carol's three daughters accompanied Carol in the limousine. When they pulled up to the first stop, there was a pandemonium that Pat Lillie says was reminiscent of the madness that characterized Carol's first national tour in 1962. Mobs of security people held back mobs of photographers and fans. Lillie opened the limo door and Carol got out, her eyes wide with terror. She grabbed on to her old friend's arm for dear life.

"As she got out of the limo, I noticed she was holding a small plastic bag," Lillie continues. "She handed it to me; there was a beautifully wrapped little box in it. 'Why are you coming to a black-tie event in your honor carrying a plastic bag?' I asked. 'This is for you,' she said as she handed it to me. It was *her* birthday and she was giving *me* a present."

Two hectic hours passed before Pat Lillie had a free moment to open the box—in it was a gold pin in the shape of a lily, with three encrusted diamonds. The next day, Pat called Carol's secretary to ask where she had managed to find such a unique gift. "She told me, 'I had absolutely nothing to do with it. It was Carol's idea...she did it herself.'"

"I can't help but wonder what this evening would have been

like if I had graduated," Carol said as she stood crying before the audience of fans and friends. "Next year, let's do this at my place!"

By the summer of 1986, Carol had just completed writing her memoirs when she began work on a project for MTM Productions and CBS-TV, a $12 million, five-part soap opera about the dark underbelly to the "glamour" of the raisin industry called *Fresno*. This was television's first comedy miniseries, and it spoofed popular nighttime soaps such as *Falcon Crest, Dynasty,* and *Dallas,* as well as the miniseries format itself. (*Fresno* was named for the California suburb known as the World's Raisin Capital, a city that ranked last in a survey measuring the quality of life in 277 cities—apparently, Fresno is so dull that only five minutes of the series were actually taped there; the rest was done in Los Angeles.)

Fresno was written by its executive producer, Barry Kemp (who created the successful *Newhart* series), and directed by Jeff Bleckner (known for his serious dramatic direction on shows like *Hill Street Blues*).

From the beginning, the project was risky because it was decided that *Fresno* would take itself seriously and not use a laugh track. Also, there was no studio audience. The only programming that could be considered close in premise and execution was Norman Lear's soap-opera spoof of 1976, *Mary Hartman, Mary Hartman*.

Carol played Charlotte Kensington, a widowed matriarch who presides over a failing raisin dynasty (her husband, Yancy, was killed in a dehydrator accident twenty years earlier). Times had been tough for this over-the-hill Southern belle; her Rolls-Royce was out of order and she had to be chauffeured around town in the back of a beat-up station wagon. But, still, she was smug in her extreme snobbery. "The world is made up of the haves and the have nots," she told her gardener. "I have and you have not."

Director Jeff Bleckner recalls of his first meeting with Carol: "I was absolutely scared to death. To me, Carol Burnett is a star, a bigger-than-life personality. 'Oh, God! What if she doesn't like me? Since I'm not known for comedy, what if she doesn't think I'm funny?' I thought. But she was gregarious, friendly, and eager for my input. We talked about the fact that we were going to take a straight approach with *Fresno,* and she said, 'Keep an eye on me. If you see me going over the top, giving too many Carol Burnett-isms, stop me.'"

The plot: Kensington Raisins has developed a revolutionary raisin (a crunchy-bran specialty) that they hope will destroy the competing Cane Enterprises, which is headed by the nefarious Tyler Cane (Dabney Coleman). "The industry hasn't seen an innovation like this in seventy-five years," Charlotte Kensington boasts. "We're not making raisins, we're making history!"

But Tyler Cane is just as determined to control the raisin industry and to destroy the Kensingtons. The ensuing struggle and Charlotte's frustrations are what the miniseries is about.

It's interesting that Carol's daughter Carrie was up for a role in *Fresno* and was one of the final three actresses considered for the part. In the end, she didn't get the job. "In this particular case, one would think she would get it because of the publicity alone," Carol admitted. "Of course, I would have liked her to be in it with me, but I didn't push for it. She's got to do it on her own merit, otherwise she's not going to have self-esteem. That's something we both agree on."

Work on the miniseries was completed October 10, and it aired the week of November 16, 1986. Despite CBS's vigorous publicity campaign touting "The Power! The Passion! The Produce!" the reviews were generally lukewarm to poor; ratings got progressively worse every night. *Fresno* was slow in getting started. It got better as it went along—but most people wouldn't stay tuned long enough to know that.

The most frequent criticism leveled at *Fresno* was that it didn't seem possible to parody an art form that is already a parody in itself, and that it was too difficult to sustain this gimmick over five nights, no matter how audacious the plot.

"I know Carol liked the show, because she called me when she saw it," Jeff Bleckner says. "But she was a little stunned by the ratings, as we all were."

Carol's disappointment about the reception of *Fresno* was somewhat tempered because, in October 1986, her book, *One More Time*, had been published to terrific sales and to great critical acclaim (*People* magazine ran a cover story with the headline CAROL BURNETT: WHAT A CLASS LADY). Her publisher reported a 275,000-copy first printing, which is believed to be the largest in history for a first-time author. The book spent weeks on the *New York Times* best-seller list, and Carol says she's prouder of *One*

More Time than anything she's ever done in her professional life. Now, Carol and Carrie are writing a book together about Carrie's drug addiction; it's tentatively entitled *Under One Roof,* and will also be published by Random House. As Carol has described it, "It will be an account of a scared mother and a scared kid who went through this separately and came out on the other side."

When Carol presented Carrie with a copy of *One More Time,* it was inscribed: "You're my dream come true." The inscription was a private joke based on the *People* magazine headline that once labeled Carrie CAROL BURNETT'S NIGHTMARE.

"She's giddy, almost like a kid," Carrie Hamilton said of her mother in an interview for *People* magazine in 1986. "It was a big exhale for her to move into her own home. She's gotten rid of a lot of excess baggage, a lot of crap."

By now, Carol was settled into a lovely, Cape Cod-style two-story home in Pacific Palisades, California, overlooking a canyon and then the Pacific Ocean. On a grand piano in Carol's living room were carefully placed framed photographs of her daughters and close friends like James Stewart and Jim Nabors. The decor is classic country—hardwood floors, shutters, and simple floral prints.

"I wish Mama could have seen this," she says of her new environment, which one reporter noted was "meticulously appointed and as neat as a movie interior awaiting action."

"She's been like a snake shedding skin," Carrie concludes. "She's got a whole new life now."

But Carol isn't sure if she will ever marry again; she enjoys being part of what she calls "the transitional generation"—women of the 1950's who were conditioned not to be independent, who never questioned total reliance on a mate for security until now. Carol has certainly enjoyed her freedom these last few years. "I never had that feeling of space, never indulged myself with independence, and I've discovered it's wonderful," she told writer Phyllis Battelle in 1986. "I think if I ever got married again," she concluded, only half jokingly, "I would insist on having my own quarters.

"I've been married twice," she added with a laugh, "and that's enough."

Even though Carol said of the six-foot-tall Peter Feibleman to a reporter for *McCall's* (June 1985), "He's terrific, just terrific. I love him. He's so supportive and so attractive and bright. I'm just crazy about him...and he loves my girls," the romance did not last long. Today, they are just friends. "The assumption that one has to be dating to be a fulfilled person is just so much prattle," Carol has decided.

Carol's February 1987 television special, *Carol, Carl, Whoopi & Robin* engendered strong ambivalence from fans and critics alike. Apparently, the special was in the planning stages for years —sketches were written and discarded, ideas were shelved.

Naturally, *Carol, Carl, Whoopi & Robin* was taped at CBS's Studio 33, and with much of the same crew Carol used on her series, including many of Joe Hamilton's employees who've become good friends over the last twenty years. "The divorce was difficult for all of us," says Bob Wright speaking for Hamilton's staff, "because it was a divorce in the family. My wife asked me, 'Well, who got you in the divorce settlement?' I told her, 'Joe gets my right hand, and Carol gets my left.' Carol relies on people in her life who have been a part of it since the beginning."

Despite the presence of four brilliant comic minds—Burnett, Reiner, Goldberg, and Williams—the program was not as funny as it was expected to be. An opening musical number explained that the premise of the show was to examine the roots of comedy and why people laugh. Strangely, that interesting concept was lost somewhere along the way and never mentioned again.

Whoopi and Carol performed a series of sketches about the full-circle evolution of mother-daughter relationships. Carol and Robin played a sketch in which she was a grieving widow and he an obnoxious, loudly dressed mourner. They performed it twice, once as scripted and then again as an improvisation.

A restaurant sketch with Carl Reiner in which he played Carol's suitor, who, through the course of the sketch, discovered that she was emotionally unbalanced, was cut from the show. Apparently, it wasn't funny enough. As a result, Reiner had mere minutes of air time, which only served to confuse viewers as to why he was a guest at all.

There were more serious problems with the special. Carol's best comedy has always been honest and never contrived. In other words, she never went for a cheap joke, a dumb laugh. On this special, there were more than a few cheap jokes: Carol's swearing during the improvisation with Williams at a point when she realized that it would elicit a rise from the audience (maybe the "new" Carol Burnett can say "bullshit" on television, but it's going to take a while before her public will be able to accept such shock fare); Carol reeling back in surprise at the sight of Robin's pink panties and black stockings when she pulls on his bow tie and his pants drop—as if she didn't expect that to happen and didn't know what he was wearing underneath.

When Carol moved into her own home in Pacific Palisades, the first place she's ever owned by herself, one of the house's main attractions for her was its spacious backyard. She'd never really had a garden, but now she was determined to put that backyard to productive use. A friend sent her an azalea bush to plant. Carol went out and bought herself a big straw hat, fifty pounds of fertilizer, and what she called a "Mary, Mary quite contrary watering can."

The tree had to be planted in just the right spot; Carol hunted around the yard until she found the perfect place. And then, carefully, she dug a hole and planted the bush. After her work was finished, she stood back proudly to take it all in. Somehow, that small azalea seemed pathetically alone standing by itself in all of that space.

Weeks passed, and she noticed that the tree adjusted to its new surroundings. Slowly but surely, it began to thrive.

And much to Carol Burnett's astonishment, it's still growing today.

Afterword

"I have a theory that there are maybe ten stars in the whole world—people like Lucille Ball, Jimmy Stewart, Cary Grant —and the rest of us are professionals in show business but not stars. I think it's a matter of longevity. I'll be a star only if I'm still around twenty years from now—and I have no idea if I will be."

—Carol Burnett
to *TV Guide*, December, 1967

GARRY MOORE ONCE CALLED CAROL BURNETT "ONE OF GOD'S greatest ad-libs." If ever Moore's description of Carol was true, it's true today. She seems to be ad-libbing her life, taking it all in slowly, feeling her way along and enjoying what she calls her "wanderlust." Where her public is concerned, this wander-lust has resulted in as many failures as successes. Such are the risks of ambition.

Generally, *Fresno* and *Carol, Carl, Whoopi & Robin* were both received poorly by critics and fans. Carol fared better with her public—if not with the critics—in December 1987, when she starred in a television revival of Neil Simon's 1968 play, *Plaza Suite*. In it, she portrayed three very different characters in a comical trilogy; Hal Holbrook, Dabney Coleman, and Richard Crenna costarred in the three acts. Carol's versatility in the sketch work was nostalgic for many viewers; it reminded them of her work on her much-beloved series. But a reviewer for a Los Angeles newspaper summed up most of the critical opinion of the special—of which Carol was co-executive producer—with a single line: "*Plaza Suite* is a vast disappointment."

"Early on, I learned not to put all my eggs in the public-

418

approval basket," she once said. "If I had, the eggs and I would have been pretty well scrambled by now."

All of this is part of Carol Burnett's metamorphosis. Mistakes are expected along the way. Her public forgives her them. And as far as she's concerned, she seems to understand that a person who never makes mistakes never accomplishes very much.

"What Carol still has today is that innate comedic sense of who Carol Burnett is," Bob Wright notes. "The judgment of how to be just plain funny, that's the essence of a Carol Burnett. Obviously, physically she has changed. She can't do the silly pratfalls that were so outrageous in the old days, the gangly comedy. Now, she is a mature woman, and her comedy is mature, but still in the realm of Carol Burnett."

Or, as Harvey Korman puts it, "She's got magic. My three-and-a-half-year-old has just discovered Carol from the reruns of our old show. And she loves her."

Carol and her production company, Kalola Productions, have entered into an agreement with the Walt Disney Studios to develop projects and motion pictures. Carol may or may not star in the projects agreed upon for production.

"I think I would like to see her do less of the *Friendly Fire* and *Beatrice* kinds of roles and more of the comedy she's known for," Tim Conway says. "Even in *Friendly Fire,* a great performance by any standards, to me it was still Carol Burnett on the screen, not Peg whatever-her-name-was. And I'm not sure I like seeing a grim, solemn Carol Burnett on the screen...."

"Carol should go back to Broadway," George Abbott offers. "To my mind, she will always be a Broadway star." Abbott laughs when he says that; for the most part, he missed Carol's television success. "I have never gotten over her as being the princess in *Once Upon a Mattress,*" he says, only half jokingly. "She has the instincts, the voice, the magic of a stage performer."

Joe Layton agrees with Abbott. "Carol, go back to the theater," he suggests. "The audience loves a star in 3-D. Find the right property and be magnificent."

Carol has said she'd go back to Broadway with no hesitation if all she had to do were the matinee shows. For years, there's been talk about Carol taking Ethel Merman's colorful role as Mama Rose in *Gypsy.* At one point, it was reported that Bernadette Peters was tapped for the title role, and Jack Klugman was set to direct. But the project never materialized.

"She wants to do that role badly," Don Crichton says. "At one point, I think she felt she was too young for it, at another she didn't want to make the commitment for a year that was required. But I know she'll do it one day. . . . It's one of her dreams, I think."

"I know I can do it," Carol says of a job in the theater. "But it's scary opening a show. Everything that so many people have worked on for so long hinges on that first performance.

"It's also exciting," she allows. "Once that curtain goes up, there is nothing but you and that audience. It's living!"

Though there is still a part of Carol that is insecure, it's heartening to see how much more self-confidence she has in herself now. Whereas she was once extremely vulnerable and confused about her appearance, today she seems self-assured and remarkably pragmatic.

"I stopped making jokes about my figure and my looks," Carol said recently. "I made those jokes because I wanted to beat everybody else to the punch, to laugh at me first. Then I began to think, 'To hell with that! I don't have to do that anymore!' My head writer said, 'What's the matter with you? You know you're good at it. You *know* it always gets a laugh.' And I said, 'Well, I don't want to do it anymore. I don't *need* to do it.' And I didn't."

Recently, Carol spent weeks viewing episodes of *The Carol Burnett Show* for inclusion in a new series of videotapes being marketed under the umbrella title *My Personal Best*. "I changed over the years of our show," she now realizes. "I watch some of those old tapes and I just *die*. I didn't start to mellow until our seventh year. I think our ninth year was probably the best because we stopped going just for laughs and more for character.

"That was when I started to mature," she concluded. "I gave up pushing for jokes. I wasn't the brassy, loud, mugging character I had always been.

"Now, I don't think it does any of us any good to put ourselves down, even in comedy," Carol observed. "If other people are going to have negative thoughts, that's their problem—I shouldn't add to it by substantiating what they might be thinking. It's anti-feminine," she concludes.

One wonders if this is really the same fragile woman who

used to tell reporters that no matter how expensive the perfume she wore, she still smelled like a horse; that regardless of how many hours she spent primping in front of the mirror, the cause was still a hopeless one. "There is a powerful woman there now," her sister, Chrissy, observes of Carol. "She's definitely her grandmother's daughter."

Carol is not "just plain folks," no matter how much she protests to the contrary. She went blindly into a profession that guarantees a subpoverty-level income for all but a very few of its members—and she came out a Broadway, television, and movie "star." She lives and works in a powerful milieu; she's made millions of dollars. But maybe for the celebrity Carol, the way it's all happened—the sometimes painful, often ironical, personal evolution of Carol Burnett—is just plain...*human.* "It's always seemed to me," she's quipped, "that God has a *wonderful* sense of humor."

It had been a long journey from 102 to *Fresno,* from "John Foster Dulles" to *Friendly Fire,* from Don Saroyan to Joe Hamilton to independence.

Carol's car was once stopped at a red light in Los Angeles when she noticed a small child and an elderly woman waiting for a bus on the corner. The girl's shoes were scuffed, her clothes were worn, the woman's coat was weather-beaten. There they stood, oblivious to the city life swirling around them, lost in their own little world; the preoccupied woman stroked the little girl's hair, the child looked up at her with big, adoring eyes. Carol couldn't help but stare. The picture was so familiar. Suddenly, in her mind, they were Nanny and her shadow—little Carol—at the bus stop.

She honked the horn and motioned for the woman to come to the car. The sound of the horn jolted the lady from her daydream. A suspicious look played on her face as she walked toward the rich lady rolling down the fancy automobile's window. "Here, take this," Carol said, pushing a folded fifty-dollar bill at her. The old woman fixed her with a stare. "I mean it, take this," Carol urged.

The woman hesitated a moment, snatched the bill quickly, and then mumbled something that sounded vaguely like a thank-you.

"You're welcome," Carol said with tears in her eyes. "And thank you, too...so much."

Someone tooted a horn behind Carol. "Get on with it, will ya, lady?"

Then she drove off, leaving a confused old woman and loving little girl far behind.

Index